One drop of strength from the Divine He[...] meetings, strategy sessions, and buildin[...] Holy Spirit, we do not have what it takes to love people and lead them to Christ. Yet, because of the Spirit's power, we have everything we need! Many Christians, however, are confused. We wonder how to have a relationship with the Spirit. Are the gifts of the Spirit for our time? For my life? If so, how do I access and use them? These are essential questions in these last days. For that reason, this book is a timely resource. Sam Storms writes with the heart of a pastor and the skill of a scholar. His preparation is impressively thorough and detailed. This book will serve as a go-to tool for all of us who seek to walk in the Spirit.

Max Lucado, pastor and bestselling author

Sam Storms has given the body of Christ a gift in *Understanding Spiritual Gifts*. This is, without doubt, the best book I have ever read on the subject. Sam brings clarity to this often-misunderstood subject, awakening us to the necessity of spiritual gifts in order to live the fruitful lives God has designed for us, and to fulfill the mission he has assigned to us. It is time for the body of Christ to function as a whole, healthy, and strong body, which is impossible without the operation of the spiritual gifts given to us by God. This is a book for this hour.

Christine Caine, founder of A21 and Propel Women

Sam Storms has written the most comprehensive book on spiritual gifts I have ever seen. I can't think of a question about the gifts that he does not address. And his answers are based on the simple statements of Scripture, not preconceived theories about the gifts. Although Sam is a scholar, this book is not a scholarly, theoretical examination of spiritual gifts. It is an eloquent, easy-to-read, practical explanation of each of the twenty-one spiritual gifts and why they are essential for the spiritual health of the church. Sam will help you discover your gift and learn how to use it effectively.

Jack Deere, author of *Why I Am Still Surprised by the Power of the Spirit*

Thank you, Sam Storms; you've done it again. You have written an important book that addresses a crucially important and practical subject that the Holy Spirit is emphasizing today. With the mind of a scholar and the heart of a pastor and as a radical lover of Jesus, my dear friend Sam Storms has written a truly comprehensive guide to the subject of spiritual gifts. I can't think of a biblical text he doesn't explain or a controversial question he doesn't seek to answer. He is fearless and tireless in this because he wants to empower and equip people to walk in their full inheritance in the Holy Spirit. You may not agree with Sam's view on everything pertaining to gifts of the Spirit, but I promise you will be challenged, encouraged, and informed by his book. And I assure you that you will get a lot of Bible! The people of God are desperately in need of a consistent experience of the power of God, and the primary way God has provided for this is through the many gifts the Spirit empowers. I can't recommend this book too highly.

Mike Bickle, International House of Prayer, Kansas City

When the opening sentence of the first chapter of this book is "Christianity is inescapably *supernatural*," readers are immediately alerted to the necessity—not the luxury, not the option—of the presence, empowerment, and gifts of the Holy Spirit. Who better than Sam Storms to walk us through this essential subject? With constant reference to Scripture, Sam tackles such pressing matters as desiring and praying for spiritual gifts in the light of God's sovereignty, and how to discover one's gift(s). And he does not shy away from controversial topics such as continuationism vs. cessationism, the nature of speaking in tongues and its related gift of interpretation, and whether there are still apostles today. From a continuationist, Calvinist perspective on spiritual gifts and in a way that shuns irresponsible (mis) representations of other viewpoints, *Understanding Spiritual Gifts* will certainly be the standard work for years to come.

Gregg R. Allison, professor of Christian Theology,
The Southern Baptist Theological Seminary

If you are wanting an introduction to the gifts of the Holy Spirit, this book is for you. If you are already knowledgeable in the gifts of the Spirit, this is the book for you as well. It is a source book for the seasoned Christian. You should secure extra copies to give away. No one is more able to produce a balanced book like this than Dr. Sam Storms. With a solid background in the Word and the Spirit, he has written a book that will be edifying and God-honoring.

R. T. Kendall, minister of Westminster Chapel (1977–2002)

UNDERSTANDING SPIRITUAL GIFTS

UNDERSTANDING
SPIRITUAL
GIFTS

A COMPREHENSIVE GUIDE

SAM STORMS

ZONDERVAN
REFLECTIVE

ZONDERVAN REFLECTIVE

Understanding Spiritual Gifts
Copyright © 2020 by Sam Storms

Requests for information should be addressed to:
Zondervan, *3900 Sparks Dr. SE, Grand Rapids, Michigan 49546*

ISBN 978-0-310-11149-8 (softcover)
ISBN 978-0-310-11595-3 (audio)
ISBN 978-0-310-11151-1 (ebook)

Cover design: Jesse Owen / 10AM Design
Cover photos: © Daniel Levis Pelusi / Unsplas
Interior design: Denise Froehlich

Printed in the United States of America

20 21 22 23 24 /LSC/ 10 9 8 7 6 5 4 3 2 1

Dedicated to
JOHN WIMBER
(1934–1997)

*Although it may seem strange to dedicate a book
to someone who is no longer alive,
I could think of no one more deserving of this honor than*
John Wimber,
*whose friendship, encouragement, and modeling
of what it means to "do the stuff"
has meant so much to me and countless thousands of others.
I will be forever grateful for your life and ministry.*

Contents

Part 1: The Nature, Purpose, and Prayerful Pursuit of Spiritual Gifts

Part 2: The Debate over the Cessation or Continuation of Miraculous Gifts of the Spirit

Part 3: Revelatory Gifts of the Spirit

Part 4: Speaking in Tongues

Part 5: Faith, Healing, and Miracles

Part 6: Other Gifts and Apostleship

Foreword

B ecause the Spirit is the third person of the Trinity, learning to depend on the Spirit is crucial to the Christian life. And because biblical teaching about gifts of the Spirit points us to dependence on God's Spirit to empower us to serve one another in the various ways that God equips us, it is teaching crucial for today's church. Few things could be more central than learning to depend on God, in our various distinctive ways, to build up fellow believers as fellow members of Christ's own body.

Those who caricaturize charismatics as biblically naive or theologically misinformed don't know Sam Storms. Sam is a sober-minded exegete committed to follow wherever Scripture may lead, a biblical scholar who is also a pastor, a balanced and respected voice. A gracious and patient dialogue partner, he knows thoroughly both sides of the cessationist/continuationist debate firsthand.

In this book, Sam argues his case logically, point-by-point, and especially with respect for Scripture. This is the Sam we would expect if we have read his other books or listened to his presidential address regarding the gift of prophecy to the Evangelical Theological Society several years ago.

Rarely do two scholars agree on every point, and this book is no exception. But I do agree with most of it, and the points where I differ, I do so respectful of my friend's careful arguments. I hope that others, too, who disagree on some points will, like me, do so respectful of Sam's irenic tone, careful reasoning, and above all commitment to the authority of Scripture.

Today many churches emphasize either the Scriptures, which pervasively attest to the centrality of the Spirit's ministries in our lives and assemblies, or the Spirit, who inspired the Scriptures that model and should guide our own experience of the Spirit today. By emphasizing merely intellectual information, as if knowledge were enough, we risk missing the experience to which Scripture invites us. By emphasizing merely experience, we risk missing understanding and embracing the right experience. In this time when unbiblical extremes are reacting against each other—either throwing out spiritual gifts or abusing them—Sam Storms's book is superbly timely.

We need Word and Spirit together, and few are as equipped as Sam to provide that balance. I highly commend this exegetically excellent and preeminently practical book.

DR. CRAIG S. KEENER
F. M. and Ada Thompson Professor of Biblical Studies
Asbury Theological Seminary

Acknowledgments

There are several people who were instrumental in the production of this book. I want to begin by thanking Ryan Pazdur, Nathan Kroeze, and Chris Beetham at Zondervan for their incredibly helpful editorial suggestions and encouragement.

I would also like to express profound gratitude to the elders, staff, and congregation at Bridgeway Church, who not only provided me with the time and opportunity to write this book but also have devoted themselves to creating an atmosphere and spiritual culture at Bridgeway that facilitates and promotes the exercise of all God's precious spiritual gifts.

Finally, there are several individuals who have exerted a special influence on me in terms of my understanding of the Holy Spirit and his work in the church today. I must begin with Jack Deere, my former classmate at Dallas Theological Seminary, who has done more than anyone to educate me in the ministry of the Spirit. Running a close second in the degree of help given to me is my dear friend (Jack's dear friend also), Mike Bickle, who provides leadership at the International House of Prayer in Kansas City.

There are others deserving of mention, such as Wayne Grudem, John Piper, Craig Keener, Brock Bingaman, Lyle Dorsett, and Christine Caine. All of these are still alive and serving the body of Christ, but one who is now with the Lord is worthy of special note as well. I was greatly encouraged and blessed by John Wimber, leader of the Association of Vineyard Churches until his death in 1997. John's friendship, support, and godly example helped me in countless ways, and I will always be in his debt. Thanks again to all of you.

SAM STORMS

Introduction

S ome of you picking up this book are thinking, *Oh, no! Not another book on spiritual gifts! Hasn't everything been said that can be said on this subject? Why do we continue to focus on an issue that seems only to divide Christians rather than unite them? Enough already!*

I understand your frustration. I often feel it myself. But mine is likely of a different sort, for a different reason. If I feel frustrated, it is because of the confusion that surrounds this topic, the bizarre and misleading interpretations that many place on certain biblical texts, as well as the way many wish to downplay the urgency of spiritual gifts for Christian living and ministry.

Consider this: Although we should avoid evaluating the importance of biblical topics based solely on how many times they are mentioned in the New Testament, we can't afford to ignore the frequency with which biblical authors address an issue. Spiritual gifts are a case in point. How often do you think they are described in the New Testament? Twenty times? Fifty? One hundred? I count no fewer than 155 biblical verses that explicitly mention, describe, regulate, or portray the exercise of spiritual gifts.[1] In addition to this, there are no fewer than 65 verses that provide narrative illustrations of signs, wonders, and miracles in operation (mostly in the book of Acts).[2] I'm not in the least suggesting that spiritual gifts are the most important topic in the New Testament. Not by a long shot! But neither are we justified in

---

1   Acts 2:1–18; 10:44–48; 11:15–18; 19:1–7; Romans 12:3–8; 1 Corinthians 1:7; 12:1–31; 13:1–13; 14:1–40; Galatians 3:5; Ephesians 4:7–16; 1 Thessalonians 5:19–22; 1 Timothy 1:18–19; 4:14; 2 Timothy 1:6–7; Hebrews 2:3–4; James 5:13–18; and 1 Peter 4:10–11.

2   Acts 3:1–10; 4:29–31; 5:12; 6:8; 8:4–8; 9:32–43; 13:1–3; 13:6–12; 14:8–11; 21:4–14; 28:1–6; 1 Corinthians 2:4; 2 Corinthians 12:12; and Romans 15:19. The four gospels contain numerous other descriptions of signs, wonders, and miracles that I have not listed.

relegating them to a peripheral role in the life of the believer and the spiritual welfare of the body of Christ.

People often ask me which is more crucial: the fruit of the Spirit or the gifts of the Spirit? Although I don't like playing these off, one against the other, the answer is obvious: the fruit of the Spirit. This is simply a reflection of a critically important principle that we tragically, and all too often, forget: *character is always more important than gifting.* Said another way, who we are now and are becoming by virtue of God's sanctifying influence in our hearts is more vital to the individual and to the corporate experience of God's people than what we do.

And yet, at the same time, we cannot ignore the way in which gifts and fruit relate to each other. As we'll see repeatedly in this book, the primary purpose of all spiritual gifts, both the more miraculous and the somewhat mundane, is to build up the body of Christ. God has graciously provided these "manifestations of the Spirit" so that we might encourage, edify, strengthen, instruct, and console one another, all with a view to our ever-increasing, incremental transformation into the image of our Lord Jesus Christ. Gifts are to fruit what means are to ends. And ends are rarely if ever attained apart from the proper implementation and use of the means that God has ordained to achieve them.

Whereas I rejoice in the house that God has provided for me and my family, I would never despise, ignore, or fail to appreciate the craftsmen and carpenters, together with their wide variety of tools, who actually constructed the place where I live. And I daresay that it would be foolish of us as Christians to expect that the house of God, the body of Christ, the church, will grow into what God has designed if we fail to make use of the tools he has supplied us by his Spirit.

Consider Paul's instruction in Ephesians 4:7–16, a text we'll look at in more detail later on. The goal toward which we all strive in God's grace is "the unity of the faith and of the knowledge of the Son of God," what Paul calls "mature manhood" or "the measure of the stature of the fullness of Christ" (v. 13). Our aim is to build up the body of Christ "in love" (v. 16). But this doesn't happen magically or automatically, apart from the contribution that each believer makes to the spiritual growth of every other believer. The means God has supplied for the attaining of this goal are the spiritual gifts of apostles, prophets, evangelists, shepherds (pastors), and teachers listed in verse 11. Of course, there are at a minimum an additional fifteen or sixteen more gifts that likewise contribute to our progressive growth into the image of Jesus, but I trust you get my point.

A Brief Biographical Note[3]

It may also help you to know that I am a *practicing continuationist*. Both the noun and the modifying adjective are important in this label. First, the noun. For the first fourteen years of my ministry, I was a convinced *cessationist*. My view of the charismatic movement was less than flattering, to say the least. But in 1987 I began to study Scripture and the arguments for the cessation of miraculous gifts of the Spirit with considerably more care and objectivity. The conclusion of my studies, one that has only solidified in the years since, is that Scripture provides no evidence whatsoever that certain of the *charismata* were intended by God to be operative in the church for a mere fifty to sixty years in the first century, only to disappear gradually over time. I repeatedly encountered text after text that described all the spiritual gifts in a thoroughly positive light as essential to the building up of the body of Christ.

Yet there are a great many evangelical Christians who are happy to embrace the noun *continuationist*, yet are admittedly *functional* cessationists. They concur that the New Testament nowhere teaches that certain gifts of a particular sort ceased with the passing of the apostolic age. But they neither *pursue* them nor *pray* for them nor *practice* them. Theologically speaking, they would agree with the conclusions in this book. However, when it comes to exercising the full range of spiritual gifts, equipping others to do so, and implementing these gifts in the day-to-day ministry of the local church, they look no different from those who believe such gifts died out centuries ago.

You should understand from the start that I am a *practicing* continuationist. I regularly, indeed daily, if not hourly, pray in tongues. I have on occasion prophesied and always encourage the people of our church to do so

---

3   My theological journey has been described in considerably more detail in two books: Sam Storms, "A Third Wave View," in *Are Miraculous Gifts for Today? Four Views*, ed. Wayne Grudem (Grand Rapids: Zondervan, 1995), and Sam Storms, *Convergence: Spiritual Journeys of a Charismatic Calvinist* (Kansas City, MO: Enjoying God Ministries, 2005).

as well. I pray for the sick and have seen many (but not all) healed. God has been pleased to use me in setting free the demonized from the oppression of evil spirits. Words of knowledge are a somewhat regular feature of our Sunday services, and we have numerous individuals who are gifted with the discerning of spirits. I say all this to inform you that what you are about to read has been written from a decidedly charismatic perspective.

I'm not saying that I'm happy about everything that transpires in the charismatic world. Fanaticism, triumphalism, and unwarranted sensationalism are all too present in certain sectors of this branch of the Christian family. I address in appendix B where I think charismatic renewal is strong, where it is weak, and what needs to change in the days ahead. That aside, I thought it important that you know where I stand before getting started.

Earlier Publications

We are now ready to dive into the deep end of the biblical pool. But before I do, I want to express my gratitude to several publishers who have granted permission for me to make use of material already in existence. As you can see from the list below, I've written on this subject in a variety of forms many times before, but never in the comprehensive manner that you will encounter in this book. The following are listed in the order in which they were published.

"A Third Wave View" in *Are Miraculous Gifts for Today? Four Views*, ed. Wayne Grudem (Grand Rapids: Zondervan, 1995).

The Beginner's Guide to Spiritual Gifts (2002; repr., Minneapolis: Bethany House, 2013).

Convergence: Spiritual Journeys of a Charismatic Calvinist (Kansas City, MO: Enjoying God Ministries, 2005).

"Are Miraculous Gifts for Today?"; "What Is Baptism in the Spirit, and When Does It Happen?"; "Should All Christians Speak in Tongues?"; and "Why Doesn't God Always Heal the Sick?" in *Tough Topics: Biblical Answers to 25 Challenging Questions* (Wheaton, IL: Crossway, 2013).

"Ephesians 2:20—The Cessationist's 'Go-To' Text," in *Strangers to Fire: When Tradition Trumps Scripture*, edited by Robert W. Graves

(Woodstock, GA: The Foundation for Pentecostal Scholarship, 2014), 69–72.

"Why NT Prophecy Does NOT Result in 'Scripture-Quality' Revelatory Words (A Response to the Most Frequently Cited Cessationist Argument against the Contemporary Validity of Spiritual Gifts)," in Michael L. Brown, *Authentic Fire: A Response to John MacArthur's Strange Fire* (Lake Mary, FL: Excel, 2014), 377–92.

Practicing the Power: Welcoming the Gifts of the Spirit in Your Life (Grand Rapids: Zondervan, 2017).

"Revelatory Gifts of the Spirit and the Sufficiency of Scripture: Are They Compatible?" in *Scripture and the People of God: Essays in Honor of Wayne Grudem*, edited by John DelHousaye, John J. Hughes, and Jeff T. Purswell (Wheaton, IL: Crossway, 2018).

The Language of Heaven: Crucial Questions about Speaking in Tongues (Lake Mary, FL: Charisma House, 2019).

PART 1

THE NATURE, PURPOSE, AND PRAYERFUL PURSUIT OF SPIRITUAL GIFTS

CHAPTER 1

Supernatural Power for Life and Ministry

Christianity is inescapably *supernatural*. That is to say, we who look to the Bible for truth believe that the physical universe is entirely the product or effect of a spiritual, nonmaterial cause, namely, the power of God. Above, beyond, and in addition to the material universe is a world of the immaterial or spiritual. God is spirit. God's power, the sort of power that dwells within every born-again believer and energizes his or her life, ministry, and whatever spiritual gifts one possesses, is not the sort of "thing" that you can touch or contain in a bottle. *It is the very energy of the life of God himself. It is the supernatural energy that emanates from God's being.*

What concerns us in these introductory comments on the subject of spiritual gifts is the glorious, but often unacknowledged, truth that *this supernatural and divine energy or power quite literally fills and indwells the bodies and souls of every born-again believer.* God does not call upon us to speculate about the nature of this power or to envision it merely as an idea. His desire is that we avail ourselves of it to partner with him in his purposes on the earth. His desire is that we cry out to him that he might intensify, expand, increase, and deepen the manifestation of this power through us in ever more demonstrative and tangible ways in our lives.

If you make any attempt to live an ordinary daily existence or to make use of the many spiritual gifts that God has provided without this power animating and energizing your body, soul, spirit, will, and affections, you will know little of the greatness and glory of God and all he is for us in Jesus. If you make any attempt to pursue Christian ministry apart from a conscious prayer for more of this power and a conscious dependence on it to enable you to do what otherwise you could never hope to do, you will never enter into the fullness of what God has designed for you and for those to whom you might minister. These may sound like rather grandiose assertions. But the Bible provides considerable evidence to back them up.

Consider Paul's prayer in Philippians 3:

> For [Christ's] sake I have suffered the loss of all things and count them as rubbish, in order that I may gain Christ and be found in him, not having a righteousness of my own that comes from the law, but that which comes through faith in Christ, the righteousness from God that depends on faith—*that I may know him and the power of his resurrection*, and may share his sufferings, becoming like him in his death, that by any means possible I may attain the resurrection from the dead. (vv. 8b–11, emphasis mine)

Paul wasn't asking God for more theoretical knowledge about the resurrection of Jesus or the powerful means by which he was brought back to life. He wasn't asking that he be provided with more arguments to prove to unbelievers that Jesus came back to life. He was asking God that he might *personally experience* the very supernatural power that was exerted by the Holy Spirit that prevented the decomposition of the body of Jesus, the supernatural energy that restored life to a corpse, the supernatural energy that overcame and reversed the entropy and decay to which the body of Jesus would otherwise be subjected. He was asking, hoping, and praying for a taste of that power; the ability to feel it in his own body, the opportunity for that very divine energy to course through his being and to heal other people's diseased bodies and to empower him for all that God had called him to do.

The Power at Work within You

Do you realize that this very power is already in you, that it is resident in your heart and mind and hands and speech? Do you realize that this very power that raised Jesus from the dead, the power of God the Holy Spirit, abides in you right now precisely so that you might transcend the limitations of your finite existence and minister to others in power and love as Jesus did?

Is this mere wishful thinking or the fruit of an overly exercised charismatic fanatic? Consider these texts, which are only a few of the many I could cite:

[I pray] that the God of our Lord Jesus Christ, the Father of glory, may give you the Spirit of wisdom and revelation in the knowledge of him, having the eyes of your hearts enlightened, that you may know what is the hope to which he has called you, what are the riches of his glorious inheritance in the saints, *and what is the immeasurable greatness of his power toward us who believe, according to the working of his great might that he worked in Christ when he raised him from the dead and seated him at his right hand in the heavenly places, far above all rule and authority and dominion, and above every name that is named, not only in this age but also in the one to come.* (Eph. 1:17–21, emphasis mine)

Here Paul is asking God the Father to impart to the Ephesian Christians the self-same power, the precise supernatural energy that God exerted when he reanimated and raised from the dead the body of Jesus. This is the self-same power and supernatural energy that exalted Jesus to the right hand of God and subjected every demon and every other human authority to his rule and reign. This is the power that God wants you to experience and put into practice when you evangelize the lost or exercise your spiritual gifts or pray for the sick.

Paul again prayed in Ephesians 3:16 that God would "grant you [and me] to be strengthened with power [not merely with ideas or exhortations or steroid injections; no, with supernatural energy] through his Spirit in your inner being." Observe closely where this power abides and operates. It is in *"your inner being"* that the Spirit operates in this powerful manner. Paul then concluded this prayer with these famous but all-too-often neglected words:

Now to him who is able to do far more abundantly than all that we ask or think, according to the power [written about in theology textbooks; well, no; talked about at Christian conferences; well, no; this power is] *at work within us*, to him be glory in the church and in Jesus Christ throughout all generations, forever and ever. Amen. (Eph. 3:20–21)

What a great and mighty God we have, a God who can infinitely exceed our highest expectations, dreams, prayers, and hopes. But *where* is it that God does all such things? Through what means? Paul said it is *"within us"*! It is *inside* and *through* Christians like you and me. No matter how high your expectations may be in reading this book, no matter how expansive your prayers are for things you hope God might do for you and through you for others, he can do infinitely and abundantly beyond it all. And he does it by means of his own supernatural and divine power that lives in and energizes you and me.

Peter echoed what Paul said repeatedly, especially in the opening verses of his second epistle: "*His divine power* has granted to us all things that pertain to life and godliness, through the knowledge of him who called us to his own glory and excellence" (2 Peter 1:3, emphasis mine). Whatever deficiency you may experience in your Christian "life" and your pursuit of "godliness" can be overcome through God's power.

When Paul prayed for the Christians in Colossae, he asked God that they be "strengthened with all power, according to his glorious might, for all endurance and patience with joy" (Col. 1:11). When he later explained to them how he managed to persevere in his ministry, this is how he said it: "For this I toil, struggling with all *his energy that he powerfully works within me*" (Col. 1:29, emphasis mine). God infuses his very own supernatural energy into his servants. This energy, said Paul, works "within" us powerfully.

This power is the Holy Spirit himself (Luke 1:35; 4:14; 5:17; Acts 10:38; Rom. 15:19). It is not an abstract, free-floating thing out there somewhere. It is an *experiential strengthening presence* that God intends for us to receive and enjoy and employ.

You can see from these many texts that experiencing the power of God the Holy Spirit is not an exceptional, rare, or sporadic phenomenon but is intended by God to be the routine, ordinary, daily reality in the life of all believers, regardless of their education, social standing, financial status, or role in the church. Every facet of the life of every child of God is designed to be an expression of spiritual power: in prayer, in the exercise of gifts, in persevering under oppression, in our resistance to temptation, in loving our spouses, in being diligent and faithful at work, and so on.

Paul said in Romans 15:13 that it is only through the "power" of the Holy Spirit that we are enabled to "abound in hope." He again said in 2 Thessalonians 1:11 that "every resolve for good and every work of faith" that you and I accomplish is by means of his "power." Power is the energy or working of God by which we are saved (Rom. 1:16; 1 Cor. 1:18, 24). And if that were not enough to convince you, the very kingdom of God in its essence consists not "in talk but in power" (1 Cor. 4:20).

We often mistakenly think that the only individuals in the church who are recipients of God's power are apostles or elders or pastors or those with a seminary degree who can read Greek and Hebrew. But consider Stephen, neither apostle nor elder nor pastor, whom Luke described as "full of grace and power," by which he did "great wonders and signs among the people" (Acts 6:8). Stephen was one of the first seven deacons. He was assigned "to serve tables" (v. 2) so that the apostles could devote themselves to preaching the Word and to prayer. The only thing that set him apart is that he was "full of faith and of the Holy Spirit" (v. 5).

Of course, it is true that the power of the Holy Spirit operated through the apostles, such as Paul. He himself said in Romans 15 in describing his ministry, "I will not venture to speak of anything except what Christ has accomplished through me to bring the Gentiles to obedience—by word and deed, *by the power of signs and wonders, by the power of the Spirit of God*" (vv. 18–19, emphasis mine).

But Stephen, a deacon, was full of the same Spirit who filled and empowered Paul—not a junior Holy Spirit, a secondary, lesser version of the Spirit. The "power" that filled Stephen was precisely the same power that filled Paul, the same power that is available to work through you and me today. There isn't one Holy Spirit who filled and empowered Paul and the other apostles, and another, somewhat weaker and less effective Holy Spirit who fills and indwells you and me. The Holy Spirit who was in Jesus, the Holy Spirit who was in Paul, is the Holy Spirit who was in Stephen and is in you and me.

We can't be certain whether Timothy was an apostle. Surprisingly, he is never called an elder, although he probably did hold that office. But when Paul urged him to "fan into flame the gift of God," he grounded this exhortation in the fact that "God gave us a spirit not of fear but of *power* and love and self-control" (2 Tim. 1:7, emphasis mine). When James urged all Christians, ordinary Christians like you and me, to "pray for one another" so that they might be healed (James 5:16), he declared that such prayer "has great *power*" (emphasis mine) as it is working.

Impartation of Power

This power is something not only that God *has* but something that he generously and abundantly *gives* to us. This is what is meant by the word *impartation*. I recently read an article by one of the many "heresy hunters" who troll the internet looking for grist for their mill. He specifically referred to the concept of impartation as something distinctive of New Age practitioners. And yet, as we've already seen in Ephesians 1 and 3, this power is given to us, dwells inside us, and works within us. We see this in numerous other places as well:

> And he called the twelve together and *gave them power* and authority over all demons and to cure diseases, and he sent them out to proclaim the kingdom of God and to heal. (Luke 9:1–2, emphasis mine)

> And behold, I am sending the promise of my Father upon you. But stay in the city until you are *clothed with power* from on high. (Luke 24:49, emphasis mine)

> But you will *receive power* when the Holy Spirit has come upon you. (Acts 1:8, emphasis mine)

And what is this "power" to which Jesus referred and promised would be ours? It is the same "power" of the Holy Spirit on which he himself consciously depended and employed to heal the sick.

> On one of those days, as he was teaching, Pharisees and teachers of the law were sitting there, who had come from every village of Galilee and Judea and from Jerusalem. And the power of the Lord was with him to heal. (Luke 5:17)

This is only one of several texts that tell us that even Jesus was the recipient of the power of the Holy Spirit, which enabled him to do everything in his ministry.[1]

> You yourselves know . . . how God anointed Jesus of Nazareth with the Holy Spirit and with power. He went about doing good and healing all who were oppressed by the devil, for God was with him. (Acts 10:37–38)

---

1 I expand on this theme in the chapter titled "How Did Jesus Perform His Miracles?" in my book *Tough Topics 2: Biblical Answers to 25 Challenging Questions* (Fearn, Ross-shire, UK: Christian Focus, 2015), 47–62.

On several occasions we read in the Gospels that "power" *went out of* Jesus. It was *transferable.* His power was *imparted* to others merely by touch:

> And Jesus, perceiving in himself that power had gone out from him, immediately turned about in the crowd and said, "Who touched my garments?" (Mark 5:30; cf. Luke 8:46)

Jesus felt the power of the Holy Spirit go out of him, and the woman felt the power of the Holy Spirit enter into her body. Indeed, we read in Luke 6:19 that "all the crowd sought to touch him, for *power came out from him* and healed them all" (emphasis mine). This isn't New Age mysticism but biblical Christianity!

This emphasis on power is far and away different from the sort of fleshly triumphalism we see so frequently in certain circles of the church of Jesus Christ. For example, when Paul visited Corinth, he declared that it was "in weakness and in fear and much trembling" (1 Cor. 2:3). His eloquence wasn't nearly up to the standards of his opponents. "My speech and my message were not in plausible words of wisdom." He said that his entire presence and ministry among them came "in demonstration of the Spirit and of *power,* so that [their] faith might not rest in the wisdom of men but in the *power* of God" (vv. 4–5, emphasis mine). Far from being a hindrance to supernatural and divine power, Paul's weakness was the platform on which it was gloriously displayed.

Again, Paul declared in 2 Corinthians 4:7 that "we have this treasure [of the gospel] in jars of clay, to show that the surpassing *power* belongs to God and not to us" (emphasis mine). Later in this epistle, after asking the Lord repeatedly that his thorn in the flesh be removed, he quoted the words of Jesus himself who spoke to him: "My grace is sufficient for you, for my *power* is made perfect in [your] weakness." Paul in turn declared, "Therefore I will boast all the more gladly of my weaknesses, so that the *power* of Christ may rest upon me" (2 Cor. 12:9, emphasis mine).

In 2 Corinthians 6 Paul spoke of his ministry as a servant of God, a ministry that brought into his experience "afflictions, hardships, calamities, beatings, imprisonments, riots, labors, sleepless nights, [and] hunger" (vv. 4–5). His ministry, he went on to say, was carried out by "the Holy Spirit" (v. 6) and by "the power of God" (v. 7). The power of God doesn't enable us to escape hardship and persecution but strengthens us to endure it without giving way to compromise or cowardice!

I earlier alluded to Colossians 1:11, where Paul prayed for the Colossian Christians in this way: "[May you be] strengthened with all power, according to his glorious might, for all endurance and patience with joy" (cf. 2 Tim. 1:7). Note carefully that the standard by which we measure this power or, perhaps better still, the reservoir from which it comes to us, is the "glorious might" of God. Once again, we see that the "power" at work within us is the energy of the omnipotent God who has Genesis 1 on his resume!

Power for Spiritual Gifts

Now, let's bring this to a conclusion by focusing on the power of the Holy Spirit for the purpose of energizing spiritual gifts, whether prophecy, healing, or tongues; the performance of signs and wonders; the encouragement of other believers; or the stunning generosity in the use of our financial resources.

Numerous times in the four gospels where the signs, wonders, and miracles of Jesus are described, the phrase "mighty works" (ESV) is the English rendering of the plural form of the word for "power" (Matt. 11:20–21, 23; 13:54, 58; 14:2; Mark 6:2, 5, 14; 9:39; Luke 19:37; Acts 2:22). We see the same thing in 1 Corinthians 2:4–5 and 1 Thessalonians 1:5. In both of these texts, power is the tangible, visible, vocal work of the Holy Spirit performing miracles through God's people.

> My speech and my message were not in plausible words of wisdom, but in demonstration of the Spirit and of power, so that your faith might not rest in the wisdom of men but in the power of God. (1 Cor. 2:4–5)

> Our gospel came to you not only in word, but also in power and in the Holy Spirit and with full conviction. (1 Thess. 1:5)

We read several times in the New Testament about the spiritual gift of miracles, or the ability to perform miracles. More will be said about miracles in subsequent chapters. For now, I want to point out that in most cases the word translated "miracles" is again the Greek word for "power." When Paul referred to "the working of miracles" as a spiritual gift in 1 Corinthians 12:10

and again in 12:28, he simply used the one word "powers." In Galatians 3:5 he asked the believers in that church, "Does he who supplies the Spirit to you and works miracles [i.e., powers] among you do so by works of the law, or by hearing with faith?"

Or consider a passage that most Christians probably know by heart, Acts 1:8: "But you will receive power when the Holy Spirit has come upon you, and you will be my witnesses in Jerusalem and in all Judea and Samaria, and to the end of the earth." Most have probably been taught that the "power" that Jesus said we will receive is primarily, if not solely, for sharing the gospel. It most assuredly does enable us to overcome fear and speak the gospel clearly. But that was not Luke's primary point. How do we know this?

Luke, who wrote both the gospel that bears his name and the book of Acts, used the word "power" (*dunamis*) twenty-five times. In twenty of those twenty-five occasions, the word describes what God did either through Jesus (ten times) or through ordinary Christians (ten times). In eight of the ten verses where "power" refers to what God did through Jesus (Luke 4:14; 4:36; 5:1; 6:19; 8:46; 10:13; 19:37; 21:27; Acts 2:22; 10:38), it has reference to his miracles, his signs and wonders. In nine of the verses where the word "power" is used to describe what God did through believers, it is with reference to miracles or signs and wonders (Luke 1:15–17 [power of Elijah in preaching]; 9:1–2; 24:49; Acts 3:12; 4:7; 4:32–33; 6:8; 8:13; 19:11). The tenth and final verse where "power" is used is Acts 1:8. Acts 1:8 structures and governs what will unfold in the book and in the experience of the church. If in the other nine times where Luke uses "power" it always refers to the working of miracles, it seems reasonable to conclude that this is what he means in Acts 1:8. Power for working miracles was an essential and expected element in the work of ministry, together with power for preaching and witnessing.

Do Spiritual Gifts Serve Only to Stir up Pride, Envy, and Rivalry among Christians?

Before we proceed any farther down this path, I think it's important to address a concern that I often hear from Christians. To put it bluntly: they are afraid of spiritual gifts. They are concerned that gifts awaken pride and create a competitive atmosphere in the life of the local church. Here is why I don't see this as a legitimate concern.

I don't think I would have enjoyed living during the time of the Old Testament, that era of redemptive history before the coming of Jesus Christ. I would not have enjoyed having to bring a blood sacrifice year after year, knowing that the offering up of bulls and goats could never truly and finally take away the guilt of my sin. I would not have enjoyed the long list of detailed and often bizarre regulations and laws that governed the lives of the people of Israel. I would not have enjoyed skipping bacon for breakfast.

But most of all, I would not have liked that only certain selected people were recipients of the presence and power of the Holy Spirit. Under the old covenant of Moses, only prophets, priests, kings, and certain individuals who were assigned special tasks experienced the power of the Holy Spirit on a regular basis. And even then, you could sin or fail in your God-given task and the Spirit would be taken from you (see 1 Sam. 16:14; Ps. 51:11).

One of the things that makes living now, under the new covenant, so wonderful is the "democratizing" of the Holy Spirit. All of God's people, everyone who knows Jesus as Savior by faith alone, are permanently indwelt and empowered by the Holy Spirit. This is what the apostle Peter described in his sermon on the day of Pentecost:

> "And in the last days it shall be, God declares,
> that I will pour out my Spirit on *all* flesh,
> and your sons and your daughters shall prophesy,
>   and your young men shall see visions,
>   and your old men shall dream dreams;
> even on my male servants and female servants
>   in those days I will pour out my Spirit, and they shall prophesy."
> (Acts 2:17–18, emphasis mine)

What I mean by the word *democratizing* is that all "flesh" receives the Spirit. Whether you are male or female, young or old, free or slave, if you know God through faith in Jesus, you receive permanently the presence and power of the Holy Spirit. This is what Paul also had in mind in 1 Corinthians 12:7. There he said that "to each [which means, to all] is given the manifestation of the Spirit for the common good." You are equipped by God to manifest the presence of his Spirit so that others can become more like Jesus.

Whereas in the Old Testament only specially selected individuals were so gifted, in the New Testament all Christians are so gifted. No one is left out. No one is unqualified or disqualified. It doesn't matter if you think or feel like you've been left out. You haven't been. If you know Jesus, you are gifted by the power of the Spirit to serve and contribute and minister to everyone else in your local church.

However, we don't always do what God has called and equipped us to do. All through 1 Corinthians 12–14, and elsewhere in Scripture, the church is described as if it were a body. And, in truth, we are Christ's body on earth. He is the head, and we are individually members of his body. But just as our physical bodies sometimes suffer from disease or certain ailments or injuries, so also the body of Christ, the local church, can suffer and fail to live as it should. Although we are all indwelt by the Spirit, gifted and empowered by the Spirit, we don't always understand this truth; we don't always embrace it and express it as we should.

There are two common spiritual afflictions in the body of Christ. And they are polar opposites of one another. On the one hand, some Christians struggle with feelings of uselessness, ineffectiveness, and sometimes envy. They think of themselves as expendable, or they feel like they contribute little of value to the church and its work. They are unqualified and unproductive. They believe they are unnecessary. They see themselves as the appendix or the wisdom teeth in the body of Christ.

At the other end of the spectrum are those who experience feelings of self-sufficiency and superiority. They believe they alone matter. They feel important. They see themselves as necessary and essential. And if others aren't just like them, then those people simply don't matter. These are the members of the body who take pride in their gifts and skills, believing that they themselves are personally responsible for their effectiveness. If the first group is the appendix or wisdom teeth of the body of Christ, these folks see themselves as the brains and heart.

And when Christians in a church start thinking this way, the body gets pathologically sick. While some feel useless and say, "You don't need me," and others feel self-sufficient and say, "I don't need you," the body suffers, which is to say, the church suffers.

Let's look at each of these spiritual afflictions and consider the remedy Paul proposed. First, Paul described those who have feelings of uselessness and ineffectiveness. In 1 Corinthians 12:14–16 he wrote,

> For the body does not consist of one member but of many. If the foot should say, "Because I am not a hand, I do not belong to the body," that would not make it any less a part of the body. And if the ear should say, "Because I am not an eye, I do not belong to the body," that would not make it any less a part of the body.

Paul was saying that there are some in the local church who believe that if they aren't like someone else, they are of no benefit or use. They look at how they have been gifted and then look at how God has gifted others, and conclude, "Because I'm not like him, I'm useless. Because I'm not like her, I'm of no benefit to anyone."

In the body of the church, those with "foot" gifts or "ear" gifts or "knee-cap" gifts look at those with "hand" gifts and "eye" gifts and say, "I'm not like that. I don't have those gifts and talents and skills. I can't do what the 'hands' and 'eyes' do, so I guess I'm not of any benefit to anyone at all. I might as well not be a part of the body. Go ahead and amputate me!"

What is the medicine or remedy Paul prescribed to heal the body of this sort of spiritual disease? In verse 17 he said, "If the whole body were an eye, where would be the sense of hearing? If the whole body were an ear, where would be the sense of smell?" His point was that if God had made everyone the same, the body would be a carnival freak show, and it wouldn't function very well. If you who have "ear" gifts had been given "eye" gifts, how would the body hear anything? You might have 20/20 or x-ray vision, but you'd be deaf! Or again, you who have "nose" gifts, if God had given you "ear" gifts, how would the body smell anything?

"If all were a single member, where would the body be? As it is, there are many parts, yet one body" (vv. 19–20). Paul's point is that if everyone in the body is the same, there is no *body*. You'd have one huge eye or one massive hand. So, as he said at the end of both verse 15 and 16, just because you aren't like everyone else in this church, that doesn't make you any less a part of the body or any less essential or useful.

Just because you compare yourself with others and don't like what you see or become envious of what they are or resentful of what you are, that doesn't make you any less a vital and important part of the body of Christ. In the same way that the foot or ear or nose contributes to the health of the physical body, so likewise, regardless of where you fit in or what role you play or how you minister, your presence is essential to the body of Christ. For there to be any body at all, there must be a diversity of members, each with its own part and role to play.

Paul's second response to those who felt useless in the church was to challenge them that their way of thinking was a denial of and a rebellion against the wisdom and goodness of God. Some might say, "Sam, you shouldn't say things like that to people who feel useless, because it will only add to their misery. Now, in addition to feeling useless, they also feel guilty!"

Or think of it this way. The person who feels useless might say, "I never said I wanted the whole body to be an eye or an ear. I realize that a properly functioning body needs ears and a nose and hands and feet and kneecaps and knuckles, and the like. I'm not questioning that. I'm just saying that I don't like being what *I* am. I want to be something different. I want to be like someone else."

Paul responded to this attitude in verse 18: "But as it is, *God* arranged the members in the body, each one of them, as *he* chose" (emphasis mine). Paul wasn't being insensitive. He was not trying to add guilt to feelings of uselessness. He was simply pointing out that you and I need to trust God regarding who we are and how we function in the body of Christ. We need to trust his wisdom and his goodness and rest confidently that what he has done is for our best interests individually and for the church's best interests corporately.

When you say, "I'm useless. I'm of no help to anyone. The church would probably be better off without me," you aren't defying other members of the body. You are defying God. You are challenging his goodness and wisdom in setting the body in place as he has chosen to do (see also 12:11). Whatever gifts we end up receiving, whatever ministries or expressions of service in the church in which we succeed, this was God's doing, not ours. It was his decision, not ours.

To those who may not have gifts that will bring you into the limelight or put a microphone in your hand, those with the gift of service or mercy or encouragement or giving, remember this: *people may not see you, but God does*. You may not feel helpful, but you are indispensable. You may not be acknowledged or praised, but your value to the body is immeasurable, and God will reward you in the age to come.

Now remember, I said there are two diseases or afflictions in the body of Christ that threaten its spiritual health. The first is a feeling of uselessness.

The second is, far from feeling useless, a feeling of utter superiority and self-sufficiency. If some say, "You don't need me; I'm useless," the others say, "I don't need you; I can do it on my own." That's the problem that Paul focused on in verses 21–26:

> The eye cannot say to the hand, "I have no need of you," nor again the head to the feet, "I have no need of you." On the contrary, the parts of the body that seem to be weaker are indispensable, and on those parts of the body that we think less honorable we bestow the greater honor, and our unpresentable parts are treated with greater modesty, which our more presentable parts do not require. But God has so composed the body, giving greater honor to the part that lacked it, that there may be no division in the body, but that the members may have the same care for one another. If one member suffers, all suffer together; if one member is honored, all rejoice together.

The problem in verses 21–26 is self-sufficiency; some people in the church are elitist. Paul's language here is difficult to unpack, and although I can't be sure, I think he was referring to our internal organs in this section. They "seem" to be less important, but only because we can't see them. They do not function visibly, in the open. Yet all would agree that the body can't survive or function without them.

The references to "less honorable" or "unpresentable" body parts are probably a veiled reference to one's sexual organs. These parts are treated with greater honor in that they are clothed or adorned for modesty's sake. Paul's point is that you can't draw conclusions about the importance of a body part based on its external appearance, whether it be clothed or unclothed. Some body parts that might appear to be weak and unpresentable, we treat with extraordinary care. Other body parts that appear important are not given much attention.

God's aim in working this way is that there would be no division in the church based on who has what gift. His aim is that all members of a local body care equally one for another. The body is a unit. Each part should care for and attend to every other part.

Paul concluded his argument in verses 27–31 by making the forceful point that no one spiritual gift is intended for all Christians. God doesn't want everyone to be an apostle. He doesn't want all to be prophets or all to be teachers or all to speak in tongues. Rather, God has appointed some to be apostles, some to be prophets, some to be teachers, and whatever appointment or assignment you have received from God, you are a vital part of the body. Don't wallow in self-pity because you don't have the gifts that someone else does. Don't exalt yourself in pride believing that you don't need others to help you grow in Christ.

Do spiritual gifts stir up pride, envy, and rivalry among Christians? Paul has made it clear: while they can, they need not. God does not want us to abuse his gifts in this way.

CHAPTER 2

Spiritual Gifts: What Are They, and Why Does God Give Them?

Here is a common definition of spiritual gifts, what I will refer to as the "traditional view":

> *Spiritual gifts are capacities or abilities imparted to Christians by the Holy Spirit to enable them to exceed the limitations of their finite humanity in order to serve other believers to the glory of God.*

Believing that the gifts enable us to exceed our human limitations does not mean there is no use for natural talents or learned skills a person may already possess. It may well be that someone who is a college professor discovers, upon his or her conversion, that they have a natural ability to communicate clearly and persuasively biblical truths in the context of a local church. A man who serves as the CEO of a massive corporation and oversees thousands of employees to ensure they are functioning at a high level of productivity may, following his conversion to Christ, be especially suited to serve as an elder in a local church with obvious giftings of administration and leadership.

But it is also possible that someone who is an instructor in a secular classroom may *not* be effective in a teaching role in the local church. And a man whose career path has led him to work as an independent electrician may well be endowed by the Spirit to serve the body of Christ at a high level of collaborative leadership. It would be a mistake, in my view, to think that there will always be a one-to-one correspondence between one's natural or learned skill set and the spiritual gift that appears to correspond closely to what that person has done well in their common vocation or in the secular workplace.

So while it is often the case that the Spirit of God makes use of an individual's abilities, skills, and talents when they enter into spiritual life in the local church, we must maintain a distinction between what we are good at doing as non-Christians and what the Holy Spirit may equip us to do in our service to the body of Christ.

A Challenge to the Traditional View

In his excellent and insightful book *What Are Spiritual Gifts: Rethinking the Conventional View*, Kenneth Berding challenges the common and "traditional view" of spiritual gifts.[1] Similar to the definition above, Berding defines the common, traditional view this way: "The spiritual gifts are abilities, or enablements, given by the Holy Spirit to individual believers to help them serve others."[2] But Berding rejects this definition. Instead, his thesis is that "so-called spiritual gifts are not special abilities; they're Spirit-given ministries."[3] To some, this may seem like a minor distinction, a different choice of words perhaps. And indeed, one might also use such terms as *roles*, *functions*, or *assignments* when describing the ministerial gifting of the Spirit. Berding concedes that the more miraculous ministries, such as healing, prophecy, tongues, and miracles, "can't be done without a special—not simply general—enablement from the Holy Spirit."[4] But here is the key insight we can gain from Berding's argument. If we think of the gifts not just as abilities God gives but as roles or assignments—ministries—to which we are called, it will change the way we think about the gifts. Berding would counsel us not to ask, "How can I discover the special abilities that the Spirit has given me," but rather, "Lord, where do you want me to serve?"

Principal among the texts he cites is Romans 12:4, where Paul spoke of the many members in the body of Christ not having the same "function" (*praxin*). The "gifts that differ according to the grace given to us" (v. 6) are

---

1   Kenneth Berding, *What Are Spiritual Gifts? Rethinking the Conventional View* (Grand Rapids: Kregel, 2006).
2   Berding, 25.
3   Berding, 32.
4   Berding, 33.

said to be the variety of "functions" or "ministry roles" to which God has called believers in the body of Christ. Berding directs our attention to this emphasis on ministry roles, a point that is often missed or overlooked. But rather than argue for or against the traditional view, I propose combining Berding's view of spiritual gifts as ministries believers are called to with the notion of empowerment and ability. In other words, the reason a person is able to fulfill a particular ministry role in equipping the body is because he or she has been empowered by a particular manifestation of the Holy Spirit.

So while I concur with Berding that spiritual gifts are given in order that one might fulfill a particular function or expression of ministry to others in the body of Christ, there is no necessary inconsistency between *function* and *power*. Power enables us to fulfill the task or ministry to which God has appointed us. It is the manifestation or revelation of the Spirit's empowering presence in and through a person that equips or enables him or her to discharge a particular ministry role. I see no reason that both cannot be included in our understanding of spiritual gifts.

So let's revise our earlier definition of spiritual gifts:

> *A spiritual gift is **when the Holy Spirit manifests his presence** and imparts his power into and through individual believers to enable them to exceed the limitations of their finite humanity so that they might **faithfully and effectively fulfill certain ministry** tasks for the building up of the body of Christ.*

Notice that I've kept the emphasis of the traditional view on the impartation of power while emphasizing that these gifts are manifestations of the Spirit's presence to fulfill specific ministry tasks.

To show why we need to retain an emphasis on the impartation of power and ability, I would like to draw our attention to several lines of evidence that support the more traditional approach to the *charismata*.[5]

Evidence for the Traditional View of Spiritual Gifts

In chapter 1 we saw that virtually everything we do as Christians is the result of the empowering presence of the Holy Spirit. The Spirit supplies us with the

---

5   *Charismata* is the English transliteration of the plural form of Paul's word for spiritual gifts.

power to persevere, to resist temptation, to rejoice in suffering, to abound in hope, as well as to perform signs and wonders and to operate effectively in whatever spiritual gift he imparts or whatever ministry assignment he wills for us to undertake. It simply won't do to diminish the role the Spirit plays in providing supernatural power or the ability to do things that we otherwise would never achieve.

Immediately preceding his discussion of spiritual gifts, the apostle Paul declared that "no one can say 'Jesus is Lord' except in [or, by] the Holy Spirit" (1 Cor. 12:3b). He was setting the stage for his explanation of how the many gifts are possible and the manner in which they operate. Although "saying" that "Jesus is Lord" is not a spiritual gift, Paul's point is that such a declaration, much like the many expressions of ministry that follow, is the result of the power of the Spirit operating in and through a born-again child of God.

Then, in describing the *charismata* in 1 Corinthians 12:6, Paul said "there are varieties of activities." This word translated "activities" (ESV) is the Greek word, *energēmatōn*. Perhaps a better translation would be, "energizings" or "empowerings." In any case, Paul immediately said that all such gifts or activities are the result of the one God "who empowers (*ho energōn*)" all of them in all of his people. It's difficult to escape the conclusion that Paul understood these gifts as the result or expression of God's energizing empowerment of the people to whom they are given.[6]

When Paul turned to his description of the *charismata*, he also said they are a "manifestation of the Spirit" (1 Cor. 12:7a). It is possible that the focus is on the Spirit who produces some effect or activity in or through a believer (what Greek scholars call a subjective genitive). However, it is far more likely that Paul was telling us that the Holy Spirit himself is manifested or disclosed in the *charismata* (an objective genitive). As David Garland has put it, "Something is exhibited that discloses the Spirit."[7]

In other words, spiritual gifts are designed to draw attention to the Holy

---

6 Much to Berding's credit, he is willing to concede that at least the nine gifts that follow in 1 Corinthians 12:8–10 are expressions of divine power or special abilities imparted by the Spirit. But why not all the gifts of the Spirit? This isn't to say that Berding is incorrect in emphasizing that some gifts are ministries or assigned roles in the church. It is simply to point out that both elements are likely involved in the full New Testament portrayal of the spiritual gifts.

7 David E. Garland, *1 Corinthians*, Baker Exegetical Commentary on the New Testament (Grand Rapids: Baker Academic, 2003), 578.

Spirit and to alert us to his presence and power. As I like to say, we should speak of such gifts as God's *presence* rather than his *presents*. In bestowing these gifts, God does not grant us something other than himself. The Spirit is himself the gift that he gives. Or again, *spiritual gifts are nothing less than the Holy Spirit himself in us*, enlightening our minds with revelatory truths, empowering our wills, and imparting to us the strength and wisdom to accomplish his gracious purposes in the church. Spiritual gifts must never be thought of as some "thing" granted to us by a distant and uninvolved deity. They are, instead, the Holy Spirit on display in and through human words and works to build up the body of Christ.

Clearly Paul believed that spiritual gifts were in some sense an expression of God working in men and women. We cannot limit spiritual gifts, as Berding does, to the appointment to specific ministries or opportunities of service. There must also be an empowering of individuals by the Spirit of God. As Paul said, whenever a person exercises a spiritual gift, he or she is manifesting the Spirit's operation in and through his or her efforts.

Paul's use of the word translated "manifestation" (*phanerōsis*) in verse 7 was his way of saying that the Spirit is himself disclosed or made visibly evident in our midst whenever the gifts are in use. Spiritual gifts are visible and vocal disclosures of *divine* activity and only secondarily *human* activity. Spiritual gifts are the way in which the Spirit himself makes evident to and through us his presence whenever we do ministry. The *charismata* are God's way of going public among his people.

When thought of in this way, it becomes clear that spurning or minimizing the spiritual gifts is nothing less than a quenching of the Spirit and the gracious divine enabling that he would otherwise bring to us. When we affirm and facilitate the exercise of these gifts, we welcome God into our midst. Does this mean that those who deny the validity of certain gifts today and labor to suppress any expression of them are resisting God? I believe that is what it means; however, I would point out that this is often not their intention. Most cessationists would not consciously resist the operation of the Holy Spirit. They, like their continuationist brothers and sisters, want everything the Spirit genuinely offers. They simply don't believe he offers certain of the more miraculous gifts beyond the time of the early church, whether that be when the canon was closed or when the last of the original apostolic company died.

In any case, the implication is that the question of whether spiritual gifts are for today is not a secondary, tangential issue that only theologians need debate. It directly touches the very mission of the church and how she lives out her calling. How we speak to the world, the way we encounter the enemy, the expectations with which we minister to the broken and wounded and despairing, are all bound up in how we answer the questions *Shall we or shall we not be the church of the Bible? Shall we or shall we not build the church with the tools God has provided?*

Finally, as we look at what Peter wrote in 1 Peter, it seems inescapable that he had in view all spiritual gifts when he encouraged every Christian to "use" whatever gift he or she has "received" to serve others in the body of Christ. Peter affirmed what we've already seen in Paul, namely, that these gifts are exercised "by the strength that God supplies," so that no one would be inclined to take credit for what any particular gift achieves. Spiritual gifts are *all* and always designed to glorify God (1 Peter 4:10–11). They are *all* the result of the strengthening presence of God the Holy Spirit. Some gifts may be more overt expressions of supernatural power. But no gift operates in the absence of God's power.

The Biblical Terminology for Spiritual Gifts

We can be greatly aided in our understanding of the nature of these gifts by looking closely at the variety of terms the Bible uses to identify them. Of course, individual words alone tell us little. We must examine how the words are used in sentences and paragraphs. Context is always decisive in the determination of meaning.

The single word in 1 Corinthians 12:1 translated "spiritual gifts" is the adjective *pneumatikos*, which appears fourteen times in 1 Corinthians. It could be either masculine, referring to "spiritual persons" or "spiritual ones," or neuter, hence "spiritual things"—in particular, the "gifts" that Paul would soon discuss in great depth. Paul used the same term again in 14:1 where it must mean spiritual things or manifestations, not persons. Some scholars translate the word as "spiritual people" and appeal to Paul's use of it in this sense earlier in the epistle (see 1 Cor. 2:13–16; it is also used in this sense in 14:37). Either view is permissible, but I'm inclined to think "spiritual things" is more accurate (as in 12:1). If people are in view, Paul's point would be to bring correction to the misunderstanding of some in Corinth who evaluated the spirituality of individuals on the basis of the "spiritual gifts" they possessed.

The Greek term *charisma* is a characteristically Pauline term, appearing sixteen times in his letters and only once elsewhere (1 Peter 4:10). It refers to a free or graciously bestowed gift. Some believe Paul shifted from *pneumatikos* to *charisma* to counter the Corinthians' notion that some particular manifestation of the Spirit is a sign of heightened spirituality. Paul's point is that all manifestations of the Spirit, regardless of how overtly miraculous or seemingly mundane they may be, are expressions of God's undeserved favor and kindness. The translation "grace-gift" is employed by many. D. A. Carson drives home the point with the rendering "concretizations of grace," that is, actual visible or vocal expressions of God's favor toward and through his people.[8] Gardner reminds us that "the noun in itself does not denote 'spiritual gift.' For it to indicate this meaning either the adjectival qualifier 'spiritual' will be needed, or the context will need to make this abundantly clear."[9] Of course, this is precisely what the broader context of chapters 12 through 14 of Corinthians does.

Charismata, the plural form of *charisma*, is the word from which we derive *charismatic*. *Charisma* refers to a gracious work of God or something God's grace has bestowed. For example, "eternal life" is a *charisma* (Rom. 6:23), as is deliverance from physical death (2 Cor. 1:10). Even celibacy (1 Cor. 7:7) is a *charisma* (see also Rom. 5:15–16; 11:29; but note esp. 1 Cor. 12:4, 9, 28, 30, 31).

Something to keep in mind here is that Peter declared as well that all spiritual gifts are stewardships of "God's varied grace" (1 Peter 4:10b). We make a mistake of some importance if we think that *grace* is merely a principle or attitude or disposition in the character and operations of God according to which he saves and sanctifies us apart from our merit. Grace is surely that, but it is much more. Grace is the power of God's presence. Grace is the power of God's Spirit converting the soul. It is the activity or movement

---

8   D. A. Carson, *Showing the Spirit: A Theological Exposition of 1 Corinthians 12–14* (1987; repr., Grand Rapids: Baker, 2019), 23.

9   Paul Gardner, *1 Corinthians*, Zondervan Exegetical Commentary on the New Testament (Grand Rapids: Zondervan, 2018), 64.

of God whereby he saves and justifies the individual through faith (see esp. Rom. 3:24; 5:15, 17). Therefore, grace is not something in which we merely believe; *it is something we experience as well.*

Grace is not only the divine act by which God initiates our spiritual life, but also the very power by which we are sustained and nourished, and proceed through that life. *The energizing and sanctifying work of the indwelling Spirit is the grace of God.* After Paul had prayed three times for God to deliver him from his thorn in the flesh, he received this answer: "My grace is sufficient for you, for my power is made perfect in weakness" (2 Cor. 12:9). Although Paul undoubtedly derived encouragement and strength to face his daily trials by reflecting on the magnificence of God's unmerited favor, in this text he appears to have spoken rather of *an experiential reality of a more dynamic nature.* It is *the operative power of the indwelling Spirit* to which Paul referred. That is the grace of God.

That grace is the power of God's presence explains why Paul opened his letters by saying, "Grace be to you," and concluded them by saying, "Grace be with you" (see Rom. 1:7; 1 Cor. 1:3; 2 Cor. 1:2; 13:14; Gal. 1:3; Eph. 1:2; Phil. 1:2; Col. 1:2; 1 Thess. 1:1; 2 Thess. 1:2; Titus 1:4). This was an earnest and constant wish of Paul that his converts might continue to experience grace, that they might know afresh the gracious power of God moving in their lives, that they might find in that grace the spiritual resources by which to live in a way pleasing to God.

If *charisma* and its plural *charismata* point us to the gracious origin of spiritual gifts, *diakonia*, often translated "ministries," points to their purpose. All spiritual gifts are designed to serve and help others. In 1 Peter 4:10–11 the verb form is used twice of gifted believers "serving" one another. The point is that spiritual gifts are less privileges than responsibilities. Gifts are not for personal adornment, status, power, or popularity. This word also supports Berding's emphasis on gifts being functions or ministries of service.

As noted above, spiritual gifts are also described by the term *energēma* (1 Cor. 12:6), translated "effects" (NASB) or "working" (NIV) or "activities" (ESV). It points to Paul's emphasis on gifts as the effect or product of divine power. All spiritual gifts are energized by the power of the Holy Spirit in and through the believer. In 1 Corinthians 12:6 Paul wrote, "There are varieties of effects (*energēmatōn*), but the same God who works (*ho energōn*) all things in all persons" (NASB). Gifts, then, are the concrete operations of divine energy through individual believers.

Paul's emphasis on the fact that it is one Spirit who is the source of the multiplicity of gifts must be noted. It stands as a strong corrective to any form of elitism. Gifts come "through the Spirit" (1 Cor. 12:8a), "according to the same Spirit" (v. 8b), "by the same Spirit" (v. 9a), "by the one Spirit" (v. 9b). Indeed, it is "one and the same Spirit" (v. 11) who distributes gifts according to his will.

If the Holy Spirit is sovereign in giving gifts, he is also sovereign in *withholding* them. All is dependent on what God desires for that moment in his church. We must be hesitant to "claim" a gift, but rather submit to his sovereign will (cf. vv. 9, 11).

When we put these words together, we discover that all spiritual gifts (*charismata*) are acts of service or ministry (*diakonia*), which are produced (*energēma*) through us by the triune God (*pneuma* [Holy Spirit] in v. 4; *kurios* [Lord Jesus] in v. 5; *theos* [God the Father] in v. 6). In light of this, we may define a spiritual gift as a God-given, and therefore gracious, Spirit-empowered capacity or ability to serve the body of Christ. It is a divinely and spiritually energized potential to minister to the body of Christ by communicating the knowledge, power, and love of Jesus.

What Is the Purpose of Spiritual Gifts?

A major misconception embraced by many is that the primary (if not the exclusive) purpose of spiritual gifts was to authenticate or supply evidentiary proof of the genuineness of the apostles and their ministry in the first century. But Paul made it quite clear that the primary purpose of all gifts is to edify or build up and spiritually strengthen other believers. He clarified this in 1 Corinthians 12:7 when he said that "to each [of us] is given the manifestation of the Spirit *for the common good*" (emphasis mine). Gifts are other-oriented. This in no way suggests that it is wrong for an individual believer to be personally edified by the exercise of his or her gift(s). It's virtually impossible to faithfully exercise one's spiritual gift, regardless of the context, and not experience a blessing of some sort. If the use of your gift sensitizes your heart to the grace of God and facilitates your maturity in Christ, you can't help but be better equipped to serve and edify others. Although the ultimate purpose of spiritual gifts is to edify others, that is not their only purpose. Jude 20 actually *commands* us to "edify" ourselves!

We must not overlook the fact that Paul's statement that spiritual gifts are for the common good (v. 7)—that is, the building up and encouragement of other Christians—has primarily (but not exclusively) in view the miraculous gifts of verses 8–10. Words of knowledge, words of wisdom, faith, healing, miracles, prophecy, discerning of spirits, and tongues and their interpretation are all designed to edify others. These are the very gifts that many cessationists contend were given primarily, if not entirely, to authenticate the apostles. But this apostle, Paul, begged to differ.

Paul continued in this vein as he described throughout 1 Corinthians 14 that all spiritual gifts, especially prophecy, are given to build up other believers. We see this in the following texts:

> "The one who prophesies speaks to people for their upbuilding [edification] and encouragement and consolation" (v. 3).
> "The one who prophesies builds up the church" (v. 4).
> Both prophecy and interpreted tongues are given "so that the church may be built up" (v. 5).
> All Christians, in the use of their gifts, are to "strive to excel in building up the church" (v. 12b).
> Prophecy in the gathered assembly is designed "to instruct others" (v. 19b).
> "What then, brothers? When you come together, each one has a hymn, a lesson [lit., a teaching], a revelation, a tongue, or an interpretation. Let all things be done for building up" (v. 26).

Observe again that miraculous phenomena like revelatory words, tongues, and interpretation of tongues are designed to build up or edify others and not simply to confirm or authenticate the ministry and message of apostles.

We noted earlier that Peter likewise viewed all spiritual gifts as being given so that Christians can serve other Christians (1 Peter 4:10).

Some cessationists have questioned whether the gift of tongues was intended to edify believers. If it were not, why did God provide the gift of interpretation so that tongues might be utilized in the gathered assembly of the church? If the gift was never intended to edify believers, why did Paul himself pray in tongues in the privacy of his own devotions? That he did so is obvious from 1 Corinthians 14:18–19.

My point is this: *all* the gifts of the Spirit, whether tongues or teaching, whether prophecy or mercy, whether healing or helps, were given, among other reasons, for the edification and building up and encouraging and instructing and consoling and sanctifying of the body of Christ. Even if miraculous gifts were no longer needed to attest and authenticate, a point I concede only for the sake of argument, such gifts would continue to function in the church for the other reasons cited.

Are There Differing Categories of Spiritual Gifts?

Some authors attempt to divide all spiritual gifts into one of three categories. The gifts listed by Paul in 1 Corinthians 12:7–10 are called *manifestation* gifts, ostensibly because of Paul's use of the word "manifestation" of the Spirit in verse 7. In the second category are the so-called *ministry* gifts. These are the ones listed by Paul in Ephesians 4:11. The purpose of these gifts is to enable the people of God to do the work of ministry. In the third category are the *motivational* gifts, found in Romans 12:6–8. The idea behind this third grouping is that we *possess* these gifts. They are gifts that God has built into us and that shape and form our personalities.

Other distinctions are sometimes made between the three categories. For example, some say that no Christian possesses a manifestation gift of the Spirit. These simply, as it were, flow through the believer at the Spirit's discretion. We can't choose when to exercise such gifts. Only God can. The motivational gifts, on the other hand, are ones that we possess and can choose to use at any time. The ministry gifts are unique in that their purpose is to enable certain persons to build up and equip other believers in the body.

I appreciate the effort made by advocates of these distinctions to better understand God's Word, but I must confess I find little exegetical basis for speaking of spiritual gifts in this way. For example, there is no reason in the text to think that only the nine gifts of 1 Corinthians 12 are manifestations of the Spirit. All spiritual gifts are the operation of the Spirit in and through believers. As for the so-called ministry gifts, it should be noted that their purpose is said to be "for building up the body of Christ" (Eph. 4:12b). But this is the very purpose stated for the so-called manifestation gifts. How can a distinction be maintained between them when the explicitly stated purpose of each of them is the same? All spiritual gifts minister to the body of Christ by edifying or building up its members. It should also be noted that the word translated "building up" in Ephesians 4:12 is the same Greek word used throughout 1 Corinthians 14 to describe how so-called manifestation gifts such as prophecy and interpreted tongues function in the lives of God's people.

Yet another shortcoming of this division of gifts into separate categories is the fact that it is quite simply wrong to say that none of the manifestation gifts are in the possession of believers to be used by them at their discretion. To say that "no one can dictate when the gift is to be operated"[10] is simply not true. One example will suffice. I have been blessed with the gift of tongues. I can speak or not speak at will. It is a gift entirely in my control. And this is confirmed by how Paul described the operation of tongues in the corporate assembly. He said in 1 Corinthians 14:27 that "only two or at most three" should speak in tongues, "and each in turn." Clearly he believed that the person with this gift could exercise control over when and how it was used. Otherwise, his instructions here make no sense. He also said that "if there is no one to interpret, let each [of those with the gift of tongues] keep silent in church and speak to himself and to God" (v. 28).

The claim is also made that the so-called ministry gifts in Ephesians 4:11 "are not the possessions—the things that belong to us—spoken of in 1 Peter 4:10. Rather they are *people* who are gifted to be equippers of the rest of the Body of Christ."[11] But I also have the gift of teaching. I am therefore a teacher. And I can exercise this gift at will anytime anywhere. If this isn't to say that it is in my "possession," I don't know how to say it is. Paul referred to Timothy's gift as being in him (1 Tim. 4:14; 2 Tim. 1:6). Furthermore, as noted before, all spiritual gifts "equip" the saints for "ministry." To isolate the four or five gifts in Ephesians 4 and claim this for them is to fail to recognize that such is the purpose of all gifts in the body of Christ.

The argument is also made that these gifts are called "motivational"

---

10 Don Fortune and Katie Fortune, *Discover Your God-Given Gifts* (Grand Rapids: Chosen, 2009), 17.
11 Fortune and Fortune, 18.

because they "are the motivating forces of our lives."[12] However, there is nothing in Romans 12 that speaks of such gifts as the motivating force of our lives. This is read into the text in order to justify creating a separate category for the seven gifts listed there. I might also add that my primary spiritual gift is that of a pastor (Eph. 4:11). That is what motivates me more than anything else. Yet the gift of pastor is not listed in Romans 12 but only in Ephesians 4 where we supposedly have only the ministry gifts.

There is one final reason why I find this attempt at categorization to be forced on the biblical text rather than read out of it. Consider the gift of prophecy. Is prophecy a motivational gift or a manifestation gift or a ministry gift? Yes! Prophecy is found in all three lists: in Romans 12, 1 Corinthians 12, and Ephesians 4. To escape the difficulty this poses, one author simply chooses arbitrarily to call prophecy in Romans 12 "perceiving" or the "perceiver." It is acknowledged that the same Greek word is used in all three lists, but that "perceiver" is chosen "to avoid confusion."[13] But there is no confusion. The spiritual gift of prophecy is the same in all three lists. If it is not, someone should bring forth exegetical evidence from the text itself that justifies differentiating the various kinds of prophecy. But there is no such evidence. Nothing in what Paul wrote justifies the conclusion that he was talking about different prophetic gifts, as if by one the person "perceives" and by another the person speaks words of encouragement and consolation. The same could be said for the gift of teaching (Rom. 12:7). It also appears in the list of so-called ministry gifts in Ephesians 4 and again in 1 Corinthians 12:29.

I can only conclude that the biblical text does not itself justify drawing these distinctions among various categories of spiritual gifts. All the gifts are themselves different from one another, but they all share most if not all of the same characteristics: they are manifestations or expressions of the Spirit's power, they all are given for the "common good" of the body, they all are expressions of God's undeserved favor, they all are to be "used" and not neglected, they all serve to equip others for the work of ministry, and they all are designed to build up or edify believers in the body of Christ.

If there is one way to differentiate one group of gifts from another, it

---

12 Fortune and Fortune, 20.
13 Fortune and Fortune, 19.

would be a distinction found in Peter's statement in 1 Peter 4:10–11. There he appears to envision what we might call "speaking" gifts and "serving" gifts. There is yet one more distinction that will be unpacked and explained in more detail later in this book. It is the difference between gifts that are residential or permanent, on the one hand, and gifts that are occasional and circumstantial, on the other. So, the person whom I earlier quoted as referring to gifts that are in our "possession" versus gifts that "flow" through us at the Spirit's discretion has actually made a valid distinction. But, as I said, I'll explain this in more detail later in the book.

Gifts Are Not Personality Traits

It's important to remember that nowhere in Scripture are gifts portrayed as personality traits or characteristics. A person who is gregarious and extroverted can receive the gift of mercy. A person who is quiet and introverted can receive the gift of teaching. A person who lacks self-confidence and is by nature somewhat hesitant to speak can receive the gift of evangelism. A person who has little faith and never expects to hear from God can be the recipient of a word of knowledge. This isn't to say there is never any overlap between a person's unique personality and the gift God bestows to them, but we must never identify any particular gift with any particular personality trait.

Again, let's take the gift of prophecy as an example. Paul said that anyone is a candidate to prophesy (1 Cor. 14:1, 5, 24, 29–32). A prophet, therefore, is someone who consistently receives spontaneous revelatory words from God that are shared with others for their "upbuilding and encouragement and consolation" (1 Cor. 14:3). But nowhere does the New Testament say that "prophet" is a particular set of personality traits. Given that any and all have the potential to prophesy, how could it be?

In other words, a prophet is never portrayed in Scripture as someone who always displays a certain demeanor or interacts with others in a particular way or responds to arguments with a unique emotional energy. A prophet is someone who consistently receives spontaneous revelatory words (pictures, dreams, impressions) from the Lord and speaks them to the edification and encouragement of others.

Quite often in some charismatic circles a person with certain personality and relational characteristics is identified as a "prophet" or a person with the gift of "mercy" when in point of fact the Spirit has never imparted that particular gift to them. They are who and what they are, in terms of their personality and character and relational development, because they are being progressively transformed by the Spirit to be more like Jesus, but not because they happen to have a particular spiritual gift that someone perceives to be linked with that sort of behavior or relational style.

As noted earlier, spiritual gifts are concrete manifestations of the Spirit through us. They are not who we are, therefore, but rather what we do in the power of the Spirit for the good of others. We should be careful always to differentiate between our particular gift(s), on the one hand, and who we are as God's children in Christ Jesus, on the other. There is, then, an important difference between our character and personality and how we are being sanctified daily to become more and more conformed to the image of Christ, and what gift the Spirit imparts to us for building up fellow believers. Simply because a person is extroverted or introverted, self-confident or timid, loves crowds or prefers solitude, is organized or disorganized, does not necessarily mean that he or she will have any particular spiritual gift that always corresponds to that particular feature of their personality or relational style. Will the two sometimes overlap? Sure. But we must never insist on a one-to-one correspondence such that because "Sally" or "Steve" displays certain personality traits they are therefore to be classified as a "mercy" or a "prophet" or a "teacher."

The danger in drawing too close a relationship between what our spiritual gift is and who we are as individual believers is that when our gift wanes or grows dormant or isn't received well by others, we would suffer shame and experience self-doubt and have fears regarding our worth as the children of the most high God. Our identity as sons and daughters of God, our identity as believers "in Christ," must never be tied to a particular "charism" or gift that the Spirit has chosen to impart to us and through us for the good of others.

CHAPTER 3

How Many Spiritual Gifts Are There, and How Many Might a Christian Receive?

Some reading this might wonder, *Why ask this question? Isn't this easy enough to answer?* After all, one need only turn to the relevant biblical texts on the subject and count them up. It's not a particularly challenging or difficult thing to do. But while we will begin with that approach, we must also ask, "Might God have provided the church with *charismata* that are not specifically identified or listed in the New Testament?" Some, I realize, will reject this question from the start. They believe that if God wanted us to receive and exercise other spiritual gifts, he would surely have mentioned them in the New Testament in conjunction with the traditional lists. Are we not undermining the sufficiency of Scripture to suggest that it has failed to mention all the possible spiritual gifts given by the Spirit? Others will insist that if we allow for certain *charismata* beyond those listed in the New Testament, we open wide the door for speculation and abuse. What's to prevent anyone from concocting or creating additional spiritual gifts that might lead us outside the governing boundaries of Scripture? These are important questions.

Let's begin with the easy answer and note the gifts that are explicitly included in the lists of the New Testament.

Romans 12:6–8

In Romans 12:6–8, Paul wrote, "Having gifts that differ according to the grace given to us, let us use them" (v. 6a). His introductory comment leads us to expect he would identify every gift of the Spirit. Instead, Paul selected seven gifts. I've added numerical identifiers to the listing of these *charismata* for clarity:

> (1) if prophecy, in proportion to our faith; (2) if service, in our serving; (3) the one who teaches, in his teaching; (4) the one who exhorts, in his exhortation; (5) the one who contributes, in his generosity; (6) the one who leads, with zeal; (7) the one who does acts of mercy, with cheerfulness. (vv. 6b–7)

Why didn't Paul list other gifts, such as those he delineated in 1 Corinthians 12:7–10? Some contend that the two lists contain different categories of gifting or different kinds of gifts. Yet the gift of prophecy is mentioned not only here in Romans 12, but also in 1 Corinthians 12:7–10, 12:28–30, and again in Ephesians 4:11. I doubt if anyone is prepared to make a case for differing kinds of prophetic ministry. It seems likely, unless a strong case can be made otherwise, that Paul was referring to a singular gift of prophecy and included it in all four lists.

The same may be said about the gift of serving, mentioned not only by Paul in Romans 12:7 but also by Peter in 1 Peter 4:11. And the same is true for the gift of teaching, which Paul listed in Romans 12:7 and again in 1 Corinthians 12:29. And although the Greek terms are different, it is unlikely that we should draw too great a distinction between "the one who leads" in Romans 12:8 and the one who has the gift of "administrating" in 1 Corinthians 12:28.

The fact that there are multiple lists of the *charismata* but only seven are mentioned in Romans 12 leads some to conclude that it would be improper and unjustified to think that the combination of all the gifts from all the lists provides us with an exhaustive delineation of the gifts that God might give. For now, I have not attempted to define or describe these gifts, but only to list them. Their nature and operation will be taken up in a subsequent chapter.

1 Corinthians 12:4–11

In 1 Corinthians 12:4–11 the apostle Paul mentioned the existence not only of a "variety" of gifts (v. 4a) but also "varieties of service" and "varieties of activities" (vv. 5–6). Are we to conclude that this "variety" includes only the nine gifts later mentioned in verses 8–10? Or could Paul again have been providing us with a sampling of gifts, leaving us to assume there are others not explicitly mentioned in the New Testament? We know with certainty that, as with the list in Romans 12, those in verses 8–10 are at most representative. Other lists include gifts not mentioned in verses 8–10. In any case, here are the nine gifts listed in 1 Corinthians 12:8–10. Once again, I have inserted numerical markers into the text to facilitate our identification of them all:

> For to one is given through the Spirit (1) the utterance [or, "word," logos] of wisdom, and to another (2) the utterance of knowledge according to the same Spirit, to another (3) faith by the same Spirit, to another (4) gifts of healing[s] by the one Spirit, to another (5) the working of miracles, to another (6) prophecy, to another (7) the ability to distinguish between spirits, to another (8) various kinds of tongues, to another (9) the interpretation of tongues. (vv. 8–10)

1 Corinthians 12:28–30

The list that appears at the conclusion of 1 Corinthians 12 is an interesting mixture of what some would call both miraculous gifts and those that are notably more mundane or routine. In other words, the former grouping includes those gifts that are more overtly miraculous or supernatural, while the latter, although likely no less the manifestation of the Spirit's power, appear more natural in operation. Here is the list, again with numeric specification inserted into the text:

> And God has appointed in the church (1) first apostles, (2) second prophets, (3) third teachers, (4) then miracles, (5) then gifts of healing, (6) helping, (7) administrating, and (8) various kinds of tongues. Are all apostles? Are all prophets? Are all teachers? Do all work miracles? Do all possess gifts of healing? Do all speak with tongues? Do all (9) interpret? (vv. 28–30)

1 Corinthians 13:1–3, 8–10

Although there is not a list to speak of in 1 Corinthians 13:1–3, 8–10, there is a reference to several spiritual gifts in this chapter. Paul mentioned tongues in verse 1, prophecy in verse 2, most likely the word of knowledge in verse 2, and also the gift of faith in verse 2. He may have been referring to the gift of giving in verse 3 ("If I give away all I have"), which he described in Romans 12:8 as "the one who contributes." A bit further down in the chapter, he again mentioned prophecy, tongues, and perhaps the word of knowledge (v. 8). Nothing new appears in this chapter, as each of these gifts has already been listed by Paul in 1 Corinthians 12.

Ephesians 4:11

Many contend that the "gifts" listed in Ephesians 4:11 are less abilities and more specific and somewhat authoritative or governing offices in the local church. Here Paul said that the risen Christ "gave (1) the apostles, (2) the prophets, (3) the evangelists, (4) the shepherds and (5) teachers" (or possibly, [4] shepherd-teachers). We find here two gifts that are not mentioned elsewhere: evangelism and shepherding or pastoring.

1 Peter 4:10–11

Peter's words in 1 Peter 4:10–11 are not technically a list, as only two general categories are noted. Some have argued that these are the only two categories and that all the gifts previously enumerated by the apostle Paul may be subsumed under them. Peter said, "As each has received a gift, use it to serve one another, as good stewards of God's varied grace: whoever speaks, as one who speaks oracles of God; whoever serves, as one who serves by the strength that God supplies—in order that in everything God may be glorified through Jesus Christ. To him belong glory and dominion forever and ever. Amen."

Was Peter suggesting that all gifts are either serving gifts or speaking gifts? In other words, was he telling us that gifts such as mercy, healing, administrating, faith, and giving, just to mention a few, are examples of what it means to serve but do not necessarily entail a special capacity to speak with eloquence or persuasive power? Likewise, would speaking gifts include things like tongues, prophecy, exhortation, and teaching? Perhaps. But the problem is that some gifts seem to overlap the two categories, while yet others struggle to find a place in either. I think it wise not to press the distinction between speaking and serving gifts, simply because in actual experience we often serve people by speaking truth to them and we communicate truth (even if not verbally) by giving and expending ourselves in their service.

Tallying Up the Gifts

From these texts we might then produce this list, in no particular order:

1. prophecy
2. service
3. teaching
4. exhortation
5. contributing or giving
6. leading
7. mercy
8. word of knowledge
9. word of wisdom
10. faith
11. gifts of healing(s)
12. miracles
13. distinguishing or discerning of spirits
14. tongues
15. interpretation of tongues
16. apostleship
17. helping
18. administrating
19. evangelism
20. pastoring or shepherding
21. pastoring-teaching

Leading and administrating may actually be the same gift. Likewise, mercy and helping, together with serving, may all be differing ways of referring to the same gift. And whereas a person might be a pastor-teacher, we should acknowledge that another may have only the gift of teaching while yet another may have only the gift of pastoring (although it is difficult to envision how one might "pastor" people without also "teaching" them). In any case, it would seem that, given the most generous reading of Scripture, there are twenty-one spiritual gifts. But might there be more gifts that the Spirit supplies according to his will (1 Cor. 12:11) that no New Testament author explicitly mentioned? And if so, how would we recognize them? Let's consider a few possibilities.

The first thing that comes to mind is intercession. Nowhere in the New Testament do we read of intercession as a spiritual gift per se, but does that necessarily preclude the possibility that it might be one? All of us, I'm sure, have known individuals who are devoted to prayer in a way that exceeds what the typical Christian might do. Yes, we must all pray and intercede at the throne of grace. But some believers appear to be uniquely energized or called to pray in such a way that they witness a remarkable track record of answered petitions. I've personally known quite a few who feel extraordinarily drawn to the prayer closet, who spend hours each day seeking God on behalf of others and their needs.

Then there is the ministry of deliverance. As with intercession, all Christians have not only been given the responsibility to pray but also have the God-given authority, in Christ and his name, to exercise power over the demonic (see Luke 10:17–20). I have had the privilege of ministering to those who were demonized or oppressed by evil spirits and have witnessed them receiving freedom. But others, once again, appear to operate at a level of authority and success in this regard in a way that far exceeds anything that I or any number of other Christians have experienced. Might there be a spiritual gift of deliverance?

Some may well push back on both of these suggestions by pointing out that all believers are to pray without ceasing and are to put on the armor of God by which we might resist the influence of our enemy. That is certainly true. But this is also the case with numerous other gifts of the Spirit. All should evangelize, but not all have the gift of evangelism. All should give, but not all do so with the generosity of those who have the gift of giving. All of us who know Jesus as Lord and Savior exercise faith, but not all experience that extraordinary, supernatural surge of confidence to believe that God is going to do things for which we don't have explicit biblical warrant. And the list of such universal responsibilities and extraordinary spiritual giftings could go on and on. So, the fact that all of us pray and proclaim victory over the demonic does not itself rule out the possibility that there may be spiritual gifts that are given to enable certain believers to operate in these ministries at an elevated level of success.

One more example comes to mind. For lack of a better way of expressing it, I would call it the spiritual gift of interpretation. I'm not talking about the gift of interpretation of tongues. Neither do I have in mind the ability to interpret Scripture. Anyone with sufficient training in the discipline of hermeneutics and its principles can interpret the meaning of Scripture without any particular spiritual gift. What I have in mind is the capacity and insight that enables a person to understand and make sense of revelatory truths that come either by means of a vision or dream or trance or other expression of the Spirit's revelatory ministry.

We first see evidence of this in the Old Testament narrative concerning Joseph, who was unjustly imprisoned with the cupbearer of the king of Egypt and his baker. The cupbearer and baker both had dreams on the same night (Gen. 40:5). They were greatly troubled, largely because there was no one who could interpret them (vv. 7–8a). "And Joseph said to them, 'Do not interpretations belong to God? Please tell them to me'" (v. 8b). Two years later Pharaoh himself had a disturbing dream that no one could interpret (Gen. 41:8). The cupbearer remembered how Joseph interpreted his dream and reported this to Pharaoh, who summoned Joseph to interpret for him. "It is not in me," said Joseph; "God will give Pharaoh a favorable answer" (v. 16).

Nothing is said here that Joseph's ability was a spiritual gift. Such language would have been anachronistic, as it was first used subsequent to the Spirit's outpouring at Pentecost. But it may well be that this Old Testament incident was an adumbration, as it were, of the Spirit-empowered ability to interpret dreams and visions in the age of the new covenant. Daniel had a similar experience. Following King Nebuchadnezzar's dream, Daniel provided him with the interpretation. We read that "the mystery was revealed to Daniel in a vision of the night" (Dan. 2:19a; cf. 2:28). It happened yet again with another of Nebuchadnezzar's dreams, and Daniel interpreted it accurately (Dan. 4:4–33).

Again, I'm not suggesting that either Joseph or Daniel possessed a "spiritual gift" of dream interpretation, but it is not beyond the realm of possibility that what God did through these two men in the Old Testament he did yet again by means of a spiritual gift in the age of the New Testament. The Spirit-enabled enlightenment by which one can interpret or make sense of some revelatory encounter may well be a gift that is operative in this age that lacks explicit biblical reference. I must also say that I've witnessed on numerous occasions both men and women who seemed extraordinarily accurate in their interpretation of dreams and visions, an ability that does not appear to be accounted for by merely natural means or insights or intelligence. It seems to be a gift from God.

As noted earlier, many will insist that it is dangerous for us to go beyond what the Bible explicitly says concerning spiritual gifts. But I'm not advocating for anything that explicitly contradicts Scripture. In fact, if there are additional spiritual gifts beyond those we see in the texts noted above, regardless of their nature, they must be held accountable to the standards and guidelines the New Testament sets forth to govern the exercise of any and all *charismata*. We should also ask what reasons might be given to conclude that God would be unwilling or disinclined to impart gifts not listed in Scripture. Might there not be new circumstances, unexpected crises, and pressing needs that emerge at various times throughout the life of local churches in the present age that call for a wider manifestation of the Spirit than that which Paul described in 1 Corinthians 12–14?

Nothing that I have said on this matter amounts to proof that there are more spiritual gifts than what we read about in Scripture. I may be entirely wrong to suggest that experiences such as intercession, deliverance, and interpretation of revelatory phenomena are spiritual gifts. But I think we should remain open to the possibility.

How Many Spiritual Gifts Might a Christian Receive?

A handful of texts address the question of how many spiritual gifts a Christian might receive, or at least provide us with principles from which we may draw our answer to this question. We begin with Romans 12:6, where Paul wrote, "Having gifts that differ according to the grace given to us, let us use them." Paul then proceeded to list seven spiritual gifts in particular. His use of the plural "gifts" in verse 6 does not itself suggest or require that each Christian has more than one, but it certainly allows for it.

When we turn our attention to 1 Corinthians, we gain a bit more insight into the answer to our question. It is undeniably the case that every Christian has at least one spiritual gift. For example, Paul said, with reference to the distribution of the many "gifts" and "varieties of service" and "varieties of activities" that "it is the same God who empowers them all in *everyone*" (1 Cor. 12:4–6, emphasis mine). No one is excluded. All believers are included in his reference to "everyone." But Paul was even more explicit in the verses that follow:

> To each is given the manifestation of the Spirit for the common good. For to one is given through the Spirit the utterance of wisdom, and to another the utterance of knowledge according to the same Spirit, to another faith by the same Spirit, to another gifts of healing by the one Spirit, to another the working of miracles, to another prophecy, to another the ability to

distinguish between spirits, to another various kinds of tongues, to another the interpretation of tongues. All these are empowered by one and the same Spirit, who apportions to each one individually as he wills. (vv. 7–11)

There are several things to note here. First, Paul declared that "to each" is given a manifestation of the Spirit. He clearly had in view each believer, each member of the body of Christ, whom he described in greater detail in verses 14–26. The words "to each" thus tell us that every born-again child of God has at least one spiritual gift.

This is confirmed as we read deeper into the text, for Paul said that "to one" is given this particular gift and "to another" yet another gift, and so on. It would be strange indeed that Paul would use such language that highlights the distribution of gifts among members of the body of Christ if any one person were excluded from being a recipient. Finally, he repeated himself at the close of verse 11 by saying once more that the Holy Spirit apportions "to each one individually as he wills." The emphasis on the all-inclusive "each one" is decisive in helping us answer our question.

That all Christians are gifted by the Spirit is confirmed yet again by what Paul said in 1 Corinthians 12:14–26. There he emphasized the essential contributing role that every member of the body of Christ has in helping others reach spiritual maturity. No one can say that he or she has no need of another. All serve everyone else in accordance with the way that God has gifted them. This would be a strange thing indeed for Paul to say if there were any in the body of Christ who did not have at least one spiritual gift.

At the close of chapter 12, Paul again emphasized that each believer is a member of the body of Christ. He then proceeded to delineate numerous gifts that have been apportioned to those members. Were it the case that some in the body were gift-less, his point about the unity of the one body and its many members and how they function together to build up one another would be meaningless.

Although it does not speak decisively to our question, Paul's exhortation in 1 Corinthians 14:26 clearly suggests that his expectation was that each believer would come to a corporate assembly with something to contribute. If there were some Christians who lacked a gift, his words of counsel would fall flat on their ears.

1 Peter 4:10–11

Perhaps the most explicit statement confirming the fact that every Christian has at least one spiritual gift is found in 1 Peter 4:10–11. There the apostle said this:

> As each has received a gift, use it to serve one another, as good stewards of God's varied grace: whoever speaks, as one who speaks oracles of God; whoever serves, as one who serves by the strength that God supplies—in order that in everything God may be glorified through Jesus Christ. To him belong glory and dominion forever and ever. Amen.

One of the greater threats to a church being and becoming all that God wants of it is the unbiblical idea that spiritual gifts and the ministry they produce are the sole responsibility of pastors and elders and those who work full-time for a local church. It is the notion that the professional clergy, to use profoundly unbiblical terms, those who've been educated in a seminary or have been officially ordained to ministry, are the only ones who've received spiritual gifts and are the only ones who are responsible to serve others in the church.

But Peter clearly said that "each" has received a gift to be used in the service of others and for the glory of God. No one is exempt. No one is unqualified. No one is left to himself or herself without the powerful enabling presence of the Spirit. We must overcome and reject the clergy/laity distinction. It isn't only pastors and elders who have spiritual gifts. Peter listed no educational qualifications.

We can say with confidence that every Christian has at least one spiritual gift and no Christian has them all (1 Cor. 12:29–30). Spiritual gifts forever shatter the myth that there are two kinds of Christians: those who minister and serve and those who are served and ministered to; those who have spiritual gifts and those who don't. All have at least one gift, and all of us are to minister and serve.

We can make several other important observations in light of Peter's declaration that all Christians have at least one gift. First, we "receive" spiritual gifts; we don't earn them. They are not a reward for holiness. They are God's gift freely given. There is no standard you have to meet, no heightened level of maturity you must first attain.

Second, we are commanded to "use" our gift or gifts. The apostle Paul agreed with Peter on this. He wrote this in Romans 12:6: "Having gifts that differ according to the grace given to us, let us *use* them" (emphasis mine). So, both Peter and Paul issued the same command to all of us: use your gift to serve. If you are not serving others by making use of the gift you've received, you are sinning. This is a command, not an option.

Third, as we noted earlier, all gifts are designed to "serve one another," not ourselves. We serve for the good of others. Paul said that all spiritual gifts, from the working of miracles to mercy, are for the "common good" (1 Cor. 12:7).

Fourth, gifts are a stewardship from God. He has entrusted to us his Spirit. Spiritual gifts are less a privilege and more a responsibility. In a very real sense, then, my gift is not really mine. It is only entrusted to me for the sake of others.

Fifth, God's grace comes in a wide variety of expressions. God's "varied grace" (1 Peter 4:10) is on display when we serve one another. The word "varied" points to the fact that no two people will always receive the same gift, and even if you have a gift that another shares, it won't always manifest itself in the same way. God's gracious enabling of us is diverse and will look different depending on the person who makes use of it. The important point to remember is that you don't have to be like others. In fact, you should never try to be like others. It also means that no two people will always operate with the same degree of accuracy or effectiveness in the exercise of their spiritual gift. So stop comparing yourself with someone else.

Sixth, I earlier directed attention to the fact that Peter divided all gifts into two broad categories: *serving and speaking*. Speaking gifts include teaching, prophecy, apostleship, tongues, interpretation of tongues, exhortation, word of knowledge, and word of wisdom; while serving gifts include giving, leading, administration, mercy, helps, healing, and miracles. Some Christians have only one speaking gift; some have only one serving gift. Some have several speaking gifts. Some have several serving gifts. Some have both several speaking gifts and serving gifts. But no one has no gift!

We should also take note of the fact that Peter didn't say that those with speaking gifts are more important or essential to the church than those with serving gifts. That is a mistake based on the idea that visibility and public recognition are important to God. They aren't. Those who serve quietly behind the scenes and never utter a word on a microphone from a platform are just as valuable and highly regarded by God as those who preach every week or prophesy.

Seventh, serving requires *God's strength* or *power*. Everything the Christian man or woman does, if it is to be virtuous and glorifying to God, must be done conscious of the fact that God is the one who supplies the strength for everything, God is the one who empowers every deed, God is the one who stirs our spirits and moves our wills and sustains our good intentions and inflames our affections.

Finally, the ultimate purpose of serving by means of one's gift is so that *God will be glorified*. He is honored when you make use of the grace he has bestowed. Therefore, it stands to reason that when you sit idle and uninvolved, you are robbing God of the glory that he might otherwise have received had you been faithful to serve others in his name. It's critical that you know this so that when someone hears you praying or sees you loving or is the recipient of your hospitality or benefits from the use of your spiritual gift, they will instinctively give the glory to God rather than to you.

This also means that it is entirely possible to appear to "serve" others all the while you are dishonoring God. If your service is not consciously undertaken in "the strength that God supplies" (1 Peter 4:11), it will end up being for your glory and not his. And if you find serving others always burdensome and weighty and just one more obligation or moral duty that you have to fulfill so that others won't think badly of you, you obviously are "serving" in the strength that you yourself supply and not in the strength "that God supplies."

Are Miraculous Spiritual Gifts the Exclusive Possession of Apostles?

Later on we'll explore in more detail the question of whether miraculous spiritual gifts are the exclusive possession of apostles, but for now we observe that the apostle Paul said that to "each," male and female, young and old (1 Cor. 12:7a), has been given the manifestation of the Spirit. And when he proceeded to provide a listing of those manifestations, he specifically included the more overtly miraculous gifts of prophecy, healing, tongues, and miracles, among others. Peter cited the prophecy of Joel on the day of Pentecost to prove that gifts such as prophecy and tongues would be given to "all flesh," including "your sons and your daughters," "young men," "old men," as well as "male servants and female servants" (Acts 2:17–18). Gifts are *not* the exclusive privilege of elders, deacons, pastors, Sunday school teachers, or some unique class of alleged supersaints.

When we read 1 Corinthians 12:7–10, nothing suggests that only apostles are endowed with these gifts. On the contrary, prophecy, faith, miracles, and other supernatural manifestations are given by the sovereign Spirit to *ordinary* Christians in the church for the daily, routine building up of the body. Not merely apostles and elders and deacons, but also homemakers and carpenters and farmers receive the manifestation of the Spirit—all "for the common good" (v. 7) of the church.

Spiritual gifts are not roles. Roles are those opportunities for ministry common to all and available to anyone. All of us are to be witnesses, but not all have the gift of evangelism. All are to give, but not all have the gift of giving. All pray, but not all have the gift of intercession. All have a responsibility to judge and weigh prophetic words and to differentiate among the "spirits" (1 Thess. 5:19–22; 1 John 4:1–6), but not all have the gift of discerning of spirits. All have faith, but not all have the gift of faith. All should teach (Col. 3:16), but not all have the gift of teaching. All can prophesy (1 Cor. 14:24), but not all are prophets. All may receive wisdom (Eph. 1:17), though all may not exercise the gift of word of wisdom.

Likewise, spiritual gifts are not offices. The term *office* is not strictly a biblical one. However, it would appear that an office in the church is characterized by: (1) an element of permanency, (2) recognition by the church (often with a title), (3) being authorized or hallowed in some way, usually through a public ceremony with the laying on of hands, and (4) remuneration for the individual who fills it.

Might a Christian Have Many Spiritual Gifts, Even If No One Has Them All?

The simple answer to the question of whether a Christian might have many spiritual gifts even if no one has all of them is yes. In all the texts noted above, we plainly saw that every Christian has at least one gift, but none of those statements requires that we conclude one cannot have more. In fact, Scripture provides several explicit indications that a believer might have several gifts.

A brief consideration of the life and ministry of the apostle Paul demonstrates that he had received numerous gifts of the Spirit. More will be said later about whether apostleship is a gift or an office, but Paul was clearly an apostle. It would appear that Paul exercised either a prophetic gift or the word of knowledge when, in Acts 13:7–12, he discerned that Elymas the magician was a "son of the devil" and "enemy of all righteousness, full of all deceit and villainy" (v. 10). No one would doubt that Paul was an extremely gifted evangelist. Luke recorded in Acts several instances where Paul operated, under God's sovereignty, in the gifts of healing (see, for example, Acts 14:9–10). He often worked miracles and testified that he spoke "in tongues more than all" the Corinthians combined (1 Cor. 14:18). He was also a teacher and an exhorter. And the list could go on. At minimum, therefore, Paul himself had been made the recipient of at least nine spiritual gifts.

There are also a few texts where the underlying assumption is that a Christian might well be the recipient of more than one gift. Paul's exhortation to the Corinthians that they should "earnestly desire the spiritual gifts, especially that you may prophesy" (1 Cor. 14:1; cf. 12:31; 14:39) clearly demonstrates that he expected these believers (and us, as well) to pray for and pursue additional gifts. If each of the Corinthians had already received at least one gift when they came to saving faith in Christ, Paul's exhortation would require us to believe that God might still impart additional gifts, always subject to the will of the Spirit (1 Cor. 12:11).

In 1 Corinthians 14:12 Paul wrote, "So with yourselves, since you are eager for manifestations of the Spirit, strive to excel in building up the church." Paul did not rebuke the Corinthian believers for this eager desire for even more manifestations of the Spirit in the form of gifts. He appears to have commended them for it. But if they had already received the only gift that God ever intended to give, his statement is meaningless. Paul's only concern was that in their desire for gifts, they pray for and pursue those that serve more readily to build up and edify the church.

In the verse that immediately follows (1 Cor. 14:13), Paul said that the person who speaks in tongues "should pray that he may interpret." In other words, here is a person who already has one spiritual gift, speaking in tongues, whom Paul exhorted to ask God for yet another, the ability to interpret for the sake of those in the church. Even if one does not believe that the gifts of tongues and interpretation are valid for the church today, this passage indicates that a Christian who has one gift can easily be the recipient of another.

Yet another textual hint that a believer may receive more than one gift is found in the exhortation that Paul gave his spiritual son, Timothy. We read this in 1 Timothy 4:14: "Do not neglect the gift you have, which was given you by prophecy when the council of elders laid their hands on you."

This is not the spiritual gift that Timothy would have received when he was first converted. This is a gift that was imparted to him by the Spirit when he was appointed, commissioned, or "ordained" to the pastoral ministry in Ephesus. When the elders laid their hands on him and prayed, he received yet another "gift" in addition to whatever gift or gifts he had earlier been given.

These texts we've examined also serve to answer another related question about spiritual gifts, namely, the time when one receives them. Some believe that when a person is converted to saving faith in Christ, he or she is given all the gifts that God intends to give. But there is no biblical statement supporting this notion. Whereas it is true, as we've just noted, that every Christian has a gift, no biblical passage says that gifts cannot or will not be granted subsequent to conversion.

I should point out that if additional spiritual gifts are given to a believer subsequent to the time of saving faith, it is not in any way connected to what many perceive to be the experience of being baptized in the Spirit. Spirit baptism, as I've explained in detail elsewhere, is something that all Christians experience at the time of conversion.[1] Contrary to what most in the classical Pentecostal tradition believe, Spirit baptism is not something that occurs "separate from" and "subsequent to" salvation. It is, instead, simultaneous with it. Jesus himself is the one who performs this spiritual baptism. Nowhere is the Holy Spirit said to baptize us into Christ; rather, Christ baptizes or submerges all believers in or with the Holy Spirit.

As noted above, on several occasions we are told to seek or pursue or earnestly desire spiritual gifts (1 Cor. 12:31; 14:1, 12–13, 39) that we obviously don't yet have. As I'll point out in chapter 4, this is not mere permission or even a suggestion: it is a command. If you are not earnestly desiring spiritual gifts, especially prophecy, you are disobeying an apostolic imperative.

---

1 See my chapter "What Is Spirit Baptism, and When Does It Happen?" in *Tough Topics: Biblical Answers to 25 Challenging Questions* (Wheaton, IL: Crossway, 2013), 252–75.

CHAPTER 4

Our Responsibility to Desire and
Pray for Spiritual Gifts

The impartation of spiritual gifts to a believing man or woman is always subject to the sovereign will of the Holy Spirit. Whatever gifts you may receive, as well as when they may be given, is always determined by the Holy Spirit, not by you. Paul makes this clear in 1 Corinthians 12:11, where he declares that "all these [spiritual gifts] are empowered by one and the same Spirit, who apportions to each one individually *as he wills*" (emphasis mine).

But some have drawn the unwarranted conclusion that since God is sovereign in the distribution of gifts, we have nothing to do in terms of desiring, praying for, and earnestly seeking them. Now, we just saw in chapter 3 that Paul commanded the person who speaks in tongues to "pray that he may interpret" (1 Cor. 14:13). This is unmistakable proof that although the Spirit sovereignly determines who does or does not receive the gift of interpretation, those with the gift of tongues are responsible to pray for it. God's sovereignty in the matter does not undermine or diminish our role in praying for a gift.

The most explicit reference to human responsibility in the matter of spiritual gifts is found in 1 Corinthians 12–14. Four texts in particular make this point:

> But earnestly desire the higher gifts. (1 Cor. 12:31b)

> Pursue love, and earnestly desire the spiritual gifts, especially that you may prophesy. (1 Cor. 14:1)

> So with yourselves, since you are eager for manifestations of the Spirit, strive to excel in building up the church. (1 Cor. 14:12)

> So, my brothers, earnestly desire to prophesy, and do not forbid speaking in tongues. (1 Cor. 14:39)

In three of these texts, the Greek word translated "earnestly desire" is the same: *zēloute*. It is the present tense, second person plural form of the verb. The interesting thing that would not be known by those who read only English is that the verb can be either indicative or imperative. If the former, Paul would have been making a statement of fact: "you are earnestly desiring" (or "you do desire"). If the latter, he would have been issuing a command: "earnestly desire." In 14:12 he employed the related noun form *zēlōtai*.

Several things should be noted. First, the exhortation to "earnestly desire" spiritual gifts (1 Cor. 12:31; 14:1, 39) is in the plural. Some conclude from this, incorrectly in my opinion, that Paul's command was directed not to individual believers but to the corporate church. They argue that this is grounds for rejecting the idea that Christians should seek any spiritual gift.

But of course the verb is plural! What exhortations or commands issued by Paul aren't, other than those in letters addressed to individuals (such as Philemon, Titus, and Timothy)? Everyone in Corinth was the focus of Paul's exhortation, and therefore each one was individually responsible to obey it. After all, is not the corporate body of Christ a collective unity of individual believers on each of whom the obligation to obey would fall? The plural of this exhortation simply indicates that *all* believers in Corinth are to heed the apostolic admonition. It is a duty *common* to everyone, including believers today. I can well imagine someone in Corinth (or today) responding to this attempt to evade Paul's obvious intent by saying, "How can we as a church pursue spiritual gifts if none of us as individuals is allowed to?"

Someone has also suggested that in 1 Corinthians 12:31a Paul was not commanding the Corinthian believers to earnestly desire the higher gifts but was simply stating a fact of reality. He was describing a state of affairs, so they argue, but was not issuing an imperative to the effect that God wanted them to earnestly desire any particular gift of the Spirit. There are at least four problems with this view.

First, the simple fact of the matter is that the Corinthians were *not* earnestly desiring the greater gifts. Much of chapter 14 is devoted to rebuking them for desiring and elevating the lower gifts, primarily the gift of tongues. They prized tongues above all other gifts, as if to suggest that tongues was a unique mark of heightened spirituality and godliness. When Paul spoke of the "higher" gifts or "greater" gifts, he meant those gifts that have a greater capacity or potential for building up and edifying other believers. That is why he urged them to desire prophecy over uninterpreted tongues, because "the one who prophesies is greater than the one who speaks in tongues, unless someone interprets, so that the church may be built up" (v. 5).

Second, the suggestion that by "higher" gifts (1 Cor. 12:31a) Paul meant more spectacular gifts, gifts that draw more attention to the individual, gifts that are more overtly supernatural or miraculous, falters on the entirety of chapter 14. There Paul provided correctives to abuse. The abuse in particular was the tendency of the Corinthians to let those with tongues dominate the gathered assembly. But in the absence of interpretation, tongues are of no benefit to those who are present. One solution to this problem in Corinth was to urge them to seek, pray for, and practice those gifts that more readily and easily and effectively edify other believers. The gift that Paul had especially in mind in this regard was prophecy.

Third, we must not overlook the context in which Paul's statement in 12:31a is found. Immediately preceding this verse is a list of spiritual gifts in which the first three are enumerated as "first," "second," and "third." Paul's evident ranking of these gifts seems not to be a reference to their chronological appearance in the life of the church but rather a way of highlighting their comparative value in building up other believers. Thus, when he then said, "But earnestly desire the higher gifts" (v. 31a), he most likely meant to "earnestly desire" those gifts that are better suited to benefit others in the body of Christ.

Fourth, and perhaps most decisive of all, is the fact that the same verb form that we find in 12:31a appears yet again in 14:1 and 39 where it is unmistakably imperative. Even those who insist that it is indicative in 12:31a concede that it is imperative in 14:1 and 39. It only makes sense that Paul would use the verb in the same sense in such close contextual proximity unless there are substantive and persuasive reasons for thinking otherwise. And as already noted, there are none.

Our Response to Paul's Command

So how should we respond to Paul's command in 1 Corinthians 14:1? There are those, like myself, who believe the New Testament explicitly affirms the ongoing contemporary validity of all spiritual gifts. For such, the command of 14:1 is morally binding, and we respond by obeying.

There are also those who believe the New Testament is explicit in its affirmation of the cessation of certain spiritual gifts, prophecy being chief among them. For them the exhortation in 1 Corinthians 14:1 and 39 is simply inapplicable to Christians beyond the time of the first century. The most we can learn from it is what God desired for the early church, but it has no relevance or binding moral authority on Christians today.

There are other cessationists who don't believe the New Testament speaks explicitly on the issue. They would say that whereas the New Testament doesn't teach the cessation of prophecy, they nevertheless believe that it is no longer given. Thus, the command of 14:1 was binding on first-century believers but not on us.

There are those who don't believe the New Testament teaches cessationism, who believe it is possible that all spiritual gifts, including prophecy, are still valid for the church today, but who disobey Paul's command. Whether their disobedience is conscious rebellion or benign neglect is difficult to discern. They may prioritize other biblical imperatives over this one and insist they only have time and energy for those more pressing or urgent. Or they are fearful of what a pursuit of spiritual gifts will bring to their church.[1]

The final response is to redefine prophecy and take it as equivalent to what we normally refer to as preaching. This allows one to obey the command and still be a cessationist. Those who hold to this idea argue that the sort of prophecy Paul exhorted us to earnestly desire is the standard practice of preaching the Word. But this doesn't solve the problem posed by Paul's exhortation that we should earnestly desire "spiritual gifts" other than prophecy—gifts such as tongues, healing, miracles, and words of knowledge. I will address this issue in a subsequent chapter where we examine whether

---

1   Andrew Wilson responds to this perspective in his excellent article "Are You Open to Spiritual Gifts? Exposing the Least Biblical Position," DesiringGod, January 17, 2019, www.desiringgod.org/articles/are-you-open-to-spiritual-gifts.

New Testament prophecy is synonymous with preaching. My conclusion there is that it is not.

I've often been asked, "What should be done when people begin to grow in their zeal for spiritual gifts like prophecy? What should be said when people are increasingly hungry for the manifestation of the Spirit's power? What should our response be when Christians display a persistent and intense desire for the supernatural work of the Spirit in their lives and in the life of the church?"

If you listen closely, you will often detect behind that question a measure of fear. Those asking the question may have a concern that people who yearn for the ministry and power of the Spirit are turning soft on doctrine or may be inclined to neglect spiritual disciplines—or perhaps they long for the miraculous as an excuse for ignoring Bible study, evangelism, and prayer.

But consider how the apostle Paul would respond to such a question, especially if the people who have this desire for spiritual gifts have already shown themselves to be somewhat immature, such as the Corinthian believers in the first century. To a body given to excess and immaturity, Paul still said, "Pursue love, and earnestly desire the spiritual gifts, especially that you may prophesy." He encouraged them to pursue the gifts. We can learn several important lessons from this.

The first is that we must affirm without hesitation that *character always takes precedence over gifting*. This isn't to diminish the importance of the Spirit's gifts. It is simply to point out that the fruit of the Spirit is preeminent. Gifts are not the goal, but rather one of the means by which we attain the goal of a transformed heart and a Christlike life. The problem in Corinth, and in many churches today, is that people were exercising the Spirit's gifts in the absence of character. But power is not necessarily a measure of piety (cf. 1 Cor. 13:1ff.).

Failure to remember this principle results in a tendency to exempt gifted people from ordinary responsibilities and biblical obligations or to hold them to a different (often lower) standard of accountability. The mistake is thinking that anyone so extraordinarily gifted must be unusually close to God, invulnerable to temptation, and so full of the Spirit as to be beyond the power of the flesh.

We would do well to remember the experience of the apostle Paul himself. He was the object of what may well have been the greatest "power encounter" in the history of the church. In 2 Corinthians 12 he described his translation into the third heaven where he heard and saw things that he was forbidden to disclose. It's hard to imagine a more stunning and breathtaking revelatory experience than that. Yet immediately on his "return," he felt pride and self-importance and elitism rising in his soul. Far from eradicating sin from his heart, this exalted experience served only to stir it up. I would have expected Paul to return from this remarkable spiritual journey free from sin, perfect in spirit, devoid of wicked motives or self-serving intentions. Far from it! Paul immediately felt the sting of self-promotion. Perhaps he thought, *Well, I must be a pretty special sort of guy for this to have happened to me. I don't know of anyone else who's had an experience remotely like mine. Sure, Peter saw a vision [Acts 10] and others have been used to heal the sick. But I was the one to whom God chose to reveal ineffable secrets of the unseen world. I guess that makes me one of a kind. And rightly so, if I do say so myself!*

Power did not automatically yield purity. Perhaps it should have. Paul's response to his heavenly transport ought to have humbled him and awakened his heart to the immeasurable glory and incomparable majesty of God. If nothing else, he might have reacted as Isaiah did upon seeing the Lord of glory enthroned and praised by adoring seraphim (Isa. 6:1ff.). But for whatever reason, it was pride and self-elation, not humility or repentance, that gripped his soul. Supernatural power and heavenly encounters of a revelatory sort are no guarantee of growth or maturity.

The second lesson comes in the form of counsel: To those who are eagerly hungry and zealous for the power of the Holy Spirit and his gifts, I say, Good! God bless you! In addition to the command in 1 Corinthians 14:1, we read in verse 5 that Paul wanted all "to prophesy." In 14:12 he acknowledged that the Corinthians "are eager for manifestations of the Spirit" and encouraged them to strive to excel in building up the church. The argument of chapter 14 would indicate that this is his way of encouraging the pursuit of prophecy, given its capacity to edify others in the body (vv. 3, 4, 5). Again in 14:12 and 14:39 Paul explicitly commanded the Corinthians to desire and pursue the gift of prophecy.

This verb translated "earnestly desire" means to have a strong affection for, to ardently yearn, to zealously long for. Or to use modern lingo, "I want you to want it really bad!" This is not an option! This is not an issue of personality, as if some are more inclined than others to experience this kind of spiritual phenomenon. This is not an issue of, "It's for that church but not this one. After all, we've got our mission statement and they've got theirs. If that's what God is calling them to pursue, fine, but we have a different divine mandate."

We cannot respond to Paul's words in this passage by saying, "Thanks, God, but no thanks. I appreciate the opportunity you've offered me, but it's just not my thing, if you know what I mean." God, through Paul, said, "Yes I know what you mean. And what you mean is that you are determined to sin by disobeying a direct order!"

All churches, no matter how different they may be, have an identical mandate when it comes to obeying Scripture. No one is exempt or special or unique in such a way that they can justify disobedience to God's Word. This is not a suggestion or mere advice or wise counsel. This is a divine command, a mandate from God himself. If you and I are not earnestly desiring spiritual gifts, especially prophecy, we are disobedient.

This is not an issue for prayer. You do not respond to this passage by saying, "Well, okay, I'll pray about it." No. *You don't pray about whether you are going to obey God. God is not giving you a choice. He's giving you a command.* The only choice you have is whether you are going to obey. Can you imagine if we responded to other commands in Scripture the way many respond to 1 Corinthians 14:1? "I don't feel led to flee fornication. I think that's meant for other Christians, but I don't sense that's my calling." Or "The prohibition against adultery just isn't compatible with where I am in God right now." Or "Being a generous giver to the needy is a wonderful calling for some churches, but we're just not into that sort of thing at this stage of our growth as a church."

I confess that I'm somewhat baffled by Paul's words to the Corinthians. I could understand this exhortation if it were given to a church with undeniable maturity like the church in Thessalonica or Philippi or Ephesus. To a church with great character and in need of power, this exhortation makes sense. But Corinth was a church with great power and little character! This counsel of Paul's strikes me as odd and unwise, if not altogether reckless. To the very people who had fallen prey to the abuse of the *charismata*, Paul said to be hungry and zealous for more. Was he not simply pouring gasoline on a raging fire? If a man is struggling with lust, you don't recommend that he watch sexually explicit movies! You don't offer a Cuban cigar to a person struggling to quit smoking.

Paul's exhortation suggests that the answer to our problems is never the suppression of spiritual zeal or laws that prohibit the exercise of legitimate gifts of the Spirit. The problem in Corinth wasn't that they were bereft of God's power. They were awash in it! Their greatest challenge wasn't the lack of power but the absence of maturity. Scripture nowhere speaks of the absence of power as if it is a desirable condition. Observe what Paul did not say: "Settle down, Corinthians. Cool it! Put on the brakes! Ease up on this supernatural stuff. Forget about spiritual gifts. Don't you realize that spiritual gifts are what got you into trouble in the first place?" The reason he didn't say that is because spiritual gifts were not the cause of their troubles: *immaturity and carnality were.* Let us never forget that spiritual gifts were God's idea. He thought them up. He gave them to the church. They are his ordained means for edifying the body and consoling the weak and encouraging those in despair. Spiritual gifts were formed and shaped by God. They operate in his power (1 Cor. 12:6b) and manifest his Spirit (12:7). If spiritual gifts are the problem, then there's no one to blame but God.

This brings me to my third lesson: the solution to the abuse of spiritual gifts is not disuse, but proper use. Paul did not recommend that the Corinthians abandon spiritual gifts or de-emphasize spiritual power. He simply gave them guidelines on how these powerful manifestations of the Spirit were to be properly exercised in the body of Christ to the edification of God's people.

The policy we implement in our churches today often turns out to be far removed from that of Paul. Here is what often happens. There are three stages. First, we see something being done badly in the church. We note someone abusing a gift, perhaps using it to manipulate another person. Or perhaps an individual is wounded by the misguided zeal of another Christian. Then we feel rising up within our souls an emotional prejudice against what was done. We feel revulsion in our hearts, we take up an offense and feel our souls recoiling and withdrawing from anything that remotely looks like what we have just witnessed. Finally, we resolve in our hearts never to get involved in anything like that again, or we pass a rule in the church forbidding that it ever be allowed. Prohibition is always easier than regulation. It is easier to legislate against something than to repair it and make it useful for the people of God.

How Do We Reconcile Our Pursuit of Spiritual Gifts with God's Sovereignty?

We saw earlier that the Holy Spirit is the one who determines who will receive what gift(s) (see 1 Cor. 12:11, 18). That being the case, what's the point of our praying for some particular gift or seeking after a specific manifestation? The answer is found in a principle that we see both in Scripture and in experience: when God desires to bestow some blessing on his people, he first awakens them to their need for it and then stirs their hearts to ask him for it. Our prayers are often the very means God employs to grant what he desires to give. If we were to justify not seeking after spiritual gifts by appealing to the priority of God's will, would we ever pray for him to save the lost or to heal the sick? After all, God "works all things according to the counsel of his will" (Eph. 1:11). The responsibility of every believer to obey every biblical injunction faithfully is not in the least undermined by an appeal to divine sovereignty.

This is a good point for us to consider the ways in which the Spirit may choose to impart his gifts to us. On the one hand, Paul referred to the Spirit sovereignly "distributing" or "apportioning" (1 Cor. 12:11) gifts to people, without saying how. That leaves the door open to any number of possibilities. Perhaps the principal way is in response to our prayers (1 Cor. 14:13). We can't be certain that Paul, in Romans 1:11, had the *charisma* of 1 Corinthians 12 in view, but he did express his desire to visit the church in Rome to impart to them some spiritual gift. It was "through prophecy" and the laying on of hands that Timothy received a spiritual gift (1 Tim. 4:14). Again, in 2 Timothy 1:6 Paul mentioned a spiritual gift that Timothy had received through the laying on of hands (the gift is said to be "in" him by this act of impartation).

We can't be certain, but it appears that in the process of praying over Timothy, someone prophesied that God's will was to grant him one or more spiritual gifts (perhaps leadership or evangelism or pastoring). This was confirmed by the elders in Ephesus and Paul as they laid hands on him. The prophetic utterance itself may have been the instrument through which the Spirit imparted this gift. On several occasions we at Bridgeway Church have prayed for a person and watched as God in that moment bestowed the very gift for which that individual had privately been praying. Contrary to what some might allege, this is not a New Age phenomenon but simply the way in which the Spirit of God has chosen to operate.

We also find in this passage in 1 Timothy some implicit guidelines for how we are to pray and what we might expect from it. Although Paul referred specifically to the "elders" praying for Timothy, I doubt if anyone would suggest that ordinary believers are prohibited from praying for one another. In our church we regularly make an appeal to people who "desire" a particular spiritual gift. Perhaps on one day the Lord impresses upon us the importance of the spiritual gift of evangelism. On another day it might be the gift of mercy or giving or prophecy. In any case, we gather around the individual who "earnestly desires" the gift, lay hands on them, wait patiently to see if the Spirit might impart some revelatory instruction regarding them (note that it was "by prophecy" that Timothy received his spiritual gift), speak forth whatever the Spirit discloses, and then pray for the Spirit's will to be fully accomplished.

Que Sera, Sera?[2]

A close friend of mine, a cessationist (yes, I have close friends who disagree with most everything I've written in this book!), once told me that he didn't believe that a Christian could receive more gifts beyond the one that he or she was given when they first came to faith in Jesus. Largely on that basis, he objected to my suggestion that we are responsible to pray for and pursue additional spiritual gifts. It soon became evident that he did not think that what a person believes about the validity of spiritual gifts has any effect at all on whether a person will receive a particular *charisma*. "If God wants you to have a gift, he'll give it to you whether or not you ask him to," he insisted.

I asked him if he was actually suggesting that one's theological convictions about the validity of cessation of tongues and other gifts have no effect on whether a person eventually experiences them. He said yes. I pushed back

---

2   The following discussion is a slightly revised version of what I wrote in my book *Practicing the Power: Welcoming the Gifts of the Spirit in Your Life* (Grand Rapids: Zondervan, 2017), 40–44, and is used here with permission.

with the argument that our beliefs control and shape our zeal, our expectations, our prayer life, and especially how we respond to and interpret claims people make regarding their experience of supernatural phenomena.

It's important that you know that my friend and I are both Calvinists. We both hold to a high view of God's sovereignty in all affairs of life and salvation. But my friend's perspective on this question borders on what can only be called a "hyper-Calvinistic" point of view. In fact, it struck me as bordering on fatalism. Needless to say, it excluded from the picture any notion of passionate prayer and human responsibility.

Let's consider how the book of Acts portrays the manner in which the gift of tongues was imparted. First of all, those present on the day of Pentecost were there in obedience to Jesus's command: "Stay in the city until you are clothed with power from on high" (Luke 24:49; cf. Acts 1:5, 8). The reason all received the gift of tongues on that day was due to at least two factors. First, they were obedient in responding to Jesus's command. There is no reason to believe, at least in my opinion, that if some had disbelieved Jesus's promise, disobeyed his command, and refused to wait with the others in Jerusalem for the outpouring of the Spirit, that they would have received tongues anyway, irrespective of their response to him.

Whether they were praying for this to occur we can't know, for the simple fact that the text says nothing to this effect. Maybe they were; maybe they weren't. I find it difficult to believe, however, that given John's and Jesus's prophecies of the impending Spirit baptism and the coming on them of divine power that they sat silently and passively and refused or at least failed to pray for the coming of what Christ had promised. In any case, no one knows what they were doing in preparation for the coming of the Spirit. For someone to say that God gave tongues to all of them irrespective of their obedience or belief or prayer is simply not substantiated by the text. The text is silent.

My second reason for finding my friend's argument misleading is that Acts 10 concerns the spread of the gospel to the Gentiles. I think most everyone acknowledges that we are dealing here with an unusual geo-ethnic expansion of the gospel that called for the same phenomenon that occurred at Pentecost to attest to the reality of their acceptance by faith. Peter and the others were clear that the experience of Cornelius and the other Gentiles in receiving the Spirit and speaking in tongues served uniquely in this case to corroborate the fact that "the gift of the Holy Spirit was poured out *even* on the Gentiles" (v. 45, emphasis mine). This led Peter to conclude that they were fit subjects for water baptism, just as were those among the Jews who believed and received the Spirit. I hardly think this example from Acts 10 is sufficient warrant for drawing the conclusion that if God wants his people to speak in tongues, they will do so irrespective of their own beliefs, prayers, desires, or state of mind and heart.

In Acts 19 the disciples of John the Baptist spoke in tongues only "when Paul had laid his hands on them" (v. 6). In the course of Paul's explanation of the gospel and the reality of Pentecost, did these men express their desire to experience what those people in Acts 2 experienced? We don't know. The text is silent. What we do know is that Paul was dealing with a situation that is altogether unrepeatable today. These "disciples" were men who had embraced the baptism of John but had lived in the overlap of the transition from the old covenant to the new covenant. They evidently lived at a distance from Jerusalem and had no access to the news of what had happened on Pentecost (no TV, no internet, no Twitter or Instagram, etc.). This is hardly a situation that we can use as paradigmatic for us today, as no one today lives in what might be called a "redemptive-historical time warp."[3]

The only other place where the gift of tongues is explicitly mentioned (outside the dubious long ending of Mark) is in 1 Corinthians. And it is important to remember that not everyone in Corinth spoke in tongues (indicating that in a time when the gift of tongues was clearly God's will for his church, some [most] Christians did not receive the gift). If they did, Paul would not have had to say in 1 Corinthians 14:5, "I wish that you all spoke in tongues" (NASB). Clearly not everyone did.

Thus my friend's argument seemed to be as follows: If spiritual gifts are designed and intended by God to function in the church throughout its existence, into the present day, then such gifts will consistently appear by divine fiat irrespective of how people live, what they believe (especially regarding the continuation or cessation of said gifts), and whether or not they pray for and

---

3 D. A. Carson points out that Paul's line of questioning presupposes "that reception of the Spirit at conversion is normal and expected; the distinctive abnormality of the Ephesians' experience could not be repeated today, since it is inconceivable that someone could be found who was a baptized follower of [John] the Baptist, an enthusiastic supporter of the Baptist's witness to Jesus, apparently also a believer in Jesus' death and resurrection, but ignorant of Pentecost" (D. A. Carson, *Showing the Spirit: A Theological Exposition of 1 Corinthians 12–14* [1987; repr., Grand Rapids: Baker, 2019], 196).

pursue such gifts and are committed to practicing them in accordance with Scripture.

This strikes me as rather presumptuous, irresponsible, and negligent of God's ordained means to achieve his ordained ends. If this view were true, it would empty prayer of its value. Why pray (as our Arminian friends would say) if God is going to do what God is going to do regardless? *Que sera, sera!* Is it not the case that God suspends the bestowal of countless blessings on our asking for them? If the principle my friend is defending is correct, why would Jesus have rebuked his disciples for their failure to pray (Mark 9:28–29) in attempting to cast the demon out of a young boy? On his belief, why wouldn't we conclude that if God wanted the boy to be delivered, he would sovereignly do it without calling for or waiting upon the prayers of others on the boy's behalf? And why should we obey Jesus who commanded us to persevere in prayer (keep on asking, keep on seeking, keep on knocking; Luke 11:9–10) to receive the gifts and blessings of the Spirit that we so desperately need (Luke 11:13)? And why would James tell us that "you do not have, because you do not ask" (James 4:2) if God typically grants gifts and blessings as sovereignly and irrespectively of our desires and prayers as my friend suggests?

Neither my friend nor I have any idea what the Corinthians did or did not do when it came to the reception of spiritual gifts. He seems to suggest that these Christians received their gifts by divine fiat apart from their desire or prayer. I would like for anyone to give me a text that says this. The text is again silent; well, almost silent. One must still account for the explicit exhortation to pray for the spiritual gift of interpretation in 1 Corinthians 14:13. But why should Paul issue such an imperative if what my friend says is correct? Why bother, if God's will is to grant the gift of interpretation? Clearly—at least it is clear to me—Paul believed that the reception of a spiritual gift is often based on one's prayer for it. Ask and you shall receive. Don't ask, and you shouldn't expect to receive.

It appears to me that perhaps my friend's position on this point is again related to his denial that a Christian, after his or her conversion, can still receive additional spiritual gifts. His attempt to evade this point as it is stated in 1 Corinthians 14:1, 13, 39; and 1 Timothy 4:14 simply doesn't ring true to me. Does it not seem that the only reason my friend might have to doubt this is the recognition that if one concedes the point his position is undermined? If Timothy could receive a spiritual gift in response to the prayers of others and through the instrumentality of prophecy, and all this subsequent to his conversion, why can't we?

My point here is that some appear to say, contrary to these texts, that a Christian receives from God as a sovereign impartation, irrespective of their own beliefs, prayers, and desires, all the gifts that he or she will ever receive at conversion. These texts clearly say otherwise.

Now, it might also be helpful to relate this matter to the issue of spiritual gifts throughout the course of nearly two thousand years of church history. One of the reasons I cite for why spiritual gifts are less frequent in certain seasons of church history than in others is simply the fact that, based on their hard cessationism (together with other factors, such as fear), people didn't seek, pursue, or passionately and incessantly pray for these gifts.

They have not because they asked not, and they asked not because they believed not! Not believing in the validity of those gifts, not believing that God would grant them, they didn't ask for them. Not asking for them, they didn't receive them. My friend evidently thinks that their asking is irrelevant. If God wants them to have the gift, then, by golly, they'll get it one way or the other. This strikes me as an illegitimate extension of our commonly held Calvinist convictions. God works through means, prayer being one of the more important of them.

I'm not suggesting that this accounts sufficiently for why certain spiritual gifts were not present in certain seasons of church life, but I am saying that it simply isn't biblical or God's way to impart gifts and blessings irrespective of our obedience to pray and ask for them. The hungry are those who are filled. The thirsty are those who are given drink. Those who ask and seek and knock are those to whom the door is opened.

Can God set aside this principle and grant gifts anyway, irrespective of our theological beliefs about their validity and irrespective of our disobedience to pray for them? Yes, of course he can. And I would venture to say (while acknowledging that I can't prove it) that this happened countless times throughout the course of church history. But that doesn't cancel out the basic principle that we cannot expect God to do things for us if we ignore the command to fulfill those conditions on which he suspends their impartation.

We should never expect God to do for us apart from prayer what he has promised in his Word to do for us only through prayer.

Some Practical Counsel on How to Discover One's Spiritual Gift(s)

Nowhere does the New Testament give us explicit guidance on how to identify or discover our spiritual gift(s). So from the outset it will appear to some that my answer to this question is speculative, based more on experience than on the assertions of any particular biblical text. When we read such passages as Romans 12:6–8 and 1 Corinthians 12:8–10, we discover that Paul seemed to assume that the believer would know which gifts he or she had received. His counsel, like that of Peter's, is that we are to "use" them for building up of the body of Christ.

Most who are reading this book have probably taken one or more of the countless spiritual gifts inventories or tests that circulate throughout churches everywhere. I certainly have. And on occasion they have proved quite accurate. Others have found them somewhat disconcerting, as their experience simply doesn't match up with what the inventory suggests should be their gifting. One individual told me that after answering all two hundred questions in a spiritual gifts inventory and later being told what his gift was, he felt locked in. He actually withdrew from opportunities for ministry and other challenges in the local church that call for little more than availability and love. Others have justified their passivity by saying, "Well, I'd like to help, but that's not my gift." Regardless of the merits or limitations of inventories or tests, I would like to propose a more practical approach to this issue.

People often share their frustration with not yet having identified their spiritual gift. Some are so obsessed with making this discovery that they are virtually paralyzed from participating in ministry and serving others until such time as they can confidently put their finger on precisely what the Holy Spirit has imparted to them. My recommendation is that Christians should stop this persistent, introspective navel gazing and simply step out and begin to love and serve others in concrete acts of ministry. In doing so, I'm confident your gift will find you.

There are times when we are confronted with people who are hurting or in need and we walk away, convinced that we don't possess the requisite spiritual gifting to serve them effectively. Let me suggest an alternative approach. Here are a few concrete illustrations I hope will make the point clear.

The next time you gather with fellow believers for a Sunday corporate celebration, or perhaps find yourself in a small group on a Wednesday night, pause momentarily and ask those present if anyone is physically ill or suffering from a chronic affliction. Once they are identified, have them sit in a chair in the middle of the room, gather around them, lay hands on them, and ask God to impart a gift for their healing. It will not do to excuse yourself by insisting that you don't have the gift of healing. As we will observe later in this book, "gifts of healings" (please note that both words are in the plural in the Greek text) are not something we permanently possess, as if we could heal anyone of any disease at any time, subject only to our will. Rather, the Spirit sovereignly chooses to impart a gift for someone's healing from a particular affliction when he wills. In other words, instead of justifying your inaction on the assumption you don't have the requisite gifting, step out in faith and pray that God would gift you at that very moment for the benefit of another.

Here's another example of how to "practice" discovering your gift. Let's say you are in a situation where you come across someone who is discouraged or depressed. The burdens of life may be overwhelming, and they are slowly losing confidence in God and his goodness to make a difference. If so, invite them to lunch or coffee and listen to their story. They probably aren't expecting you to provide a detailed and erudite theological explanation for why they are suffering. They simply want someone who cares enough about their situation to pray for them and to offer a few words of encouragement. If you should step out in faith to comfort them in their sorrow, you may well discover that the Holy Spirit has chosen to grant you the gift of encouragement or perhaps of mercy. But you will be a blessing to that individual regardless. Consider the alternative: "I don't have the spiritual gifts they need to have their hope restored and their faith renewed, so I won't do anything at all."

Or it may be that someone has fallen on difficult times financially. Bills are past due and they can't see any hope for an increase in income. Offer to pray for them, and as you do, pray for yourself, that God would alert you to what you personally might do to alleviate their burden. The spiritual gift of giving is in operation when someone feels a powerful internal urge to assist someone in trouble and gives generously to their need, even if there doesn't appear to be enough money available to do so. And as you give, trust God to supply you with the monetary resources necessary to make it happen.

Perhaps a friend of yours is battling temptation and sin, and not doing well in finding the strength to resist. As you pray for them, ask the Lord to give you words of wisdom that will supply them with guidance in how best to avoid temptation in the first place. Pray that the Spirit would reveal a word of encouragement or that he would enable you to recall a similar time in your life when you, likewise, were struggling with sin. If you sense something from the Spirit or a thought comes to mind, share it with them. It might be the key that opens the door to their heart and brings freedom from bondage.

Most of us at various times are confused by particular texts in Scripture. As much as we have prayed and studied, we've seen little breakthrough in terms of understanding. In such times, sit down with a friend and together explore the Scriptures, making use of whatever resources are available, especially prayer, and ask the Holy Spirit to shed light on your thinking. It may well be that in doing so you are given the insight and ability to teach your friend in a way that is life-changing.

I often encounter people who report hearing voices in their heads and feel as if they are being bombarded by the fiery missiles of the evil one. They feel tormented and often struggle with crippling shame and self-contempt. They wonder, *What kind of person must I be that I would be the focus of Satan's attack?* If your friend is experiencing something like this, open up your Bibles together and read Luke 10:1–20. Remind each other of the authority that we've been given over the power of the demonic. Speak the Word of God to this person regarding the defeat of the enemy, as described by Paul in Colossians 2:13–15. In the name of Christ, command any demonic spirits to leave and never to return. Pray for the person to be filled afresh with the Holy Spirit.

Consider doing some research among the people in your church and identify those who are unable to do long overdue yard work or whose garage desperately needs deliverance from piles of clutter, or perhaps an elderly widow who simply needs someone to do her laundry and fold and put away her clothes. You may well discover in the midst of your efforts that a glorious joy in showing mercy has erupted in your heart.

I realize that little of what I've just said sounds supernatural or even remotely spectacular. But that doesn't mean it isn't biblical. I'm simply suggesting that as we spend less time obsessed with some introspective search to identify our spiritual gift(s) and more time actually praying and giving and helping and teaching and serving and exhorting those around us, the likelihood greatly increases that we will walk headlong into our gifting without ever knowing what happened. God will more likely meet us with his gifts in the midst of trying to help his children than he would while we're taking a spiritual gifts analysis test.

So let me highlight the practical takeaway for you. If the focus of your spiritual energy is consistently introspective, you will rarely see the abundance of hurting people that surround you. Open your eyes and look for those who are weeping. Ask the Spirit to guide your steps to those who are weak, afflicted, and destitute. And as you go, listen for the voice of God to grant you a prophetic word that will encourage and console the suffering. Take your hands out of your pockets and lay them on the sick, beseeching the Lord of mercy for healing. Instead of first asking, "What is my gift?" ask, "Who is in need?" I am increasingly persuaded that if God's people will look outward before they look inward, they will encounter the charismatic and empowering presence of the Spirit to equip them for every good deed. As I've said many times before, if you're still bewildered by what may or may not be your spiritual gift, act first and ask later.

PART 2

THE DEBATE OVER THE CESSATION OR CONTINUATION OF MIRACULOUS GIFTS OF THE SPIRIT

CHAPTER 5

Biblical and Theological Arguments
in Support of Cessationism

As we begin this chapter, a defining of terms is necessary. I've used these terms several times already in this book, but in this chapter I want to help you understand the position commonly referred to as cessationism. A *cessationist* must be distinguished from a *secessionist*. The latter term refers to an individual who believes the South had a right to secede from the Union in the middle of the nineteenth century! I say this because the terms are often confused or mispronounced. A *cessationist* is someone who believes that certain spiritual gifts, typically those of a more overtly supernatural nature, *ceased* to be given by God to the church sometime late in the first century AD (or more gradually through the course of the next few centuries). Cessationists do not deny that God can on occasion still perform miracles, such as physical healing. But they do not believe the spiritual gift of miracles or the gift of healing is given to believers today. Whereas "healing" still exists in the life of the church, "healers" do not. God's people may still experience miracles, but God no longer empowers "miracle workers." A *continuationist*, by contrast, is a person who believes that all the gifts of the Spirit *continue* to be given by God and are therefore operative in the church today and should be prayed for and sought after.

Most cessationists and continuationists concede that at least some gifts continue and at least one gift has ceased. Cessationists believe that gifts such as teaching, evangelism, mercy, service, and giving are designed by God to continue until the end of the age. And many (perhaps most) continuationists believe that at least one spiritual gift, that of apostleship, has ceased or has been withdrawn from the life of God's people. Needless to say, this latter point will depend entirely on how one defines apostleship and whether it is a spiritual gift or an office or perhaps an appointment to a particular kind of ministry. These questions will be taken up later in the book.

Biblical and Theological Arguments for Cessationism

Before we look at the biblical arguments in favor of cessationism, I want to share a conversation I had with a close friend who is a committed cessationist. When I asked him why he embraced this view of spiritual gifts, his first response wasn't to cite the biblical texts or theological principles that I will discuss below. Of course, he eventually got around to them, but they were not his first line of defense. Instead, he pointed out that the doctrine of continuationism and the pursuit and practice of the miraculous gifts of the Spirit is, in his mind, inseparable from the Word of Faith movement, as well as the more extreme expressions of the so-called prosperity gospel. He also mentioned the offensive and excessive flamboyance of certain TV evangelists and their manipulative tactics disguised as ministry. He was also quite honest about his own fear of "losing control" if he were to embrace continuationism. And then there was the evident disparity between what he read in the New Testament about the operation of miraculous gifts of the Spirit and what he observes in the charismatic movement of our own day: If the former were still valid and operative, why don't we see the same quality and quantity of miracles today?

I mention these factors in his answer simply to point out that there is sometimes more at work under the radar, so to speak, in the minds of many cessationists than simply the appeal to certain biblical texts. This may not be true for all cessationists, but it is important to keep it in the forefront of our thinking as we examine the arguments cited in defense of this position.

Although it is becoming less frequent these days, some cessationists still appeal to Paul's comments in 1 Corinthians 13:8–12 as evidence that God did not intend for miraculous gifts to continue in the life of the church. There we read,

Love never ends. As for prophecies, they will pass away; as for tongues, they will cease; as for knowledge, it will pass away. For we know in part and we prophesy in part, but when the perfect comes, the partial will pass away. When I was a child, I spoke like a child, I thought like a child, I reasoned like a child. When I became a man, I gave up childish ways. For now we see in a mirror dimly, but then face to face. Now I know in part; then I shall know fully, even as I have been fully known.

In his book *Spiritual Gifts: What They Are and Why They Matter*, New Testament scholar Tom Schreiner has a chapter titled "Unconvincing Arguments for Cessation of the Gifts." The first argument Schreiner cites is this passage in 1 Corinthians 13. Tom points out how in the past, many cessationists identified the coming of "the perfect" with the final composition or perhaps the later canonization of the New Testament Scriptures. Once the inspired and altogether sufficient Scriptures were in the hands of the church, there was no longer any need for the revelatory gifts such as prophecy or other miraculous gifts such as speaking in tongues or healing. Other cessationists suggest that the "perfect" is not a reference to canonical Scripture but to the spiritual maturity of the church.[1]

Schreiner, himself a committed cessationist, then proceeds to cite numerous exegetical and theological arguments for why this interpretation of the "perfect" is wrong, and why it is in all probability "another way of describing 'face to face,' and seeing 'face to face' most naturally refers to Christ's second coming."[2] Or perhaps a more accurate understanding is that the "perfect" is that glorious state of final consummation that is brought about by the second coming of Christ, that time when we will "know fully" even as we have "been fully known." Thus, "if anything," notes Schreiner, "Paul teaches that the spiritual gifts persist and last until the second coming. In fact, I think this is the best argument for the spiritual gifts continuing until today."[3]

Yet another common argument for cessationism is the belief that signs

---

1 For a thoroughgoing refutation of the arguments for these views, see D. A. Carson, *Showing the Spirit: A Theological Exposition of 1 Corinthians 12–14* (1987; repr., Grand Rapids: Baker, 2019), 87–92.

2 Thomas R. Schreiner, *Spiritual Gifts: What They Are and Why They Matter* (Nashville: B&H, 2018), 151.

3 Schreiner, 153.

and wonders as well as certain spiritual gifts served primarily, perhaps even only, to confirm or authenticate the original company of apostles. When the apostles passed away, so did the gifts. We are told that when Paul and Barnabas arrived in Iconium, "they remained for a long time, speaking boldly for the Lord, who bore witness to the word of his grace, granting signs and wonders to be done by their hands" (Acts 14:3). Paul also testified that the Gentiles were brought to obedience "by word and deed, by the power of signs and wonders, by the power of the Spirit of God" (Rom. 15:18b–19a). God used the apostles' signs and wonders to give their words and works a stamp of authority.

Some cessationists would also direct our attention to the words of Jesus in Matthew 12:39 and 16:4. In addressing the scribes and Pharisees who asked "to see a sign" from him, Jesus responded, "An evil and adulterous generation seeks for a sign, but no sign will be given to it except the sign of the prophet Jonah" (Matt. 12:39). The longing for the supernatural, they say, is a sign of spiritual immaturity and a weak faith. James Boice, in his contribution to the book *Power Religion*, quotes with approval this sentiment from John Woodhouse, that "a desire for further signs and wonders is sinful and unbelieving."[4]

Another point often made is that since we now have the completed canon of Scripture, we no longer need the operation of so-called miraculous gifts. If the Bible is itself truly sufficient to supply us with everything we need to live godly and Christ-honoring lives, what possible purpose would miraculous gifts continue to have? In other words, cessationists are arguing that acknowledging the validity of revelatory gifts such as prophecy and words of knowledge would likely, if not necessarily, undermine the finality and sufficiency of Holy Scripture. How can we affirm that the Holy Spirit is still speaking to us by means of revelatory gifts without threatening the authoritative written Word of God? On this point, Schreiner speaks for many cessationists when he writes, "Now that the church has the authoritative guidance for faith and practice in the Scriptures, the gifts and miracles which were needed to build up the early church are no longer needed, and they are not common. This is not to say, however, that God never does miracles

---

4 James Montgomery Boice, "A Better Way: The Power of Word and Spirit," in *Power Religion*, ed. Michael Scott Horton (Chicago: Moody, 1992), 126.

today."[5] Gifts and miracles may happen, but they are no longer needed or common, says Schreiner.

Appeal is also made to Ephesians 2:20, where Paul said that the church of Jesus Christ is "built on the foundation of the apostles and prophets." This, says Schreiner, is "the basis for cessationism."[6] Prophets, along with apostles, "played a key role in the founding and establishing of the church."[7] Schreiner concludes that "the sole and final authority of Scripture is threatened if so-called prophets today give revelations which have the same authority as Scripture."[8] Of course, he is entirely correct. But this argument is persuasive *only* if it can be demonstrated that the sort of prophecies that continuationists affirm do, in fact, "have the same authority as Scripture." That is a major point of contention that I will address later in the book.

Another objection sometimes heard from evangelical cessationists is that we typically don't see miracles or gifts today that are equal in *quality or intensity* to those in the ministries of *Jesus* and the *apostles*, and God doesn't intend for *any* miraculous gifts of a *lesser quality or intensity* to operate in the church among ordinary Christians. Surely, if God intended for the sort of miraculous ministry that we see in the New Testament to continue into the present day, we would regularly witness instantaneous and irreversible healings, the complete cleansing of lepers, and even resurrections from the dead. In sum, contemporary claims to supernatural phenomena simply don't measure up to the standards that are consistently portrayed in the New Testament.

Earlier I shared that I was a cessationist for the first fifteen years of my public ministry. I read virtually all of their literature and participated in countless one-on-one conversations with many of the chief representatives of this view. And I am convinced that this argument exerts a greater influence on their theological conclusions than any other. I realize that a number of cessationists take issue with this suggestion. They insist that the other arguments cited in this chapter, those grounded in biblical texts together with their belief in the Bible's sufficiency, are the principal reason why they

---

5   Schreiner, *Spiritual Gifts*, 167.
6   Schreiner, 157.
7   Schreiner, 159.
8   Schreiner, 160.

do not believe miraculous gifts are valid today. But they will still admit that a belief in the perceived comparative infrequency of present-day miracles and spiritual gifts is a compelling, if not determinative, force behind their cessationist convictions.

I find this ironic, because one of the most oft-heard criticisms of the contemporary charismatic movement is that we who identify with it base our theology on our experience and not on Scripture. But as I examine Schreiner's argument (and the one mentioned below made by Steve Timmis), I find him questioning the validity of miraculous gifts today *because we don't see them in our experience.* In this case, it is the cessationists' lack of experience in witnessing New Testament miraculous gifts that drives their opposition.

I'll cite one more example of what I have in mind. In his review of my book *Practicing the Power*, my good friend Steve Timmis[9] denies being a cessationist but then acknowledges that my book wasn't written for him. Storms, he says, is "writing for those persuaded by the reality of and need for the so-called miraculous gifts of the Spirit." Timmis clearly identifies himself as one who *isn't* persuaded by the reality of these gifts or our need for them. To my mind, this sounds like cessationism.

Later in his review, Timmis speaks about what he perceives as a "discrepancy between" what we experience today and what is described in the New Testament. He suggests that I seem to be "happy to accept a lower standard of 'success'" when it comes to divine healing. "If the gifts are operative for today," says Timmis, "then it seems reasonable to expect them to reflect what we see in the New Testament." He adds that my book "sets out to challenge its readers to faith and expectancy, yet it inadvertently encourages them to be satisfied with something less than the New Testament Christianity it claims to espouse." In other words, "when experience falls short of what happened in the New Testament," says Timmis, "the cracks are papered over and the discrepancies dismissed." Timmis concludes that "the anecdotal evidence cited by good friends is underwhelming."

To be fair, there isn't anything wrong in raising this objection to the validity of miraculous gifts today, but I find it entirely misguided. What is

9   Steve Timmis, "A Friendly Critic on the Best New Resource for Charismatics," TGC, March 29, 2017, www
.thegospelcoalition.org/reviews/practicing-power-sam-storms/.

missing in Timmis's review, as well as from far more detailed and technical defenses of cessationism, is any concrete textual declaration that the gifts in question were only intended for the first fifty or sixty years of the church's existence. We should not miss this point: it is in the absence of such biblical argumentation that "functional" cessationists revert to an appeal to the absence of "anecdotal evidence" in our day of New Testament–level displays of supernatural ministry. This challenge—the lack of evidence—will be addressed in chapter 6.

Another defense put forth is sometimes called the "cluster" argument. According to this argument, miracles and supernatural phenomena were concentrated or "clustered" at specific times in biblical history and therefore should not be expected to appear as a regular or normal phenomenon in other periods of history. Three eras in particular are often cited. John MacArthur explains,

> Most biblical miracles happened in three relatively brief periods of Bible history: in the days of Moses and Joshua, during the ministries of Elijah and Elisha, and in the time of Christ and the apostles. None of those periods lasted much more than a hundred years. Each of them saw a proliferation of miracles unheard of in other eras. . . . Aside from those three intervals, the only supernatural events recorded in Scripture were isolated incidents.[10]

Schreiner also argues for a modified version of the cluster argument:

> I believe God gave gifts and miracles, signs and wonders, in remarkable ways at certain points in redemptive history to authenticate his revelation. . . . [However], miracles aren't limited to such high points in redemptive history, as any careful reading of the Old Testament shows, but they are clustered at central eras in the Scriptures.[11]

Although this argument initially has the appearance of truth, I will demonstrate in chapter 6 how it fails to recognize the presence of the miraculous in virtually every period of Old Testament history.

---

10 John F. MacArthur, *Charismatic Chaos* (Grand Rapids: Zondervan, 1992), 112.

11 Schreiner, *Spiritual Gifts*, 167.

Richard Gaffin and Additional Arguments for Cessationism

Perhaps the most articulate spokesman for cessationism is Richard Gaffin. His case can be found in his contribution to *Are Miraculous Gifts for Today? Four Views*.[12]

Gaffin makes his case for cessationism based on the idea that "the whole of Acts is unique."[13] In other words, "Acts intends to document a *completed* history, a unique epoch in the history of redemption—the once-for-all *apostolic* spread of the gospel 'to the ends of the earth.'"[14] Gaffin believes that "it is in terms of this controlling perspective that the miraculous experiences of those at Pentecost and elsewhere in Acts have their meaning. These miracles attest the realization of the expanding *apostolic* program announced in Acts 1:8."[15] Thus "Acts 2 and the subsequent miraculous events that Luke narrates are not intended to establish a pattern of 'repetitions' of Pentecost to continue on indefinitely in church history. Rather, together they consti-tute ... an event-complex complete with the finished apostolic program they accompany."[16]

In light of this understanding of the nature and purpose of Acts, "to observe that in Acts others than apostles exercise miraculous gifts (e.g., 6:8) is beside the point. To offer as evidence that such gifts continue beyond the time of the apostles pulls apart what for Luke belongs together. Others exer-cise such gifts *by virtue of the presence and activity of the apostles*; they do so under an 'apostolic umbrella,' so to speak."[17]

Gaffin speaks for most cessationists when he affirms that miracles, as well as physical healing, still occur. "I do question [however] ... whether the gifts of healing and of working miracles, as listed in 1 Corinthians 12:9–10, are given today."[18] Whatever such miracles occur in Acts "accompany the

---

12 Richard B. Gaffin Jr., "A Cessationist View," in *Are Miraculous Gifts for Today? Four Views*, ed. Wayne Grudem (Grand Rapids: Zondervan, 1995). Gaffin also builds his case for cessationism in Richard B. Gaffin Jr., *Perspectives on Pentecost* (Phillipsburg, NJ: Presbyterian and Reformed, 1979), 89–116.

13 Gaffin, "A Cessationist View," 37.

14 Gaffin, 38.

15 Gaffin, 38.

16 Gaffin, 38.

17 Gaffin, 39.

18 Gaffin, 42.

unique and finished apostolic spread of the gospel that concerns Luke."[19] As with other cessationists, Gaffin believes that "the apostles and prophets belong to the period of the foundation,"[20] during which time the inspired revelatory will of God was given. "With this foundational revelation completed, and so, too, their foundational role as witnesses, the apostles and, along with them, the prophets and other associated revelatory word gifts, pass from the life of the church."[21]

In sum, although this is not a biblical or theological argument, cessationists argue that the miraculous gifts of the Spirit gradually disappeared from the life of the church following the death of John, the last apostle. At this point, I will simply say that this is a questionable hypothesis, and we will examine the evidence for it, or lack thereof, in chapter seven. It is undeniable that the leaders of the Protestant Reformation in the early sixteenth century embraced the cessation of the gifts. And for the next three hundred years following the Reformation, miraculous manifestations of the Spirit were at best sporadic, until such time as the emergence of the Pentecostal revival in the early 1900s.

2 Corinthians 12:12

Cessationists appeal to 2 Corinthians 12:12, where Paul said that "the signs of a true apostle were performed among you with utmost patience, with signs and wonders and mighty works." If these latter phenomena were "the signs of a true apostle," it would only make sense that once the apostles were themselves no longer present, the supernatural signs that bore witness to them would likewise disappear. In other words, signs, wonders, and miraculous gifts of the Holy Spirit such as tongues, interpretation, healing, and the discerning of spirits were designed to confirm, attest, and authenticate the apostolic message. It seems only reasonable to conclude, therefore, that "the 'signs of an apostle' passed away with the times of an apostle."[22] Richard Mayhue appeals to this argument in his defense of cessationism:

---

19 Gaffin, 42.
20 Gaffin, 43.
21 Gaffin, 44.
22 Norman Geisler, *Signs and Wonders* (Wheaton, IL: Tyndale, 1988), 118.

The Scriptures teach that miracles through human agents served a very specific purpose. That purpose focused on authenticating the prophets and apostles of God as certified messengers with a sure word from heaven. When the canon of Scripture closed with John's Revelation, there no longer existed a divine reason for performing miracles through men. Therefore, such kinds of miracles ceased according to the Scriptures.[23]

Paul's second letter to the church in Corinth is largely devoted to a defense of his apostolic calling and authority. The false apostles in Corinth had argued that someone lacking verbal eloquence, like Paul, who also failed to demand financial support for his ministry, couldn't possibly be a true apostle. When Paul turned to defend himself, he didn't appeal to the criteria the Corinthians had come to expect as essential for apostolic authority. Instead, Paul pointed to those things that "show[ed]" his "weakness" (2 Cor. 11:30). He hoped that the believers in Corinth would come to recognize that he was "not at all inferior to these super-apostles" (2 Cor. 12:11). In fact, "the signs of a true apostle were performed among" the Corinthians "with utmost patience, with signs and wonders and mighty works" (v. 12).

But does this text refer to the miraculous as "signs" of the apostles? There is reason to doubt this is what the text means. Unfortunately, the NIV translation contributes to the confusion by translating as follows: "I persevered in demonstrating among you the marks of a true apostle, including signs, wonders and miracles." This rendering leads one to believe that Paul is identifying the "signs" or "marks" of an apostle with the miraculous phenomena performed among the Corinthians.

A closer look at the Greek text can be helpful here. The word translated "signs" or "marks" (*sēmeia*) is in the nominative case, as one would expect. But the terms "signs, wonders and miracles" are all three in the dative. This means, contrary to what many have thought, that Paul did *not* say the insignia of an apostle *are* signs, wonders, and miracles. Rather, as the English Standard Version more accurately translates, he asserted that "the signs of a true apostle were performed among you with utmost patience, with [or better still, *accompanied by*] signs and wonders and mighty works." Mark Seifrid

---

23 Richard Mayhue, *The Healing Promise* (Eugene, OR: Harvest House, 1994), 184.

rightly confirms this point by noting that "unfortunately, both the NIV and the NRSV basically ignore the datives (*sēmeiois te kai terasin kai dunamesin*), equating them with the 'signs of an apostle.' The ESV rightly connects them to Paul's perseverance."[24]

This critical grammatical point is something I mentioned in my contribution to the book *Are Miraculous Gifts for Today? Four Views*. There I pointed out that whereas "the instrumental dative is grammatically possible," it is conceptually unlikely.[25] After all, what could it possibly mean to say that Christlike perseverance was present or on display "*by means of* signs and wonders and mighty works"? Murray Harris nevertheless argues for the instrumental dative and connects the miraculous phenomena not to Paul's "perseverance" but to the "signs of a true apostle." The associative dative, which designates accompanying circumstances, seems more fitting.[26] On this view, as Harris notes, Paul "largely distinguishes the 'marks' from the miracles, even if . . . the latter together constitute one of those 'marks.'"[27] The important point is that "Paul does not equate the marks of apostleship with miracles as if to suggest that *only* the former do the latter."[28]

None of this should be taken as a denial that signs, wonders, and mighty works marked the existence of an apostle of Jesus Christ. There can be no doubt that such phenomena accompanied the ministries of men such as Peter and Paul. What, then, is the apostle telling us about himself and his ministry in Corinth? According to Harris,

Paul is appealing to God's working of miracles during his ministry at Corinth as divine accreditation of his apostleship. By the "signs, marvels, and powerful deeds" that accompanied Paul's service, God was testifying to his authentic apostolicity.[29]

24 Mark A. Seifrid, *The Second Letter to the Corinthians* (Grand Rapids: Eerdmans, 2014), 458n454.
25 Sam Storms, "A Third Wave View," in *Are Miraculous Gifts for Today? Four Views*, ed. Wayne Grudem (Grand Rapids: Zondervan, 1995), 194n23.
26 See F. Blass and A. Debrunner, *A Greek Grammar of the New Testament* (Chicago: University of Chicago Press, 1961), 195, 198.
27 Murray J. Harris, *The Second Epistle to the Corinthians: A Commentary on the Greek Text* (Grand Rapids: Eerdmans, 2005), 876.
28 Storms, "A Third Wave View," 194n23.
29 Harris, *The Second Epistle to the Corinthians*, 876.

But Harris also proceeds to point out,

> In themselves these miracles were no evidence of apostleship, for signs and wonders could be counterfeited and the working of miracles was not a privilege reserved for apostles but a gift of the Spirit that might be given to anyone in the congregation (1 Cor. 12:10–11, 28–29). But for Paul miracles were not the sole basis for apostolic accreditation.[30]

For those who are a bit lost in all the discussion about Greek noun cases, what I think Paul was saying, here and elsewhere in the New Testament, is that miraculous phenomena were a *necessary* sign of apostolic authority but not a *sufficient* one. One could hardly claim to be an apostle of Jesus Christ (at least in the sense in which the original Twelve, plus Paul and a handful of others, were apostles) in the absence of these supernatural works. But the mere presence of such works was not in itself sufficient to prove that one was an apostle. Signs, wonders, and miracles were, undoubtedly, attendant elements in Paul's apostolic work. But they were not themselves the "signs of an apostle," as if to say that only apostles performed them.

What, then, did Paul have in mind when he spoke of "the signs of a true[31] apostle"? The signs of an apostle, the distinguishing marks of true apostolic ministry were, among other things:

1. the fruit of his preaching, that is, the salvation of the Corinthians themselves (cf. 1 Cor. 9:1b–2, "Are not you my workmanship in the Lord? If to others I am not an apostle, at least I am to you, for you are the seal of my apostleship in the Lord"; cf. 2 Cor. 3:1–3);
2. his Christlike life of simplicity, godly sincerity, holiness, humility, and the like (cf. 2 Cor. 1:12; 2:17; 3:4–6; 4:2; 5:11; 6:3–13; 7:2; 10:13–18; 11:6, 23–28); and
3. his sufferings, hardship, and persecution (cf. 2 Cor. 4:7–15; 5:4–10; 11:1–33; 13:4). The "first commendation of an apostle," notes Seifrid, is "perseverance" or "endurance" in the midst of affliction.[32] Paul

---

30 Harris, 876–77.
31 The word "true" (ESV) is not in the original Greek text.
32 Seifrid, *Second Letter to the Corinthians*, 457.

patiently, in perseverance, displayed these "signs" of his apostolic authority. And this was accompanied by signs, wonders, and miracles he performed in their midst.[33]

Let us also remember that Paul did not refer to the "signs" of an apostle nor to the miraculous phenomena that accompanied his ministry as a way of differentiating himself from other, nonapostolic Christians, but from the false apostles who were leading the Corinthians astray (2 Cor. 11:12–15, 23). "In short," writes Wayne Grudem, "the contrast is not between apostles who could work miracles and ordinary Christians who could not, but between genuine *Christian* apostles through whom the Holy Spirit worked and *non-Christian* pretenders to the apostolic office, through whom the Holy Spirit did not work at all."[34]

As noted above, I'm not suggesting that signs, wonders, and miraculous deeds did not, in fact, serve to authenticate or attest to the truthfulness of the message the apostles proclaimed. They most assuredly did. But nowhere in the New Testament are such supernatural phenomena said to be the signs or an authenticating seal on the apostles themselves. That would have been impossible, given the fact that numerous nonapostolic Christians operated in the ministry of signs and wonders. We cannot easily ignore the fact that more than one hundred nonapostolic believers on the day of Pentecost were recipients of the gift of tongues. And the clear implication of Peter's words is that they would experience dreams and visions as a result of which they would prophesy.

I've already mentioned a few incidents where nonapostolic believers were recipients of miraculous gifts of the Spirit, but it wouldn't hurt to remind ourselves once again. Stephen, a deacon, "full of grace and power, was doing great wonders and signs among the people" (Acts 6:8). Stephen also experienced a glorious revelatory vision of "the glory of God, and [of] Jesus standing at the right hand of God" (Acts 7:55). But no one would have said these supernatural phenomena were a confirming sign that Stephen was an apostle.

---

33 A much more detailed analysis of the characteristics and requirements for apostleship will be undertaken in chapters 17 and 18.

34 Wayne Grudem, "Should Christians Expect Miracles Today? Objections and Answers from the Bible," in *The Kingdom and the Power*, ed. Gary S. Greig and Kevin N. Springer (Ventura, CA: Regal, 1993), 67.

Philip, another deacon (Acts 6:5), performed many miraculous signs, healed the sick, drove out demons (Acts 8:7), and displayed "great miracles," yet no one argues that on this basis he was an apostle. Nonapostolic Christians in Antioch prophesied (Acts 13:1–3), as did anonymous disciples of the John the Baptist (Acts 19:6–7). The aforementioned Philip was blessed with four daughters, all of whom prophesied. Paul expected the average Christians in Rome to prophesy (Rom. 12:6) but never suggested that operating in this miraculous ministry meant that they were apostles. The miraculous gifts and powers in 1 Corinthians 12:8–10 are said to be distributed to average believers in Corinth, none of whom would ever have been thought to be apostles. Paul also described how the Holy Spirit worked "miracles" among the Galatians (Gal. 3:5), apparently in the complete absence of an apostle.

My point in citing these instances is simply to highlight once again the fact that miraculous gifts and powerful signs were not restricted to the apostles. This confirms that whatever else Paul may have meant in 2 Corinthians 12:12, he was not saying that "signs and wonders and mighty works" were the exclusive domain and authenticating mark of apostles alone.

One final comment is in order, and this may catch some readers by surprise. The phrase "sign gift" appears nowhere in Scripture. I mention this because cessationists often create a special category for certain miraculous gifts and speak of them as "sign gifts," believing that this will provide grounds for arguing that such gifts served a unique purpose in the first century but have since been withdrawn. Yet while the word "sign" does often appear, and likewise the word "gift" (charisma), no spiritual gift is explicitly called a "sign gift." And no author ever speaks of this as a separate category of gifts in order to differentiate them from the more ordinary or less miraculous charismata. I earlier noted that in Romans 12:6–8 the gift of prophecy (one of the cessationists' so-called sign gifts) is listed alongside serving and teaching and mercy. No attempt is made to single it, or any other miraculous gift, out as if it were of a different nature and purpose from those gifts that all Christians acknowledge continue in the life and ministry of the church today.

It is true that in 1 Corinthians 14:22 Paul said that "tongues are a sign not for believers but for unbelievers." However, as we'll see in chapter 12, to speak in tongues without interpretation in the presence of unbelievers is a negative sign of judgment that Paul did not want the Christian community to give. He did not use the word *sign* to set apart tongues into a different category. He was rebuking the Corinthian Christians for a misuse of tongues, not identifying the actual purpose of tongues in the life of the believing community. And notice that where Paul immediately mentioned prophecy, the word *sign* does not appear in the original text.[35]

The word for "sign" (*sēmeion*) appears often in Acts, but it is usually with reference to "signs and wonders." The latter typically refer to the abundance of miracles that were associated with Jesus and the original company of apostles (see Acts 2:43; 4:30; 5:12; 6:8; 7:36; 8:13; 14:3; 15:12; also Rom. 15:19). Could a particular healing serve as a "sign" in some capacity? Yes (see Acts 4:16, 22; 8:6), but neither healing nor tongues nor prophecy is ever described as a "sign gift" to indicate that it was temporary and in a different category from other gifts that were designed by God to be permanent. Again, although on occasion a healing may serve as a "sign," at no time is healing called a "sign gift."[36]

Thus, to speak of certain spiritual gifts as "sign" gifts does not serve us well. It suggests a narrow and temporary purpose for some gifts, something not corroborated elsewhere in the New Testament.

Hebrews 2:3–4

Perhaps the second most oft-cited text in defense of cessationism is Hebrews 2:3–4. The author of Hebrews said that the gospel message "was declared at first by the Lord, and it was attested to us by those who heard, while God also bore witness by signs and wonders and various miracles and by gifts of the Holy Spirit distributed according to his will." The urgency of paying close attention to this great salvation and fixing our faith on Jesus alone is of massive importance because of the way God confirmed the truth of the gospel. Notice that there are three stages in this process of confirmation.

1. Jesus Christ himself declared that he had come to save sinners. His word of forgiveness and redemption for those who trust and

---

35 The translators of the ESV include the word "sign" but direct the reader's attention to a footnote where they indicate that the "Greek lacks *a sign.*"

36 The only possible exception to this is in the long ending to Mark's gospel, a paragraph that the majority of New Testament scholars do not believe is part of the original text of Scripture (see Mark 16:17–18).

treasure him was proclaimed loudly and clearly and with the self-authenticating power of his divine authority.

2. Those who were eyewitnesses to Jesus while he was on the earth, who saw him and heard him and walked with him, in turn told us about their experience. They bore testimony that all he did and said was real and true. They were present when he cleansed the lepers and drove out demons and walked on water and refuted the Pharisees and raised the dead.

3. In turn, God the Father also bore witness to the truth of this message of salvation by granting signs and wonders and various miracles and gifts of the Holy Spirit. Such displays of divine power confirmed and attested to the reality of all that Jesus claimed to be.

All Christians agree on these points. But what of the claim that this suggests, perhaps even requires, that "signs and wonders and various miracles and . . . gifts of the Holy Spirit" served their purpose in the first century and should not be expected or prayed for subsequent to the death of the original apostles? John MacArthur believes that this passage "confirms that validation of the prophets was the chief purpose for biblical miracles."[37] He argues yet again that "we see Scripture attesting that signs, wonders, miracles, and miraculous gifts were God's confirmation of the message of Christ and his apostles ('those who heard')."[38] MacArthur also believes that the past tense of the verb "it was attested" is "a clear biblical word that the miracles, wonders, and sign gifts were given only to the first-generation apostles to confirm that they were messengers of new revelation."[39]

But several things should be said in response to this argument. First, even if we should concede that "validation of the prophets was the chief purpose for biblical miracles," this in no way suggests, and far less requires, that it was the only purpose. The New Testament consistently testifies to several other purposes or effects of miraculous ministry.

Second, the author of Hebrews did not limit his text to the apostles. In fact, the word *apostle* doesn't even occur in this passage. Now, it is certainly

---

37 MacArthur, *Charismatic Chaos*, 118.
38 MacArthur, 119.
39 MacArthur, 119.

the case that the apostolic company were among those in view when he spoke of "those who heard." But there is no reason why it should be limited or restricted to them. Numerous others, beyond the Twelve, heard Jesus preach and watched him perform miracles. And many more than the Twelve exercised spiritual gifts.

Third, the text does not say to what or to whom God "bore witness" by signs and wonders. The NIV goes beyond what is in the original text by inserting the words "to it." However, the most likely interpretation is that "the great salvation" mentioned in verse 3 is in view.

Fourth, there is something else our author didn't say that many have simply assumed he did: he nowhere said that the miracles that attested to or confirmed (or "validated") the message were performed only by those who originally heard the Lord. The word translated "bore witness" sounds as if it is in the past tense, as if to suggest that God used to do this, that in the past he formerly bore witness by signs and wonders, but that he no longer does so in the present day. But the participle translated "bore witness" is in the present tense in Greek. Although that doesn't prove my point, it certainly makes room for it (both grammatically and theologically). It means that it is entirely within the realm of possibility that even in the time during which the recipients of this letter were living, God was still bearing witness to the truth of the gospel through signs, wonders, miracles, and spiritual gifts. In other words, as William Lane has noted, our author's language suggests "that the corroborative evidence was not confined to the initial act of preaching, but continued to be displayed within the life of the community."[40] Tom Schreiner acknowledges this possibility and says that "perhaps the miracles described here were also ongoing in the life of the readers."[41]

Fifth, there is nothing in this passage that suggests God cannot, does not, or will not continue to attest to and confirm the truth of the gospel through supernatural spiritual displays of power. Some argue that since we have the Bible, we no longer need such miracles or spiritual gifts to confirm the truth of the gospel. But the Bible itself nowhere says that. Nowhere in Scripture are we told that the Bible replaces miracles or that the gospel cannot still be confirmed by supernatural displays of power. If supernatural displays of

---

40 William Lane, *Hebrews 1–8*, Word Biblical Commentary (Dallas: Word, 1991), 39.
41 Thomas R. Schreiner, *Commentary on Hebrews* (Nashville: B&H, 2015), 83.

power and the operation of spiritual gifts confirmed the truth of the gospel of salvation in the first century, why could they not continue to do so today?

Sixth, even if God no longer uses miraculous events to confirm or attest to the truth of the gospel (although I believe he does), such spiritual gifts have other purposes they serve. As we've already noted on several occasions, Paul clearly teaches that all spiritual gifts, even the more overtly miraculous ones, serve the "common good" or are for the benefit and building up of the body of Christ (see 1 Cor. 12:7–10). The gift of prophecy is designed by God to encourage, console, and edify believers (1 Cor. 14:3). Every spiritual gift is used to strengthen and build up believers in the church. And that is a purpose they serve that will never come to an end until Jesus himself returns in the clouds.

In other words, while acknowledging that supernatural displays of miraculous power served to authenticate and confirm the truth of the gospel, we must never think that such was their only purpose. Nowhere does the New Testament reduce the purpose of the miraculous to attestation and confirmation.

Finally, it is worth noting that the standard word for spiritual gifts (*charisma*) doesn't even appear in this text. It literally reads, "distributions of the Holy Spirit" (v. 4). As I have written elsewhere,

> Perhaps the author is not even describing "gifts" per se, in which case *pneumatos hagiou* [Holy Spirit] may be an objective genitive referring to the Spirit himself as the one whom God distributed or supplied to (cf. Gal. 3:5) his people. If, on the other hand, "gifts" are in view, note that he distinguishes between "various miracles" (lit., "powers," *dynamesin*) and "gifts" of the Spirit. This would suggest that by "gifts" he intends more than what we would call miraculous *charismata*. Is anyone prepared to restrict *all* spiritual gifts to the first century simply because they served to authenticate and attest to the gospel message? In view of these factors, I am not persuaded that this passage supports cessationism.[42]

---

42 Storms, "A Third Wave View," 191n21.

Excursus: A Response to Jonathan Edwards on the Cessation of the *Charismata*

Why are so many evangelical Christians opposed to or skeptical of the suggestion that God still speaks by means of revelatory gifts like prophecy and word of knowledge? Whenever I speak about this subject in mainstream Protestant churches, some cringe in fear while others get angrily defensive. Having spoken with many of them about this, I've concluded that the primary reason for their reaction is their belief that if God were to speak outside the Scriptures or were to bestow the gift of prophecy to the church, it would undermine both the finality and sufficiency of the Bible, God's written Word.

Cessationists insist that prophecy in the New Testament is the infallible report of a divinely inspired revelation, no different in quality from Old Testament prophecy and therefore equal to the Bible itself in authority. Prophecy, they argue, consists of the very words of God himself. Prophecy, therefore, is infallible and binding on the theological and moral convictions of all Christians.

If such prophecy were still being given, the finality of the Word of God would be seriously threatened. If such prophecy were still being given, or if God were to speak to his people through other means, on what grounds could one insist that the biblical canon is closed? Would we not be forced to open the canon and begin inserting new verses in new chapters in new books bearing the names of contemporary "prophets"?

Furthermore, cessationists believe that if people begin to act and believe in response to their claim of having "heard God" or having received a prophetic utterance, their reliance on the sufficiency of the Bible for all of life would be undermined. It would result in people living their lives and often justifying bizarre (or at least unwise) behavior based on subjective impressions rather than on the objective and infallible written Word of God. People will neglect or ignore the counsel of Scripture because of something "God told" them. Worse still, they'll be prone to control and manipulate others on the "authority" of some divinely revealed directive.

One must admit that this is indeed a potential problem. In fact, it's more than potential. I have known a number of people who were inclined to neglect Scripture as the source of truth and direction because they valued the "present-tense" voice of God above his "past-tense" voice. Jonathan Edwards (1703–58), during the revival known as the First Great Awakening, was forced to deal with the claims of people to having heard God speak outside of the Bible. He found it to be a uniquely problematic issue. Listen to his description:

> And one erroneous principle, than which scarce any has proved more mischievous to the present glorious work [his way of referring to the revival], is a notion that 'tis God's manner now in these days to guide his saints, at least some that are more eminent, by inspiration, or immediate revelation; and to make known to 'em what shall come to pass hereafter, or what it is his will that they should do, by impressions that he by his Spirit makes upon their minds, either with or without texts of Scripture; whereby something is made known to them, that is not taught in the Scripture as the words lie in the Bible.[1]

Edwards proceeded to identify no fewer than five negative consequences of this. Given my profound appreciation for Edwards, we would do well to listen and respond carefully to his concerns.

Satanic Deception?

First, Edwards argued that "by such a notion the Devil has a great door opened for him; and if once this opinion should come to be fully yielded to and established in the church of God, Satan would have opportunity thereby

---

1   Jonathan Edwards, *The Great Awakening*, ed. C. C. Goen (New Haven, CT: Yale University Press, 1972), 432.

to set up himself as the guide and oracle of God's people, and to have his word regarded as their infallible rule, and so to lead 'em where he would, and to introduce what he pleased."[2] Evidently Edwards believed that it was virtually impossible, or at least extremely difficult, to discern the voice of God and distinguish it from the voice of Satan.

Edwards undoubtedly believed, as do all cessationists, that in the first century AD, prior to the closing of the biblical canon, God spoke to his people through dreams, visions, words of knowledge, and other forms of prophetic revelation. But what was to prevent satanic speech through these revelations at that time? Would not his objection that Satan can use it deceptively apply equally to *that* day and age? In other words, if the mere existence of extrabiblical revelation gives Satan the "opportunity ... to set up himself as the guide and oracle of God's people," then that would have been as great a problem to the churches in first-century Corinth and Thessalonica and Colossae, for example, as it was to Edwards's own eighteenth-century church in Northampton, Massachusetts, or is to the twenty-first-century church in Oklahoma City or Chicago or Paris. And if that alleged "problem" was, in God's mind, *insufficient* reason to withhold such extrabiblical revelation then, why should it be any different in Edwards's day or our own?

Evidently the first-century church did quite well in discerning God's will and ways when extrabiblical revelation was prevalent. Why can't we do this equally well? Insofar as we have the final authoritative canon of Scripture by which to assess and judge all claims of prophetic revelation, we can arguably do even better. If Edwards's argument is valid, it proves too much: it would weigh against the existence of extrabiblical revelation *at any and all times*, including the apostolic era, something Edwards would by no means countenance.

The potential threat of satanic deception through extrabiblical revelatory guidance is nowhere explicitly mentioned in the New Testament. If this were a significant problem, as Edwards would have us to believe, it is stunning that no warnings or guidelines or instructions were given by the apostles to alert believers in the first century. Certainly there are numerous descriptions of Satan's activity among unbelievers, blinding and hardening and deceiving them concerning the person of Jesus. There are also warnings

2   Edwards, 432.

about demonic temptations aimed at believers, but nowhere do the New Testament authors question the validity of extrabiblical revelation or the spiritual gift of prophecy because of some satanic capacity to "guide" and "lead" us contrary to the will of God. In other words, if there is a potential for Satan to dupe and deceive believers, the Bible does not relate this to the presence of extrabiblical or subjective revelatory activity of the Spirit.

One passage of Scripture that may shed light on the issue is 1 John 4:1–6, a text that Edwards reflected on in addressing the issue of revival in his day. He found in this passage several criteria by which to judge the source and validity of the various physical and emotional "manifestations" during the First Great Awakening. The passage also speaks to the question of how to discern between the work of God and that of the enemy and demonstrates that Edwards's resistance to prophetic gifts based on a fear of satanic deception was unfounded, assuming that the believer avails himself or herself of the resources God has provided. Let's look at it more closely.

> Beloved, do not believe every spirit, but test the spirits to see whether they are from God, for many false prophets have gone out into the world. By this you know the Spirit of God: every spirit that confesses that Jesus Christ has come in the flesh is from God, and every spirit that does not confess Jesus is not from God. This is the spirit of the antichrist, which you heard was coming and now is in the world already. (1 John 4:1–3)

The background to this passage is the abundance of supernatural activity and phenomena in the early church: tongues, healings, prophecies, deliverance, and so on. John's readers were apparently given to the *uncritical acceptance* of anything supernatural. It remained for the apostle to inform them that *the supernatural is not always divine*! The emphasis here is not so much on the character of the spirit, whether it be false or genuine, but on its origin, whether it be divine or diabolical. John was clearly concerned with the "two spirits" that inspire contrary confessions of the Lord Jesus Christ.

This text tells us that the primary distinguishing feature of the enemy is denial of the incarnation of Christ and reassures us that we need not fall prey to his deception. But it also speaks of the confidence we have for victory over the efforts of Satan to mislead and distort. In other words, we have a solid basis on which to know the difference between the spirit of antichrist and the Spirit of God. The confession of Jesus as Christ incarnate is the means by which to determine the origin of a "spirit," whether it be of God or the devil.

All believers, said John, have the responsibility to test the spirits to determine their origin (1 John 4:1). "Unbelief," noted John Stott, "can be as much a mark of spiritual maturity as belief."[3] In other words, Christians must resist the temptation to be naive and gullible about supernatural and miraculous phenomena. The fact is, "many false prophets" have gone out into the world. Neither Christian faith nor love is to function indiscriminately. It is the duty of us all to judge, weigh, assess, and evaluate, and to exercise our discernment.

John gave two negative signs of "not being of God." In 1 John 3:10 the one who does not practice righteousness is "not of God" and in 4:3 the one who does not confess Jesus is "not of God." Furthermore, such a one is not merely "not of God," but is, positively speaking, *of the devil* (3:10) and *of the antichrist* (4:3). The "of" suggests both allegiance and ownership, hence "belonging to," as well as the idea of "spiritual dependence."

> Little children, you are from God and have overcome them, for he who is in you is greater than he who is in the world. They are from the world; therefore they speak from the world, and the world listens to them. We are from God. Whoever knows God listens to us; whoever is not from God does not listen to us. By this we know the Spirit of truth and the spirit of error. (1 John 4:4–6)

Here we see that Christians are assured of a theological victory over false prophets and heretics. They have not succeeded in deceiving you. You know the truth and have rejected their lies. Why? Indeed, how? Because "he who is in you is greater than he who is in the world"! Having contrasted Christians ("you") with the heretics ("them"), John next compared the spiritual forces who are *in* the respective antagonists. Yes, Satan is great, but God is greater! Yes, Satan is powerful, but God is infinitely more powerful!

The "he" who is in the Christian is God the Father (1 John 3:20; 4:12–13), God the Son (1 John 2:14; 3:24), or God the Holy Spirit (1 John 2:20, 27), or the triune God in the fullness of his divine presence. John did not say "greater are *you*" but "greater is *he*." It isn't you, but *God in you* that brings the assurance of victory.

---

3   John R. W. Stott, *The Epistles of John: An Introduction and Commentary* (Grand Rapids: Eerdmans, 1976), 153.

Some may argue that I have misapplied this passage, that the only thing of which John assured us is the ability to know if someone is true or false based on their confession or denial of the incarnation. This is far and away different, for example, from being able to discern whether an "impression" directing us to take some specific action is of God or of the enemy. That is true, but if we can confidently know when a "spirit" is or is not of the truth by noting where it stands on the doctrine of the incarnation, can we not also apply other biblical standards to judge the origin of any purported "voice" or "impression"? I think the answer must be yes.

John continued by arguing that the response of the audience to the respective messages reveals their true character and is yet another criterion by which to know the Spirit of truth and the spirit of error (4:5–6). At first glance, these verses sound like the height of arrogance. John said that *if you know God, you will listen to what I say*! If you don't listen to what I say and receive my teaching, then you are in bondage to the spirit of error. No ordinary individual Christian could ever make such a bold claim. But John was here speaking as an apostle with the full authority and inspiration of Christ behind his words. Stott explained,

> He is carrying a stage further the argument of the first three verses. There the test of doctrine was whether it acknowledged the divine-human person of Jesus Christ; here the test is whether it is accepted by Christians and rejected by non-Christians. There is a certain affinity between God's Word and God's people. Jesus had taught that His sheep hear His voice (Jn. 10:4, 5, 8, 16, 26, 27), that everyone who is of the truth listens to His witness to the truth (Jn. 18:37), and that "he who is of God hears the words of God" (Jn. 8:47). In the same way John asserts that since "we are of God" (6) and "ye are of God" (4), you listen to us. There is a correspondence between message and hearers. The Spirit who is in you (4) enables you to discern His own voice speaking through us (2). So you can recognize God's Word because God's people listen to it, just as you can recognize God's people because they listen to God's Word.[4]

So, my reason for citing this text in 1 John was simply to emphasize that so

4 Stott, 158.

long as we avail ourselves of the truth of apostolic teaching, we can be confident that Satan will neither dupe nor deceive us. This isn't to say we are utterly invulnerable or beyond the potential to be misled. Our capacity for yielding to the truth of the Word is often compromised by fleshly self-indulgence. But we need not be spiritually paralyzed or resort to a denial of God's present tense voice for fear that such will expose us to the destructive influence of the enemy, for "greater is he who is in you than he who is in the world."

In the volume *Are Miraculous Gifts for Today? Four Views*, Richard Gaffin (as Edwards preceding him) objects to the possibility of postcanonical revelation on the grounds that we would be bound to attend and submit to it no less than to Scripture.[5] Aside from the fact that this wrongly presupposes that contemporary prophecy yields infallible, Scripture-quality words from God, the problem is one Gaffin himself must face. For were not the Thessalonian Christians, for example, "bound to attend and submit to" (lit., "hold fast"; 1 Thess. 5:21) the prophetic words they received, no less than to the Scripture in which this very instruction is found? Evidently Paul did not fear that their response to the spoken prophetic word would undermine the ultimate authority or sufficiency of the written revelation (Scripture) that he was in process of sending them. The point is this: noncanonical revelation was not inconsistent with the authority of Scripture then, so why should it be now? This is especially true if contemporary prophecy does not necessarily yield infallible words of God.

Someone might ask, "But how should we in the twenty-first century, in a closed-canonical world, respond to noncanonical revelation?" The answer is, "In the same way Christians responded to it in their first-century, open-canonical world, namely, by evaluating it in light of Scripture" (which was emerging, and therefore partial, for them, but is complete for us). Such revelation would carry for us today the same authority it carried then for them. Furthermore, as noted earlier, we are in a much better position today than the early church, for we have the final form of the canon by which to evaluate claims to prophetic revelation. If they were capable of assessing prophetic revelation then (and Paul believed they were; witness his instruction in 1 Cor.

---

5 Gaffin's argument is found on pp. 46–48 in his chapter, "A Cessationist View," and my response is found on pp. 81–82 in my chapter, "A Third Wave Response" (from which the following discussion has been adapted), in *Are Miraculous Gifts for Today? Four Views*.

14:29ff. and 1 Thess. 5:19–22 to do precisely that), how much more are we today! If anything, contemporary claims of prophetic revelation should be easier to evaluate and respond to than such claims in the first century.

Therefore, if noncanonical revelation was not a threat to the ultimate authority of Scripture in its emerging form, why would it be a threat to Scripture in the latter's final form? If first-century Christians were obligated to believe and obey Scripture in the open-canonical period, simultaneous with and in the presence of noncanonical prophetic revelation, why would noncanonical revelation in the closed-canonical period of church history pose any more of a threat?

Gaffin argues that contemporary prophecy cannot, in fact, be evaluated by Scripture because of its purported specificity. But this is no more a problem for us today than it would have been for Christians in the first century. Didn't *they* evaluate prophetic revelation in spite of the latter's specificity and individuality? If they were obedient to Paul's instruction, they certainly did (1 Cor. 14:29; 1 Thess. 5:21–22). Why, then, can't we? And are we not, in fact, better equipped than they to do so insofar as we, unlike them, hold in hand the final form of canonical revelation whereby to make that assessment?

Neglect of Scripture?

Edwards was also convinced that admitting the existence of extrabiblical revelation would soon "bring the Bible into neglect and contempt. Late experience in some instances has shown that the tendency of this notion is to cause persons to esteem the Bible as a book that is in a great measure useless."[6] But again, the Bible itself nowhere warns us that extrabiblical revelatory activity will lead to the neglect of the written Word. If Paul or the other New Testament writers believed this was a credible threat, why didn't they supply us with some warning to that effect? Why would Paul have written extensively on the nature and operation of revelatory gifts but failed to mention the potential for this sort of abuse? When he did address himself to abuse, it was the temptation to suppress prophecy and treat it with disdain that evoked his stern rebuke (1 Thess. 5:19–22). Nowhere, either in 1 Thessalonians 5 or any other text, did he say, "Listen, folks, I'm concerned

6   Edwards, *The Great Awakening*, 432.

that if you embrace and exercise revelatory gifts you will end up elevating them and their authority above that of the written words of this epistle and the others that I have written to a number of other churches." That a few fanatical folk who are probably already inclined to ignore the clear teaching and authority of Scripture fall into error on this point is no argument that we should deny what the Bible itself says about the ongoing voice of the Spirit beyond the close of the canon.

Incorrigible?

A third objection raised by Edwards is that "as long as a person has a notion that he is guided by immediate direction from heaven, it makes him incorrigible and impregnable in all his misconduct: for what signifies it for poor blind worms of the dust to go to argue with a man, and endeavor to convince him and correct him, that is guided by the immediate counsels and commands of the great Jehovah?"[7] Again, however much a problem this may have been in Edwards's day or is in ours, it is no justification for dismissing the teaching of the New Testament. People who are determined to follow sinful ways will do it irrespective of what the Bible says. Whether or not one believes in postcanonical revelation is ultimately irrelevant.

I might also add that people who embrace Edwards's view can also do the same thing with the written Word. I have witnessed countless instances where someone dogmatically and inflexibly held to a particular interpretation of a text (as baseless as it might be) to justify a decision or to rationalize unwise behavior. These people were convinced that they "were guided by immediate counsels and commands of the great Jehovah" as set forth in his *written* Word. The only way to address this kind of abuse is the same way we should address those who appeal to God's voice to rationalize unwise and errant behavior: careful and more extensive and deliberate analysis of the meaning and significance of the biblical text.

7 Edwards, 432–33.

Failed Prophecies?

Edwards also pointed to numerous instances of failed prophecies. He was surprised that "such multiplied, plain instances of the failing of such supposed revelations in the event don't [sic] open everyone's eyes. I have seen so many instances of the failing of such impressions, that would almost furnish an [sic] history."[8] Two points should be made here.

First, we've misunderstood the nature of New Testament prophecy if we think of it as primarily predictive in nature. The purpose of the gift is less foretelling the future than forth-telling the heart of God for a particular person. If people, as was perhaps the case in Edwards's day, focus on foretelling or predicting future events, they will invariably go astray.

Second, there are many instances of "the failing of such impressions," but Edwards's response comes perilously close to what Paul himself warned against in 1 Thessalonians 5:19–22. Very likely the "failure" of some to accurately foretell the future was leading some people in Thessalonica to the point of "despising" prophetic utterances. Paul's counsel was to resist the temptation to do so; otherwise one would be in danger of "quenching the Holy Spirit." The proper biblical response to the abuse of prophecy is not to reject it, despise it, discard it, or forbid it, but to judge it, weigh it, evaluate all such claims, and then follow the apostle's advice: "Hold fast what is good. Abstain from every form of evil" (1 Thess. 5:21–22).

Discontent?

In Edwards's fifth and final point, he made this plea:

> And why can't we be contented with the divine oracles, that holy, pure Word of God, that we have in such abundance and such clearness, now since the canon of Scripture is completed? Why should we desire to have anything added to them by impulses from above? Why should not we rest in that standing rule that God has given to his church, which the Apostle

---

8   Edwards, 433.

teaches us is surer than a voice from heaven? And why should we desire to make the Scripture speak more to us than it does?[9]

Believing in extrabiblical revelatory activity of the Spirit is not because of lack of contentment with Scripture. In fact, it is precisely what Scripture itself teaches concerning the activity of the Spirit that leads us to embrace so-called impulses from above. I believe in the ongoing revelatory activity of the Spirit *because* I am unreservedly "contented" with the absolute truthfulness of everything Scripture says.

Note one thing that characterizes all of Edwards's arguments: *not one of them is biblical!* That is to say, none of his points is derived from an explicit statement in Scripture. Each one is based on supposed negative consequences or the fanatical behavior of people who already had a deficient view of biblical authority and a low esteem for the canonical Word.

---

9   Edwards, 434.

CHAPTER 6

Biblical and Theological Arguments in Support of Continuationism

In chapter 5 we reviewed the case for cessationism. In this chapter we'll consider if there are biblical reasons for believing that God intends miraculous gifts of the Spirit to be present and operative in the lives of his people today, both individually and in the corporate experience of the local church. Since we've already looked at the cessationist arguments against this, and I hold to a continuationist position, my explanation will primarily take the form of a response to each of the arguments put forward by cessationists.

The Case for Continuationism[1]

Cessationists typically argue that because certain miraculous gifts functioned to authenticate the apostolic message, we should not expect them to be operative in today's church. But there is no reason to think these gifts in the twenty-first century church couldn't function in the same way when we

---

1 As noted in the introduction, I have written elsewhere on this topic in a number of publications and have drawn upon them extensively in the composition of this chapter. See Sam Storms, "A Third Wave View," in *Are Miraculous Gifts for Today? Four Views*, ed. Wayne Grudem (Grand Rapids: Zondervan, 1995), 175–223 (along with my responses to the other contributors in this book); "Are Miraculous Gifts for Today?" in Storms, *Tough Topics: Biblical Answers to 25 Challenging Questions* (Wheaton, IL: Crossway, 2013), 232–51; "Appendix 2: Are Miraculous Gifts for Today?" in Storms, *Practicing the Power: Welcoming the Gifts of the Spirit in Your Life* (Grand Rapids: Zondervan, 2017), 244–69; and chapter 12 in Storms, *The Language of Heaven: Crucial Questions about Speaking in Tongues* (Lake Mary, FL: Charisma House, 2019).

proclaim the same gospel. Nowhere in the Bible are we told that because we now have the Bible we no longer need or might profit from what miraculous gifts of the Spirit can achieve.

If signs, wonders, and the power of the Holy Spirit were essential in bearing witness to the truth of the gospel *then*, why not *now*? The miracles that confirmed the preaching of the gospel in the first century serve no less to confirm the gospel in subsequent centuries, even our own. And if signs, wonders, and miracles were essential in the ministry of the Son of God as he walked this earth, how much more so now in his physical absence. Surely no one wants to suggest that the Bible, for all its glory, is sufficient to do what Jesus couldn't. Jesus thought it necessary to utilize the miraculous phenomena of the Holy Spirit to attest and confirm his ministry. If it was essential for him, how much more so for us.

We must also resist the tendency toward reductionism. Just because "spiritual gift A" serves us well in one particular capacity does not mean it cannot serve us well in another. Believing that signs and miracles attested to the divine ministry of Jesus and the apostles does not mean they cannot serve other functions beyond the first century and even into the twenty-first. Paul made it quite clear that the primary task of all spiritual gifts, both the so-called more miraculous as well as the so-called more mundane gifts, is to build up and strengthen the body of Christ. This is especially clear from 1 Corinthians 12:7–10, where we find what are typically called "miraculous" or "supernatural" gifts of the Spirit. There Paul explicitly declared that these gifts are given by the Spirit "for the common good" (v. 7).

For the cessationist argument to persuade, one must demonstrate that authentication or attestation was the *sole and exclusive purpose* of such displays of divine power. However, *nowhere in the New Testament is the purpose or function of the miraculous or the* charismata *reduced to that of attestation.* The miraculous, in whatever form in which it appeared, served several other distinct purposes. For example, the miraculous served to *glorify* God and to draw attention to his power and compassion. This was the primary reason for the resurrection of Lazarus, as Jesus himself made clear in John 11:4 (cf. 11:40). The doxological purpose of the miraculous is also found in John 2:11; 9:3; and Matthew 15:29–31. Miracles also served an *evangelistic* purpose (see Acts 9:32–43). This isn't to say that miraculous gifts or signs and wonders are responsible for the conversion of souls, but they surely can be used by

God as a form of pre-evangelism to break down resistance in the unbelieving heart and to awaken a person to the reality of a sovereign, supernatural God. Much of our Lord's miraculous ministry was an expression of his *compassion* and *love* for the hurting multitudes. He healed the sick and even fed the five thousand principally because he felt compassion for the people (Matt. 14:14; Mark 1:40–41).[2]

Several texts indicate that one primary purpose of miraculous phenomena was to *edify* and *build up* the body of Christ (1 Cor. 12:7; 14:3, 4, 5, 26). Simply stated, *all* the gifts of the Spirit, whether tongues or teaching, whether prophecy or mercy, whether healing or helps, were given, among other reasons, for the edification, building up, encouraging, instructing, consoling, and sanctifying of the body of Christ. Even if the ministry of the miraculous gifts to attest and authenticate has ceased, a point I concede only for the sake of argument, such gifts would continue to function in the church for the other reasons cited.

Yet another text that tells us about the sanctifying effect of spiritual gifts is Ephesians 4:11–13. Here is what Paul wrote:

> And he gave the apostles, the prophets, the evangelists, the shepherds and teachers, to equip the saints for the work of ministry, for building up the body of Christ, until we all attain to the unity of the faith and of the knowledge of the Son of God, to mature manhood, to the measure of the stature of the fullness of Christ.

Paul spoke of the operation of spiritual gifts (together with the office of apostle), and in particular the gifts of prophecy, evangelism, pastoring, and teaching, as functioning in the building up of the church "until we all attain to the unity of the faith and of the knowledge of the Son of God, to mature manhood, to the measure of the stature of the fullness of Christ" (v. 13). That word "until" is crucial. Until *what* time or when will we no longer need the operation of these gifts? Not "until" the body of Christ attains to mature manhood and measures up to the stature of the fullness of Christ. Since the latter most assuredly has not yet been attained by the church, and won't

---

2 For an extensive demonstration of this truth, see my article "Why Did Jesus Heal the Sick?" *Enjoying God* (blog), April 15, 2019, www.samstorms.org/enjoying-god-blog/post/why-did-jesus-heal-the-sick.

be until Jesus comes back, we can confidently anticipate the presence and power of such gifts until that day arrives.

There may well be additional support for continuationism in something Paul wrote in the first chapter of his first epistle to the Corinthians:

> I give thanks to my God always for you because of the grace of God that was given you in Christ Jesus, that in every way you were enriched in him in all speech and all knowledge—even as the testimony about Christ was confirmed among you—so that you are not lacking in any gift, as you wait for the revealing of our Lord Jesus Christ, who will sustain you to the end, guiltless in the day of our Lord Jesus Christ. God is faithful, by whom you were called into the fellowship of his Son, Jesus Christ our Lord. (vv. 4–9)

The significance of this text is not merely Paul's affirmation that the Corinthians "[were] not lacking in any gift," but the eschatological time frame within which he envisioned their experience of these gifts. We must remember that Paul believed he might well live until the second coming of Christ, and this appears to be the basis on which he made this assertion concerning the Corinthian believers. The gifts (*charismata*) they had received from the Lord are envisioned as lasting until such time as Jesus is revealed from heaven at his parousia. As Paul Gardner explains it, "the gifts are given to help the church live appropriately until the time when they shall see 'face to face' (13:12)."[3] It's "as you wait" for his return that you enjoy the presence and power of these gifts. Paul said nothing, hinted at nothing, that would suggest he believed these gifts would be withdrawn prior to "the revealing of our Lord Jesus Christ," something he later reaffirmed in even more explicit detail (see 1 Cor. 13:8–12).

Neither did Paul differentiate among the many spiritual gifts with which the Corinthians had been blessed, as if there was a distinction in his mind between so-called foundational or temporary sign gifts, on the one hand, and permanent, ministry gifts on the other. We should also note that Paul's reference to the second coming of Christ was a not-so-veiled rebuke of those in Corinth who believed that their possession of certain gifts, particularly

---

3 Paul Gardner, *1 Corinthians*, Zondervan Exegetical Commentary on the New Testament (Grand Rapids: Zondervan, 2018), 62.

tongues, was an indication that they had attained some heightened state of spirituality prior to the consummation.

Continuationism and the Sufficiency of Scripture

Another cessationist argument we considered was that the ongoing operation of revelatory gifts of the Spirit would undermine the sufficiency of Scripture. The sufficiency of Scripture is the doctrine that the Bible contains every theological truth and every ethical norm that is required for living a Christ-exalting and God-glorifying life. What the Bible contains and teaches is "enough" to enable us to lead godly lives in this present age. Wayne Grudem argues that "the sufficiency of Scripture guarantees that God will not give any new revelation in this age that adds to *the moral standards that he requires for all Christians to obey* during the church age."[4] More recently, in his excellent treatment of *sola scriptura*, Matthew Barrett defined the sufficiency of Scripture in these terms:

> The sufficiency of Scripture means that all things necessary for salvation and for living the Christian life in obedience to God and for his glory are given to us in the Scriptures. Not only is the Bible our supreme authority, it is the authority that provides believers with all the truth they need for reconciliation with God and for following after Christ.[5]

This raises the question: "What precisely does the Bible say that God has done or provided to enable us to be edified and built up and thoroughly equipped for every good work?" (2 Tim. 3:16–17). Among the many things it says God has done and provided is the blessing of the spiritual gifts, those in 1 Corinthians 12:7–10 in particular. The "all-sufficient" Word of God explicitly commands us to earnestly desire "the higher gifts" (1 Cor. 12:31a), which Paul went on to identify primarily as prophecy. He again commanded us to "earnestly desire the spiritual gifts, especially that you may prophesy" (1 Cor. 14:1). Again, "Now I want you all to speak in tongues, but even more to prophesy" (1 Cor. 14:5a). And if there is any doubt about Paul's meaning, he

---

4   Wayne Grudem, *The Gift of Prophecy in the New Testament and Today* (Wheaton, IL: Crossway, 2000), 257.

5   Matthew Barrett, *God's Word Alone: The Authority of Scripture* (Grand Rapids: Zondervan, 2016), 334.

closed this chapter with the exhortation, "So, my brothers, earnestly desire to prophesy, and do not forbid speaking in tongues" (1 Cor. 14:39).

I emphasize once again: it is in the all-sufficient Scriptures that we find these exhortations. They are found in the Bible that tells us everything we need for Christian growth and godliness. Do we believe the Bible tells us what to embrace and what to avoid? Yes. Do we believe the Bible is altogether sufficient to give us every command that we need to obey and every warning that we need to heed? Yes. Do we believe the Bible warns us about those misguided beliefs and practices that may well threaten its own sufficiency? Yes.

What then does the Bible say about revelatory gifts of the Spirit? It says we need them because they serve "the common good" (1 Cor. 12:7). It says prophecy is given to God's people "for their upbuilding and encouragement and consolation" (1 Cor. 14:3). It says that when we come into the corporate gathering of God's people, "each one has a hymn, a lesson [or teaching], a revelation, a tongue, or an interpretation," and that all things should "be done for building up" (1 Cor. 14:26). And yet nowhere does it ever remotely suggest, much less explicitly assert, that the ongoing validity of the very gifts it endorses is a dangerous threat to the reality of Scripture's own sufficiency.

In light of this, I would like to pose several questions to my cessationist friends. From where do you think continuationists derive our belief in the ongoing validity of miraculous gifts of the Spirit? We didn't concoct the idea on our own. We get our view from Scripture! It is the Scriptures, the all-sufficient Scriptures that teach us to earnestly desire spiritual gifts, especially that we might prophesy (1 Cor. 14:1). It is the Scriptures, the all-sufficient Scriptures that teach us that such gifts are not merely given to authenticate the apostolic message but also to build up God's people (1 Cor. 12:7; and all of 1 Cor. 14). It is the Scriptures, the all-sufficient Scriptures that tell us to "earnestly desire to prophesy," and not to "forbid speaking in tongues" (1 Cor. 14:39). It is the Scriptures, the all-sufficient Scriptures that tell us that in the new covenant age inaugurated at Pentecost, God's people, young and old, male and female, will experience revelatory dreams and visions and will prophesy (Acts 2). And *nowhere* in the Scriptures, the all-sufficient Scriptures, are we told that these revelatory gifts will last only for about fifty or sixty years and then disappear.

Belief in the sufficiency of Scripture means that we believe what it says and obey its commands. *But in the cessationists' appeal to the notion of the Bible's sufficiency, they end up denying the Bible's functional authority.* This is the great irony. My cessationist friends say they believe the Bible is inerrant and sufficient to tell us all we need to know to live godly lives, but they deny the Bible's teaching concerning the operation of spiritual gifts and their capacity to enable us to live godly lives. If we believe in the Bible's sufficiency, we would expect it to plainly tell us that the revelatory gifts of the Spirit and other miraculous *charismata* were designed only for the few decades of the first century.

Some cessationists have argued that God gave prophets to receive revelation until the apostolic message reached its final maturity and then ceased. With the completion of the message, the need for the revelatory gifts was also complete. But where in the New Testament does any author ever say that? What text or texts might you cite to support that assertion? One cessationist has mentioned Ephesians 2:20; 3:5; 4:11 (the latter of which, by the way, says that apostles and prophets and evangelists and pastor-teachers were given "until" we reach our final and consummate maturity as conformed to Christ, and I daresay that won't happen until the Second Coming). But where in any of these texts or in any others are we told that the spiritual gift of prophecy is not needed because we have the "completion of the message"?

If, as cessationists undoubtedly believe, the Bible is sufficient for all instruction and sufficient to provide inerrant guidance for whatever we might need to grow in godliness, why does the all-sufficient Bible not say what cessationists continually assert? Wouldn't it have been prudent for the apostles to have told us that their teaching on revelatory gifts would only operate for a mere fifty or sixty years of church life? In my experience, cessationists who affirm the sufficiency of the Bible seem reluctant to admit that *this very Bible* fails to provide us with a single text in which we are told that the many gifts it encourages us to pursue and practice were temporary or were characterized by some inherent obsolescence.

I must repeat myself here. If the Bible is sufficient to give us all we need to live godly lives, and I certainly believe it is, then why does it not give us a single, solitary text in which it tells us to ignore the exhortations to earnestly desire spiritual gifts, especially prophecy, or a single, solitary text in which it tells us that the revelatory gifts that were given to edify and encourage the people of God were not meant for any generation of Christians beyond those of the first century? Why does the written Word only tell us to make good use of such gifts for the edification of the body and not tell us that such was only meant for the early church? I simply don't know how my cessationist friends can affirm biblical sufficiency when they disregard without textual support the many examples and exhortations concerning the use of these gifts.

So, in summary, I contend that if you believe in the sufficiency and the functional authority of Scripture, you *must necessarily* believe in the ongoing validity and edifying power of revelatory gifts of the Spirit.

Miscellaneous Arguments Addressed

If cessationism is true, what are we to do with the consistently positive portrayal of gifts of the Spirit that we see in the inspired Word of God? When we look to the many New Testament epistles and their description of life as believers in the local church, what do we find? We read about spiritual gifts operating in Thessalonica (1 Thess. 5:19–22), in Antioch (Acts 13:1–2), in Caesarea (Acts 10:44–48; 21:8–9), in Rome (Rom. 12:3–8), in Samaria (Acts 8:4–8), in Ephesus (Acts 19:1–7; 1 Tim. 1:18; 4:14), in Galatia (Gal. 3:1–5), and of course in Corinth (1 Cor. 12–14). Given this consistently positive portrayal of how the gifts should operate, someone must mount up an overwhelming case for why we should not pray for, pursue, and practice such gifts in the church today.[6]

We often hear it said that the miraculous gifts of the Spirit were somehow uniquely tied or tethered to the original apostles. In the absence of those men, we should not expect the gifts to be found. But the apostles were hardly the *only* ones who operated in the power of signs and wonders. The New Testament describes numerous nonapostolic Christians exercising with great success and spiritual benefit to others the many gifts that we are supposed to believe no longer exist in the church. One thinks immediately of the 70 (72?) nonapostolic followers of Jesus who were authorized and empowered to cast out demons (Luke 10:19–20), as well as at least 108 men and women among the 120 who were present in the upper room on the day of Pentecost (Acts 2:1–17). I've already had occasion to mention individuals

---

6   Let's be sure not to forget that the problem in Corinth wasn't with spiritual gifts, but with "unspiritual" or immature people. One cannot indict spiritual gifts or lay a charge at their feet without simultaneously indicting God. He is, after all, the one who thought up the idea of spiritual gifts and the one who bestowed them on his people. If spiritual gifts per se are the problem, the problem is with the God who authored them. Surely no one would want to say the latter.

such as Stephen (Acts 6–7), Philip (Acts 8), and Ananias (Acts 9). We also read about prophets in the church at Antioch (Acts 13:1) and several unnamed individuals in Tyre who "through the Spirit . . . were telling Paul not to go on to Jerusalem" (Acts 21:4). When Paul baptized several unnamed disciples of John the Baptist, they prophesied and spoke in tongues (Acts 19:6). Then there were the "four unmarried daughters" of Philip who are said to have "prophesied" (Acts 21:8–9), the unnamed brethren of Galatians 3:5, together with believers in Rome (Rom. 12:6–8), believers in Corinth (1 Cor. 12–14), and Christians in Thessalonica (1 Thess. 5:19–20).

As noted in chapter 3, when we read 1 Corinthians 12:7–10 it does not sound as if Paul was saying that only apostles are endowed with the *charismata*. On the contrary, gifts of healings, tongues, miracles, and so on were given by the sovereign Spirit to ordinary Christians in the church at Corinth for the daily, routine building up of the body. Carpenters, shepherds, and housewives, as well as apostles and elders and deacons received the manifestation of the Spirit, all "for the common good" of the church.

I earlier noted how Richard Gaffin argues that the experience of the early church as recorded in Acts must be viewed as a distinct and unique period that cannot be reproduced or copied today. After all, the early church had the presence of the apostles, and we obviously don't. But I would argue instead for the fundamental continuity or spiritually organic relationship between the church in Acts and the church in subsequent centuries. No one denies that there was an era or period in the early church that we might call "apostolic." We must acknowledge the significance of the personal physical presence of the apostles and their unique role in laying the foundation for the early church. But nowhere does the New Testament ever suggest that certain spiritual gifts were uniquely and exclusively tied to them or that with their passing came the passing of such gifts. The universal church or body of Christ that was established and gifted through the ministry of the apostles is the same universal church and body of Christ that exists today (something that only the most extreme of hyper-dispensationalists would deny). We are, together with Paul and Peter and Silas and Lydia and Priscilla and Luke, members of the same one body of Christ, indwelt and empowered by the same Holy Spirit.

A counterargument is often made to the effect that signs and wonders and miraculous *charismata* in Acts were closely connected to the apostles or to those who were themselves associated with the apostolic company. But we must remember that the book of Acts is, after all, the Acts of the *Apostles*. We title it this way because we recognize that the activity of the apostles is the principal focus of the book. We should hardly be surprised or try to build a theological case on the fact that a book *designed* to report the acts of the apostles describes signs and wonders performed by the apostles.

Furthermore, to say that Stephen and Philip and Ananias don't count because they are closely associated with the apostles proves nothing. Virtually *everyone* in Acts has some degree of association with the apostolic company. It is difficult to think of one person, who figures to any degree of prominence in the book of Acts, who is *not* associated with at least one of the apostles. But wasn't there a remarkable concentration of miraculous phenomena characteristic of the apostles as special representatives of Christ? There was indeed (cf. Acts 5:12). But the prevalence of miracles performed by the apostles in no way proves that *no* miracles were performed by or through others.

Spiritual Gifts, Then and Now

As noted in the previous chapter, the one argument I hear more often than others is that we today do not operate at the same level of accuracy or effectiveness as the early church. Jack Deere has responded to this point:

> It is simply not reasonable to insist that all miraculous spiritual gifts equal those of the apostles in their intensity or strength in order to be perceived as legitimate gifts of the Holy Spirit. No one would insist on this for the non-miraculous gifts like teaching or evangelism. . . . We should, of course, expect the healing ministry of the apostles to be greater than that of others in the body of Christ. They were specially chosen by the Lord to be his handpicked representatives, and they were given authority and power over all demons and over all disease. . . . They possessed an authority that no one else in the body of Christ possessed. . . . If we are going to say that the apostolic ministry sets the standard by which we should judge the gifts in Romans 12 and 1 Corinthians 12, we might be forced to conclude that no gifts, miraculous or non-miraculous, have been given since the days of the apostles! For who has measured up to the apostles in any respect?[7]

---

7   Jack Deere, *Surprised by the Power of the Spirit* (Grand Rapids: Zondervan, 1993), 67.

The most we can conclude from not seeing *apostolic* healing or *apostolic* miracles is that we are not seeing healings and miracles at the level they occurred in the ministry of the *apostles*. It does not mean that God has withdrawn gifts of healing or the gift of working miracles (1 Cor. 12:9–10) from the church at large.

Andrew Wilson makes a similar point in a blog article responding to Steve Timmis. Wilson cites the following:

> Jesus himself didn't always heal instantaneously. There are actually far more instantaneous and dramatic miracles these days than you guys give God credit for. Tongues in Paul's letters were probably a prayer language rather than an earthly language. New Testament prophecy can be fallible, too. You're speaking from within a Western, functionally materialist society, which misses out [on] much of the global picture. Paul didn't heal everyone, and arguably Jesus didn't either. And so on.
>
> But the best response, I think, is as follows. Yes, the apostles were more successful at healing than we are. There is, indeed, a discrepancy between our experience and what's described in the New Testament. But the apostles were also more successful at evangelism. And church planting. And leadership. And cross-cultural mission. And church discipline. And teaching. And standing firm under persecution. And handling disappointment. Yet in none of these cases do we conclude that the gulf is so wide, their "success" so much greater than ours, that to write a book telling people how to share the gospel, or teach, or lead more effectively, is to encourage people to be satisfied with sub-biblical Christianity. Rather, we acknowledge the disparity, and seek to learn from it. What did they do? How did they do it? What can we learn? What are we missing? Which contemporaries of ours is God using in this area at the moment? What can we learn from them? And so on.
>
> This is also the most charismatic response, in the best sense of that word: it is the response that places the strongest possible emphasis on *charisma*, on gift. Some people's healing and prophetic gifts, like some people's evangelistic and leadership and pastoral gifts, are more developed than others. I see fewer people healed than my friend Simon Holley, who sees fewer people healed than Heidi Baker, who sees fewer people healed than Peter, who saw fewer people healed than Jesus. When I preach the

gospel, fewer people come to faith than when my friend Adrian Holloway does, who sees fewer people come to faith than when Billy Graham did. My teaching gift isn't John Piper's, and his isn't John Calvin's, and his isn't Paul's. Gifts vary. "As it is, God arranged the members in the body, each one of them, as he chose" (1 Cor 12:18).

So is there a discrepancy between the quality, quantity and immediacy of New Testament miracles and ours? Yes. Does that mean the miraculous gifts are not for today? No. Unless teaching is not for today either, that is. In which case, you probably shouldn't be reading this in the first place.[8]

In sum, Wilson agrees that the sort of miracles we see today are rarer than those found in Acts, "but then so are sermons that see 3,000 people saved, and so are missionaries who plant churches from Jerusalem round to Illyricum. That is not a reason to seek those things less; it is a reason to seek them more."[9]

A Continuationist Response to the Cluster Argument[10]

What does the continuationist say in response to the "cluster" argument? If you recall, this is the argument that miracles and signs have clustered in three periods of redemptive history. At most, this might suggest that in these clusters of redemptive history, miraculous phenomena were *more* prevalent than in other times, but it does *not* prove that miraculous phenomena in other times were nonexistent. Nor does it prove that an increase in the frequency of miraculous phenomena could not appear in subsequent phases of redemptive history.

To make a substantive argument, one would need to explain not only why miraculous phenomena were prevalent in these three periods but also why they were, allegedly, infrequent or, to use John MacArthur's term,

---

8   Andrew Wilson, "On Acts 29 and Spiritual Gifts," *Think* (blog), April 19, 2017, www.thinktheology.co.uk. One should also consult Wilson's paper delivered at the annual meeting of the Evangelical Theological Society, Denver, Colorado, 2018. He has expanded on this theme in his book *Spirit and Sacrament* (Grand Rapids: Zondervan, 2019). See also Max Turner, "Spiritual Gifts Then and Now," *VoxEv* 15 (1985): 48–50.

9   Andrew Wilson, "A Response to Tom Schreiner," *Themelios* 44.1 (2019): 37.

10   My response to the "cluster" argument here is adapted from my treatment of it in "A Third Wave View" in *Are Miraculous Gifts for Today? Four Views*, 186–90.

"isolated," in all other periods. If miraculous phenomena were infrequent in other periods, a point I concede here only for the sake of argument, one would need to ascertain why. Could it be that the relative infrequency of the miraculous was due to the rebellion, unbelief, and apostasy rampant in Israel throughout much of their history (cf. Pss. 74:9–11; 77:7–14)? Let us not forget that even Jesus "could do no mighty work there [in Nazareth], except that he laid his hands on a few sick people and healed them" (Mark 6:5), all because of their unbelief (at which, we are told, Jesus "marveled," v. 6). The point is that the comparative isolation of the miraculous in certain periods of Old Testament history could be due more to the recalcitrance of God's people than to any supposed theological principle that dictates as normative a paucity of supernatural manifestations.

It's also worth pointing out *there were no cessationists in the Old Testament.* No one is ever found to argue that since miraculous phenomena were "clustered" at selected points in redemptive history, we should not expect God to display his power in some other day. In other words, *at no point in Old Testament history did miracles cease.* It is possible that they may have *subsided.* But this proves only that in some periods God is pleased to work miraculously with greater frequency than he is in others.

The fact that miracles do appear throughout the course of redemptive history, whether sporadically or otherwise, proves that miracles never ceased. How does the prevalence of miracles in three periods of history support the argument for cessationism? How does the existence of miracles in every age of redemptive history serve to argue against the existence of miracles in our age? The occurrence of miraculous phenomena throughout biblical history, however infrequent and isolated, cannot prove the *nonoccurrence* of miraculous phenomena in postbiblical times. The *continuation* of miraculous phenomena *then* is *not* an argument for the *cessation* of miraculous phenomena *now.* The fact that in certain periods of redemptive history few miracles were recorded proves only two things: first, that miracles *did* occur and, second, that few of them were recorded. It does not prove that only a few actually occurred.

In addition, the assertion that miraculous phenomena outside these three special periods were isolated is not altogether accurate. One can make this argument only by defining the miraculous so narrowly as to eliminate a vast number of recorded supernatural phenomena that otherwise might qualify. MacArthur insists that to qualify as a miracle the extraordinary event must occur "through human agency" and must serve to "authenticate" the messenger through whom God is revealing some truth. In this way one is able to exclude as miraculous any supernatural phenomenon that occurs apart from human agency and any supernatural phenomenon unrelated to the revelatory activity of God. If no revelation is occurring in that period of redemptive history, no supernatural phenomena recorded in that era can possibly meet the criteria for what constitutes a miracle. With such a narrow definition of a miracle, it's easy to declare them isolated or infrequent.

But if "human agency" or a "gifted" individual is required before an event can be called miraculous, what becomes of the virgin birth and resurrection of Jesus? What about the resurrection of the saints mentioned in Matthew 27:52–53 or Peter's deliverance from jail in Acts 12? Was the instantaneous death of Herod in Acts 12:23 not a miracle because the agency was angelic? Was the earthquake that opened the prison in which Paul and Silas were housed not a miracle because God did it himself, directly? Was Paul's deliverance from the venom of a viper (Acts 28) not a miracle simply because no human agency was utilized in his preservation? To define as a miracle only those supernatural phenomena involving human agency is arbitrary. It is a case of special pleading, conceived principally because it provides a way of reducing the frequency of the miraculous in the biblical record.

That miracles confirm and authenticate the divine message is certainly true. But to *reduce* the purpose of miracles to this one function is to ignore other reasons for which God ordained them. The association of the miraculous with divine revelation becomes an argument for cessationism *only* if the Bible *restricts* the function of a miracle to attestation. And the Bible does not do this.

The Old Testament reveals a consistent pattern of supernatural manifestations in the affairs of humanity. In addition to the multitude of miracles during the lifetime of Moses, Joshua, Elijah, and Elisha, we see numerous instances of angelic activity, supernatural visitations and revelatory activity, healings, dreams, visions, and the like. Once the arbitrary restrictions on the definition of a miracle are removed, a different picture of Old Testament religious life emerges.[11]

---

11 See especially Deere's treatment of miraculous phenomena in the Old Testament in *Surprised by the Power*

Two other factors indicate that miraculous phenomena were not as isolated and infrequent as some allege. First, we have the assertion of Jeremiah 32:20, in which the prophet spoke of God who had "shown signs and wonders in the land of Egypt, and to this day in Israel and among all mankind, and have made a name for yourself, as at this day." This text alerts us to the danger of arguing from silence. The fact that from the time of the exodus to the captivity fewer instances of signs and wonders are recorded does not mean they did not occur. Jeremiah insisted they did. One might compare this with the danger of asserting that Jesus did not perform a particular miracle or do so with any degree of frequency simply because the Gospels fail to record it. John told us explicitly that Jesus performed "many other signs in the presence of the disciples" that John did not include in his gospel account (John 20:30), as well as "many other things that Jesus did" that were impossible to record in detail (John 21:25).

Second, most cessationists insist that New Testament and Old Testament prophecy are the same. They also readily acknowledge that New Testament prophecy was a "miracle" gift. If Old Testament prophecy was of the same nature, then we have an example of a miraculous phenomenon recurring throughout the course of Israel's history. In every age of Israel's existence in which there was prophetic activity, there was miraculous activity. What then becomes of the assertion that miracles, even on the narrow definition, were infrequent and isolated?

Is It Okay to Pray for Signs, Wonders, and Miraculous Gifts?

Is a longing for signs and wonders a sign of weak and immature faith? If so, how does one account for Acts 4:29–31, which records the prayer of the church in Jerusalem that God might stretch out his hand "to heal," and to perform "signs and wonders" through the name of Jesus?

---

of the Spirit, 255–61. One also thinks of Daniel who ministered well beyond the time of Elijah and Elisha. Yet "proportionately Daniel's book contains more supernatural events than the books of Exodus through Joshua (the books dealing with the ministries of Moses and Joshua) and 1 Kings through 2 Kings 13 (the books dealing with the ministries of Elijah and Elisha)" (Deere, 263). What makes Deere's listing of miraculous phenomena in the Old Testament even more shocking is that he doesn't even mention the numerous supernatural events in the Major or Minor Prophets. One need only read through the book of Ezekiel to see yet again how pervasive dreams, visions, prophetic utterances, and a wide variety of other miraculous occurrences and experiences were taking place.

Clearly it is good to pray for signs and wonders. It is not evil or a sign of emotional and mental imbalance to petition God for demonstrations of his power. This passage also demonstrates that there is no necessary or inherent conflict between miracles and the message, between wonders and the word of the cross. Our Lord's denunciation in Matthew 12:39 and 16:4 was directed at unbelieving scribes and Pharisees, not the children of God. Their demand for the miraculous was simply a way to cover up their unwillingness to believe. But if our desire is that God be glorified in the display of his power, asking him in prayer to work signs and wonders in our midst is not only permissible, it is essential.

A Response to Richard Gaffin[12]

New Testament scholar Richard Gaffin argues that "Acts intends to document a *completed* history, a unique epoch in the history of redemption—the once-for-all, *apostolic* spread of the gospel 'to the ends of the earth.'"[13] But Luke nowhere said this. Even if it were true, where did Luke assert that what the Holy Spirit did in that "history" was not to be done in subsequent "histories"? Again, Luke nowhere asserted that Acts was "unique." Were we to concede that in certain respects it was, why conclude that the uniqueness and therefore unrepeatable characteristics of Acts is principally in its portrayal of the charismatic work of the Spirit? Luke never suggested, far less asserted, that the way God related to and was active among his people in that particular "history" was finished. Gaffin has articulated a premise that may have a measure of truth but lacks textual evidence on which to support the theological conclusion he draws from it.

One searches in vain for a text in which the charismatic and supernatural work of the Holy Spirit that attended the expansion of the gospel, and subsequently characterized the life and ministry of the churches that were planted, is not meant by God to attend the expansion of the gospel into the

---

12 The following response to Richard Gaffin is adapted from my chapter, "A Third Wave Response" in *Are Miraculous Gifts for Today? Four Views*, 72–85.

13 Gaffin, "A Cessationist View," in *Are Miraculous Gifts for Today? Four Views*, ed. Wayne Grudem (Grand Rapids: Zondervan, 1995), 37–38.

rest of the world in subsequent centuries or is not meant to characterize the life of such churches.

We must also consider what Peter said in Acts 2 concerning the operation of so-called miraculous gifts as characteristic of the new covenant age of the church. As D. A. Carson has said, "The coming of the Spirit is not associated merely with the *dawning* of the new age but with its *presence*, not merely with Pentecost but with the entire period from Pentecost to the return of Jesus the Messiah."[14] Or again, the gifts of prophecy and tongues (Acts 2) are not portrayed as merely *inaugurating* the new covenant age but as *characterizing* it (and let us not forget that the present church age = the latter days).

Gaffin places emphasis on the inaugural breakthrough of the gospel into Samaria and to the Gentiles and insists that the miraculous phenomena that occurred on those occasions played an essential role of attesting to this expansion. I agree. But we must also focus on the churches that were planted and emerged and endured in the aftermath of these so-called epochal stages in redemptive history. What I read in Acts, 1 Corinthians, Romans, Ephesians, 1 Thessalonians, and Galatians indicates that the miraculous phenomena that accompanied the beginning and founding of these churches are to characterize their up-building and growth as well. It appears that Gaffin is asking us to believe that *because* signs, wonders, and miraculous gifts helped launch the church by serving to attest the original proclamation of the gospel, those phenomena have no additional or ongoing function to sustain and nurture the church itself. But this is a non sequitur lacking in biblical evidence.

Gaffin's argument is reductionism gone to seed. He isolates one function of miraculous phenomena, ties it in with the period in which it occurs, and then concludes that it can have no *other* functions in any *other* period of church history. And he does this without one biblical text that explicitly asserts it.

Gaffin says that "Acts 2 and the subsequent miraculous events Luke narrates are not intended to establish a pattern of 'repetitions' of Pentecost to continue on indefinitely in church history. Rather, together they constitute, as already intimated, an event-complex, complete with the finished apostolic program they accompany."[15] But why can't the miraculous events and

---

14 D. A. Carson, *Showing the Spirit: A Theological Exposition of 1 Corinthians 12–14* (1987; repr., Grand Rapids: Baker, 2019), 203.
15 Gaffin, "A Cessationist View," 38.

charismata continue without one thinking that this means a "repetition" of Pentecost? Again, the once-for-all-ness of Pentecost as a redemptive historical *event* does not require, or even suggest, the restriction of miraculous *charismata* to that period. What Gaffin persists in concluding by theological inference the Bible itself nowhere asserts.

"It would certainly be wrong to argue, on the one hand," says Gaffin, "that Luke intended to show that miraculous gifts and power experiences ceased with the history he documented."[16] I find this confusing in view of his affirmation that the miraculous events in Acts subsequent to Pentecost are *not* intended by Luke to tell us what the rest of church history is to be like. Rather, such events (presumably, prophecy, tongues, and healing) "constitute . . . an event-complex, complete with the finished apostolic program they accompany."[17]

He then asserts that "in this respect, to observe that in Acts others than apostles exercise miraculous gifts (e.g., 6:8), is beside the point. To offer that as evidence that such gifts will continue beyond the time of the apostles pulls apart what for Luke belongs together."[18] I disagree. I believe it is *precisely* the point—the point being that the miraculous ministry of the Holy Spirit is designed not solely for the apostles nor solely for the foundational work they performed. If, as Gaffin contends, miraculous phenomena and apostolic ministry belonged together in Luke's mind, why then did others than the apostles perform miracles? It will not suffice for Gaffin simply to assert that nonapostolic miracles are beside the point. It is a vitally important point that cessationism cannot explain. Let us remember that it is, in fact, Luke himself who pulled apart the two. Perhaps he did so because that was his point!

Gaffin says that "others exercise such gifts *by virtue of the presence and activity of the apostles*; they do so under an 'apostolic umbrella,' so to speak."[19] Where did Luke ever say this? What biblical text ever asserts it? And even if it should be granted, why would we conclude that God didn't want the church to experience such gifts after the apostles were gone? Again, universally applicable conclusions have been deduced without textual warrant.

---

16 Gaffin, 38–39.
17 Gaffin, 38.
18 Gaffin, 39.
19 Gaffin, 39.

In reflecting on the book of Acts, I find nothing in the perpetuity of signs, wonders, and miraculous gifts that threatens the integrity or uniqueness of the apostolic era. The uniqueness of the apostolic era is that it was first and foundational, not that it was miraculous.

In a desire to retain a close connection between apostolic ministry and signs and wonders, Gaffin says it is a "disjunction foreign to Luke"[20] to argue that signs and wonders attest the message (gospel) and not necessarily the messenger. But such a distinction was hardly foreign to Luke, for he spoke of many nonapostolic Christians performing signs and wonders, and nowhere explicitly attributed their power to any relationship or physical contact with the apostles. Neither Luke nor any New Testament author said that God could not or would not attest the message with signs and wonders when it is proclaimed by ordinary believers. When this is combined with the fact that several ordinary, nonapostolic believers did signs and wonders, the distinction that Gaffin alleges is "foreign" to Luke appears quite familiar to him.

Gaffin also argues that the New Testament itself records these gifts in operation only in Acts. And these "accompany the unique and finished apostolic spread of the gospel."[21] But nowhere does Acts or the New Testament ever say that what was unique about the apostles was the signs and wonders they performed. How can it be argued that because signs and wonders accompany the apostolic spread of the gospel, they cannot accompany the nonapostolic spread of the same gospel? The fact that the first-century apostles finished *their* work in spreading the gospel doesn't mean that others, in subsequent generations, are finished. Also, I find it hard to understand how the exercise of miraculous gifts by average, nonapostolic, Christian men and women in the church at Corinth, all for the purpose of edifying and encouraging and consoling and helping one another be more like Jesus, can in *any* sense be regarded as exclusively tied up with the alleged "unique and finished apostolic spread of the gospel." These people weren't planting churches or extending the gospel across ethnic boundaries. They were just ordinary believers struggling with life and ministering to the daily needs and pains and problems of other Christians like themselves. The same may be said of believers in Thessalonica (1 Thess. 5:19–22), Rome (Rom. 12:3–6a),

---

20 Gaffin, 39.
21 Gaffin, 42.

Galatia (Gal. 3:5), and elsewhere. How can anyone argue that such miraculous gifts lost their validity and practical value in accomplishing that for which God ordained them simply because at some point in the first century the apostles died?

Gaffin argues that because of the alleged exclusivistic link between apostolic ministry and miraculous gifts (a link nowhere asserted in Scripture), the continuation of the latter "into the postapostolic era may not simply be presupposed."[22] To the contrary, when it is observed that Paul described ordinary church life in 1 Corinthians 12:7–10 as involving miraculous gifts, gifts whose purpose is to edify believers and sanctify their souls, gifts which are nowhere exclusively (or even primarily) tied to the apostles or whose function is reduced to accompanying and attesting to their ministry, the continuation of such gifts is *precisely* what should be presupposed.

What Is the Meaning of "the Perfect" in 1 Corinthians 13:8–12, and What Does It Teach Us about the Cessation or Continuation of Miraculous Gifts of the Spirit?[23]

Toward the end of Paul's famous "love chapter," we read this:

> Love never ends. As for prophecies, they will pass away; as for tongues, they will cease; as for knowledge, it will pass away. For we know in part and we prophesy in part, but when the perfect comes, the partial will pass away. When I was a child, I spoke like a child, I thought like a child, I reasoned like a child. When I became a man, I gave up childish ways. For now we see in a mirror dimly, but then face to face. Now I know in part; then I shall know fully, even as I have been fully known. (1 Cor. 13:8–12)

People who embrace cessationism point out that whereas Paul said in verses 8 and 10 that prophecy and knowledge will "pass away" or "be done away with" when the "perfect" comes, tongues, on the other hand, simply "cease." They take this to mean that the spiritual gift of speaking in tongues

---

22 Gaffin, 42.

23 Much of this analysis of 1 Corinthians 13:8–12 is adapted from my book *The Language of Heaven: Crucial Questions about Speaking in Tongues* (Lake Mary, FL: Charisma House, 2019), and is used here with permission.

simply dies out of its own accord. There is something intrinsic to the character of tongues speech, so they say, that alone accounts for why it will cease. No one has to take any action against tongues to cause them to cease. They just stop. This is often based on the fact that the verb "cease" is in the middle voice. But as D. A. Carson points out, the verb *pauō* regularly appears in the middle voice and "never unambiguously bears the meaning 'to cease of itself' (i.e., because of something intrinsic in the nature of the subject)."[24] Simply put, most New Testament scholars are in agreement that no theological conclusions can be drawn about the duration or cessation of any of these gifts based on the verbs that are used.[25]

Neither is it popular even among cessationists to argue that the "perfect" is anything less than the state of spiritual consummation that will be introduced at the second coming of Christ. Cessationist Richard Gaffin is certainly correct when he says, "To argue, as some cessationists do, that 'the perfect' has in view the completion of the New Testament canon or some other state of affairs prior to the Parousia [the second coming of Christ] is just not credible exegetically."[26]

Gaffin rightly links up the "perfect" of 1 Corinthians 13:10 with the "unity/fullness" of Ephesians 4:13 and concludes that Paul had in view "the situation brought by Christ's return."[27]

Paul declared that when the "perfect" comes, spiritual gifts such as prophecy and words of knowledge will pass away. I would also include tongues in this, along with all the spiritual gifts. Spiritual gifts are wonderful and we need them, but even at the highest and most effective level, they can bring us only partial knowledge of God. As Paul said, "We know in part and we prophesy in part" (13:9). Spiritual gifts, for all their value and power, cannot

---

24 D. A. Carson, *Exegetical Fallacies*, 2nd ed. (Grand Rapids: Baker, 1996), 77.

25 Says Gordon Fee, "The change of verbs is purely rhetorical [i.e., it is merely a stylistic variation that carries no special theological significance]; to make it otherwise is to elevate to significance something in which Paul shows no interest at all. Just as one can scarcely distinguish between 'cease' and 'pass away' when used in the same context, neither can one distinguish between *katargeō* [translated 'pass away'] and *pauō* [translated 'cease'] in this context (although NIV's choice of 'be stilled' for tongues is felicitous). The middle voice came along with the change of verbs" (Gordon Fee, *The First Epistle to the Corinthians*, rev. ed. [Grand Rapids: Eerdmans, 2014], 713n375).

26 Gaffin, "A Cessationist View," 55n81.

27 Gaffin, 55.

bring us into the full experience of knowing God as God knows us. For that we must await the arrival of the "perfect" (v. 10).

So, what is the "perfect"? Cessationists typically embrace one of two interpretations. Some argue that the "perfect" refers to *the completed canon of Scripture*. Tongues, prophecy, and knowledge, among other miraculous gifts, ceased when the book of Revelation was written. Few serious New Testament scholars hold this view today for a number of reasons. First, there is no evidence that even Paul anticipated the formation of a "canon" of Scripture following the death of the apostles. In fact, Paul seems to have expected that he himself might survive until the coming of the Lord (1 Cor. 15:51; 1 Thess. 4:15–16). Second, there is no reason to think that Paul could have expected the Corinthians to figure out that he meant the "canon" when he used the term *to teleion*.[28] Third, as Max Turner points out, "the completed canon of Scripture would hardly signify for the Corinthians the *passing away of merely 'partial' knowledge* (and prophecy and tongues with it), and the arrival of 'full knowledge', for the Corinthians already had the Old Testament, the gospel tradition (presumably), and (almost certainly) more Pauline teaching than finally got into the canon."[29]

A fourth reason the cessationist argument fails is that in verse 12b Paul said that with the coming of the "perfect," our "partial knowledge" will give way to a depth of knowledge that is matched only by the way we are known by God. That is to say, when the perfect comes we will *then* see "face to face" and will know even as we are now known by God. Few people any longer dispute that this is language descriptive of our experience in the eternal state, subsequent to the return of Christ. As Turner says, "However much we respect the New Testament canon, Paul can only be accused of the wildest exaggeration in verse 12 if that is what he was talking about."[30] The cessationist view rests on the assumption that prophecy was a form of divine revelation designed to serve the church in the interim, until such time as the canon was formed. But a careful examination of the New Testament reveals

---

28 Says Fee, "It is a primary exegetical axiom that what neither Paul himself nor the Corinthians could have understood can possibly be the meaning of what Paul was writing to them" (*First Epistle to the Corinthians*, 715n381).

29 Max Turner, *The Holy Spirit and Spiritual Gifts* (Peabody, MA: Hendrickson, 1998), 294.

30 Turner, 295.

that prophecy had a much broader purpose that would not in the least be affected by the completion of the canon.

Others argue that the "perfect" refers to *the maturity of the church*. When the church has advanced beyond its infancy and is fully established, the need for spiritual gifts like prophecy and tongues will have ended. However, in verses 11–12 Paul wasn't talking about relative degrees of maturity, but of absolute perfection.

Thus, it seems clear to me that by "perfect" Paul was referring to that *state of affairs brought about by the second coming of Jesus Christ at the end of human history*. The "perfect" is not itself the coming of Christ but rather that experience or condition of perfection that we will enjoy in the new heavens and new earth. Paul's point is really rather simple: spiritual gifts like prophecy, word of knowledge, and tongues, and all the others as well, in my opinion, will pass away at some time future to Paul's writing, referred to by him as "perfection." This state of "perfection" again clearly points to the eternal state following Christ's return. We know this from two things that Paul said in verse 12.

In verse 12b Paul said, "Now I know in part; then [When? When the "perfect" comes] I shall know fully, even as I have been fully known." Paul didn't mean we will be omniscient in the eternal state, as if to say we will know absolutely everything in exhaustive detail. He meant that we would be free from the misconceptions and distortions associated with this life in a fallen world. Our knowledge in the age to come will in some ways be comparable to the way God knows us now. God's knowledge of us is immediate and complete. Our knowledge of God will be the same when we enter his presence in the new heavens and new earth. Paul's distinctions "are between 'now' and 'then,' between what is incomplete (though perfectly appropriate to the church's present existence) and what is complete (when its final destiny in Christ has been reached and 'we see face to face' and 'know as we are fully known')."[31]

Notice also in verse 12a that Paul said, "For now [during the present church age, before the arrival of the "perfect"] we see in mirror dimly, but then [when the "perfect" comes; we will see] face to face." The words "face to face" are standard biblical language for the appearance of a human in the

---

31 Fee, *First Epistle to the Corinthians*, 715.

immediate presence of God, beholding him in an unmediated way (see Gen. 32:30; Ex. 33:11; Num. 14:14; Deut. 5:4; 34:10; Judg. 6:22; Rev. 22:4). Paul had in mind direct personal communication, such that awaits us in the age to come. In this life we suffer from the limitation of seeing in a mirror, dimly, whereas when the perfect comes we will behold God directly without any intermediary or obscuring of his glory. Attempts to make the "perfect" refer to a time in the present age, before the coming of Christ and the eternal state when all sin will be abolished, minimizes the language of verse 12.

As Paul said in verse 11, living now in the present church age is akin to being a child; we are limited, and our knowledge is imperfect. But when the "perfect" comes, we will have advanced into adulthood; sin will be abolished, evil and corruption and the limitations of this life will have passed away; we will see God "face to face" and we will then know even as we have been fully known. There is a massive qualitative and quantitative difference between what we know now by means of the gifts of the Spirit and what we will know in the consummation. Only in the consummation brought about by the return of Christ, and not until then, will spiritual gifts cease to operate. No one has explained this better than David Garland:

> The "perfect" is shorthand for the consummation of all things, the intended goal of creation; and its arrival will naturally displace the partial that we experience in the present age. Human gifts shine gloriously in this world but will fade to nothing in the presence of what is perfect. But they also will have served their purpose of helping to build up the church during the wait and to take it to the threshold of the end. When the anticipated end arrives, they will no longer be necessary.[32]

Paul was explaining the difference between what is true and appropriate for us now, in this present age, and what will be our experience later, in the age to come. Life in the present church age yields only knowledge that is partial. It is never altogether free from error. But life in the age to come, the state of perfection, will be characterized by an unmediated relationship to God that is devoid of error or mistake or misconception. The perfection

---

32 David E. Garland, *1 Corinthians*, Baker Exegetical Commentary on the New Testament (Grand Rapids: Baker Academic, 2003), 623.

that is to come is not an experience in the present age but refers to life and joy and knowledge in the new heaven and new earth (Rev. 21–22). "At the coming of Christ the final purpose of God's saving work in Christ will have been reached; at that point those gifts now necessary for the building up of the church in the present age will disappear, because 'completeness' will have come."[33]

What we've seen in our examination of 1 Corinthians 13:8–12 is that Paul envisioned the ongoing operation of all spiritual gifts until the time of Christ's second advent and the inauguration of the eternal state. Far from being a passage that proves cessationism, it clearly affirms continuationism.

33 Fee, *First Epistle to the Corinthians*, 716.

CHAPTER 7

The Evidence from Church History[1]

After studying the documentation that supports the ongoing presence of charismatic gifts throughout church history, New Testament scholar D. A. Carson has concluded, "There is enough evidence that some form of 'charismatic' gifts continued sporadically across the centuries of church history that it is futile to insist on doctrinaire grounds that every report is spurious or the fruit of demonic activity or psychological aberration."[2]

Some may be surprised to discover that we have in-depth knowledge of only a small fraction of the events and circumstances in the history of the church. It is presumptuous for us to conclude that the gifts of the Spirit were absent from the lives of people about whom we know virtually nothing. The absence of evidence is not necessarily the evidence of absence!

We simply don't know what was happening in the thousands upon thousands of churches and home meetings of Christians in centuries past. No, I cannot say with confidence that believers regularly prayed for the sick and saw them healed any more than you can say they didn't. You cannot say they never prophesied to the comfort, exhortation, and consolation (1 Cor. 14:3) of the church any more than I can say they did. Neither of us can say with any confidence whether countless thousands of Christians throughout the

---

1   This chapter is a somewhat expanded version of what may be found in two of my books: *Practicing the Power: Welcoming the Gifts of the Holy Spirit in Your Life* (Grand Rapids: Zondervan, 2017), 255–69; and *The Language of Heaven: Crucial Questions about Speaking in Tongues* (Lake Mary, FL: Charisma House, 2019), and is used here with permission.

2   D. A. Carson, *Showing the Spirit: A Theological Exposition of 1 Corinthians 12–14* (1987; repr., Grand Rapids: Baker, 2019), 218.

inhabited earth prayed in tongues in their private devotions. These are not matters that were extensively documented or recorded. We must remember that printing with movable type did not exist until the work of Johann Gutenberg (1390–1468). The absence of documented evidence for spiritual gifts in a time when documented evidence for most of church life was, at best, sparse is poor grounds for concluding that such gifts did not exist.

Here is why I raise this point. *If* the gifts were sporadic (and I'm not persuaded they were), there may be an explanation other than the cessationist argument that they were restricted to the first century. Remember that prior to the Protestant Reformation in the sixteenth century, the average Christian did not have access to the Bible in his or her own language. Biblical ignorance was rampant. This is hardly the sort of atmosphere in which people would be aware of spiritual gifts (their name, nature, function, and the believer's responsibility to pursue them), and because they didn't have the ability to read and know the Bible, we would not expect them to seek and pray for such phenomena or to recognize them if they manifested. If the gifts were sparse—and this is debatable—it could likely have been due to ignorance and the spiritual lethargy it breeds.

In the first centuries of the church, it's important to note the growing concentration of spiritual authority and ministry in the office of bishop and priest, particularly in the emerging Church of Rome. By the early fourth century AD (and even earlier, according to some), there was already a move to limit the opportunity to speak, serve, and minister in the life of the church to the ordained clergy alone. Lay folk were silenced and marginalized and left almost entirely dependent on the contribution of the local priest or monarchical bishop.

Although Cyprian (bishop of Carthage, AD 248–58) spoke and wrote often of the gift of prophecy and received visions from the Spirit,[3] he was also responsible for the gradual disappearance of such *charismata* from the life of the church. He, among others, insisted that only the bishop and priest of the church should be permitted to exercise these revelatory gifts. In the words of James Ash, "The charisma of prophecy was captured by the monarchical

---

3 *The Epistles of Cyprian* 7.3–6 (*The Ante-Nicene Fathers* [hereafter *ANF*], ed. Alexander Roberts and James Donaldson, 10 vols. [repr., Peabody, MA: Hendrickson, 1994], 5:286–87); 7.7 (*ANF* 5:287); 68.9–10 (*ANF* 5:375); 4.4 (*ANF* 5:290).

episcopate, used in its defense, and left to die an unnoticed death when true episcopate stability rendered it a superfluous tool."[4]

If we concede, for the sake of argument, that certain spiritual gifts were less prevalent than others in certain seasons of the church, their absence may well be due to unbelief, apostasy, and other sins that serve only to quench and grieve the Holy Spirit. If Israel experienced the loss of power because of repeated rebellion, if Jesus himself "could do no mighty work there, except that he laid his hands on a few sick people and healed them" (Mark 6:5), all because of their "unbelief" (v. 6), we should hardly be surprised at the infrequency of the miraculous in periods of church history marked by theological ignorance and both personal and clerical immorality.

We must also remember that God mercifully blesses us with both what we don't deserve and what we refuse or are unable to recognize. I am persuaded that numerous churches today that advocate cessationism still experience these gifts but dismiss them as something less than the miraculous manifestation of the Holy Spirit.

For example, someone with the gift of discerning of spirits may be described as "possessing remarkable sensitivity and insight." Someone with the gift of words of knowledge is rather said to have "deep understanding of spiritual truths." Someone who prophesies is said to have "spoken with timely encouragement to the needs of the congregation." Someone who lays hands on the sick and prays successfully for healing is told that God still answers prayer but that "gifts of healing" are no longer operative. These churches wouldn't be caught dead labeling such phenomena by the names given them in 1 Corinthians 12:7–10, because they are committed to the theory that such phenomena don't exist.

If this occurs today (and it does, as it did in a church in which I ministered for several years), there is every reason to think it has occurred repeatedly throughout the course of history subsequent to the first century. Consider this hypothetical example. Let us suppose that a man had been assigned to write a descriptive history of church life in what is now southern France in, say, AD 845. How might he label what he saw and heard? If he were ignorant of spiritual gifts, being untaught, or perhaps a well-educated cessationist, his record would make no reference to prophecy, healing, tongues, miracles, or

---

4   James Ash, "The Decline of Ecstatic Prophecy in the Early Church," *Theological Studies* 36 (June 1976): 252.

word of knowledge. Such phenomena might well exist, perhaps even flourish, but would be identified and explained in other terms by our hypothetical historian.

Centuries later we discover his manuscript. Would it be fair to conclude from his observations that certain spiritual gifts had ceased subsequent to the apostolic age? Of course not! My point is that in both the distant past and present the Holy Spirit can empower God's people with gifts for ministry that they do not recognize or may explain in terms other than those of 1 Corinthians 12:7–10. The absence of explicit reference to certain *charismata* is a weak basis on which to argue for their permanent absence from church life.

Here is the question most commonly asked: If the Holy Spirit wanted the church to experience the miraculous *charismata*, would they not have been more visible and prevalent in church history? Again, I'm only conceding, for the sake of argument, that they were not. Let's take the principle underlying that argument and apply it to several other issues.

We all believe the Holy Spirit is the *Teacher* of the church. We all believe the New Testament describes his ministry of *enlightening* our hearts and *illuminating* our minds to understand the truths of Scripture (see Eph. 1:15–19; 2 Tim. 2:7; 1 John 2:20, 27; et al.). Yet within the first generation after the death of the apostles, the doctrine of justification by faith was compromised. Salvation by faith plus works soon became standard doctrine and was not successfully challenged (with a few notable exceptions) until Martin Luther's courageous stand in the sixteenth century. If God intended for the Holy Spirit to continue to teach and enlighten Christians concerning vital biblical truths beyond the death of the apostles, why did the church languish in ignorance of this most fundamental truth for more than thirteen hundred years? Why did Christians suffer from the absence of those experiential blessings this vital truth might otherwise have brought to their church life?

And this applies to other important doctrines as well. If God intended for the Holy Spirit to illumine the minds of his people concerning biblical truths after the death of the apostles, why did the church languish in ignorance of the doctrine of the priesthood of all believers for almost a thousand years? Those of you who believe in a pretribulation rapture of the church must also explain the absence of this "truth" from the collective knowledge of the church for almost nineteen hundred years!

No one would say this proves the Holy Spirit ceased his ministry of teaching and illumination. Or that God ceased to want his people to understand such vital doctrinal principles. The alleged relative infrequency or absence of certain spiritual gifts during the same period of church history does not prove that God was opposed to their use or had negated their validity for the remainder of the present age. Both theological ignorance of certain biblical truths and a loss of experiential blessings provided by spiritual gifts can be, and should be, attributed to factors other than God intending such knowledge and power *only* for believers in the early church.

Finally, I would add that what has or has not occurred in church history is ultimately irrelevant to what *we* should pursue, pray for, and expect in the life of our churches today. The final criterion for deciding whether God wants to bestow certain spiritual gifts on his people today is the Word of God. I'm disappointed to hear people cite the alleged absence of a particular experience in the life of an admired saint from the church's past as reason for doubting its present validity. As much as I respect the giants of the Reformation or other periods in church history, I intend to emulate the giants of the New Testament who wrote under the inspiration of the Holy Spirit. I greatly admire and have learned much from John Calvin and Jonathan Edwards, but I obey the apostle Paul.

In sum, neither the failure nor success of Christians in days past is the ultimate standard by which we determine what God wants for us today. We can learn from their mistakes as well as their achievements. But the only question of relevance for us is "What saith the Scripture?"

Miraculous Spiritual Gifts in Church History

We are now ready for a brief survey of church history (from the apostolic fathers to Augustine). I believe the representative examples cited demonstrate that the miraculous gifts of the Spirit were, and are, still very much in operation. Indeed, before Chrysostom in the East (AD 347–407) and Augustine in the West (AD 354–430), no church father ever suggested that any or all of the *charismata* had ceased in the first century. And even Augustine later retracted his earlier cessationism (see below). So let's conduct a quick overview.[5]

---

5 For helpful documentation, see Stanley M. Burgess, *The Spirit and the Church: Antiquity* (Peabody, MA:

The Epistle of Barnabas (written sometime between AD 70 and AD 132) says this of the Holy Spirit: "He himself prophesying in us, he himself dwelling in us."[6] The author of *The Shepherd of Hermas* claimed to have received numerous revelatory insights through visions and dreams. This document has been dated as early as AD 90 and as late as AD 140–55.

Justin Martyr (c. AD 100–165), perhaps the most important second-century apologist, was especially clear about the operation of gifts in his day:

> Therefore, just as God did not inflict His anger on account of those seven thousand men, even so He has now neither yet inflicted judgment, nor does inflict it, knowing that daily some [of you] are becoming disciples in the name of Christ, and quitting the path of error; who are also receiving gifts, each as he is worthy, illumined through the name of this Christ. For one receives the spirit of understanding, another of counsel, another of strength, another of healing, another of foreknowledge, another of teaching, and another of the fear of God.[7]

> For the prophetical gifts remain with us, even to the present time. And hence you ought to understand that [the gifts] formerly among your nation have been transferred to us. And just as there were false prophets contemporaneous with your holy prophets, so are there now many false

---

Hendrickson, 1984); Stanley M. Burgess, ed., *Christian Peoples of the Spirit: A Documentary History of Pentecostal Spirituality from the Early Church to the Present* (New York: New York University Press, 2011); Ronald A. N. Kydd, *Charismatic Gifts in the Early Church* (Peabody, MA: Hendrickson, 1984); Paul Thigpen, "Did the Power of the Spirit Ever Leave the Church?" *Charisma*, September 1992, 20–29; Richard M. Riss, "Tongues and Other Miraculous Gifts in the Second through Nineteenth Centuries," *Basileia*, 1985; Jeff Oliver, *Pentecost to the Present: The Holy Spirit's Enduring Work in the Church*, 3 vols. (Newberry, FL: Bridge Logos, 2017); Eddie L. Hyatt, *2000 Years of Charismatic Christianity* (Lake Mary, FL: Charisma House, 2002); Kilian McDonnell and George T. Montague, *Christian Initiation and Baptism in the Holy Spirit: Evidence from the First Eight Centuries* (Collegeville, MN: Liturgical Press, 1991); Cecil M. Robeck Jr., *Prophecy in Carthage: Perpetua, Tertullian, and Cyprian* (Cleveland, OH: Pilgrim, 1992); and J. D. King, *Regeneration: A Complete History of Healing in the Christian Church*, vol. 1, Post-Apostolic through Later Holiness (Lee's Summit, MO: Christos, 2017). Then, of course, one must reckon with the massive documentation of miraculous gifts throughout the course of church history as compiled by Craig S. Keener in his two-volume work, *Miracles: The Credibility of the New Testament Accounts* (Grand Rapids: Baker Academic, 2011).

6   *The Epistle of Barnabas* 16.9 (translated by J. B. Lightfoot, www.earlychristianwritings.com/text/barnabas-lightfoot.html).

7   Justin Martyr, *Dialogue with Trypho*, chap. 39.

teachers amongst us, of whom our Lord forewarned us to beware; so that in no respect are we deficient, since we know that He foreknew all that would happen to us after His resurrection from the dead and ascension to heaven.[8]

For numberless demoniacs throughout the whole world and in your city, many of our Christian men, exorcising them in the name of Jesus Christ, who was crucified under Pontius Pilate, have healed and do heal, rendering helpless and driving the possessing devils out of the men, though they could not be cured by all the other exorcists, and those used incantations and drugs.[9]

Irenaeus (approx. AD 120–202),[10] certainly the most important and influential theologian of the late second century, wrote,

Wherefore, also, those who are in truth His disciples, receiving grace from Him, do in His name perform [miracles], so as to promote the welfare of other men, according to the gift which each one has received from Him. For some do certainly and truly drive out devils, so that those who have thus been cleansed from evil spirits frequently both believe [in Christ], and join themselves to the Church. Others have foreknowledge of things to come: they see visions, and utter prophetic expressions. Others still, heal the sick by laying their hands upon them, and they are made whole. Yea, moreover, as I have said, the dead even have been raised up, and remained among us for many years. And what shall I more say? It is not possible to name the number of the gifts which the Church, [scattered] throughout the whole world, has received from God, in the name of Jesus Christ, who was crucified under Pontius Pilate, and which she exerts day by day for the benefit of the Gentiles, neither practicing deception upon any, nor taking any reward from them [on account of such miraculous interpositions]. For as she has received freely from God, freely also does she minister [to others].[11]

8 Justin Martyr, *Dialogue with Trypho*, chap. 39.
9 Justin Martyr, *Second Apology* 6 (*ANF* 1:190).
10 See *Christian Peoples of the Spirit: A Documentary History of Pentecostal Spirituality from the Early Church to the Present*, ed. Stanley M. Burgess (New York: New York University Press, 2011).
11 Irenaeus, *Against Heresies* 2.32.4.

He wrote further:

> Nor does she [the church] perform anything by means of angelic invocations, or by incantations, or by any other wicked curious art; but, directing her prayers to the Lord, who made all things, in a pure, sincere, and straightforward spirit, and calling upon the name of our Lord Jesus Christ, she has been accustomed to work miracles for the advantage of mankind, and not to lead them into error.[12]

And a bit later in the same work he wrote:

> In like manner we do also hear many brethren in the church, who possess prophetic gifts, and who through the Spirit speak all kinds of languages [i.e., tongues], and bring to light for the general benefit the hidden things of men, and declare the mysteries of God, whom also the apostle terms "spiritual," they being spiritual because they partake of the Spirit.[13]

Tertullian (d. 225) spoke and wrote on countless occasions of the operation of the gifts of the Spirit, particularly those of a revelatory nature such as prophecy and word of knowledge.

> But from God—who has promised, indeed, "to pour out the grace of the Holy Spirit upon all flesh, and has ordained that His servants and His handmaids should see visions as well as utter prophecies"—must all those visions be regarded as emanating. . . .[14]

He described the ministry of one particular woman as follows:

> For, seeing that we acknowledge spiritual charismata, or gifts, we too have merited the attainment of the prophetic gift, although coming after John (the Baptist). [This woman has been] favoured with sundry gifts of revelation [and] both sees and hears mysterious communications; some men's

---

12 Irenaeus, *Against Heresies* 2.32.5.

13 Irenaeus, *Against Heresies* 5.6.1; Eusebius, *Ecclesiastical History* 5.7.6.

14 Tertullian, *A Treatise on the Soul* 47 (*ANF* 3:225–26).

> hearts she understands, and to them who are in need she distributes rem-
> edies. . . . After the people are dismissed at the conclusion of the sacred
> services, she is in the regular habit of reporting to us whatever things she
> may have seen in vision (for her communications are examined with the
> most scrupulous care, in order that their truth may be probed). . . . Now
> can you refuse to believe this, even if indubitable evidence on every point
> is forthcoming for your conviction?[15]

Tertullian contrasted what he had witnessed with the claims of the her-
etic Marcion:

> Let Marcion then exhibit, as gifts of his god, some prophets, such as have
> not spoken by human sense, but with the Spirit of God, such as have both
> predicted things to come, and have made manifest the secrets of the
> heart; . . . Now all these signs (of spiritual gifts) are forthcoming from my
> side without any difficulty, and they agree, too, with the rules, and the
> dispensations, and the instructions of the Creator.[16]

The Montanist Controversy[17]

Montanism arose in Phrygia in about AD 155, although Eusebius and Jerome
both date the movement to AD 173. What did the Montanists believe and
teach that had such a significant impact on the ancient church and its view
of spiritual gifts?[18] Several items are worthy of mention.

First, Montanism at its heart was an effort to shape the entire life of the

---

15 Tertullian, *A Treatise on the Soul* 9 (*ANF* 3:188).
16 Tertullian, *Against Marcion* 5.8 (*ANF* 3:446–47). We also have extensive evidence of revelatory visions in operation in the life of two contemporaries of Tertullian, the martyrs Perpetua and her handmaiden Felicitas (AD 202). See Cecil M. Robeck Jr. *Prophecy in Carthage: Perpetua, Tertullian, and Cyprian* (Cleveland, OH: Pilgrim, 1992), 11–94; and J. E. Salisbury, *Perpetua's Passion: The Death and Memory of a Young Roman Woman* (New York: Routledge, 1997).
17 Two excellent sources for quotes by Montanus are *New Testament Apocrypha*, ed. Edgar Hennecke and Wilhelm Schneemelcher (Philadelphia: Westminster, 1963); and *Christian Peoples of the Spirit: A Documentary History of Pentecostal Spirituality from the Early Church to the Present*, ed. Stanley M. Burgess (New York: New York University Press, 2011), 27–28.
18 The most helpful and fair-minded treatment of Montanism is the book by Christine Trevett, *Montanism: Gender, Authority and the New Prophecy* (New York: Cambridge University Press, 1996).

church in keeping with the expectation of the immediate return of Christ. Thus, they opposed any developments in church life that appeared institutional or would contribute to a settled pattern of worship. Needless to say, those who held official positions of authority within the *organized* church would be suspicious of the movement.

Second, Montanus himself allegedly spoke in terms that asserted his identity with the Paraclete of John 14:16. The prophetic utterance in question is as follows: "For Montanus spoke, saying, 'I am the father, and the son and the paraclete.'"[19]

However, many have questioned whether Montanus was claiming what his critics suggest. More likely he, as well as others in the movement who prophesied, was saying that one or another or perhaps all of the members of the Trinity are speaking through them. For example, in yet another of his prophetic utterances, Montanus said, "You shall not hear from me, but you have heard from Christ."[20]

Third, Montanus and his followers (principally, two women, Prisca and Maximilla) held to a view of the prophetic gift that was a departure from the apostle Paul's teaching in 1 Corinthians 14, insofar as they practiced what can only be called "ecstatic" prophecy, in which the speaker either lost consciousness or fell into a trancelike state, or perhaps was but a passive instrument through which the Spirit might speak. One of the prophetic utterances that survived (there are only sixteen), found in Epiphanius, confirms this view: "Behold, a man is like a lyre and I pluck his strings like a pick; the man sleeps, but I am awake. Behold, it is the Lord, who is changing the hearts of men and giving new hearts to them."[21]

If this is what Montanus taught, he would be asserting that when a person prophesied, God was in complete control. The individual was little more than an instrument, such as the strings of a lyre, on which God plucked his song or message. The man or woman was asleep, in a manner of speaking, and thus *passive* during the prophetic utterance.

This concept of prophecy is contrary to what we read of in 1 Corinthians 14:29–32 where Paul asserted that "the spirits of prophets are subject to

---

19 Found in the writings of Didymus, *On the Trinity* 3.41.
20 Quoted in Epiphanius, *Panarion* 48.12.873.
21 *Haer.* 48.4 (www.earlychristianwritings.com/info/montanists-cathen.html).

prophets" (v. 32). The Montanists cannot be charged with having originated this view, for it is found among the Greek apologists of this period. Justin Martyr and Theophilus both claimed that the Spirit spoke through the Old Testament prophets in such a way as to possess them. Athenagoras said of Moses, Isaiah, Jeremiah, and other Old Testament prophets that they were "lifted in ecstasy above the natural operations of their minds by the impulses of the Divine Spirit, [and that they] uttered the things with which they were inspired, the Spirit making use of them as a flute player breathes into a flute."[22] The point is that, at least on this one point, the Montanists were not espousing a view of prophecy that was significantly different from what others in the mainstream of the church of that day were saying.

Fourth, the gift of tongues was also prominent among the Montanists, as was the experience of receiving revelatory visions. Eusebius preserved a refutation of Montanism written by Apollinarius in which the latter accused these "prophets" of speaking in unusual ways. For example, "He [Montanus] began to be ecstatic and to speak and to talk strangely."[23] Again, Maximilla and Prisca are said to have spoken "madly and improperly and strangely, like Montanus."[24] Finally, he referred to the Montanists as "chattering prophets." We cannot be certain, but the word translated "chattering," found nowhere else in all of Greek literature, may refer to speaking at great length in what sound like languages, that is, speaking in tongues.

Fifth, Montanus did assert that this outpouring of the Spirit, of which he and his followers were the principal recipients, was a sign of the end of the age. The heavenly Jerusalem, said Montanus, would soon descend near Pepuza in Phrygia. They also stressed monogamy and insisted on chastity between husband and wife. They were quite ascetic in their approach to the Christian life (which is what attracted Tertullian into their ranks). They strongly emphasized self-discipline and repentance.

Finally, although Montanism was often treated as heresy, numerous authors in the early church insisted on the overall orthodoxy of the movement. Hippolytus spoke of their affirmation of the doctrines of Christ and creation, and the "heresy hunter" Epiphanius (AD 315–403) conceded that

---

22 Athenagoras, *A Plea for the Christians*, 9.
23 Quoted in Kydd, *Charismatic Gifts in the Early Church*, 35.
24 Kydd, 35.

the Montanists agreed with the church at large on the issues of orthodoxy, especially the doctrine of the Trinity.[25]

Epiphanius wrote that the Montanists were still found in Cappadocia, Galatia, Phrygia, Cilicia, and Constantinople in the late fourth century. This assessment was confirmed by Eusebius, who devoted four chapters of his monumental *Ecclesiastical History* to the Montanists. Didymus the Blind (AD 313–98) wrote of them, and the great church father Jerome (AD 342–420) personally encountered Montanist communities in Ancyra when he was traveling through Galatia in 373. My point is that Montanism was alive and influential as late as the close of the fourth century.

Ironically, and tragically, one of the principal reasons why the church became suspect of the gifts of the Spirit and eventually excluded them from the life of the church was because of their association with Montanism. The Montanist view of prophecy, in which the prophet entered a state of passive ecstasy in order that God might speak directly, was widely considered inconsistent with Paul's teaching in 1 Corinthians 14. Other unappealing aspects of the Montanist lifestyle, as noted above, provoked opposition to the movement and hence to the *charismata* as well. In sum, it was largely the Montanist view of the prophetic gift, in which a virtual "Thus saith the Lord" perspective was adopted, that contributed to the increasing absence in church life of the *charismata*.

Other Important Figures in the Life of the Early Church

The work of Theodotus (late second century) is preserved for us in Clement of Alexandria's *Excerpta ex Theodoto*. In 24:1 we read, "The Valentinians say that the excellent Spirit which each of the prophets had for his ministry was poured out upon all those of the church. Therefore the signs of the Spirit, healings and prophecies, are being performed by the church."

Clement of Alexandria (d. AD 215)[26] spoke explicitly of the operation in his day of those spiritual gifts listed by Paul in 1 Corinthians 12:7–10. Origen (d. AD 254) acknowledged that the operation of the gifts in his day is not

---

25 Kilian McDonnell and George T. Montague, *Christian Initiation and Baptism in the Holy Spirit: Evidence from the First Eight Centuries* (Collegeville, MN: Liturgical Press, 1991), 106–21, 136–37.
26 Clement of Alexandria, *The Instructor* 4.21 (*ANF* 2:434).

as extensive as was true in the New Testament, but they are still present and powerful: "And there are still preserved among Christians traces of that Holy Spirit which appeared in the form of a dove. They expel evil spirits, and perform many cures, and foresee certain events, according to the will of the Logos."[27]

The pagan Celsus sought to discredit the gifts of the Spirit exercised in churches in Origen's day, yet the latter pointed to the "demonstration" of the validity of the gospel, "more divine than any established by Grecian dialectics," namely, that which is called by the apostle the "manifestations of the Spirit and of power." Not only were signs and wonders performed in the days of Jesus, but "traces of them are still preserved among those who regulate their lives by the precepts of the Gospel."[28] Many believe Celsus was referring to prophecy and tongues in the Christian community when he derisively described certain believers "who pretend to be moved as if giving some oracular utterances" and who add to these oracles "incomprehensible, incoherent, and utterly obscure utterances, the meaning of which no intelligible person could discover."[29] This, of course, is precisely what one would expect a pagan skeptic to say about prophecy and tongues.

Hippolytus (d. AD 236) set forth guidelines for the exercise of deliverance ministry, insisting that "if there is someone who has a demon, such a one shall not hear the Word of the teacher until purified."[30] Novatian wrote in *Treatise Concerning the Trinity* (AD 245),

> Indeed this is he who appoints prophets in the church, instructs teachers, directs tongues, brings into being powers and conditions of health, carries on extraordinary works, furnishes discernment of spirits, incorporates administrations in the church, establishes plans, brings together and arranges all other gifts there are of the charismata and by reason of this makes the Church of God everywhere perfect in everything and complete.[31]

---

27 Origen, *Against Celsus* 1.46 (*ANF* 4:415).

28 Origen, *Against Celsus* 1.2 (*ANF* 4:397–98).

29 Origen, *Against Celsus* 7.9 (*ANF* 4:615).

30 Hippolytus, *Apostolic Tradition* 15 (www.stjohnsarlingtonva.org/Customer-Content/saintjohnsarlington/CMS/files/EFM/Apostolic_Tradition_by_Hippolytus.pdf).

31 Novatian, *Treatise Concerning the Trinity* 29.10.

I earlier mentioned Cyprian (bishop of Carthage, AD 248–58), who spoke and wrote often of the gift of prophecy and the receiving of visions from the Spirit.[32]

Gregory Thaumaturgus (AD 213–70) is reported by many to have ministered in the power of numerous miraculous gifts and to have performed signs and wonders. Eusebius of Caesarea (AD 260–339), theologian and church historian in the court of Constantine, opposed the Montanists' abuse of the gift of prophecy, but not the gift's reality. He affirmed repeatedly the legitimacy of spiritual gifts but resisted the Montanists, who operated outside the mainstream church and thus contributed, said Eusebius, to its disunity.

Cyril of Jerusalem (d. 386) wrote often of the gifts in his day: "For He [the Holy Spirit] employs the tongue of one man for wisdom; the soul of another He enlightens by prophecy, to another He gives power to drive away devils, to another he gives to interpret the divine Scriptures."[33]

Although Athanasius nowhere explicitly addressed the issue of charismatic gifts, many believe he is the anonymous author of *Vita S. Antoni*, or *The Life of St. Anthony*. Anthony was a monk who embraced an ascetic lifestyle in AD 285 and remained in the desert for some twenty years. The author (Athanasius?) of his life described numerous supernatural healings, visions, prophetic utterances, and other signs and wonders. Even if one rejects Athanasius as its author, the document does portray an approach to the charismatic gifts that many, evidently, embraced in the church of the late third and early fourth centuries. Another famous and influential monk, Pachomius (AD 292–346), was known to perform miracles and empowered to converse "in languages he did not know."

The influential and highly regarded Cappadocian Fathers (mid to late fourth century) must also be considered. Basil of Caesarea (b. AD 330) spoke often of the operation in his day of prophecy and healing. He appealed to Paul's description in 1 Corinthians 12 of the "word of wisdom" and "gifts of healing" as representative of those gifts that are necessary for the common good of the church.

---

32 *The Epistles of Cyprian* 7.3–6 (*ANF* 5:286–87); 7.7 (*ANF* 5:287); 68.9–10 (*ANF* 5:375); 4.4 (*ANF* 5:290).

33 Cyril of Jerusalem, *Catechetical Lectures* 16.12 (*Nicene and Post-Nicene Fathers*, Series 2 [hereafter *NPNF2*], ed. Alexander Roberts, James Donaldson, Philip Schaff, and Henry Wace, 14 vols. (Peabody, MA: Hendrickson, 1996), 7:118.

Is it not plain and incontestable that the ordering of the Church is effected through the Spirit? For He gave, it is said, "in the church, first Apostles, secondarily prophets, thirdly teachers, after that miracles, then gifts of healing, helps, governments, diversities of tongues," for this order is ordained in accordance with the division of the gifts that are of the Spirit.[34]

Spiritual leaders in the church, such as bishops or presbyters, says Basil, possess the gift of discernment of spirits, healing, and foreseeing the future (one expression of prophecy).[35]

Gregory of Nyssa (b. AD 336; Basil's younger brother) spoke on Paul's words in 1 Corinthians 13: "Even if someone receives the other gifts which the Spirit furnishes (I mean the tongues of angels and prophecy and knowledge and the grace of healing), but has never been entirely cleansed of the troubling passions within him through the charity of the Spirit, [he is in danger of failing]."[36]

He also described numerous miracles, especially of healing, in his *Life of St. Macrina* (who happened to be his sister). One in particular concerned the healing of a young child's eyes:

And the mother gazed intently at the child's eyes and then loudly exclaimed with joy and surprise, "Stop being angry at our negligence! Look! There's nothing missing of what she promised us, but the true medicine with which she heals diseases, the healing which comes from prayer, she has given us and it has already done its work, there's nothing whatsoever left of the eye disease, all healed by that divine medicine!" And as she was saying this, she picked the child up in her arms and put her down in mine. And then I too understood the incredible miracles of the gospel, which I had not believed in, and exclaimed: "What a great thing it is when the hand of God restores sight to the blind, when today his servant heals such sicknesses by her faith in Him, an event no less impressive than those miracles!" All the

---

34 Basil of Caesarea, *On the Holy Spirit* 16.39 (*NPNF²* 8:25).

35 Basil of Caesarea, *The Longer Rule* 24, 35, 42, 55.

36 Saint Gregory of Nyssa, "On the Christian Mode of Life," in *Saint Gregory of Nyssa: Ascetical Works*, trans. Virginia Woods Callahan, Fathers of the Church 58 (Washington, DC: The Catholic University of America Press, 1967), 141.

while he was saying this, his voice was choked with emotion and the tears flowed into his story. This then is what I heard from the soldier.

All the other similar miracles which we heard about from those who lived with her and who knew in detail what she had done I do not think it prudent to add to our narrative. For most people judge the credibility of what is told them by the yardstick of their own experience, and what goes beyond the power of the hearer, this they have no respect for, suspecting that it is false and outside of the truth. For this reason I pass over that incredible farming miracle at the time of the famine, how the grain was distributed according to need and showed no sign of diminishing, how the volume remained the same both before it was given out to those who asked for it and after the distribution, and other miracles still more extraordinary, the cure of sicknesses, the casting out of demons, true prophecies of things to come; all of these are believed to be true by those who knew the details of them, even if they are beyond belief. But for those who are more bound to this world of flesh, they are considered to be outside the realm of what can be accepted, that is by those who do not know that the distribution of graces is in proportion to one's faith, abundant for those who have in them a lot of room for faith.

In order therefore that those who have too little faith, and who do not believe in the gifts of God, should come to no harm, for this reason I have declined to make a complete record here of the greater miracles, since I think that what I have already said is sufficient to complete Macrina's story.[37]

The final Cappadocian, Gregory of Nazianzen (b. AD 330), provides extensive descriptions of the physical healing that both his father and mother experienced as well as several visions that accompanied them.[38]

Hilary of Poitiers (AD 356) speaks of "the gift of healings" and "the working of miracles" that "what we do may be understood to be the power of God" as well as "prophecy" and the "discerning of spirits." He also referred to the importance of "speaking in tongues" as a "sign of the gift of the Holy Spirit" together with "the interpretation of tongues," so "that the faith of those that

37 Kevin Corrigan, "Saint Macrina: The Hidden Face Behind the Tradition," *Vox Benedictina: A Journal of Translations from Monastic Sources* 5.1 (1988): 13–43.
38 Gregory of Nazianzen, *On the Death of His Father* 28–29 (*NPNF*² 7:263–64; 31 (*NPNF*² 7:264).

hear may not be imperiled through ignorance, since the interpreter of a tongue explains the tongue to those who are ignorant of it."[39]

By the late fourth century the gifts of the Spirit were increasingly found among ascetics and those involved in the monastic movements. The various compromises and accommodations to the wider culture that infiltrated the church subsequent to the formal legalization of Christianity under Constantine drove many of the more spiritually minded leaders into the desert.

Something must be said about Augustine (AD 354–430), who early in his ministry espoused cessationism, especially with regard to the gift of tongues.[40] However, in his later writings he retracted his denial of the ongoing reality of the miraculous and carefully documented no fewer than seventy instances of divine healing in his own diocese during a two-year span.[41] After describing numerous miracles of healing and even resurrections from the dead, Augustine wrote:

> What am I to do? I am so pressed by the promise of finishing this work, that I cannot record all the miracles I know; and doubtless several of our adherents, when they read what I have narrated, will regret that I have omitted so many which they, as well as I, certainly know. Even now I beg, these persons to excuse me, and to consider how long it would take me to relate all those miracles, which the necessity of finishing the work I have undertaken forces me to omit.[42]

Again, writing his *Revisions* (also titled *Retractions*), at the close of life and ministry (ca. AD 426–27), he conceded that tongues and the more spectacular miracles, such as people being healed by the mere shadow of Christ's preachers as they pass by, had ceased. He then said:

> But what I said should not be understood as though no miracles should be believed to be performed nowadays in Christ's name. For I myself, when I was writing this very book, knew a blind man who had been given his sight

---

39 Hilary of Poitiers, *On the Trinity* 8.30 (*NPNP* 9:146).

40 Ambrose, who highly influenced Augustine, also believed in the operation of tongues in his day (*The Holy Spirit* 2.150).

41 See Augustine, *City of God* 22.8–10.

42 Augustine, *City of God* 22.8.489.

> in the same city near the bodies of the martyrs of Milan. I knew of some other miracles as well; so many of them occur even in these times that we would be unable either to be aware of all of them or to number those of which we are aware.[43]

Later in the *Revisions*, he poses this question, "Why do the miracles Jesus performed not happen with the same frequency in our day?" Augustine's response: "Because they would not be striking unless they were marvelous, but if they were familiar occurrences they would not be marvelous." He then clarifies his answer by saying that "there are not such great nor so many [miracles] nowadays, not because none happen nowadays."[44]

Augustine also made reference to a phenomenon in his day called *jubilation*. Some believe he was describing singing in tongues. He wrote:

> Words cannot express the things that are sung by the heart. Take the case of people singing while harvesting in the fields or in the vineyards or when any other strenuous work is in progress. Although they begin by giving expression to their happiness in sung words, yet shortly there is a change. As if so happy that words can no longer express what they feel, they discard the restricting syllables. They burst into a simple sound of joy; of jubilation. Such a cry of joy is a sound signifying that the heart is bringing to birth what it cannot utter in words. Now who is more worthy of such a cry of jubilation than God himself, whom all words fail to describe? If words will not serve, and yet you must not remain silent, what else can you do but cry out for joy? Your heart must rejoice beyond words, that your unbounded joy may be unrestrained by syllabic bonds.[45]

A Strange and Unpersuasive Argument for Cessationism

In November of 2018 I attended the annual meeting of the Evangelical Theological Society in Denver, Colorado, together with some 2,700 others.

---

43 Augustine, *Revisions*, The Works of Saint Augustine: A Translation for the 21st Century (Hyde Park, NY: New City, 2010), Kindle edition, book one, 13, 7.

44 Augustine, *Revisions*, Kindle edition, book one, 14, 5.

45 Augustine, cited by Oliver, *Pentecost to the Present*, 1:142–43.

The theme of that year's gathering was the Holy Spirit. On the first day of our meeting, I participated in a three-hour panel conversation (debate?) with three good friends: Andrew Wilson, Tom Schreiner, and Ligon Duncan. Andrew and I defended continuationism while Tom and Ligon argued for cessationism.

Among the many things said, one brief exchange was especially fascinating. Andrew Wilson presented what I believe is an incontrovertible case that all spiritual gifts continued to operate well into the patristic age, some four hundred to five hundred years following the death of the apostles. An argument was then put forth by our dialogue partners that although these pastors, church leaders, and theologians of the patristic period spoke often of the presence and operation of all spiritual gifts, none of them claimed to have such gifts themselves. In other words, the argument, evidently, is that since these prominent church fathers didn't explicitly claim personally to have the gifts that they say were present among others, that such gifts, in fact, were not operative.

I find that a rather strange and altogether unpersuasive argument that ultimately has no bearing on the debate between continuationists and cessationists. Here is why.

First, the fact that these individuals did not claim to have such gifts by no means proves that others didn't. In point of fact, they repeatedly testified that others did have such gifts, and they provided eyewitness testimony to their presence in the patristic age. One need only read the words of Augustine, perhaps the most prominent theologian of this period, who went to great lengths to bear witness to the miraculous operation of such gifts in his own church and city.

If one denies that such gifts were present and operative during the patristic age, notwithstanding the repeated and consistent testimony of respected church fathers and theologians that they were, the question of motivation must also be considered. That is to say, *why* would people lie about these manifestations of the Spirit? Were they simply deceived into thinking the gifts were present when they actually were not? Were they so naive and uninformed that they simply didn't know any better? If that is the case, why should cessationists believe anything else they might have said? If they can't be trusted or believed on the matter of spiritual gifts, why should anyone trust them when they speak on other spiritual or theological or historical matters?

The alleged silence of such individuals about the presence of these gifts in their own experience may simply be confirmation of what we read in 1 Corinthians 12:27–31. There the apostle Paul said that not all prophesy, not all speak in tongues, not all possess gifts of healings, and so on. Perhaps the reason these people did not claim such gifts for themselves is because, as Paul said, the Spirit had chosen not to grant them any particular miraculous gift. Their silence regarding such gifts in their own lives would simply be an example of the truth of 1 Corinthians 12:27–31, namely, that not everyone possesses every gift. It is an unreasonable stretch to conclude that their silence about their own gifting is proof that other gifts were absent among others.

Finally, consider the panel for the debate itself. At no time during the course of reading two papers in defense of continuationism did Andrew Wilson ever say that *he* regularly speaks in tongues.[46] What might someone conclude who, two hundred years later, reads Andrew's papers while engaged in a debate over the continuation or cessation of spiritual gifts? Might the cessationist, two centuries hence, argue that there is no evidence that such gifts were operative in 2018 because Andrew Wilson, who was alive at that time, nowhere claimed in his written lectures that he himself operated in the power of such miraculous *charismata*?

Perhaps he would. But I hope you can see how baseless such an argument would be. The fact that Wilson didn't explicitly mention those gifts he possesses in no way suggests, much less requires, that they weren't present in his life or in the lives of others who lived at the same time. The reality is that Andrew and I both are blessed with the gift of tongues. And we both speak often of others we know and have seen who operate in miraculous gifts. Our failure or reluctance to describe our own experience in this regard hardly suggests that no one else operates in these *charismata* of the Spirit. The silence of certain church fathers regarding their own personal experience of the miraculous *charismata* is a weak argument for their cessation.

---

46 You can read both of Wilson's papers, along with those of Thomas Schreiner, in *Themelios* 44.1 (2019): 16–40.

Miraculous Spiritual Gifts in the Middle Ages

There is less evidence of the miraculous gifts as we enter the period of the Middle Ages (for reasons I've already noted), yet at no time did the gifts disappear altogether. Due to limitations of space, I list only the names of those in whose ministries are numerous documented instances of the revelatory gifts of prophecy, healing, discerning of spirits, miracles, and tongues, together with vivid accounts of dreams and visions.[47] They include the following:

John of Egypt (d. 394)

Leo the Great (400–461; he served as bishop of Rome from 440 until 461)

Genevieve of Paris (422–500)

Benedict of Nursia (480–547)

Gregory the Great (540–604)

Gregory of Tours (538–94)

The Venerable Bede (673–735; his *Ecclesiastical History of the English People*, written in 731, contains numerous accounts of miraculous gifts in operation)

Aidan, bishop of Lindisfarne (d. 651) and his successor Cuthbert (d. 687; both of whom served as missionaries in Britain)

Ansgar (800–865), one of the first missionaries to Scandinavia

Bernard of Clairvaux (1090–1153), who wrote a treatise on the *Life and Death of Saint Malachy the Irishman* (1094–1148)

Richard of St. Victor (d. 1173)

Dominic, founder of the Dominicans (1170–1221)

Anthony of Padua (1195–1231)

Bonaventure (1217–74)

Francis of Assisi (1182–1226; documented in Bonaventure's *Life of St. Francis*)

Thomas Aquinas (1225–74)

---

47 For extensive documentation, see Stanley M. Burgess, *The Holy Spirit: Medieval Roman Catholic and Reformation Traditions (Sixth-Sixteenth Centuries)* (Peabody, MA: Hendrickson, 1997). See also Paul Thigpen, "Did the Power of the Spirit Ever Leave the Church?" *Charisma*, September 1992, 20–29; and Richard M. Riss, "Tongues and Other Miraculous Gifts in the Second through Nineteenth Centuries," *Basileia*, 1985.

Peter Waldo, founder of the Waldenses (d. 1217)

Virtually all of the medieval mystics, among whom are several women:

Hildegard of Bingen (1098–1179)

Gertrude of Helfta (1256–1301)

Bergitta of Sweden (1302–73)

St. Clare of Montefalco (d. 1308)

Catherine of Siena (1347–80)

Julian of Norwich (1342–1416)

Margery Kempe (1373–1433)

Dominican preacher Vincent of Ferrier (1350–1419)

Teresa of Ávila (1515–82)

John of the Cross (1542–91)

If one objects that these are all Roman Catholics, we must not forget that during this period in history there was hardly anyone else. Aside from a few splinter sects, there was little to no expression of Christianity outside the Church of Rome (the formal split with what became known as Eastern Orthodoxy did not occur until AD 1054).

Moving closer to the time of the Reformation, we should note Ignatius of Loyola (1491–1556), founder of the Jesuits and author of the *Spiritual Exercises*. Spiritual gifts, especially tongues, are reported to have been common among the Mennonites, the Moravians, especially under the leadership of Count von Zinzendorf (1700–1760), as well as among the French Huguenots in the late seventeenth century and the Jansenists of the first half of the eighteenth century. John Wesley (1703–91) defended the ongoing operation of tongues beyond the time of the apostles. One could also cite George Fox (1624–91), who founded the Quaker Church.[48]

---

48 For documentation of Wesley's beliefs, see *Christian Peoples of the Spirit: A Documentary History of Pentecostal Spirituality from the Early Church to the Present*, ed. Stanley M. Burgess (New York: New York University Press, 2011), 177–86. For Fox, I recommend *George Fox: An Autobiography*, ed. Rufus M. Jones (Richmond, IN: Street Corner Society, 1976).

Miraculous Spiritual Gifts in the Scottish Reformation

Those who insist that revelatory spiritual gifts such as prophecy, discerning of spirits, and word of knowledge ceased to function beyond the first century also have a difficult time accounting for the operation of these gifts in the lives of many who were involved in the Scottish Reformation, as well as several who ministered in its aftermath. Jack Deere, in his book *Surprised by the Voice of God*,[49] has provided extensive documentation of the gift of prophecy at work in and through such men as George Wishart (1513–46; mentor of John Knox), John Knox himself (1514–72), John Welsh (1570–1622), Robert Bruce (1554–1631), and Alexander Peden (1626–86).

I strongly encourage the reader to obtain Deere's book and closely examine the account of their supernatural ministries, not only in prophecy but often in gifts of healings. Deere also draws our attention to one of the historians of the seventeenth century, Robert Fleming (1630–94), as well as one of the major architects of the Westminster Confession of Faith, Samuel Rutherford (1600–1661), both of whom acknowledged the operation of the gifts in their day.

This brief survey of church history demonstrates that the standard cessationist claim that miraculous gifts of the Spirit disappeared following the death of the original apostles is false. Substantial evidence exists that the Holy Spirit continued to impart the *charismata* and that, in those periods where the gifts are not as frequently found, a reasonable explanation can be given other than appealing to some form of inherent obsolescence in the nature and purpose of the gifts themselves.

We now turn our attention from spiritual gifts in church history to the nature of each individual gift and its purpose in the life of the church.

---

49 Jack Deere, *Surprised by the Voice of God* (Grand Rapids: Zondervan, 1996), 64–93.

PART 3

REVELATORY GIFTS OF THE SPIRIT

CHAPTER 8

Word of Wisdom and Word of Knowledge

We face a problem from the outset in our efforts to understand the spiritual gifts of word of knowledge and word of wisdom. The problem is that neither Paul nor any other New Testament author ever bothered to define them. Although the terms *knowledge* and *wisdom* both appear frequently in 1 Corinthians and in other New Testament letters, the only place where "the word of knowledge" and "the word of wisdom" occur is in 1 Corinthians 12:8. There they appear at the head of a list of nine gifts of the Spirit:

> For to one is given through the Spirit the utterance of wisdom, and to another the utterance of knowledge according to the same Spirit, to another faith by the same Spirit, to another gifts of healing by the one Spirit, to another the working of miracles, to another prophecy, to another the ability to distinguish between spirits, to another various kinds of tongues, to another the interpretation of tongues. (1 Cor. 12:8–10)[1]

No reason is given anywhere in Scripture why these two gifts should be noted but left unexplained. It may well be that the Corinthians were so familiar with their nature and purpose that Paul felt no pressure or need to provide additional details. Others, as we will shortly note below, believe that these gifts are specifically and directly related to Paul's comments in this letter regarding "knowledge" and "wisdom." Thus, any suggestion that

---

1   The ESV translates these as "the *utterance* of wisdom" and "the *utterance* of knowledge," ostensibly to highlight that these are *spoken* gifts.

they stand alone in chapter 12 without further explication fails to take into consideration what Paul had already said elsewhere in 1 Corinthians.

We may ask how, if at all, one should differentiate these two gifts from the gift of prophecy. On two occasions in 1 Corinthians, Paul simply referred to a "revelation" coming to a believer unrelated to any specific gift (see 1 Cor. 14:6, 26; in 14:30 the "revelation" comes in conjunction with prophecy). Might these revelatory disclosures be Paul's somewhat cryptic way of referring back to both word of knowledge and wisdom, or did he have the gift of prophecy specifically in mind?

Biblical Precedents

The specific language Paul employed here provides us with virtually no help in understanding the nature of these two spiritual gifts. The terms *word* (or "utterance"), *wisdom*, and *knowledge* are common enough in the New Testament, but their meaning must be gleaned both from the broader context in which they appear, as well as likely examples of these gifts in actual operation. However, it must be conceded that in cases of the latter, the terminology of *word*, *wisdom*, and *knowledge* are nowhere to be found. There is, therefore, no way that we can with any degree of certainty be assured that the examples cited below are actual instances of the two gifts under consideration.

That being said, the Gospels record several instances where Jesus is described as "knowing" the thoughts of the scribes and religious leaders:

> But Jesus, knowing their thoughts, said, . . . (Matt. 9:4)

> Knowing their thoughts, he said to them, . . . (Matt. 12:25)

> But he knew their thoughts, and he said . . . (Luke 6:8)

Jesus is also portrayed as knowing the thoughts of his own disciples:

> But Jesus, knowing the reasoning of their hearts, . . . (Luke 9:47)

In John 1:43–51 we read about the calling of Nathanael, where Jesus, without having met the man, knew his moral character and declared, "I saw you" (v. 48). The most frequently cited example is our Lord's encounter with the Samaritan woman in John 4. Jesus proceeded to disclose her secret sins (vv. 16–18), which led her to conclude that he was a prophet (v. 19). Later she spread the news about a man "who told me all that I ever did" (v. 29).

I'm not suggesting that these incidents are examples of our two spiritual gifts. But they may be analogous to them. Many people would attribute the knowledge Jesus displayed to his divine nature. He is, after all, the omniscient God incarnate. Others, myself included, would point instead to the revelatory ministry of the Holy Spirit in the life of Jesus. To live a fully human life, God the Son voluntarily suspended the exercise of certain divine attributes (such as omniscience). He in no sense ceased to be fully God, but he chose not to make use of those attributes that would have proven inconsistent with a genuine human life of weakness and finitude. The relationship of the incarnate Christ to the Holy Spirit and his utter dependence on the latter for his ability to know such things and to work miracles is a vast subject that cannot detain us here. I would simply direct your attention to such texts as Matthew 12:28; Luke 4:1–2, 14–15, 16–19; 5:17; 8:46; 10:21; John 3:34–35; Acts 1:1–2; 10:38.[2] My point in this is that Jesus displayed a supernatural knowledge of what he could not otherwise have known, by virtue of the ministry of the Holy Spirit. This would at least alert us to the possibility of what Paul may have had in mind when he spoke of the "word of knowledge" and "word of wisdom."

Could it be that Peter's response to Ananias and Sapphira was by a word of knowledge? No indication is given as to how or by what means Peter gained his insight into the motivation of their hearts, but it may well have been by virtue of his having been given one or both of these spiritual gifts. We see something similar in Acts 8:26–40. Philip was first instructed by an angel to "go toward the south to the road that goes down from Jerusalem to Gaza" (v. 26). He was later told by the Holy Spirit to join the Ethiopian eunuch in his chariot, where he proceeded to share the gospel with him (v. 29). Could Philip have been the recipient of a word of wisdom by which he was led into this encounter?

In Acts 9:10–19 Ananias experienced a vision from the Lord in which he was granted knowledge about a man named Saul. He was also given divine guidance and instruction on what to say to this man who had done "much evil" to the Lord's "saints at Jerusalem" (v. 13). Were the revelatory experiences

---

2 I address this issue at considerable length in the chapter titled "How Did Jesus Perform His Miracles?" in my book *Tough Topics 2: Biblical Answers to 25 Challenging Questions* (Fearn, Ross-shire, UK: Christian Focus, 2015).

of Cornelius and Peter in Acts 10 examples of word of knowledge? And what of the revelatory word of guidance that came to the church at Antioch concerning the mission of Paul and Barnabas? Only prophets and teachers are mentioned in the text, so it may be that this is simply a prophetic revelation, not a word of knowledge or wisdom. Yet again we see the difficulty in distinguishing among the three gifts.

A more likely example of the word of knowledge may be found in Paul's encounter with Elymas the magician in Acts 13:6–12. There the apostle was "filled with the Holy Spirit" (v. 9) and proceeded to disclose the secret and malicious intentions of Elymas. How did he come by this knowledge? Might it be the result of a spiritual gift granted to Paul as he was filled with the Spirit? A similar instance occurs one chapter later, in Acts 14:8–10, where Paul is described as "seeing" that a man "crippled from birth and had never walked" had "faith to be made well" (vv. 8–9). How did Paul "see" or "perceive" or have knowledge of this truth? Again, we cannot be certain that the word of knowledge is in operation, but it would not be unreasonable to think so.

Consider the incident in Acts 16:16–18 that took place in Philippi. Paul was met by a slave girl "who had a spirit of divination" (v. 16). Not wanting his ministry to be associated with demonic advertisement, he commanded the demon "to come out of her" (v. 18). One cannot help but wonder how Paul knew she was under the influence of "a spirit of divination."

Are these merely instances of revelatory activity of a general sort (as noted above), or are they occurrences of the gift of prophecy? Or could they be examples of the word of wisdom or word of knowledge? Yet again, perhaps they are instances of the gift of discerning of spirits. Might they be expressions of miraculous activity that is a combination of some or all of these revelatory events? Each of these instances is undoubtedly revelatory in nature, which is to say that God disclosed information otherwise unattainable. But should we call any of these incidents "word of wisdom" or "word of knowledge"?

Wisdom and Knowledge in Corinth

Some believe the key to understanding these two spiritual gifts is to be found in how the terms are used in 1 Corinthians.[3] It would appear that the

---

3   The following discussion is adapted from my book *The Beginner's Guide to Spiritual Gifts* (Minneapolis:

people in Corinth were influenced by an incipient gnosticism that emphasized both wisdom and knowledge as the keys to true spirituality. British New Testament scholar James Dunn refers to these two terms as "slogans of the faction opposing Paul in Corinth."[4] Dunn argues that "this is why *gnosis* [knowledge] keeps recurring within the Corinthian letters and only rarely elsewhere, and why 1 Corinthians 1–3 is so dominated by discussion of *sophia* [wisdom]."[5] Remarkably, it was actually in the name of wisdom that the Corinthians were rejecting both Paul and his gospel.

When we look closely at 1 Corinthians 1:18–27, we see that in the span of these ten verses the word *wisdom* and its derivatives occur twelve times. In 1 Corinthians 2:1 Paul said that when he preached to the Corinthians, it was not with "superiority of speech (*logos*) or of wisdom (*sophia*)" (NASB; interestingly, these are the same Greek terms used in 1 Cor. 12:8), but rather "in demonstration of the Spirit and of power" (2:4). See also 2:5–8, 13 for additional references and allusions to wisdom. Especially noteworthy is 1 Corinthians 1:17 where Paul said that Christ did not send him to proclaim the gospel "in cleverness [*sophia*, i.e., wisdom!] of speech (*logos*)." Again, in 1 Corinthians 2:4 Paul insisted that he did not preach with persuasive "words (*logos*) of wisdom (*sophia*)." The same two words are found together yet again in 2:13.

The word *wisdom* can be used in both a good and a bad sense. Evil wisdom is the rhetorical skill, eloquence, and natural reasoning used to undermine the gospel. Worldly wisdom is the perspective of the unbelieving mind that knows nothing of the realm of the Spirit and regards the idea of a crucified Messiah as absurd. Spiritual wisdom, on the other hand, refers primarily to the mysterious purposes of God whereby he redeems his people through the foolishness of the cross (see esp. 1 Cor. 2:6–9).

Perhaps our interpretation of the gift of "word of wisdom" in 12:8 should reflect Paul's emphasis on the "message" (word) of "wisdom" in 1 Corinthians 1–3. In that case, the focus would be less on a revelation of some otherwise hidden truth about a person and more on the purpose of God in redemptive history. That is to say, the "word" revealed would explain or unfold God's "wisdom"

Bethany House, 2015), 45–49, and is used here with permission.

4   James D. G. Dunn, *Jesus and the Spirit* (Philadelphia: Westminster, 1975), 217.

5   Dunn, 217.

in bringing salvation to a lost world through the life, death, and resurrection of a carpenter from Nazareth. Or again, word of wisdom may be the ability to articulate life-changing insights into God's mysterious, saving purposes for mankind, both on a global plane as well as in application to individuals.

The same may be noted of the word *knowledge*. In 1 Corinthians 8:1–4, 7, 10 *knowledge* appears four times (see also 13:2, 8). Knowledge, according to Paul, is insight into the unfathomable depths of God's gracious work in Christ. Thus, the word of knowledge may be the Spirit-empowered ability to communicate insight into the unfathomable depths of God's gracious work in Christ.

If so, it may be that when Paul came to 1 Corinthians 12, he decided to reclaim for distinctly Christian use both the terms *wisdom* and *knowledge* and apply them in a way that would build up the church. Dunn agrees and defines the word of wisdom as "some charismatic utterance giving an insight into, some fresh understanding of, God's plan of salvation or of the benefits it brings to believers."[6] He defines word of knowledge in similar fashion, focusing on the idea of insight into the nature of the world, both spiritual and natural, with special reference to the relationship between God and man. A word of knowledge, says Dunn, was simply an utterance spoken under inspiration that communicated an insight into "cosmical realities and relationships."[7] It might even more closely approximate the idea of inspired teaching, in which the speaker is granted extraordinary insight into the meaning of Scripture.

If these definitions are accurate, and I'm not entirely convinced they are, we may need to refer to those revelatory insights into the details, data, and secrets of a person's life, not as word of knowledge or word of wisdom, but as prophecy or simply as a revelation.

Revelatory Words?

So then, are the word of wisdom and word of knowledge *revelatory* gifts? Does the insight or illumination or knowledge come immediately and spontaneously from the Holy Spirit apart from natural means, or is it the reasoned conclusion to which any Christian, through observation and study of the Scriptures, might come?

---

6   Dunn, 220.
7   Dunn, 218.

Observe that Paul did not call wisdom and knowledge spiritual gifts per se. He spoke of the word (*logos*) of wisdom and the word (*logos*) of knowledge. As Dunn explains, "For Paul wisdom and knowledge as such are not to be thought of as *charismata*; only the actual utterance which reveals wisdom or knowledge to others is a charisma."[8] Dunn wants to distinguish between that general wisdom and knowledge that all Christians possess (or *may* possess) and the gift of utterance in relation to wisdom and knowledge, which is restricted in scope.

It may well be that word of wisdom and word of knowledge are not revelatory in nature.[9] However, we should note that Paul's use of *knowledge* later in his discussion of spiritual gifts (13:2, 8–12; 14:6) would seem to support the supernatural, spontaneous, and revelatory nature of this gift. In 1 Corinthians 13:2 Paul mentioned having all knowledge in the same breath with prophecy and faith, both overtly supernatural giftings. Again, in verses 8–12, knowledge is linked with tongues and prophecy to make the point regarding the continuation of the *charismata* until the second coming of Christ. Although no reference is made to the *word of* knowledge, it seems likely that Paul's use of *knowledge* points back to 12:8. We especially note 14:6, where *knowledge* is sandwiched, so to speak, between *revelation* and *prophecy*. My sense is that this knowledge is the fruit of a revelatory event that 12:8 indicates is to be spoken ("word" or "message" of knowledge) for the edification of the church.

The customary Pentecostal, charismatic, third-wave understanding of the word of wisdom and the word of knowledge is that they refer, respectively, to the articulation of revelatory insight into the *how* (wisdom) and *what* (knowledge) of a person's life. Word of wisdom, so it has been said, pertains to *instruction*, and word of knowledge pertains to *information*. But in view of Paul's use of the terms *word*, *wisdom*, and *knowledge* elsewhere in 1 Corinthians, we may need to be more cautious and less dogmatic in how we define these gifts. In the light of what we've seen, how would *you* classify or describe the following three examples?

8 Dunn, 221.

9 See Wayne Grudem, *Systematic Theology: An Introduction to Biblical Doctrine* (Grand Rapids: Zondervan, 1994), 1080–82.

A Gifted Baptist

I have often pointed in previous publications to the experience of Charles Spurgeon (1834–92), Baptist pastor in London, who tells of an incident in the middle of his sermon where he paused and pointed at a man whom he accused of taking an unjust profit on Sunday, of all days! The culprit later described the event to a friend:

> "Mr. Spurgeon looked at me as if he knew me, and in his sermon he pointed to me, and told the congregation that I was a shoemaker, and that I kept my shop open on Sundays; and I did, sir. I should not have minded that; but he also said that I took ninepence the Sunday before, and that there was fourpence profit out of it. I did take ninepence that day, and fourpence was just the profit; but how he should know that, I could not tell. Then it struck me that it was God who had spoken to my soul through him, so I shut up my shop the next Sunday. At first, I was afraid to go again to hear him, lest he should tell the people more about me; but afterwards I went, and the Lord met with me, and saved my soul."[10]

Spurgeon then added this comment:

> I could tell as many as a *dozen* similar cases in which I pointed at somebody in the hall without having the slightest knowledge of the person, or any idea that what I said was right, except that I believed I was moved by the Spirit to say it; and so striking has been my description, that the persons have gone away, and said to their friends, "Come, see a man that told me all things that ever I did; beyond a doubt, he must have been sent of God to my soul, or else he could not have described me so exactly." And not only so, but I have known many instances in which the thoughts of men have been revealed from the pulpit. I have sometimes seen persons nudge their neighbours with their elbow because they had got a smart hit, and they have been heard to say, when they were going out, "*The preacher told us just what we said to one another when we went in at the door.*"[11]

10 Charles Spurgeon, *The Autobiography of Charles H. Spurgeon* (n.p.: Curts & Jennings, 1899), 2:226–27.
11 Spurgeon, 2:226–27.

On another occasion, Spurgeon broke off his sermon and pointed at a young man, declaring, "Young man, those gloves you are wearing have not been paid for: you have stolen them from your employer."[12] After the service the man brought the gloves to Spurgeon and asked that he not tell his mother, who would be heartbroken to discover that her son was a thief!

What are we to make of this? By all accounts, Spurgeon was a cessationist. If asked, he likely would have denied that revelatory gifts such as word of knowledge and prophecy were still operative in the church. And yet his own experience in the pulpit stands as witness against his theology, a theology that we have come to see is lacking in biblical support. The most probable explanation is that a "manifestation" of the Holy Spirit (1 Cor. 12:7) was present through Spurgeon, like unto that of which we read in 1 Corinthians 14:24–25. Although he would not himself have labeled it as such, I'm inclined to think that Spurgeon exercised either the gift of prophecy or the word of knowledge (1 Cor. 12:8). Failure to precisely identify the phenomenon does not alter the reality of what the Holy Spirit accomplished through him.

---

12 *C. H. Spurgeon Autobiography: The Full Harvest* (Carlisle: Banner of Truth Trust, 1973), 2:60.

CHAPTER 9

The Nature and Purpose of the
Spiritual Gift of Prophecy

One would be hard-pressed to identify a more controversial and disputed spiritual gift than prophecy. There is a sense in which it has become the focal point of debate among Christians who differ on the perpetuation and validity of spiritual gifts today.[1] My hope is that a careful analysis of what the New Testament says about prophecy will help diminish some of the heat that it provokes and heal the divide that it has caused among otherwise unified evangelical believers.

My approach will be to delineate several distinguishing characteristics of this spiritual gift. And it would appear that the place to begin is where the New Testament does: on the day of Pentecost.

Prophecy at Pentecost

We learn from the events described in Acts 2 that one of the primary characteristics of the Spirit's work in "the last days" is empowering people to prophesy. Citing the words of Joel, Peter declared,

> "'And in the last days it shall be, God declares,
> that I will pour out my Spirit on all flesh,

---

1 Hence the title to Thomas R. Schreiner's article "It All Depends upon Prophecy: A Brief Case for Nuanced Cessationism," in *Themelios* 44.1 (2019): 29–35.

and your sons and your daughters shall prophesy,
>   and your young men shall see visions,
>   and your old men shall dream dreams;
> even on my male servants and female servants
>   in those days I will pour out my Spirit, and they shall prophesy."
>   (vv. 17–18)

There is much to learn from the events of Pentecost, but our concern at this stage is the way Peter described what is to be characteristic of the present church age.

Contrary to what many Christians have been led to believe, "the last days" is not a reference to the final days or even years immediately preceding the second coming of Christ. The "last days" that Joel had in view when he uttered this prophecy back in the late seventh or early sixth century BC was the entire present age in which we now live. In other words, the "last days" began on the day of Pentecost and extend all the way until Jesus returns. The "last days," or the era of the new covenant, have now extended for nearly two thousand years (see 2 Tim. 3:1; Heb. 1:1–2; 9:26; James 5:3; 1 Peter 1:20; 1 John 2:18; cf. also 1 Cor. 10:11; 1 Tim. 4:1).

It is during this present church age that the Spirit will be poured out "on all flesh," that is to say, not just on kings and prophets and priests but on every child of God: every man and woman, every son and daughter, young and old (see Acts 2:17). Peter's (and Joel's) language is unmistakable when it comes to this new covenant universalizing of the Spirit's empowering presence: "all flesh" (v. 17), that is, irrespective of age ("old men" and "young men"), gender ("sons" and "daughters" and "male servants" and "female servants"), social rank ("servants"), or race ("all flesh"; cf. v. 39; i.e., both Jew and Gentile).

I need to explain my use of the word *characteristic* when I speak of prophecy in the church age. This is justified in light of Peter's reference to the "last days." Some have tried to argue that the events that occurred on the day of Pentecost in the first century were designed solely to launch or inaugurate or in some sense jump-start the age of the new covenant. Now, make no mistake, the coming of the Spirit in power on Pentecost most assuredly did inaugurate the new covenant age in which we now live. But what the Spirit did on that day centuries ago is also designed by God to characterize the experience of God's people throughout the course of this age until Jesus comes back. In other words, what we are reading in Acts 2:17–21 is a description of what the Holy Spirit does in and through and on behalf of God's people throughout the entire course of this present age. Prophecy, whatever it may mean, is designed by God to be a normative experience for all God's people in this age in which we live, as we await the return of the Lord.

Prophecy and Revelation

The foundation or basis of all prophetic ministry is the *revelatory* work of the Spirit. In other words, prophecy is always the communication of something the Holy Spirit has "revealed" or disclosed to a person. In Acts 2 this revelatory work of the Spirit is expressed in dreams and visions (Acts 2:18). In 1 Corinthians 14:26 Paul said that when Christians "come together" for a corporate assembly, "each one has a hymn, a lesson, a *revelation*, a tongue, or an interpretation" (emphasis mine). Later, in 14:30, Paul made it clear that a person prophesies upon reception of a spontaneous revelation from the Spirit. I use the word *spontaneous* in this case because Paul envisions "a revelation" coming to someone sitting in the meeting while yet another has already begun to speak.

Evangelicals often have a knee-jerk reaction to the use of the word *revelation* based on the mistaken assumption that all divine revelation is canonical. The idea that God might still be providing his people with "revelation" of any sort is thought to suggest, if not require, a repudiation of the notion that what we have already received in canonical and inspired form in the Bible is sufficient. If God has supplied us in Scripture itself with everything necessary for life and godliness, what need would there be for him to reveal anything beyond what we already possess?

Part of the problem is in the way that we employ the term *revelation* and the verb "to reveal." The verb "to reveal" (*apokaluptō*) occurs twenty-six times in the New Testament, and the noun "revelation" occurs eighteen times. In every relevant instance, the reference is to divine activity; never to human communication. However, not every act of divine revelation is equal in authority. The tendency among some is to improperly assume that anytime a "revelation" is granted, it bears the same universally binding authority, sufficient to warrant its inclusion in the biblical canon. But divine "revelation" comes in a variety of different forms. For example, consider Paul's statement in Philippians 3:15. There were present in Philippi some who took issue with certain elements in Paul's teaching. He appealed to all who were "mature" to "think" as he did. If some did not, Paul was confident that "God [would] reveal" to them the error of their way and bring them into conformity with apostolic truth. We see from a text like this that God can "reveal" to a Christian or in some manner disclose to their minds truths that no one would ever regard as canonical or bearing the authoritative weight of inspired biblical texts. The Spirit, instead, would bring something to mind spontaneously, some insight or truth designed exclusively for them and never intended by God to be taken as universally authoritative or binding on the conscience of other believers.

Jesus employed the verb "to reveal" to describe his own gracious activity in making known the Father to those who previously had no saving knowledge of him (Matt. 11:25–27). But surely no one would insist that the insight given to such folk should be written down and preserved as canonical for subsequent generations of Christians. Paul again used the language of "revelation" to describe the activity of God in making known the reality of divine wrath against those "who by their unrighteousness suppress the truth" (Rom. 1:18). Thus, God's act of divine disclosure is again unrelated to the inspiration of texts that carry an intrinsic authority.

In view of this, D. A. Carson has rightly pointed out that not all "revelatory" activity of God comes to us as Scripture-quality, divinely authoritative, canonical truth. Thus, says Carson, "when Paul presupposes in 1 Corinthians 14:30 that the gift of prophecy depends on a revelation, we are not limited to a form of authoritative revelation that threatens the finality of the canon. To argue in such a way is to confuse the terminology of Protestant systematic theology with the terminology of the Scripture writers."[2]

Defining Prophecy

We're now able to define prophecy more specifically as the speaking forth in merely human words something the Holy Spirit has sovereignly and often spontaneously revealed to a believer. Prophecy, therefore, is not based on a

---

2   D. A. Carson, *Showing the Spirit: A Theological Exposition of 1 Corinthians 12–14* (1987; repr., Grand Rapids: Baker, 2019), 214.

hunch, a supposition, an inference, an educated guess, or even on sanctified wisdom. Prophecy is not based on personal insight, intuition, or illumination. Prophecy is the human *report* of a divine *revelation*. This is what distinguishes prophecy from teaching. Teaching is always based on a text of Scripture. Prophecy is always based on a spontaneous revelation.

Some have tried to make the case that prophecy is actually just another name for preaching. For numerous reasons we cannot equate the two. First, as we've already noted, in Acts 2 Peter, quoting Joel, declared that prophecy is the direct result of revelatory visions and dreams and is the experience of young and old, both male and female.

We also see that in Acts 13:1–2 there were in Antioch both "prophets and teachers" (v. 1). If all teaching/preaching is an expression of prophecy, this seems odd. On what basis or for what reason would Luke have drawn a distinction between the two if they were essentially synonymous? Note also Luke's reference in Acts 21 to four daughters of Philip, all of whom had the gift of prophecy. Are we to conclude that his daughters regularly preached in the local church of which they were a part? Whereas evangelical egalitarians are inclined to say yes, we who are complementarians would embrace another perspective.

Another hint that prophecy and preaching cannot be equated comes from what Paul said in 1 Corinthians 14:6. There he differentiated between "revelation" and "knowledge" and "prophecy" and "teaching." As noted earlier, prophecy is based on a "revelation," whereas teaching is rooted in a text.

We also saw that in 1 Corinthians 14:26 Paul described how Christians are to approach the corporate gathering of the local church. "Each one," said Paul, "has a hymn, a lesson [lit., a teaching], a revelation, a tongue, or an interpretation." Here he clearly differentiated between a "teaching" and a "revelation." The former is based on a biblical text while the latter is the basis for prophecy. As noted above, this is confirmed in 1 Corinthians 14:29–30 where Paul explicitly said that prophecy is based on a spontaneous revelation from the Spirit. Teaching/preaching, on the other hand, is the exposition and application of a biblical text.

If prophecy and preaching or teaching are synonymous, one must explain why Paul differentiated between "prophets" and "pastors and teachers" or more likely "pastor-teachers" in Ephesians 4:11. Two passages in 1 Timothy also strongly suggest that prophecy is not preaching but the report or exhortation or encouragement given by one individual to another for the latter's edification. Paul encouraged Timothy to draw upon the prophecies spoken over him as a way to "wage the good warfare" (1 Tim. 1:18). And in 1 Timothy 4:14 he urged him not to neglect the gift he had that was given to him "by prophecy" when the council of elders laid hands on him.

Finally, there are those instances in Acts that, although not explicitly called prophecies, appear to be such—things such as Peter's supernaturally given knowledge about the sin of Ananias and Sapphira (Acts 5:1–11), the revelation from the Spirit that Paul and Barnabas were to be set apart for missionary service (Acts 13:1–3), Paul's awareness that a paralyzed man had faith to be healed (Acts 14:8–10), the counsel given to Paul by disciples at Tyre (Acts 21:4), and the word given to Paul by Agabus (Acts 21:7–14).

Thus, preaching/teaching is grounded in an inspired text. Prophecy is the fruit of a revelation that often (but not always) comes spontaneously to a person. People may "learn" (1 Cor. 14:31) from prophecy no less than from preaching, but the fact that the *results* of each may be identical does not mean the *roots* are.

Who Can Prophesy?

There is nothing in Scripture to indicate that the gift of prophecy is gender specific. In fact, several texts explicitly speak of women prophesying to the edification of other believers (see Acts 2:17–18; 21:9; 1 Cor. 11:2–16). This does not necessarily mean that everyone, both male and female, will in fact prophesy. As Paul made clear, not all are prophets (1 Cor. 12:29). At the same time, he expressed his desire that "all" would prophesy (1 Cor. 14:5) because "the one who prophesies builds up [edifies] the church" (1 Cor. 14:4). In two other texts he seemed to envision the possibility that any Christian might speak prophetically (1 Cor. 14:24, 31). But again, we shouldn't conclude from this that everyone will. My sense is that Paul was drawing a distinction between, on the one hand, "prophets" who consistently display a facility and accuracy in this gift and, on the other, those who merely on occasion "prophesy." Thus, not all will be "prophets" (cf. 1 Cor. 12:29; Eph. 4:11), but it would appear that all *may* prophesy.

The Content of Prophetic Words

What might God disclose that would serve as the basis for prophetic utterances? The Scriptures provide us with few examples, but among them are revealing the "secrets" of the unbeliever's heart (1 Cor. 14:24–25), and a warning about impending persecution (Acts 21:4, 10–14). It may be that the Spirit would bring to mind a Scripture passage that applies especially at a particular moment in time to a person's life. Paul explicitly stated that whatever form prophetic revelation might take, it will typically serve to exhort, edify, and console another person (1 Cor. 14:3). In Acts 13:1–3 it appears that a prophetic word served to disclose the Spirit's will for the ministry of Saul and Barnabas. As Paul was preaching, he was the recipient of a revelation that a paralyzed man had the sort of faith that would lead to healing (Acts 14:9–10). And it would appear that it was by means of a prophetic revelation that Timothy received a spiritual gift (1 Tim. 4:14).

I see no reason why we should limit the range of prophetic activity to these few examples. The Spirit could conceivably make use of this gift to accomplish any number of goals. Although some believe the incident in Acts 5 is an example of the gift of word of knowledge (see the previous chapter), it is just as likely that the Spirit's revelation to Peter of the heart motivation in both Ananias and Sapphira was the basis for his prophetic discipline that ensued.

What Is the Purpose of Prophecy?

Paul said that prophecy *builds up* (*edifies*), *encourages*, and *consoles* (1 Cor. 14:3). When people are suddenly confronted with the inescapable reality that God truly knows their hearts and has heard their prayers and is intimately acquainted with all their ways, they are encouraged to press on and to persevere. I have often spoken with believers who, in spite of what they knew theologically to be true, *felt* as if God had forgotten them. Their prayers seemed never to be heard, much less answered. Then, often quite without warning, they receive a prophetic word from a total stranger that could be known only by God himself, and their faith is bolstered and their spirit consoled.

In January of 1991 I attended a large conference in Anaheim, California. At the time, I knew very little and had experienced even less of the so-called revelatory gifts of the Spirit. On the final day of the conference, I was invited to join about fifty other people in a private room. There I watched and listened attentively as a group of some four individuals prophesied to each of those in the room. When my turn came, I had no expectation that anything supernatural was about to occur. One of the four men, none of whom I had ever met or heard of before, looked intently at me and said, "I'm going to tell you what you've been praying in your hotel room these past few nights. And I have a strong sense from the Lord that he intends to answer your requests."

Well, he certainly had my attention. What followed was my first encounter with the gift of prophecy. This man quoted back to me my prayers, verbatim. I'm not talking about a general summary or a paraphrase, but the precise words that I had privately prayed the previous two nights. He then proceeded to describe what was happening in the church in Oklahoma where I was serving as pastor. If I may use the words of the apostle Paul, I was profoundly encouraged, edified, and consoled (1 Cor. 14:3)!

There was no attempt on this man's part to dazzle me with his insight. There was nothing overtly sensational about what happened that day, aside from the fact that the God to whom I had had prayed chose to reveal my requests to a man I'd never met. He hardly drew attention to himself, as only a handful of people were present and most likely none of them even heard what was spoken. What happened that day was a simple but undeniably supernatural display of the love of God for a struggling pastor. God made use of a prophetic gift to confirm his presence and power in my life and to show his providential care.

Prophecy can also function to disclose the secrets of the hearts of the unbelieving, leading them to repentance and faith in Christ (1 Cor. 14:24–25). On occasion a prophetic word can provide us with specific guidance on when to go, where to go, and with whom to go (we see this in Acts 13:1–3). Some suggest that Paul and Barnabas already knew they were called on mission and even where they were to go. This prophetic revelation was simply confirmation to them of what God had already revealed. We must remember that while God can make use of a prophetic revelation to guide and direct us, prophecy is not the primary means by which we make decisions in the Christian life. Prophecy is often more of a confirmation to us of what we have already discerned in reading Scripture or have heard from the wise counsel of close friends.

Yet another function of the prophetic gift is to provide us with the resources to wage war against Satan and the flesh and to encourage us in the Christian life. Consider what Paul said in 1 Timothy 1:18–19. There we discover that prophecy is one of the most powerful and reassuring tools God has given us by which we are to wage war in our ongoing battle with the world, the flesh, and the devil. "This charge I entrust to you, Timothy, my child, in accordance with the prophecies previously made about you, that *by them* [i.e., by means of the "prophecies" spoken to you] you may wage the good warfare, holding faith and a good conscience" (vv. 18–19a, emphasis mine).

Paul's appeal to young Timothy resounds with ear-shattering clarity: "Timothy, please, I implore you as my spiritual son, don't even think about trying to fight Satan, the enemy of our faith, without drawing strength and encouragement and power from the prophetic words delivered to you! Never attempt to face opposition in the church apart from the reassurance that flows from those revelatory words you received. Timothy, there is strength and confidence for you in the truth and certitude of those Spirit-prompted utterances that came to you at your ordination. By all means fight. Never fear. But fight fearlessly through the power of those prophetic words."

How do you wage a good war? How does one fight and resist the seductive allure of the passing pleasures of sin? By "holding faith and a good conscience." Paul had in mind both theological and ethical integrity, both right belief and right behavior, both orthodoxy and orthopraxy, both truth in our doctrinal affirmations and purity in our lives. This is no easy task! We are assaulted daily by those who would undermine our confidence in God and his Word. We struggle with anxiety, with provocations to lust, with greed, with despair and doubt and the temptation to quit. With what shall we fight? What shall we bring to bear against the deceitful promises of sin? Paul was clear: it is by means of the prophecies made about you that strength to stand firm is found.

Paul's exhortation is quite instructive given the fact that many think the spiritual gift of prophecy is inconsistent with sound doctrine or that if too much emphasis is placed on it that a person will go soft on theology and emphasize only experience. But Paul couldn't have said it with any greater clarity: The way you hold to the foundational truths of the Christian faith and resist the temptation to abandon them, the way you maintain a good conscience before God, is by thinking about and reflecting on and drawing strength from the prophetic words given to you by the Spirit!

We don't know what these prophetic utterances were, but there is no shortage of possibilities. Paul may have had in mind certain spiritual gifts that were promised to young Timothy, gifts on which he could rely and should now draw strength to fulfill his calling. Perhaps prophetic words were spoken over Timothy related to ministry opportunities or open doors that would expand his influence. There may well have been simple affirmations of Timothy in terms of his identity in Christ and God's purpose for his life. I've known people who received unique prophetic promises of God's presence and protection in the face of unusual danger. In Timothy's case, perhaps someone spoke powerfully of a biblical promise, drawn from a particular biblical text, that applied directly to him. Someone may have had a vision or dream that reinforced to Timothy his fitness and giftedness for ministry that would prove especially helpful when those older than him began to question his qualifications. We could speculate further, but no need. Timothy obviously would have known what Paul meant, even if we don't.

How does one appeal to such prophetic words to wage a good war? By constantly reminding oneself of God's commitment and presence and unshakable purpose to enable Timothy (and us) to fight doubt and anxiety and fear and despair. It is incredibly reassuring to recall tangible, empirically verifiable evidence of God's existence and power and presence communicated through a prophetic utterance.

I suspect that, perhaps long ago, some of you received words you believed were from God. But for whatever reason you've lost confidence in his promise. You've begun to wonder if it was really the Spirit who spoke. I encourage you to recover and revisit those words, rehearse them in your mind, meditate on them, put legs under them to see if God intended all along for you to be the means by which they are fulfilled. Pray them back to God (as did David in the Psalms) and hold him to his word. But whatever you do, never attempt to fight the battles of faith apart from the strength such words provide.

Is Prophecy an Ecstatic Experience?

The answer to this question depends on one's definition of *ecstasy*. It may mean that a person experiences a sense of mental detachment wherein they become unaware of their surroundings and, in varying degrees, oblivious to sight or sound. This may or may not entail complete loss of consciousness.

Others define *ecstasy* as something akin to divine seizure, in which the Holy Spirit overrides and usurps control of one's faculties of thought and speech. This was evidently the approach taken by Montanus in the early church and those associated with his ministry. However, in 1 Corinthians 14 the apostle Paul didn't teach that *ecstasy* is a part of the prophetic experience. Several factors support this conclusion.

- Paul assumed that the person prophesying was capable of recognizing from some form of signal that someone else had received a revelation and was ready to speak (v. 30). Clearly, then, the person was not oblivious to their surroundings.
- The person prophesying was also expected to cease speaking upon recognition that another had received a revelation ("let the first be silent," v. 30). The prophet could both speak and keep silent at will. Also, the second prophet didn't burst into speech but somehow indicated to the first, then waited until that person had stopped.
- Paul said that all who prophesied could do so in turn, "one by one" (v. 31), indicating the sensible and voluntary control of their faculties.
- In 1 Corinthians 14:32 Paul said that "the spirits of prophets are subject to prophets." He was likely referring to the many different manifestations of the one Holy Spirit through the spirit of each individual prophet (see also 14:12, 14–16). This means that the Holy Spirit will never force or compel a prophet to speak, but subjects his work to the wisdom of each individual. The Spirit voluntarily submits in this one respect for the sake of order. This isn't a theological declaration that we are in some sense superior to or more powerful than the Holy Spirit. It isn't the nature of the Spirit to incite confusion or to coerce the will; thus, he subordinates his inspiration to the prophet's own timing. This verse also answers a potential objection to Paul's instructions in verse 30. Someone might object by saying they were forced to prophesy, being unable to restrain herself or himself and thus unable to defer to a second (v. 30). Paul's answer was that the Holy Spirit remains subject to the prophets, never forcing a person to speak in a disorderly or chaotic way. The Spirit is neither impetuous nor uncontrollable.
- The case of tongues is in many respects parallel. The tongues speaker

could speak or be silent at will and was expected to follow a prescribed "order of service" in the exercise of the gift (vv. 27–28), something out of the question if he/she were in any sense mentally disengaged from events in the meeting.

Having ruled out ecstasy does not mean that the prophetic experience lacks an emotional dimension. The reception and communication of divine revelation may well entail spiritual excitement, a sense of urgency, and even an unmistakable sense of the presence of God.

Yet another hint that prophecy is not ecstatic is that it is always subject to and under the oversight of God and his sovereign will. This is what we see in Revelation 22:6: "And he said to me, 'These words are trustworthy and true. *And the Lord, the God of the spirits of the prophets*, has sent his angel to show his servants what must soon take place'" (emphasis mine).

The word "spirits" is what grammarians call an "objective" genitive. The idea can be paraphrased: "God *over* the spirits of the prophets" or "God *ruling* or *inspiring* the spirits of the prophets." In any case, God is clearly portrayed as sovereign over what prophets prophesy. God, as it were, owns, operates, and oversees the ministry of true prophets. This confirms what we saw in the previous point in 1 Corinthians 14, that the prophetic is entirely dependent on God, always awaiting his anointing and activity. Prophets may prophesy at will, but they only receive revelation by the initiative of God. Thus, more so than with the gift of teaching, prophets are somewhat *passive*, being *instruments or conduits* for the revelatory word of God, whereas teachers are more *active*, drawing directly from the Scriptures and expounding what they interpret. This is, in fact, the primary distinction between the prophetic gift and the teaching gift: the former is dependent on a spontaneous revelation while the latter is dependent on an inscripturated text. However, this should not be taken to mean that the Spirit is not also active in the exercise of other spiritual gifts, such as teaching.

Is the word "spirits" a reference to the human spirit of each prophet, or is it a reference to the Holy Spirit? Some find it problematic to suggest that the Holy Spirit would be mentioned in the plural. But remember: (1) the plural is used for the Holy Spirit in Revelation 1:4; 4:5; 5:6; and (2) when the human spirit is energized by a charismatic manifestation of the Holy Spirit (i.e., when a spiritual gift is in operation), Paul seems to have in mind both;

in 1 Corinthians 14 it is difficult to know when one should translate *pneuma* as "Spirit" and when as "spirit." Gordon Fee simply renders it "S/spirit."[3]

Paul used the same terminology in 1 Corinthians 14:32 ("the spirits of prophets are subject to prophets"; the only difference is that in Revelation the definite article appears: "*the* spirits of *the* prophets"). There he has in mind the control by the prophet of the manifestation of the Spirit, confirming what we saw earlier, that contrary to those who think prophecy is an ecstatic and uncontrollable phenomenon that overwhelms and overrides the will of the prophet, each individual is capable of consciously refraining from prophetic utterance in accordance with the rules and decorum for prophetic ministry in the church.

Ephesians 2:20[4]

Cessationists typically make much of Ephesians 2:20, where Paul said that the church is "built on the foundation of the apostles and prophets, Christ Jesus himself being the cornerstone." They typically insist that *all* New Testament prophets functioned foundationally. That is to say, together with the original apostles, prophets always spoke in such a way that they were contributing to the once-for-all theological and ethical foundation of the universal body of Christ.

But there is nothing to suggest that "the prophets" in Ephesians 2:20 is an exhaustive reference to all possible prophets in the church. Why should we conclude that the only kind of prophetic activity is "foundational" in nature, especially in light of what the New Testament says about the extent and effect of prophetic ministry? Suffice it here to say that many cessationists seem to believe that once apostles and prophets ceased to function foundationally, they ceased to function altogether, as if the only purpose for apostles and prophets was to lay the foundation of the church. Nowhere does the New Testament say this, least of all in Ephesians 2:20. This text need say no more than that apostles and prophets laid the foundation once and for all and then

---

3   Gordon D. Fee, *God's Empowering Presence* (Peabody, MA: Hendrickson, 1994), 229.

4   I have written on this text in my chapter "Ephesians 2:20—The Cessationist's 'Go-To' Text," in *Strangers to Fire: When Tradition Trumps Scripture*, ed. Robert W. Graves (Woodstock, GA: Foundation for Pentecostal Scholarship, 2014), 69–72. See also chapter 10 in this book for a more extensive treatment of this text.

ceased to function *in that capacity.* But nothing suggests that they ceased to function in other capacities, much less that they ceased to exist altogether. It is certainly true that *only* apostles and prophets lay the foundation of the church, but it is anything but certain that such is the *only* thing they do.

In a word, the portrayal in Acts and 1 Corinthians of who could prophesy and how it was to be done in the life of the church simply does not fit with the cessationist assertion that Ephesians 2:20 describes all possible prophets, every one of whom functioned as part of the once-for-all foundation of the church. Rather, Paul was there describing a limited group of prophets who were closely connected to the apostles, both of which groups spoke Scripture-quality words essential to the foundation of the church universal.

From this brief analysis of the nature and function of prophecy, we can see why Paul declared that it is good for upbuilding, encouragement, and consolation (1 Cor. 14:3). But is this New Testament expression of prophecy identical with what we see in the Old Testament? Now that we have a grasp of the New Testament spiritual gift of prophecy, we turn our attention to the highly controversial question of whether it is identical with or different from Old Testament prophecy.

CHAPTER 10

Is the New Testament Spiritual Gift of Prophecy Different from Old Testament Prophecy?

Virtually all cessationists insist that the New Testament gift of prophecy is the same as prophecy in the Old Testament. Since the latter was always infallible, the former must also be without error.[1] Thus, any notion of a fallible prophetic word, a word that contains both elements of truth and potential error, is ruled out right from the start. Continuationists, on the other hand, believe that the New Testament gift of prophecy is of a lesser authority than that which we see in the Old Testament. It often comes as a mixture of infallible divine revelation and human, potentially fallible interpretation and application.

Since I am a continuationist, I embrace the view that what we see in the New Testament exercise of the prophetic gift carries the potential for error. Of course, the question that must be answered is whether substantial reasons exist in the New Testament documents themselves to justify this understanding. I believe there are.

---

1 In this regard, one should consult Andrew Wilson's article "The Continuation of the Charismata," in *Themelios* 44.1 (2019): 16–22. Wilson makes a strong case for concluding that not all prophesying in the Old Testament was infallible divine revelation. He develops his argument based on the equally insightful comments of Iain M. Duguid, "What Kind of Prophecy Continues? Defining the Differences between Continuationism and Cessationism," in *Redeeming the Life of the Mind: Essays in Honor of Vern Poythress*, ed. John Frame, Wayne Grudem, and John Hughes (Wheaton, IL: Crossway, 2017), 112–28.

Arguments That Suggest New Testament Prophecy Is Different from Old Testament Prophecy

I should acknowledge from the beginning that the distinction between Old Testament prophecy and the New Testament spiritual gift of prophecy is not based on an explicit assertion in any particular text but is rather the cumulative inference drawn from observations on how the gift of prophecy is described in the New Testament.

The shift from Old Testament prophecy to the New Testament spiritual gift is first seen in the events of Pentecost. We've already had occasion to note what might be called the democratization of the Spirit. Unlike what was true under the old covenant, all believers in the age of the new covenant are recipients of the permanent indwelling presence of the Holy Spirit. Young and old, male and female, indeed "all flesh" from every socioeconomic and educational dimension of life who know and love Christ are baptized in the Spirit and indwelt by him. The result of this, said Peter (quoting Joel), is that they are the recipients of revelatory dreams and visions that form the basis of their prophetic utterances.

Under the terms of the old covenant, only select individuals were enabled to prophesy. But a characteristic feature of the new covenant is that its members all have at least the *potential* to prophesy. Whether all actually do was addressed in an earlier chapter. Although the universalizing of the Spirit's presence does not in itself prove that the authority of New Testament prophecy is of a lesser nature than that of Old Testament prophecy, it unmistakably alerts us to a quite significant and substantial change in how the Spirit of God operates in the lives of God's people. It strikes me as odd, if not implausible, to say that every Christian in the age of the new covenant has the potential to speak infallible and inerrant words from God, which, as most cessationists contend, would constitute the abiding and morally obligatory foundation on which the universal body of Christ is built. So let's explore this issue in a bit more detail.

In his book on spiritual gifts, cessationist Tom Schreiner cites Ephesians 2:20 and concludes that "New Testament prophets have the same authority as the apostles" and that all prophetic ministry was designed to establish the theological and ethical principles on which the church of Jesus Christ would be built.[2] Again, he insists that "if prophecy still exists today, it is hard to resist the conclusion that the foundation established by the apostles and prophets hasn't been completed."[3] Again, says Schreiner, "We see in Ephesians 2:20 that the words of the prophets play a decisive role in the shaping of the doctrine and life of the church. . . . They [the prophets] play a foundational role in establishing the church of Jesus Christ."[4] Let's be sure, right from the start, what this view entails. On Schreiner's understanding of the gift of prophecy, Philip's four daughters (see Acts 21:8–9) spoke with "the same authority as the apostles." Likewise, every single one of the "sons" and "daughters" and "young men" and "old men" and "male servants" and "female servants" whom Peter cited as prophesying (Acts 2:17–18) spoke with "the same authority as the apostles." Are we really prepared to say that? Does the way the spiritual gift of prophecy is portrayed in the New Testament correspond to this assertion? In other words, when we look at how prophecy actually functioned in practice in the lives of God's people, does it lead us to conclude that Schreiner's understanding of Ephesians 2:20 is true, that all New Testament prophecy is infallible and morally binding foundational truth? I believe the answer to that is no.

Let me remind you again of Schreiner's assertion, namely, that all prophetic revelation was inerrant and foundational to the universal church of Jesus Christ. Yet, as just noted, we read in Acts 2 that when the Spirit is poured out on "all flesh. . . your sons and your daughters shall prophesy," which according to Schreiner means that every son and daughter who prophesied was contributing infallible revelation essential to the building up of the universal church of Christ. Likewise, we would conclude the same about the "young men" and "old men" and the "male servants" and "female servants." Do we really believe that all of the prophetic utterances that came forth from all God's people listed here are essential to the foundation of the universal body of Christ? Since you and I are a part of that body and are required by God to submit our lives to whatever theological and ethical truths are contained in that foundation, it would be quite helpful for us to know what they are. But nowhere in Scripture are any of these revelatory experiences recorded.

---

2 Thomas R. Schreiner, *Spiritual Gifts: What They Are and Why They Matter* (Nashville: B&H, 2018), 104.

3 Schreiner, 107.

4 Schreiner, 108.

I would also like to know what was said by the prophets at Antioch (Acts 13:1), since all prophetic revelation is allegedly essential to the constitution and formation of the universal church. But neither I nor anyone else knows what they said in their prophetic utterances. Are we being asked to believe that the revelation they received was foundational to the beliefs and behavior of all Christians in every age? I find that hard to believe.

It would also be extremely beneficial to my spiritual life to know what was prophesied by the unnamed disciples of John the Baptist in Acts 19. If their words were foundational and universally binding on the conscience of all Christians in every age, it would behoove us to know what they were. But nowhere in Scripture are we told anything they said. And what about Philip's four daughters who, according to Luke, "prophesied" (Acts 21:9). It would seem we are required to believe that these four single women spoke infallible truth into the foundation of the universal body of Christ. Aside from the fact that I find that quite implausible, how would complementarians feel about four young women speaking authoritative theological truth into the life of all men in the body of Christ?

I would also like to know what the prophets in the church at Rome (Rom. 12:6) had to say, since according to cessationists, everything they said constituted a contribution to the foundation of the church. The same may be said of the numerous prophetic utterances described in 1 Corinthians 14 (see v. 26). And how could the encouragement, edification, and consolation of believers in first-century Corinth, none of which I or anybody else knows about, serve to establish the theological parameters of the universal church of Jesus Christ? I'm particularly curious about how the disclosure of an unbeliever's sin in 1 Corinthians 14:24–25 could be foundational to the universal church. The same could be said about the hundreds, if not thousands, of unrecorded prophetic utterances in the churches at Thessalonica (1 Thess. 5), Ephesus (1 Timothy), Caesarea (Acts 21), Philippi, Colossae, and elsewhere.

To be even more specific, are we being asked to believe that the "prophecies" given personally to Timothy, by which, said Paul, he was to "wage the good warfare, holding faith and a good conscience" (1 Tim. 1:18–19), are essential to the beliefs and behavior of all Christians in every age? If so, it would have been helpful if Paul or Timothy or anyone had recorded and preserved them for us. And how does the prophetic utterance over Timothy at his "ordination" (1 Tim. 4:14) serve to build the universal body of Christ? In what possible sense could that have been foundational to the church?

Thus, to say that all prophetic revelation in the New Testament is infallible, inerrant, and served to establish the principles and practices of the universal church, simply does not measure up to the way the spiritual gift of prophecy actually functioned in the lives of God's people.

Yes, some prophets functioned foundationally, but not all. Yes, some revelation that formed the basis and content of some prophecy was designed by God to constitute the theological and ethical foundation of the universal body of Christ. But by no means all. The way in which prophetic ministry is described in the many churches of the first century necessarily leads me to conclude that Ephesians 2:20 speaks only of those prophets who functioned foundationally. It certainly can in no way be inclusive of every other instance of prophetic ministry recorded for us in the New Testament.

Another indication that the New Testament spiritual gift of prophecy differs from Old Testament prophecy concerns the parallel change in the nature of the office of priest. In the Old Testament, the priests were taken only from the tribe of Levi, and only a very few in each generation were selected to minister in the temple of God. The priesthood was a limited, restricted office, and those who were priests had a special privilege of access into the presence of God in the temple that was not allowed for others in Israel.

But in the new covenant we have all become priests: "But you are a chosen race, a royal priesthood" (1 Peter 2:9). We all have confidence to enter the very holy of holies because we have obtained the rights that were restricted to the priests in the Old Testament (see Heb. 10:19–22; 12:22–24). The apostle John wrote, "To him who loves us and has freed us from our sins by his blood and made us a kingdom, priests to his God and Father, to him be glory and dominion forever and ever" (Rev. 1:5–6; see also 5:10).

Wayne Grudem has concluded from these passages that, according to cessationists, the office of priest in the New Testament has to be exactly the same as the office of priest in the Old Testament. Therefore, only a very few people can be priests, and they must descend from only one family. They need to offer sacrifices in a temple just as the priests did in the Old Testament. Of course, such an argument would be foolish, for we see in the New Testament that the office of priest has expanded to all of God's people. Under the terms of the new covenant, the functions of the office of priest have changed significantly. We all are priests now, but we no longer serve in an earthly temple or offer earthly sacrifices, for we all have direct access to God in prayer through the way that has been opened to us by our Great High Priest, Jesus Christ.

Just as the office of priest has changed significantly from the old covenant to the new covenant, so there is significant evidence that the office of prophet has also changed significantly. Thousands of God's people are now "prophets," but they no longer speak the very words of God to be added to the Bible. Rather, they report things that have been shown to them or revealed to them by God, yet their words have merely human authority, not the absolute divine authority of the very words of God. Their prophecies do not belong to Scripture. They have to be tested and evaluated (1 Cor. 14:29; 1 Thess. 5:20–21).[5]

So my question, once again, is this: If such words, each one of them, were the very "Word of God" and thus equal to Scripture in authority, what happened to them? Why were the New Testament authors so lacking in concern for whether other Christians heard them and obeyed them? Why were they not preserved for subsequent generations of the church? I'm not suggesting this proves that these "revelatory gifts" operated at a lower level of authority, but it certainly strikes me as odd that the New Testament would portray the operation of the gift of prophecy in this manner if in fact all such "words" were Scripture quality and essential to building the foundation for the universal body of Christ.

As best I can tell, the only two recorded prophecies that were preserved and included in the canonical text of Scripture were both from Agabus (Acts 11:27–30 and 21:10–12). Does it not strike you as odd that no effort was made to retain and impose on the conscience of all Christians everywhere so much as a single, solitary syllable from all those alleged "Scripture-quality" and divinely inspired words?

In his book Schreiner attempts to dismiss this point by arguing that there was a lot of prophetic revelation in the Old Testament that was never inscripturated, or included in the biblical canon, so why should we expect anything different in the New Testament? The answer is obvious: nowhere are we told

---

5 The preceding was adapted from an unpublished paper written by Wayne Grudem and made available to me. It is cited here with his permission.

in the Old Testament that all prophetic revelation was foundational to the universal church of Jesus Christ. But that is precisely what Schreiner argues in the case of all New Testament prophecy. The situations, therefore, are decidedly different. My good friend Tom Schreiner cannot so easily dismiss the absence from Scripture of potentially tens of thousands of prophetic words since he believes that every single one of those prophetic words is infallible, authoritative (in a way that is equal to that of the apostles themselves), and foundational to the life and beliefs of the universal body of Christ.

Prophecy in the New Testament

As we continue to pursue an answer to this question of whether the New Testament gift of prophecy is different from Old Testament prophecy, our attention turns to Paul's counsel to the church at Thessalonica. He exhorted them to not "quench the Spirit" by "despis[ing] prophecies" (1 Thess. 5:19–20). Rather, they were to "test everything"; that is, they were to weigh, judge, evaluate, or assess what purports to be a prophetic word and then "hold fast what is good" and "abstain from every form of evil" (vv. 21–22).[6]

Paul effusively praised the church in Thessalonica for the high regard in which they held the Word of God. When they heard the word that Paul proclaimed, they "accepted it not as the word of men but as what it really is, the word of God, which is at work in you believers" (1 Thess. 2:13). If these Christians believed (as cessationists tell us they should have) that prophetic words in their church were equal in authority to Scripture, they would have esteemed them highly and would never have "despised" them. If Paul had taught them (as cessationists tell us he did) that such "words" were revelation on a par with and possessing equal authority to the very Scripture that he was writing to communicate this concept (namely, the letter of 1 Thessalonians itself), would the Thessalonian Christians have been guilty of despising them?

I think it far more likely that these believers were tempted to "despise" prophetic utterances because they knew that such "words" were a mixture of divine revelation and fallible human interpretation and application, and that, for whatever reason, people in their midst had in some way abused the

---

6 The parallel text in 1 Cor. 14:29, where Paul exhorted his readers to "weigh what is said," also points to a difference between Old Testament and New Testament prophecy. I'll take up this text in chapter 11.

gift or had used such words to manipulate others or promote themselves or had predicted some event(s) that had not come to pass.

If the prophetic utterances in Thessalonica were equal in authority to Scripture and altogether infallible, would not Paul have harshly rebuked the Thessalonians for not receiving them as such but for treating them as dispensable and unimportant? If such "words" were perfectly infallible revelation on a par with Scripture, would he not have simply said, "Submit to them without hesitation and obey them" rather than "test" them to see what is in them that is good and what is in them that is bad?

One must also wonder about the difference, between the two testaments, in the consequences for having prophesied "falsely." Much is made of the fact that in the Old Testament a false prophet would be subject to the death penalty by stoning. But what is said in the New Testament about how to respond to those whose words are determined to be less than fully accurate? We know that Paul commanded the church to "weigh" prophetic words (1 Cor. 14:29) and to "test" prophetic utterances (1 Thess. 5:20–21). But what is said should be done if such words turn out on assessment to be false? Nothing. The people who delivered such words are not rebuked. They are not disciplined. They are not excommunicated. And neither are they called "false prophets"! The terminology of "false prophet" is reserved exclusively in the New Testament for the non-Christian, the unregenerate man or woman who denies the fundamental truths of the faith, in particular the doctrine of the incarnation of Christ (see Matt. 7:15–23; 24:11; Mark 13:22; Luke 6:26; Acts 13:6–12; 2 Peter 2:1–3; 1 John 4:1–3; and note that 2 John 7 does not contain the words "false prophets" but rather "deceivers" and is clearly parallel to 1 John 4:1–3).

What I'm suggesting is that not everyone who prophesied "falsely" is necessarily a "false prophet." One can misinterpret a revelation from God and perhaps misapply it to God's people but not for that reason stand in jeopardy of death or even church discipline. If New Testament prophecy was always as inerrant and infallible as Old Testament prophecy, one would expect some measure of parallel in our response to and treatment of it. I'm not saying that the death penalty for false prophets in the Old Testament should be carried over into the New Testament. I'm simply saying that the New Testament speaks loudly when, instead, there is complete and utter silence about how to deal with someone in the new covenant who speaks with less than perfect accuracy.

In 1 Corinthians 14:30–31 Paul wrote, "If a revelation is made to another sitting there, let the first be silent. For you can all prophesy one by one, so that all may learn and all be encouraged."[7] Paul appeared to be indifferent toward the possibility that the first prophecy might be lost and never heard by the church. Some object and say that the first prophetic word wouldn't necessarily be lost. The person could simply remain silent until the second had finished and then resume his speech. But as Wayne Grudem has pointed out,

> If the first prophet was expected to resume speaking, why then would Paul command this first prophet to be silent at all? If the first prophet could retain his revelation and speak later, then so could the second prophet. And in that case it would make much more sense for the second prophet to wait, instead of rudely interrupting the first prophet and making him give his speech in two parts.[8]

Again, Paul's apparent lack of concern for the loss of such prophetic words seems incompatible with a belief that they were equal in authority with Scripture itself.

Two additional texts in 1 Corinthians 14 may provide additional support for the notion that New Testament prophecy operates at a lower level of authority than that of Old Testament prophecy (although cessationists dispute my interpretation of both texts). In verse 36 Paul asked, "Or was it from you that the word of God came?" This question was designed to prevent the church from making up guidelines for public worship based on an alleged prophetic word, contrary to what he had just stated. His point is that a Scripture-quality, authoritative "word of God" had not, in fact, been forthcoming from the Corinthian prophets. Paul did not deny that they had truly prophesied, but he denied that their "words" were equal in authority to his own. Such "words" were in fact of a lesser authority.

Related to the above is 1 Corinthians 14:37–38, where Paul wrote, "If anyone thinks that he is a prophet, or spiritual, he should acknowledge

---

7 The force of "all" here has been disputed. Interpretations range from "all" the prophets, to "all" without distinction as to gender or social standing (rather than a universal "all" without exception), to "all" potentially, but not in actual practice. The latter strikes me as the more likely view.

8 Wayne Grudem, *The Gift of Prophecy in the New Testament and Today* (Wheaton, IL: Crossway, 2000), 63.

that the things I am writing to you are a command of the Lord. If anyone does not recognize this, he is not recognized." Paul was clearly claiming a divine authority for his words that he was just as obviously denying to the Corinthians. "According to Paul, the words of the prophets at Corinth were not and could not have been sufficiently authoritative to show Paul to be wrong."[9] And yet Paul believed the prophecy at Corinth to be a good and help-ful gift of God, for he immediately thereafter exhorted the Corinthians once again to "earnestly desire to prophesy" (v. 39)! It would appear that the apostle believed that the spiritual gift of congregational prophecy, which operated at a lower level of authority than did the apostolic, canonical, expression of it, was still extremely valuable to the church. No one has articulated this with greater clarity than D. A. Carson. He writes:

> The presupposition seems to be that if a prophecy is in any sense revelatory, it must be true, and thus authoritative—and therefore what is there to pre-vent a contemporary "prophet" from, say, annulling various components of the new covenant in much the same way that the New Testament writers claim to fulfill and therefore transcend certain aspects of the old cove-nant? But the remarkable fact is that Paul takes the prophecy *of his own day* to be in some sense revelatory (14:30) and yet to have less authority than his own written word. One cannot fail to perceive that those interpretations of New Testament prophecy that insist it enjoys the same authority status as Old Testament canonical prophecy see in the phenomenon a great deal more than the apostle himself allows. Conversely, of course, this verse pre-supposes not only considerable authority vested in the apostle Paul, but his self-conscious awareness of it. Some of the protestations over the obscurity of this verse are located, I think, in the failure to recognize this fact.[10]

A close look at Paul's own personal experience as recorded in Acts 21 should also prove helpful.[11] We are told that when he arrived in Tyre that

---

9 Grudem, 68.

10 D. A. Carson, *Showing the Spirit: A Theological Exposition of 1 Corinthians 12–14* (1987; repr., Grand Rapids: Baker, 2019), 172–73.

11 See the discussion of this story in my article "Revelatory Gifts of the Spirit and the Sufficiency of Scripture: Are They Compatible?" in *Scripture and the People of God: Essays in Honor of Wayne Grudem*, edited by John DelHousaye, John J. Hughes, and Jeff T. Purswell (Wheaton, IL: Crossway, 2018), 91–93.

"through the Spirit [*dia tou pneumatos*[12]] they [the disciples at Tyre] were telling Paul not to go on to Jerusalem" (Acts 21:4). Upon arriving in Caesarea several days later, he was the recipient of a prophetic word from a man named Agabus to the effect that, if he were to go to Jerusalem, he would be bound by the Jews and delivered over to the Gentiles. It is entirely likely that Agabus was joined in this word to Paul by the "four unmarried daughters" of Philip, each of whom "prophesied" (Acts 21:9). In any case, Agabus prefaced his word with the statement, "Thus says the Holy Spirit" (v. 11a). The specific way in which the Spirit "spoke" through the disciples at Tyre and revealed this scenario to Agabus is not made known. Agabus, unlike those in Tyre, did not himself tell Paul not to continue his journey to Jerusalem, but upon hearing his revelatory vision concerning Paul, Luke and the people in Caesarea "urged him not to go up to Jerusalem" (v. 12b).

Here we see the connection with 1 Thessalonians 5. Paul chose *not* to heed the advice given to him (v. 13). In the final analysis, following what must have been highly emotional dialogue (see vv. 13–14) in which no agreement could be reached (v. 14a), the apostle retained his prior commitment to finish the journey. The conclusion of all concerned was mutual: "Let the will of the Lord be done" (Acts 21:14b).

At no time did Paul dispute with either the Christians in Tyre or Agabus and insist that the Spirit did not reveal that his arrival in Jerusalem would bring harsh persecution. He did not suggest that the revelatory vision or word that Agabus claimed came from the Spirit was in fact fabricated or misguided. Why, then, did Paul choose to act contrary to what the disciples in Tyre had said? The answer is found earlier in Acts 19:21. There we read that "Paul resolved in the Spirit to pass through Macedonia and Achaia and go to Jerusalem, saying, 'After I have been there, I must also see Rome.'" Paul's decision to go to Jerusalem was as much a product of the Spirit's revelatory ministry as was that of the Christians in Tyre and of Agabus who warned him of persecution should he go there. He had resolved "in the [Holy] Spirit" to make the journey. This understanding is confirmed in Acts 20:22 where Paul declared, "And now, behold, I am going to Jerusalem, constrained by the Spirit, not knowing what will happen to me there, except

---

12 This same Greek phrase appears in Acts 11:28 to describe the means, manner, or perhaps better still, the source and power through which Agabus delivered his prophetic word concerning an impending famine.

that the Holy Spirit testifies to me in every city that imprisonment and afflictions await me."

How do we account for Paul's decision to resist the urging of his friends that he not go to Jerusalem?[13] Clearly the Spirit who spoke to believers in Tyre and to Agabus and the four daughters of Philip had also revealed to Paul that he *should* go, notwithstanding what others might say. Indeed, he was "constrained" by the Spirit to finish this journey to Jerusalem.

I believe the best way to account for this is by recognizing that in any particular "prophetic utterance" there are at least three elements. There is (1) the divine *revelation* from the Spirit, which in all instances is inspired and infallible. There is also (2) the human *interpretation* of what that revelation means. Finally, there is an attempt to make (3) *application* to the person(s) involved.

The likelihood is that several Christians at Tyre had received a revelation from the Holy Spirit (perhaps in a vision or dream) that troubles awaited Paul in Jerusalem. If he were to proceed with his travel plans to visit the city, he would probably be severely persecuted. His life might well be in danger. This *revelation*, being as it was from God, was altogether accurate and infallible. But the *interpretation* they drew from it was not. They inferred that it was God's will for Paul not to go. With that conclusion, they then (mis)*applied* this revelation to Paul by fervently appealing to him that he make alternative travel plans. As far as they were concerned, it simply could never be God's will for Paul to venture into a territory where life-threatening persecution awaited him. Their love for the apostle and understandable concern for his safety led them to urge him not to go.

And what was Paul's response? He did precisely what he instructed the Thessalonians to do whenever a prophetic utterance was delivered. He *tested* it. He weighed and analyzed it against the standard of his own experience with the Spirit. Based on earlier, repeated guidance from the Spirit, Paul knew that the Christians in Tyre and Agabus and the others were correct that should he go to Jerusalem he would be sorely persecuted. But he obviously concluded that they had either misinterpreted or more likely still, out of understandable concern for his welfare, had misapplied the revelation by insisting that he not continue his trip.

---

13 I have addressed several possible explanations in my book *Practicing the Power: Welcoming the Gifts of the Holy Spirit in Your Life* (Grand Rapids: Zondervan, 2017), 113–14, and won't rehearse them here.

Thus, we see that Paul's own personal practice as a recipient of a prophetic utterance indicates that he did not regard the revelatory word as bearing Scripture-quality authority. Whereas the revelation itself was altogether true (having come from God, it must of necessity be true), it must be communicated by fallible human men and women. It strikes me as most plausible to conclude that Paul believed all prophetic utterances to be a mixture of sorts in which the infallible divine revelation is processed through the fallible interpretive grid of Christian men and women who in turn, on occasion, make applications that are inconsistent with what either Scripture might already have made clear or what one's own experience under the guidance of the Spirit had previously established.

I would also draw attention to Schreiner's attempt to reconcile Acts 21:4 with his view of all prophecy as infallible and authoritative. He argues that the prophecy in 21:4 is that "Paul would suffer"[14] in Jerusalem. He then says that their urging Paul not to go to Jerusalem was only an "inference."[15] But the text does not say that Paul would suffer in Jerusalem. It says he *should not go* to Jerusalem. Again, here is what we read in Acts 21:4: "And having sought out the disciples, we stayed there for seven days. And through the Spirit they were telling Paul not to go on to Jerusalem." The text does not say what Schreiner says it says. It does not say that "through the Spirit they were telling Paul he would suffer in Jerusalem." What Schreiner calls the "inference" is in fact the very prophecy itself. And it was inconsistent with what the Holy Spirit had repeatedly told Paul. As I pointed out above, in Acts 19:21 we read that "Paul resolved in the Spirit to . . . go to Jerusalem." Again in 20:22 he said, "And now, behold, I am going to Jerusalem, constrained by the Spirit."

Again, Schreiner writes, "Thus the prophecy that Paul would face suffering in Jerusalem was accurate and Spirit-inspired; the conclusion that people drew from the prophecy—that Paul should not travel to Jerusalem—was mistaken."[16] But I humbly point out one final time: that is not what the text says. The disciples in Tyre "through the Spirit" were not telling Paul that suffering awaited him. No, they were telling Paul "not to go up to Jerusalem." What Schreiner calls the "inference" or "conclusion" is in fact the very prophetic word itself.

---

14 Schreiner, *Spiritual Gifts*, 117.
15 Schreiner, 117.
16 Schreiner, 117.

The conclusion from this must be that Agabus and company's prophetic utterance was neither infallible nor authoritative for Paul's life, something Paul himself must have concluded based on his own prior revelatory encounter with the Spirit concerning his missionary journeys. The revelation concerning what would happen to Paul in Jerusalem was infallible and accurate. But it was misinterpreted and thus misapplied. What, then, should they have done? Once they received the revelation, they should have prayed about it, discussed it among themselves, and then sat down with Paul and shared it with him without interpreting it and applying it. I can only conclude that whereas Paul didn't question the validity of the revelation they received, neither did he believe that they were speaking to him the very words of God such that disobedience would constitute a sin. In other words, based on previous and oft-repeated guidance from the Spirit, Paul knew that whereas they had heard God correctly, they had to some extent misinterpreted and assuredly misapplied what he said.

My next argument comes from an implication regarding Paul's permission that women can prophesy but his prohibition of them from teaching men or participating in the public evaluation of prophetic utterances. Clearly women can prophesy (see Acts 2:17–18; 21:9; 1 Cor. 11:5). But if that is true, what did he mean in 1 Corinthians 14:34 when he said, "The women should keep silent in the churches. For they are not permitted to speak"? The likely answer is that Paul was prohibiting women from participating in the passing of judgment on or the public evaluation of the prophets (14:29). Evidently he believed that this entailed an exercise of authority restricted to men only (see 1 Tim. 2:12–15).

If one should ask why Paul would allow women to prophesy but not evaluate the prophecies of others, the answer is in the nature of prophecy itself. Prophecy, unlike teaching, does not entail the exercise of an authoritative position within the local church. The prophet was but an instrument through whom revelation is reported to the congregation. "Those who prophesied did not tell the church how to interpret and apply Scripture to life. They did not proclaim the doctrinal and ethical standards by which the church was guided, nor did they exercise governing authority in the church."[17]

But to publicly evaluate or criticize or judge prophetic utterances is

---

17 Grudem, *The Gift of Prophecy in the New Testament and Today*, 121–22.

another matter. In this activity one could hardly avoid explicit theological and ethical instruction of other believers. If we assume that in 1 Timothy 2 Paul prohibited women from teaching or exercising authority over men, it's understandable why he would allow women to prophesy in 1 Corinthians 11:5 but forbid them from judging the prophetic utterances of others (especially men) in 14:34.

Simply put, how can complementarians deny women a teaching ministry that entails the exercise of authority, on the one hand, and then affirm that women prophesied with an authority equal to that of the apostles, on the other? It would seem that either they must abandon their complementarian convictions, or that they must recognize that there was a form of prophecy that was not foundational in nature and did not entail an authority equal to that of the apostles. And if they opt for the latter, there would then be no conflict between the ongoing validity of prophecy today and the finality and sufficiency of the biblical canon.

So, again, my question is this: If all New Testament prophets exercised an authority equal to that of the apostles, and women prophesied, how could Paul prohibit women from exercising the apostolic authority that is inherent within the New Testament gift of prophecy? We continuationist complementarians have no problem with this, for we recognize that not all New Testament prophecy was foundational and not all New Testament prophecy carried the same authority as that of the apostles. Therefore, for Paul to endorse women prophesying and yet prohibit women from exercising authority over men is entirely understandable.

My final question grows out of the exhortation of Paul that Christians should "earnestly desire the higher gifts" (1 Cor. 12:31), included among which (perhaps even most of all) being the gift of prophecy. Again, in 1 Corinthians 14:1, he wrote, "Pursue love, and earnestly desire the spiritual gifts, especially that you may prophesy." And as much as Paul wanted them all to speak in tongues, he desired "even more" that they should "prophesy" (1 Cor. 14:5). Finally, he closed this chapter in 1 Corinthians with the exhortation: "So, my brothers, earnestly desire to prophesy, and do not forbid speaking in tongues" (v. 39).

Paul's instruction to the churches throughout the first-century world would undoubtedly have been identical to his instruction to the Corinthians. The apostle did not embrace one perspective on revelatory gifts that would apply to the Corinthians and yet another, different perspective for the churches in Macedonia and Italy and elsewhere. Likewise, the same set of practical guidelines imposed on the Corinthians would have been required of all Christians in every other city and church.

If Paul actually viewed the revelation on which prophecy was based as infallible, morally authoritative, and essential to establishing the foundation of the universal church, we must be willing to say that the apostle urged every Christian in every local congregation to earnestly desire that he or she might be the recipient of inspired and authoritative revelation that would both enable them to speak with the authority of an apostle and also serve to lay the foundation for the body of Christ throughout all ages. I'm not willing to do that.

CHAPTER 11

Judging Prophetic Utterances, and the
Spiritual Gift of Discerning of Spirits

In reading the chapter title, you may at first think it strange that I'm addressing how to judge prophetic words in the same chapter with my discussion of the spiritual gift of discerning of spirits. But not a few would argue that they are the same thing. They point to the fact that the gift of distinguishing of spirits in 1 Corinthians 12:10 appears to be coupled with the gift of prophecy in much the same way "interpretation" is coupled with the gift of tongues. Thus, to discern or distinguish between spirits, so goes the argument, is simply Paul's way of describing the passing of judgment or the assessment of a prophetic utterance. I don't believe this is the case (see below). But you can now understand why I thought it helpful to address both phenomena in the same chapter.

How Do We Judge or Evaluate Prophetic Words?

The word of God never calls on Christians to suspend their critical faculties and naively or gullibly embrace as truth everything that purports to be from the Holy Spirit. We are repeatedly exhorted to make use of our minds and to exercise discernment. This is certainly the case when it comes to our response to prophetic words. Twice the apostle Paul spoke to this point.

Christians often struggle to strike a proper biblical balance between two essential truths that we find in Scripture. On the one hand, we long to give the Spirit full rein to work in our midst; we have no desire to quench the "fire" of his presence and power. Yet, on the other hand, we acknowledge the importance of diligently assessing or judging the biblical validity of what purports to be a revelatory disclosure through some prophetic utterance. Paul was keenly aware of this tension and provided us with this helpful instruction: "Do not quench the Spirit. Do not despise prophecies, but test everything; hold fast what is good. Abstain from every form of evil" (1 Thess. 5:19–22).

You will immediately notice that, whereas we might quench the Spirit in any number of ways, Paul specifically had in mind how it happens in our response to prophecy. The imagery of "quenching" the Spirit reminds us that his work in our midst is compared to a fire, a burning presence that we must never douse with the water of denominational rules or fear or skepticism. But that does not mean that anything goes, as if no rules or boundaries should ever be placed on what is permitted to occur in our corporate gatherings. The alternative to quenching the Spirit is biblically informed, humble evaluation of what is said. We are to "test," or examine, "everything." The word "everything" undoubtedly refers to the "prophecies" or "prophetic utterances" mentioned in verse 20. The "good" in verse 21 to which we are to hold fast, and the "evil" in verse 22 from which we are to abstain or avoid, also have in view the prophecies mentioned in verse 20.

How do we "hold fast what is good" (v. 21b)? After careful analysis yields the conclusion that the utterance is most likely from the Spirit, we should embrace it, believe it, and obey whatever admonitions may be entailed by it. Some are bothered by Paul's use of the term "evil." But "evil" can come in varying degrees of severity! In using this word, Paul likely meant an utterance that fails to edify or is inconsistent with what Scripture teaches. We need not think of "evil" in the sense of malicious or wicked, but simply a purported prophetic "word" that fails to build up, encourage, and console others (see 1 Cor. 14:3), and instead misleads and disheartens the people of God.

This instruction by Paul alerts us to the fact that, much like today, not everyone in the first century was excited about and supportive of prophetic ministry in the church. Paul didn't tell us why, but I suspect people then were disenchanted with revelatory gifts for the same reason that many are today. Perhaps some in Thessalonica were pointing to their prophetic gifting as grounds for promotion in the church or a reason they should be granted greater authority and acclaim. I suspect that some were disillusioned when a prophetic utterance didn't come to pass in the way they expected. Or maybe a few were making use of their gifting to manipulate and control others. Whatever the case, it is quite remarkable given the fact that Paul had spoken so highly of the Thessalonians and regarded them as one of the more godly and mature congregations where he had ministered (see 1 Thess. 1:1–10).

This is a critical reminder to us all that we must never despise or minimize the importance of prophecy in the church based solely on the grounds that some have abused or misapplied the gift. If I may be allowed to say it as forcefully as I think Paul said it: *it is a sin to despise prophecy!* We are not permitted to treat prophetic utterances with contempt or to legislate the gift out of the life of the local church. What we see in 1 Thessalonians is similar to Paul's counsel to the Corinthians in chapter 14 of his first letter to them, namely, that the solution to abuse isn't disuse. Instead, we must bring wise correction to those who would either despise prophecy or fail to weigh and assess properly the things that are spoken. Unqualified openness is not the solution. Neither is cynical suppression of the gift. Rather, we must employ biblically informed discernment.

We must also determine what Paul had in mind when he spoke of "prophecies" or "prophetic utterances" (*prophēteia*). Was he talking about the *person* who prophesies, the *charisma* of prophecy itself, or the *verbal utterances* of the prophet? Most likely, the latter, as the use of the plural and the absence of the definite article suggest. This is confirmed in verse 21a where the alternative to despising "prophecies" is that "everything" should be tested. Again, the plural "everything" (or "all things") that must be tested has for its antecedent the "prophecies" in the immediately preceding verse. Much to our dismay, Paul "[did] not specify what criteria should be used in determining whether something is good or evil, but presumably he expected his readers to weigh supposed Spirit-inspired words and deeds against the doctrinal and ethical norms they had received from him."[1] Gordon Fee believes the answer is found in two additional Pauline texts. We know that many in the church in Thessalonica were disturbed by a false report regarding the arrival of the day of the Lord (2 Thess. 2:2). In response Paul urged them to "stand firm and hold to the traditions that you were taught by us, either by our spoken word or by our letter" (v. 15). Perhaps, then, "the first test is the apostolic proclamation

---

1   Charles A. Wanamaker, *The Epistles to the Thessalonians: A Commentary on the Greek Text* (Grand Rapids: Eerdmans, 1990), 203.

of/teaching about Christ. This is a test that has to do with the theological or doctrinal content of the utterance."[2] The second test derives from Paul's teaching in 1 Corinthians 14:3 where he said that prophecy has for its purpose "upbuilding and encouragement and consolation. "This," says Fee, "is the test of purpose, as well as content, and has to do with its helpfulness to the believing community."[3]

1 Corinthians 14:29[4]

We need to look briefly at 1 Corinthians 14:29, the other primary text on judging prophetic words. There Paul described what may well have been the dynamics of a first-century church service. He wrote, "Let two or three prophets speak, and let the others weigh what is said."

Does Paul's statement that we are to "let two or three prophets speak" in a meeting imply that more would be in violation of God's Word? If so, his point would be to limit the number to three, lest those with this gift dominate the meeting. Similar instruction can be found in verse 27 concerning those who speak in tongues. On the other hand, verses 24 and 31 seem to suggest that many might prophesy in a meeting. In that case, there should be no more than three at a time before the others weigh carefully what is said. In other words, verse 29 may be designed to restrict how many may speak in sequence, but not the total number of prophecies given in any one service.

Who are the "others" in this passage who are to pass judgment or weigh what is said? Some insist "the others" are the other prophets. However, the term Paul used for "others" (*hoi alloi*) usually means "others different from the subject," that is, others beyond the prophets whose utterances are to be evaluated (i.e., the others who make up the larger group; i.e., the congregation as a whole). If Paul meant "the rest" of the prophets present at the meeting, he would more likely have used a different term, *hoi loipoi*, which carries the meaning "the rest of the same class."

As I briefly noted at the start of this chapter, it could be that Paul was

---

2   Gordon D. Fee, *The First and Second Letters to the Thessalonians* (Grand Rapids: Eerdmans, 2009), 222.

3   Fee, 222.

4   Much of my discussion of this passage is dependent on Wayne Grudem's excellent book *The Gift of Prophecy in the New Testament and Today*, rev. ed. (Wheaton, IL: Crossway, 2000); see esp. 54–62.

referring to those who had the gift of distinguishing of spirits (12:10). In 1 Corinthians 12:10 the word translated "the ability to distinguish" is the noun *diakrisis*. In 14:29 the word translated "pass judgment" (NASB) is the related verb form *diakrinō*. Thus, "the ability to distinguish between spirits" in 12:10 appears to be coupled with the gift of prophecy in much the same way "interpretation" is coupled with the gift of tongues. Given the fact that the gift of speaking in tongues is followed immediately by the gift of interpreting tongues, it may well be that Paul intended for us to view prophecy and distinguishing between spirits likewise as a pair.

But then why wouldn't Paul simply have said, "and let those who distinguish between spirits pass judgment," if in fact he had such a group in mind? Also, if we take "the others" to refer either to a special group of prophets or those with the gift of discerning of spirits, what is the majority of the congregation to do when prophecies are being uttered and evaluated? It seems they would be compelled to sit passively waiting for the prophecy to end and be judged before knowing whether to believe it or not. Furthermore, these first two views would require us to believe that teachers, pastors, and other church leaders without either the gift of prophecy or discerning of spirits must sit passively awaiting the verdict of an elite group. None of this seems plausible. Grudem explains,

> As a prophet was speaking, each member of the congregation would listen carefully, evaluating the prophecy in the light of the Scripture and the authoritative teaching which he or she already knew to be true. Soon there would be an opportunity to speak in the response, with the wise and mature no doubt making the most contribution. But no member of the body would have needed to feel useless, for every member at least silently would weigh and evaluate what was said.[5]

---

5   Grudem, 57. Max Turner concurs: "Here [in 1 Cor. 14:29], clearly, it is not a matter of deciding whether it is *true* prophecy or *false* prophecy, and then stoning the prophet (or at least exorcising her) in the latter case. It is a matter of deciding what is from God, and how it applies, and of separating this from what is merely human inference. Indeed, the human element and human error appears to have been so apparent that in 1 Thessalonians 5:19, 20 Paul has to warn the congregation, 'Do not *despise* prophecies, but *test everything*; hold fast to what is good' [emphasis his]. Arguably, then, prophecy in the New Testament is thus a mixed phenomenon" (Max Turner, *The Holy Spirit and Spiritual Gifts* [Peabody, MA: Hendrickson, 1998], 214).

Paul's exhortation to "weigh" (*diakrinō*) what is said by the prophets most likely means that all believers have a responsibility to sift the word and identify what is of God and what is the human and thus fallible admixture. Anthony Thiselton provides this helpful explanation:

> **The others** are to **distinguish between** (i) *prophetic speech which is God-given and coheres with the gospel of Christ and the pastoral situation and* (ii) *speech which is merely self-generated rhetoric reflecting the speaker's disguised self-interests, self-deceptions, or errors,* albeit under the guise of supposed "prophecy." We have argued . . . that this includes a claim to communicate *gospel preaching pastorally contextualized.* The authentic is to be **sifted** from the inauthentic or spurious, in the light of the Old Testament scriptures, the gospel of Christ, the traditions of all the churches, and critical reflections. Nowhere does Paul hint that preaching or "prophecy" achieves a privileged status which places them above critical reflection in the light of the gospel, the Spirit, and the scriptures. *It is never infallible.*[6]

I find it difficult to believe that Paul would have commanded this sort of assessment if all prophetic words were by definition inerrant Scripture-quality revelation from God. Thus, David Garland is likely correct in his assessment of what Paul means:

> The assumption is that the prophets do not speak with unquestionable divine authority. The congregation is not to accept everything that is said just because a person claims to speak under the influence of the Spirit. The prophet's words invite appraisal and discussion. . . . This is quite different from ascertaining whether the individual is a true or a false prophet. Presumably, the speakers reside in their midst, and the congregation would not need to examine them week after week, but they do need to evaluate what they say. . . . Prophets must allow the content of their revelation to be tested in the community and may need reminding that their "prophecy" is only partial and temporary (13:9–10).[7]

---

6 Anthony C. Thiselton, *The First Epistle to the Corinthians: A Commentary on the Greek Text* (Grand Rapids: Eerdmans, 2000), p. 1140 (emphasis in original).

7 David E. Garland, *1 Corinthians* Baker Exegetical Commentary on the New Testament (Grand Rapids: Baker

So, what then is the nature of this judgment to be passed? It isn't the determination of whether the utterance is of the Spirit or of the devil, but whether what is said is compatible with what the Spirit has already said (in Scripture, in the apostolic tradition, etc.). If New Testament congregational prophecy is often a mixture of divine revelation and human interpretation and application (see Acts 21:4–6, 10–14, 27–35), it is essential that the church evaluate and analyze what is said, rejecting what is wrong and accepting what is right (cf. 1 Thess. 5:19–22; see also 1 John 4:1–6). Only on the assumption that some of what the prophets say is their own contribution, and therefore possibly erroneous or misleading, could Paul command that their utterances be evaluated.[8]

The Criteria for Judging Prophetic Words

I make no claim at being exhaustive here, but I suggest that the following six criteria or standards of judgment should be brought to bear on any prophetic utterance.

1. The early church was to evaluate them in the light of the apostolic traditions (2 Thess. 2:15) bequeathed them by Paul. The reference to what they were "taught . . . by word of mouth" (NASB) obviously alludes to the oral instruction received from Paul during his stay in Thessalonica. The "letter" he mentioned is likely a reference either to 1 Thessalonians or 2 Thessalonians.

2. For us today, all prophetic words must be in absolute conformity with Scripture. In the wilderness, Jesus tested Satan's "words" against what the rest of Scripture said and exposed how he was misapplying

---

Academic, 2003), 662.

8 I agree with Roy E. Ciampa and Brian S. Rosner that "Paul could mean the evaluation of the prophets themselves, but more likely he has in mind the evaluation of the messages given by them" (Roy E. Ciampa and Brian S. Rosner, *The First Letter to the Corinthians* [Grand Rapids: Eerdmans, 2010], 715). Carson concurs, pointing out that "the word *diakrinō* . . . suggests that the prophecy be evaluated, not simply accepted as totally true or totally false" (D. A. Carson, *Showing the Spirit: A Theological Exposition of 1 Corinthians 12–14* [Grand Rapids: Baker, 2019 (1987)], 122). He also directs our attention to Grudem, who demonstrates that the verb *diakrinō* "commonly (though not consistently) bears in Hellenistic Greek the connotation of sifting, separating, evaluating; whereas the simple *krinō* is used for judgments where there are clear-cut options (guilty or innocent, true or false, right or wrong), and never for evaluative distinction (Carson).

texts (Matt. 4:1–11). I was present at one gathering when a woman known for her prophetic gift said this: "I have a sense from the Lord tonight that he is lonely. He longs for your fellowship and love." Now, it doesn't take a seminary education to know that this is biblically misguided. God is never lonely! Our great triune God is altogether self-sufficient and in need of nothing (see Acts 17:24–25). The fellowship and love among the persons of the Godhead assures us that God has never known solitude or stood in need of anything we humans might supply.

It wasn't this woman's desire to mislead the congregation. Her intent was to emphasize how delighted God is when we draw near to him and how abundant and effusive he is in pouring out his affection for us. God created us for fellowship with him, but not because he is in need, rather, to glorify himself by generously supplying our desperately needy hearts with what only he can provide. When this was later pointed out to the woman, she humbly received correction and affirmed to the congregation that in her desire to bless them, she had not spoken consistently with the infallible revelation of Scripture.

3. We also measure prophetic words by their tendency to edify or build up (1 Cor. 14:3). We must always ask: does it build up, strengthen, or tear down and create disunity and fear and doubt and self-contempt? Does the word have a tendency to exhort and encourage (v. 3)? Does the word have a tendency to console (v. 3), or does it lead to despair? If the word is predictive, empirical examination is in order to determine whether it comes to pass as prophesied.

4. We must also apply the test of love (1 Cor. 13) by which all spiritual gifts are to be measured and subordinated. Paul didn't appear to care much for any gift of the Spirit if it violated the dictates of love. Always ask the question: "Does this prophetic utterance seem to be motivated by selfishness and a grab for power and prestige on the part of the speaker, or does it come across as selfless and designed to bless and encourage the one to whom it is addressed?"

5. The test of community is also important. Wisdom demands that we always run the word by others who have skill and experience in evaluating prophetic revelation.

6. Finally, there is the test of personal experience. When Paul was given

a word about the danger that awaited him in Jerusalem (Acts 21:3–4, 10–14), he evaluated and then responded in the light of what God had already told and shown him (20:22–23). In effect, Paul said, "Yes, we all received the same revelation, that suffering awaits me in Jerusalem, but we differ on its interpretation and application."

This means that there is a vast difference between prophesying falsely and being a false prophet. All of us have at one time or another, some more, some less, prophesied falsely. We have spoken words we thought were from God that, in fact, were not. But that doesn't make us false prophets. It just makes us human! False prophets in the New Testament were non-Christian enemies of the gospel (cf. Matt. 7:15–23; 24:10–11, 24; 2 Peter 2:1–3; 1 John 4:1–6).

The takeaway from this is simple. Anytime you are the recipient of a prophetic word, open your Bible and carefully assess what was said. To do so isn't a sign of unbelief or cynicism or pride, far less suspicion of the person who spoke it. It's your Christian obligation. My hope is that each of us will determine in our hearts neither to be skeptics who end up putting out the Spirit's fire nor fools who gullibly believe everything we are told.

Some Practical Guidelines

On occasion you will experience an immediate check or hesitation in your heart regarding the authenticity of an utterance allegedly from God. This doesn't mean you are by nature a cynic or that you have questions regarding the validity of the gift of prophecy in our day. It more likely indicates that your knowledge of Scripture, together with common sense, has detected something amiss in what was said. If that should occur, I suggest the following steps.

First, some alleged prophetic "words" need immediate correction, especially if they are biblically misguided. In every case, be gentle, kindhearted, and encouraging. Don't crush the spirit of the person or respond in a way that would make them fearful and hesitant ever to prophesy again. If their word is contrary to what is clearly taught in Scripture, it will be difficult to bring correction without incurring some measure of relational discomfort.

There will often be times when a "prophetic word" is general or vague or merely a repetition of some biblical text or principle already well known. But this is no reason to dismiss it or regard it as of no use. Not all prophetic revelation needs to be as specific and overtly supernatural as the word spoken to me by that man in Anaheim. Sometimes the best way forward is to commit as a group to pray about what was said and revisit it at a later time.

If the word is weird or unintelligible or might be embarrassing to that person, simply say, "Thanks for sharing. Let's discuss this in private at a later time. I'm not sure this is the direction the Spirit is leading us at this time." But don't be surprised if you subsequently discover that the "weird" or slightly "embarrassing" word was genuinely of God and proves to be beneficial to those for whom it was intended.

I would also encourage you not to employ prophecy as a way to criticize or correct church leadership publicly by name. Take such words privately to the elders: "Do not admit a charge against an elder except on the evidence of two or three witnesses" (1 Tim. 5:19).

Be careful about prophesying such personal matters as marriages, babies, moves, or job changes. It seems reasonable that if God desires to make known something of this nature to a person, he will communicate it in some manner directly to the individual himself. We should also be cautious in "prophesying" public, political, and natural disasters. It doesn't take prophetic gifting to declare that California or Alaska is going to endure a devastating earthquake at some time in the future!

If God reveals to you someone's physical affliction, do not automatically assume it is his will to heal them then and there. God may have revealed this to you so that you can come to their assistance to accomplish tasks they otherwise can't perform. Or it may be to inform and energize your intercession on their behalf.

It's always wise to avoid using prophecy to establish doctrines, practices, or ethical principles that lack explicit biblical support. The purpose of prophecy isn't to provide others with guidance on what they should wear, which movies they should or shouldn't watch, or whether they should drink alcohol in moderation. And one doesn't need prophetic revelation to know that drunkenness is forbidden to the Christian!

Finally, be cautious about excessive dependence on prophetic words for making routine, daily decisions in life. There are, of course, certain exceptions to this "rule." Instead, "reckon" with the circumstances of any situation

(1 Cor. 6:5; Phil. 2:25), consider the needs of people, the principles of Scripture, and the counsel of wise people. Make a sober evaluation of what is fitting or advisable. In some texts Paul appealed to "knowledge," "discernment," and "spiritual wisdom and understanding" (Phil. 1:9–10a; Col. 1:9) as essential in the decision-making process. Revelatory insight from the Lord can be crucial in such deliberation, but God does not want us to be paralyzed in its absence.[9]

The Gift of Discerning of Spirits

Our approach to the gift of discerning of spirits will be much the same as our attempt to define the word of knowledge and word of wisdom. As with those two latter gifts, the only place in the New Testament where this gift is explicitly mentioned is 1 Corinthians 12:8–10. The English Standard Version renders it as "the ability to distinguish between spirits" (v. 10). The preposition "between" is the translator's attempt to make sense of what Greek grammarians call the objective genitive. In the most literal sense possible, the gift is "distinguishing of spirits." This would likely be the Spirit-empowered ability not simply to recognize the existence of "spirits" (be they demonic or otherwise) but the ability to differentiate between spirits. More on this below.

I'm inclined to believe that this is the ability to distinguish between what the Holy Spirit does and what another "spirit" (demonic), or perhaps even the human spirit, does. Not all miracles or supernatural displays are produced by the Holy Spirit. Whereas all Christians are responsible to "test the spirits to see whether they are from God" (1 John 4:1), Paul has in mind here a special ability that is fundamentally *intuitive* or *subjective* in nature. Given the contextual flow in 1 John, all should test the spirits by evaluating their message; in particular, do they confess that "Jesus Christ has come in the flesh" (4:2)? This requires no special gifting. But the spiritual gift of distinguishing of spirits is probably a supernaturally enabled *sense* or *feeling* concerning the nature and source of the "spirit."

We are once again led to look into the book of Acts for some possible instances where this gift is in operation. In chapter 8 on word of knowledge and word of wisdom, I suggested that these texts may well describe those

---

9 For a more detailed presentation of how to judge prophetic utterances, see my book *The Beginner's Guide to Spiritual Gifts* (Minneapolis: Bethany House, 2012), 135–50.

two gifts. But they may just as readily be descriptive of the ability to distinguish between spirits.

- Acts 16:16–18, where Paul discerned that the power of a certain slave girl is in fact a demonic spirit.
- In Acts 13:8–11 Paul discerned that Elymas the magician was demonically energized in his attempt to oppose the presentation of the gospel.
- In Acts 14:8–10 again Paul discerned ("seeing") that a man had faith to be healed.
- This gift is also in operation when a person is able to discern whether a problem in someone's life is demonic or merely the consequence of other emotional and psychological factors, or perhaps a complex combination of both.
- People with this gift are often able to detect or discern the presence of demonic spirits in a room or some such location.
- In Acts 8:20–24 Peter is said to "see" (not physically, but to "perceive" or sense) that Simon Magus was filled with bitterness and iniquity.
- It would seem that Jesus exercised something along the lines of this gift when he looked at Nathanael and described him as a man "in whom there is no deceit" (John 1:47). John 2:25 says that Jesus "knew what was in man." Was this a gift of "discernment" or "distinguishing of spirits"?

If we have properly identified this gift as the ability or capacity to differentiate between when, where, and what the Holy Spirit is doing or saying, on the one hand, and what demonic or merely human spirits are doing or saying, on the other, it would appear that this gift is desperately needed in the life of the local church today. I can well imagine that Christian counselors stand greatly in need of this discerning power.

Some argue that the plural "spirits" in 1 Corinthians 12:10 is synonymous with *pneumatikōn* in 12:1; 14:1, 37, and has in view the *charismata* themselves. Thus, to discern between "spirits," so they say, is the ability to ascertain which particular gifts have been distributed to which persons, or perhaps the ability to determine "the varied ways in which the Spirit of God is working, in such a way as to distinguish various consequences and patterns."[10] On this

---

10 Thiselton, *First Epistle to the Corinthians*, 967.

view, it is the capacity to discern or trace out the ways of the Spirit, what he is doing, why, and what may ultimately be the fruit of his activity.

Opposition to the view I've taken here is based on the observation that Paul almost never used *pneuma* or its plural form to refer to demonic entities. But this in no way indicates that Paul did not himself envision demonic beings as "spirits." Furthermore, when Paul preached in Philippi, he discerned that the young slave girl "had a spirit [*pneuma*] of divination." Although Luke was the one who used the word, clearly Paul knew precisely what he was dealing with. In fact, in verse 18 Luke recorded Paul as saying "to the spirit, 'I command you in the name of Jesus Christ to come out of her'" (Acts 16:18). We see much the same thing in Acts 19:11–20 where Paul's "extraordinary miracles" (v. 11) are described. The language of "evil spirits" (or the singular, "evil spirit") is used no fewer than four times in the span of six verses. Clearly this language in reference to demonic beings was quite familiar to both Luke and Paul. It also should come as no surprise that Paul chose not to regularly refer to demons as "spirits," given his preference for the standard terminology of "rulers," "authorities," "thrones," "dominions," and the like (see Eph. 1:21; Col. 1:16; 2:15). I should also point out that 2 Thessalonians 2:2 would also appear to be a clear instance where Paul used the word "spirit" to refer to a demonic being.

One final question that must be asked, even if we are uncertain of the answer, is how this sense or conviction of discernment actually operates. In other words, what does the believer see, sense, feel, or know? There has been considerable speculation on this point, and I do not intend to join the chorus in trying to provide an answer. However, a few speculative observations are in order.

In Acts 13:9 we read that Paul "looked intently" at Elymas and then drew the conclusion concerning his wicked purposes. Did Paul "see" something by means of a vision or perhaps "hear" the voice of the Spirit? Or did he simply have an overwhelming inward conviction concerning this man? We don't know.

Later, in Acts 14:9, Paul is described in virtually the same language as "looking intently" at the crippled man. But Luke also recorded that Paul in some manner "saw" that he had faith to be healed. Nothing indicates that the man himself signaled Paul to this effect. In fact, how could one make known he had "faith to be made well"? More likely the verb translated "seeing" should be taken as descriptive of some spiritual perception or internal knowing. Perhaps the Holy Spirit impressed on Paul's heart in an undeniably powerful and inescapable manner that this man believed that he could be healed.

When Peter is said to "see" that Simon Magus was "in the gall of bitterness and in the bond of iniquity" (Acts 8:23), this may simply mean that the apostle concluded this to be true based on Simon's own words (in vv. 18–19), where he made an effort to purchase the power of the Spirit with money. On the other hand, it could as easily be the case that the Holy Spirit had imparted to Peter the gift of discerning between spirits, by which he understood what was in the heart of Simon Magus.

All this goes to show how subjective this particular spiritual phenomenon is. Perhaps only those who have been the recipient of this gift, whether in the early church or today, can adequately explain how they sense or know that a particular supernatural event or intent is of God or the enemy.

Perhaps a personal example will help. During the time I was on staff at a church in Kansas City, it was common for the church members to engage in "prayer walking." There's nothing particularly unusual about this practice. We would divide up into groups of four or five and pray for our neighborhoods, schools, and other churches in the area. On one particular day I was praying in the company of three other individuals. As we approached an elementary school, I suddenly sensed the presence of evil. How, you ask? I don't know. But there was an unmistakable, quite tangible and disconcerting awareness that occultic activity of some sort had occurred in the area we were approaching. I told those with me what I was sensing, and another confirmed that she, too, was actually beginning to feel nauseated and disoriented. As we turned the corner of the school building, we saw it: satanic symbols spray-painted on the walls of the school, together with the remnants and paraphernalia of what appeared to be occultic rituals. Needless to say, we spent considerable time praying for the children of that school, that none would be adversely affected by what had taken place in such close proximity to their classrooms.

Might this have been an instance when God imparted to me (and a woman in our group) the gift of discerning of spirits? I think so. I've had a few similar encounters since that day and have grown in my awareness of what the Spirit is indicating in such circumstances. Some of you may be uncomfortable with the inescapable subjectivity of this spiritual gift.

I understand your concern. But we are dealing with "spiritual" gifts, not empirical science. You may prefer that we have some sort of objective, verifiable standard by which to judge the reality and accuracy of such phenomena. As far as I can tell, the only objective plumb line, if you will, is the Word of God. But Scripture itself does not tell us when such "feelings" or "sensations" are of the Spirit. They are unavoidably elusive and difficult to define. I can't explain why the Spirit would impart to me the emotional reaction that I had on that day as an indication of demonic activity. I can only bear witness to the occurrence and pray that I would not be led astray by it. Not everyone who is a recipient of the gift of discerning of spirits will always experience it in precisely the way I did. As noted earlier, nowhere in Scripture are we told how this gift operates or in what manner the Spirit would alert us to the presence of evil. Others may be empowered to "discern" demonic activity in ways that are decidedly different from how the Spirit awakens me to it. In every case, of course, one's "experience" of this gift must not violate what is explicitly taught in Scripture regarding the person of the Holy Spirit and the principles that govern the exercise of all spiritual gifts.

PART 4

SPEAKING IN TONGUES

CHAPTER 12

Deciphering the Gift of Speaking in Tongues[1]

The cessationist insists that all tongues speech, whether in the first or twenty-first century, is always a legitimate human language spoken somewhere in the world but previously unknown to the speaker. This conclusion is based on the nature of tongues speech on the day of Pentecost. Virtually all commentators acknowledge that the "tongues" spoken on the day of Pentecost was an example of xenolalia, which is to say, the ability to speak real human languages. The variety of nations represented (Acts 2:8–11) would certainly suggest this. The word translated "tongue" (*glōssa*) refers either to the literal organ in our mouths or to real human language. The word translated as "language" in Acts 2:6, 8 is *dialektō* (dialect), most likely a reference to human languages known throughout the world (cf. Acts 1:19; 21:40; 22:2; 26:14).

Given the fact that linguistic experts insist that the "tongues" spoken by Christians in our own day are not actual languages, the conclusion, according to cessationists, seems obvious: the spiritual gift of tongues no longer exists in the life of the local church. In other words, all New Testament tongues speech was some form of human language, contemporary tongues speech is not, therefore contemporary tongues speech is not biblical, but psychological emotivism or nonsense gibberish. This position is based on

---

1   Both the material in this chapter and the one that follows have been adapted from my book *The Language of Heaven: Crucial Questions about Speaking in Tongues* (Lake Mary, FL: Charisma House, 2019), and is used here with permission. If you wish to dig more deeply into the vast array of issues relating to the gift of tongues, I urge you to obtain *The Language of Heaven*, in which I address in considerable detail thirty crucial questions relating to this controversial topic.

the assumption that the phenomenon in Acts 2 governs all other instances of this spiritual gift. Whatever is true in Acts 2 regarding tongues must be true in every other case of its occurrence.

The continuationist response is that tongues may come in a variety of species or expressions, both known human languages and heavenly speech that is crafted by the Holy Spirit for those believers to whom the gift is given. If the cessationist argument is to hold up, we would need to be shown that the other occurrences of tongues in Acts (and in 1 Corinthians) are parallel to Acts 2 and display the same characteristics. But this is precisely what is lacking.

Tongues Speech in Acts and 1 Corinthians

Several lines of evidence suggest that the gift of tongues may be more than the ability to speak in real human languages. First, if tongues speech is always in a foreign language intended as a sign for unbelievers or as an evangelistic tool, why are the tongues in Acts 10 and Acts 19 spoken in the presence of believers only? If tongues is always an actual human language so that it might serve to communicate the gospel to unbelievers, why is it that in Acts 10 and Acts 19 no unbelievers are present? Why would the Spirit energize or lead believers to speak in tongues in the absence of the very people for whom this alleged evangelistic tool is designed?

Second, Paul described various "kinds" or "species" of tongues in 1 Corinthians 12:10 and 12:28. His words suggest that there are differing categories of tongues speech, perhaps human languages, angelic dialects, and heavenly languages that are uniquely formed by the Spirit for each person to whom the gift is granted.

Those who insist that all tongues speech is necessarily a human language of some sort push back and argue that in saying that tongues come in a variety of kinds or species, Paul meant that there are a variety of human languages, such as English, French, Japanese, Mandarin, and so on. But no one, to my knowledge, has ever suggested that all tongues speech was one specific human language. We already know from Acts 2 that when tongues appeared at Pentecost, they came as differing human dialects. It seems highly unlikely that Paul would have labored to point out that tongues are never just one human language but a multiplicity of such.

The countless dialects or languages that humans around the world speak when communicating with one another could be considered at least one "kind" or "species" of tongues, namely, human languages. Another kind or species would be nonhuman languages, such as the variety of ways in which angels might communicate with one another or with God. I find it almost impossible to believe that among the myriads and myriads of angels, they all speak one single language. Yet regardless of however many different languages angels employ, they would all be subsumed under the rubric of one "species" or "kind," namely, angelic speech.

Another "species" or "kind" of tongues is the sort the Holy Spirit constructs or enables a human being to speak in the course of his or her prayer and praise to God. Each of these expressions of tongues would be unique to each individual, all of which, however, would together constitute yet another "kind" or "species" of tongues.

Third, perhaps the most persuasive argument against tongues being known human languages is what Paul said in 1 Corinthians 14:2. There he asserted that whoever speaks in a tongue "speaks not to men but to God." Let's consider this. What is a human language, whether it be Russian or German or Norwegian? Is it not a means by which one human being communicates with or speaks to another human being? But Paul very clearly denied that this is what is happening when a person speaks in tongues. This person is most decidedly *not* doing what human language typically does. To speak in tongues is *not* to speak to other humans. Rather, it is a way of speaking directly to God. Therefore, the "species" or "kind" of tongues that Paul had in view in 1 Corinthians 12–14, unlike the species that Luke described in Acts 2, is not a human language.

Fourth, and very much related to the previous point, if tongues speech is always a human language, how could Paul say that when one speaks in tongues "no one understands him" (1 Cor. 14:2)? If tongues are human languages, many could potentially understand, as they did on the day of Pentecost (Acts 2:8–11). This would especially be true in Corinth, a multilingual cosmopolitan port city that was frequented by people of numerous dialects. Thus, "if Paul came speaking in tongues, in a non-Greek or non-Latin language, he surely would have been able to communicate with someone."[2]

2   David E. Garland, *1 Corinthians*, Baker Exegetical Commentary on the New Testament (Grand Rapids: Baker Academic, 2003), 584.

Try to imagine a scenario in which a person with the gift of tongues in Corinth stands up to speak, utilizing his Spirit-empowered ability, let's say, to speak in the language of the Parthians (see Acts 2:9). Paul might then take advantage of the situation to teach on the subject. "What you've just heard," says Paul, "is one expression of the gift of tongues. And since what he just said is mysterious and incoherent in the absence of interpretation, he obviously was not speaking to you and me but to God alone." At this point a visitor to the service might stand up and say, "Wait a minute, Paul. With all due respect, you are wrong. What he said was not mysterious or incoherent. I understood perfectly what he said. He was, after all, speaking my own native language!"

This hypothetical scenario is not all that hypothetical. In fact, if tongues in Corinth were always a known human language, it could conceivably happen again and again anytime a person who spoke that particular language was present. My point is simply that Paul would be repeatedly wrong in saying that "no one understands" the person speaking in tongues. Conceivably, and not hypothetically, numerous individuals would understand what was being said, just as they did on the day of Pentecost. Clearly, then, the tongues that Paul envisioned being given to Christians in Corinth (or any other city of that day and time) were not identical to the tongues given at Pentecost. They were, in fact, a different species or kind of tongues, namely, the sort that cannot be understood by any human being unless supernaturally enabled to understand by means of the spiritual gift of interpretation.

Fifth, one reason that no one understands what is being said in tongues is because "he utters mysteries in the Spirit." Those who stand opposed to the legitimacy of tongues today contend that the word "mysteries" in 1 Corinthians 14:2 refers to what Paul had in mind in Ephesians 3:2–6 when he spoke of the "mystery of Christ," to wit, that "the Gentiles are fellow heirs, members of the same body, and partakers of the promise in Christ Jesus through the gospel." There is no mistaking the fact that the word "mystery" (singular) here in Ephesians 3 is a technical term for the truth concerning Gentile salvation, something largely hidden during the time of the Old Testament but now revealed to Paul and to us. Or, as Anthony Thiselton defines it, the word denotes "what was once hidden but has now been disclosed in the era of eschatological fulfillment" (see 1 Cor. 2:1, 7; 4:1; 15:51).[3]

---

3 Anthony C. Thiselton, *The First Epistle to the Corinthians: A Commentary on the Greek Text* (Grand Rapids:

But Thiselton also goes on to point out that "every writer uses terminology in context-dependent ways that may modify a more usual meaning," and that is evidently what Paul was doing here.[4] In other words, we must look first and foremost at how an author used a word in a specific context to determine its meaning. And there are several reasons why Paul's use of the word in 1 Corinthians 14:2 is different from how he used it in Ephesians 3.

We first observe that in verse 2 the word is plural, "mysteries," not singular as in Ephesians 3. A singular and deeply profound mystery was made known to Paul concerning Gentile salvation and equality in the body of Christ. But there are multiple "mysteries" to which those who speak in tongues give utterance. My conclusion is that this use of the word means something unintelligible, something incomprehensible, something that is not known to us unless brought into the vernacular by means of the gift of interpretation. The content of the tongues speech remains a "mystery" to all because it is a species of heavenly language evoked by the Holy Spirit and spoken back exclusively to God himself.

Yet another important observation is that no such descriptive information concerning the content of the "mysteries" is given in 1 Corinthians 14. In Ephesians 3 we are told explicitly what the "mystery" was. It was the "mystery of Christ" (v. 4) and the manner in which his death and resurrection and the inauguration of the new covenant have brought Gentiles into equal standing in the covenants of promise. But this is far and away different from 1 Corinthians 14:2, in which we find "mysteries" that "no one understands." We "understand" the mystery of Christ, but "no one understands" the "mysteries" uttered by the tongues speaker. Clearly we are dealing with two different senses in which the word *mystery* may be used. Paul was not speaking of doctrinal or ethical truths that comprise the foundation on which the church of Jesus Christ is built but simply of utterances that are unknown to those who hear them because they are spoken in a tongue that "no one understands."

Finally, we should consider other texts where "mystery" is used in the sense of something unknown, something whose meaning is difficult to decipher or comprehend, something the meaning of which is beyond us

Eerdmans, 2000), 1085.
4   Thiselton, 1085.

unless it is revealed. Paul wrote in 1 Corinthians 13:2 of prophecy and said that even though he might "understand all mysteries," his understanding was useless without love. John spoke of the "mystery of the seven stars," which he then explained to his readers as being a reference to "the angels of the seven churches" (Rev. 1:20). He likewise referred to the "mystery of the woman" or the "great prostitute" who oppresses the people of God. Her identity was a "mystery" or something unknown until such time as John explained her.

Paul Gardner also points out that the gist of 1 Corinthians 14:2 "is simply that the person who speaks 'in a tongue' . . . cannot be understood by normal people but only by God because what he speaks is a 'mystery' given him by God's Spirit."[5] But if tongues is always a known human language, then countless numbers of "normal people" would be able to understand what is being spoken. Anyone who spoke the particular language being uttered by the tongues speaker would instantly recognize his own native dialect and make sense of its meaning. It would hardly be a "mystery" to him or her.

We now return to the sixth reason for believing that not all tongues speech is a human language. If tongues speech always is in a human language, then the gift of interpretation would be one for which no special work or enablement or manifestation of the Spirit would be required. Anyone who was multilingual, such as Paul, could interpret tongues speech simply by virtue of his educational talent. No supernaturally energized gift of the Spirit was needed by those who were present in Jerusalem on the day of Pentecost. Since the tongues in Acts 2 were human languages, any and all who spoke a particular language could instantly recognize what was being said. But Paul clearly described the gift of interpretation of tongues as one that is sovereignly and supernaturally given to some believers (1 Cor. 12:8–10).

Again, try to envision this not unlikely scenario in first-century Corinth. At a corporate meeting of the church, a person stands up and begins to speak in tongues. Upon finishing, another person stands up and provides a clear and intelligible interpretation or rendering of the meaning of what was said. One of the elders at Corinth then might respond by saying, "Let us praise

---

5 Paul Gardner, *1 Corinthians*, Zondervan Exegetical Commentary on the New Testament (Grand Rapids: Zondervan, 2018), 591.

God for the way his Holy Spirit has imparted a supernatural and miraculous gift of interpretation so that we might benefit and be built up by what was said in tongues." At that moment the man who provided the interpretation could conceivably stand up and say, "Well, not exactly. I can speak several languages. I've studied them intently and have lived in a variety of places. So when I heard the brother speak in a tongue, I instantly recognized what he was saying by virtue of my exceptional education."

But is this what we read in 1 Corinthians regarding interpretation? It would appear that Paul believed this to be a miraculous gift by which a man or woman is enabled by the Holy Spirit to understand and communicate the truth of an utterance that otherwise they would not comprehend. However, if all tongues speech is some human language spoken somewhere in the world, a great many people who hear it would be capable of making sense of what is said without any help or gifting from the Spirit at all. In addition, if tongues speech is always a human language, it would make no sense for Paul to suggest that interpretation should be prayed for, since the ability to translate a foreign language comes through instruction and rote practice, not prayer (see 1 Cor. 14:13).

Seventh, in 1 Corinthians 13:1, Paul referred to "the tongues of men and of angels." While he might have been using hyperbole, he just as likely might have been referring to heavenly or angelic dialects for which the Holy Spirit gives utterance. Stop and ask yourself this question: "What language do angels speak?" Or again: "Do all angels speak the same language?" Surely you don't believe that angels speak only English! When the angel spoke to Daniel in Daniel 10, he would have had to speak either Hebrew or Aramaic. When the angel spoke to Peter in Acts 13, it was most likely in Greek. It would appear that angels are capable of speaking in whatever human language is needed to communicate with the human they are addressing.

Now, how many angels are there? We don't know, but several biblical texts speak of myriads upon myriads or ten thousand upon ten thousand. If each believer has a "guardian" angel (and this is by no means certain; see, however, Heb. 1:14), and there are, as some experts say, 2.2 billion Christians in the world, that would mean there are at least 2.2 billion angels. I can't prove that, but I suspect there are likely even more. All of us would agree that angels communicate. They hear from God, they interact with humans, and they interact with each other. Assuming that angels differ in power and rank and role,[6] does it not seem highly likely that they communicate in a variety of different dialects suitable to their identity and station as angelic beings? So, with Paul's speaking of the "tongues of angels" in 1 Corinthians 13:1, we should not be at all surprised. Could it be possible, then, that he actually envisioned angelic tongues as one species or kind of tongues that the Spirit enables human beings to speak when they pray and praise God?

Gordon Fee cites evidence in certain ancient Jewish sources that the angels were believed to have their own heavenly languages or dialects and that by means of the Spirit one could speak them.[7] In particular we take note of the Testament of Job 48–50, where Job's three daughters put on heavenly sashes given to them as an inheritance from their father, by which they are transformed and enabled to praise God with hymns in angelic languages.

Some have questioned this account, however, pointing out that this section of the Testament of Job may have been the work of a later Christian author. Yet, as Christopher Forbes points out, "What the Testament does provide . . . is clear evidence that the concept of angelic languages as a mode of praise to God was an acceptable one within certain circles. As such it is our nearest parallel to glossolalia."[8] The fact that tongues are said to cease at the second coming of Christ (1 Cor. 13:8–9) leads Anthony Thiselton to conclude that it cannot be angelic speech, for why would a heavenly language terminate in the eschaton?[9] But it would not be heavenly speech per se that ends, but heavenly speech on the part of "humans" designed to compensate "now" for the limitations endemic to our fallen, preconsummate condition.

Craig Keener cites several documents from Qumran where different angels lead the heavenly worship on successive Sabbaths, making use of different languages. He suggests that since these angels are called "princes," it

---

6   For evidence of this, see my chapter "What Can We Know about Angels?" in *Tough Topics* (Wheaton, IL: Crossway, 2013), 120–36.

7   Gordon Fee, *The First Epistle to the Corinthians*, rev. ed. (Grand Rapids: Eerdmans, 2014), 69. See also Richard B. Hays, *First Corinthians* (Louisville: John Knox, 1997), 223.

8   Christopher Forbes, *Prophecy and Inspired Speech: In Early Christianity and Its Hellenistic Environment* (Peabody, MA: Hendrickson, 1997), 185–86. *Glossolalia* is a term for speaking in tongues that is built on the Greek word *glossa* ("tongue, language") and either *laleō* ("to speak or talk") or *lalia* ("what is said; manner of speech").

9   Thiselton, *First Corinthians*, 973, 1061–62.

is possible that they are those whom God appointed to oversee the nations whose languages they employ (cf. Dan. 10:13, 20–21; 12:1).[10]

Eighth, some say the reference in 1 Corinthians 14:10–11 to earthly, foreign languages proves that all tongues speech is also human languages. But Paul's point is that tongues function *like* foreign languages, not that tongues *are* foreign languages. His point is that the hearer cannot understand uninterpreted tongues any more than he can understand the one speaking a foreign language. If tongues were a foreign language, there would be no need for an analogy.

Ninth, if tongues speech is always a human language, Paul's statement in 1 Corinthians 14:23 wouldn't necessarily hold true. His argument in this passage is that if tongues are to be used in the corporate assembly of God's people there must be accompanying interpretation. Otherwise, if "outsiders or unbelievers enter, will they not say that you are out of your minds?" My response is, not necessarily. That is to say, if the tongues being spoken are languages known throughout the world at that time, any unbeliever who would know the language being spoken would more likely conclude the person speaking was highly educated rather than "mad" or "out of your minds."

My conclusion, then, is that the spiritual gift of tongues in 1 Corinthians was *not* the ability to speak in a known human language. What, then, are tongues?

Exploring the Purpose of Tongues Speech

As noted above, there is a variety of differing species of tongues. On some occasions, such as at Pentecost, they are actual human languages spoken somewhere in the world, dialects such as those employed by Parthians and Medes and Elamites and people from Cappadocia, just to mention a few (see Acts 2). On other occasions, primarily in the daily experience of local churches throughout the ancient world and in our day as well, they may be one of the many dialects spoken by the angelic hosts.

But I suspect that more times than not, the tongues Paul had in mind in 1 Corinthians 12–14, the tongues in which I regularly speak and pray today, are a heavenly language, a language that derives from the supernatural

---

10 Craig S. Keener, *Acts: An Exegetical Commentary, Volume 1* (Grand Rapids: Baker Academic, 2012), 808.

enablement of the Holy Spirit. Such tongues are not a language that anyone on earth could study in grad school or encounter while on a mission trip to a remote third-world country. Thus, tongues are not in the same category of such phenomena as English or German or Swedish but function to communicate desires, requests, declarations of praise, and thanksgiving that God fully grasps. Therefore, we can say that tongues are linguistic, in the sense that they are genuine speech that communicates information. Or as Robert Graves has said, tongues are "structured, articulate speech."[11] Remember, Paul said that the one speaking in tongues is speaking to God, and he later would contend that uninterpreted tongues is a form of giving thanks to God (1 Cor. 14:16–17). So there is substantive content to what is being spoken. But it comes in a form uniquely and especially crafted or shaped by the Holy Spirit, who is its source. Thus, the only way that either I or any other human might know what is actually being said is if the same Holy Spirit provides the interpretation.

There is no question, then, that tongues speech conveys meaning. If tongues speech is meaningless, it would be a futile and fruitless experience. The purpose of tongues speech is to communicate with God (1 Cor. 14:2). That neither the speaker nor those listening understand what is being said (unless, of course, the gift of interpretation should accompany it) is no objection to the legitimacy of tongues. It only matters that God understands, that the "coded" speech of the believer contains meaningful, substantive truths that are known to God because they have their source in God. Therefore, I agree with David Garland when he says that "Paul understands [tongues] to be a language inspired by the Spirit and not a noncognitive, nonlanguage utterance. It is not simply incoherent babbling in the Spirit. . . . Tongues consist of words . . . , which, though indecipherable, are not meaningless syllables strung together."[12]

---

11 Robert W. Graves, *Praying in the Spirit* (Tulsa, OK: Empowered Life Academic, 2016), 122.

12 Garland, *1 Corinthians*, 584. Mark J. Cartledge provides an extremely helpful survey of the status of scholarly research on the nature of tongues in his article "The Nature and Function of New Testament Glossolalia," *Evangelical Quarterly* 72.2 (2000): 135–50. His conclusion, with which I generally concur, is that "Luke considered glossolalia to be real unlearned human languages (xenolalia), while Paul understood glossolalia to be either real unlearned human languages (xenolalia) or a mysterious kind of heavenly language which he called the 'language of angels'" (149). See also Mark J. Cartledge, *Charismatic Glossolalia: An Empirical-Theological Study*, Ashgate New Critical Thinking in Theology and Biblical Studies (Aldershot, UK: Ashgate, 2002).

Our focus here will be on what Paul said in 1 Corinthians 12–14 regarding the spiritual gift of tongues. When we look closely at what the apostle said, we discover that tongues function in a variety of different ways.

All spiritual gifts, including tongues, serve to build up or edify the body of Christ. Paul said clearly that these gifts, even those of a more miraculous nature, are manifestations of the Spirit designed "for the common good" (1 Cor. 12:7). What becomes quite clear in 1 Corinthians 14 is that, in the case of tongues speech, the only way this can happen is if there is an interpretation provided. Unintelligible speech cannot edify another person. If we are to learn and be encouraged and grow up in spiritual maturity, we must be able to comprehend what is being said by another believer. This is what accounts for Paul's insistence that tongues are to be followed by interpretation (1 Cor. 14:27). "But if there is no one to interpret, let each of them [i.e., each of those who have the gift of tongues] keep silent in church and speak to himself and to God" (v. 28).

This truth is the reason why Paul earlier affirmed his preference for the gift of prophecy when the local church gathers for worship. "The one who speaks in a tongue," said Paul, "builds up himself, but the one who prophesies builds up the church" (1 Cor. 14:4). This doesn't mean that Paul was opposed to the gift of tongues. In fact, he followed verse 4 immediately with a reminder that he wanted "all" in Corinth "to speak in tongues" (v. 5a). But prophecy remains a more effective way to build up other Christians because, unlike tongues, it doesn't require interpretation. However, if "someone interprets" the utterance in tongues, "the church may be built up" no less so than if someone prophesies (v. 5).

Paul clearly believed that speaking in tongues was a good thing. "The one who speaks in a tongue builds up himself" (1 Cor. 14:4a). This is not an indictment against tongues but an affirmation of it. Self-edification is a good thing. It's simply not the best thing. It is one indirect effect of this particular spiritual gift. But the more immediate and primary goal of every gift is to build up others. I trust that the reason you are reading this book is to edify yourself. If self-edification were sinful, you should put down this book and never read another. We memorize Scripture to build up ourselves. We engage in various spiritual disciplines, such as fasting and prayer and meditation, in order that we might be edified. And Jude makes it explicit: "But you, beloved, building yourselves up in your most holy faith and praying in the Holy Spirit, keep yourselves in the love of God" (Jude 20–21a). Every Christian should hope that every other Christian is laboring in God's grace to build up or edify himself or herself, for each of us stands to benefit greatly from his or her maturity and insight and Spirit-empowered efforts to encourage and instruct us in becoming more like Jesus.

So we must forever put to rest the idea that the spiritual edification that one gains from speaking in tongues is bad. Paul's point is simply that it is inappropriate in the assembly of God's people if there is no one to interpret. Paul reaffirmed this later in the chapter when he described his own practice of speaking or praying in tongues. If one has the gift of tongues, he or she should pray that God would also grant the gift of interpretation so that what is spoken might be understood by others, so that they, too, might be edified (1 Cor. 14:13). Paul then said this: "For if I pray in a tongue, my spirit prays but my mind is unfruitful" (v. 14). His mind was "unfruitful" in the sense that he didn't understand what he was saying, and neither did anyone else (unless another interpreted). At first glance, many think this would be an excellent reason never to speak or pray in tongues at all. After all, what possible spiritual good can come from praying words that one's mind doesn't comprehend? But Paul did not draw that conclusion. Far from it. Here is what he said he would do:

> What am I to do? I *will* pray with my spirit [i.e., I will pray in tongues], but I *will* pray with my mind also [i.e., in my normal language that both I and others can understand]; I will sing praise with my spirit [a reference, no doubt, to singing in tongues], but I will sing with my mind also [in a language that I and others can understand]. (v. 15, emphasis mine)

We know that by praying and singing "with" his "spirit," Paul was describing praying and singing in tongues, because he proceeded to observe that if someone were to give thanks "with" his "spirit," no one present would understand. Hearers would not be able to "say 'Amen'" to the person's "thanksgiving" because they would not know what the person was saying (1 Cor. 14:16). All of this, of course, assumes that no one is present to interpret. But that doesn't mean that the person speaking or praying or singing in tongues isn't putting forth something meaningful and spiritually substantive. How do we know this? We know it because Paul immediately said that "you may be giving thanks well enough, but the other person is not being built up" (v. 17). Your tongues speech, whether in prayer or praise, is genuine, authentic gratitude to God. It makes perfectly good sense to God, and he is honored by your expression of thanksgiving, even if your mind is unfruitful.

One more important point should be noted. Let's not forget that we are trying to determine if uninterpreted prayer in tongues is beneficial to the speaker. It's certainly not beneficial to those around you in the gathered assembly of the church. For that, it must be interpreted. But Paul was resolutely determined to pray and praise and give thanks in private in uninterpreted tongues. We know this from what he said in the immediately following verses: "I thank God that I speak in tongues more than all of you. Nevertheless, in church I would rather speak five words with my mind in order to instruct others, than ten thousand words in a tongue" (1 Cor. 14:18–19).

Paul had the gift of tongues. He exercised his gift regularly, indeed, more often and more fluently than all the Corinthians combined. But if he refused to speak in uninterpreted tongues in church, insisting instead on only speaking "with" his "mind," so that others may be instructed, where did he pray in tongues? Where did he sing and give thanks in tongues? The only viable answer is that he did it in private, in the context of his own personal prayer life. In doing so, as he said earlier in verse 4, he "[built] up himself." But if he was to build up others, he had to speak in a way they could understand.[13]

---

13 Another attempt to deny that either Paul spoke in tongues in private or that he encouraged others to do so is that when he spoke in tongues outside the public gathering of the church, he did so in the same way the early disciples did in Acts 2. This argument proposes that there are multiple scenarios in which Paul found himself that were like that which occurred on the day of Pentecost. Thus, we are being asked to believe that on countless occasions Paul found himself in a crowd of people gathered around the inhabited world, all of whom spoke only in their native languages, and that Paul declared to each in their own dialect the "mighty deeds of God" (Acts 2:11 NASB). This view has several insurmountable problems. One is that it would have to ignore all the other evidence I've provided in this chapter that demonstrates the legitimate use of tongues as a private prayer language that also serves to praise and give thanks to God. Another problem is that it fails to account for Paul's language in 1 Corinthians 14:18 where he declared, and gave thanks to God for the fact, that he spoke in tongues "more than all of you." It seems we are being asked to believe that Paul spoke in tongues in scenarios identical to Acts 2 far more frequently than the Corinthians did in their private devotions or in their corporate church gatherings. I find that highly improbable, if not impossible, to believe. Furthermore, Paul had just described his tongues speech as being prayer, praise (singing in tongues), and the giving of thanks. So are we now asked to believe that when Paul found himself in the midst of numerous people who didn't speak his language that he would pray in tongues publicly in front of them, sing praises to God in tongues in front of them, and express his

We are now prepared to summarize the various functions or purposes of tongues speech. We have already seen that Paul described it as a form of prayer. He said in 1 Corinthians 14:2 that the person "who speaks in a tongue speaks not to men but to God." That, after all, is precisely what prayer is: speaking to God. He said explicitly in verse 14 that when he prayed in a tongue his "spirit [prayed]." He was determined to "pray" with his "spirit" (v. 15). So there is no escaping the fact that even though Paul did not know what he was saying, when he "prayed" in tongues, he was articulating very real, very substantive requests and petitions to God. As far as Paul was concerned, it was only important that God knew what he was saying.

Paul also told us that tongues can be a form of singing our praise to God. In other words, singing in tongues is worship. Paul was determined not only to sing with his mind, that is, in words that he and others understood, but also to "sing praise" with his "spirit" (i.e., in tongues). Those with the gift of tongues will testify to the fact that often they seize the opportunity to put their tongues speech in a more melodious and musical form. They "sing praise" with their "spirit" (v. 15b).

Finally, the gift of tongues is also a way in which a believer can express his gratitude to God. When you speak in tongues, said Paul, "you may be giving thanks well enough" (1 Cor. 14:17). It isn't necessary that you understand precisely how your gratitude is being expressed. As far as Paul was concerned, it is evidently only important that God knows. But Paul's lack of comprehension was no barrier to his determination to pray and sing in tongues and in doing so to say "thank you" to God. Of course, if uninterpreted, this must be done only in private. If it is done in public, in the assembly of God's people,

---

heartfelt personal gratitude to God in tongues in front of them, all with a view to lead them to Christ? I don't think so. And let's not forget that Paul expressed his desire that all the Corinthians (and all Christians) speak in tongues (1 Cor. 14:5). Are we then being asked to believe that what Paul desired for the people in Corinth (or any other church) is that all of them would likewise find themselves in scenarios similar to Acts 2 so they could then speak in tongues somewhere other than inside the church gathering? I would also point out that there is not one verse, nor even a single syllable in the New Testament to suggest that Paul spoke in tongues in public settings or scenarios proposed by this theory. Where in the New Testament, in Acts or anywhere else that describes Paul's public ministry, do we ever get so much as a hint that he spoke in tongues in the presence of people from foreign lands in the way we read in Acts 2? Since Paul himself said he spoke in tongues more than all the tongues-happy Corinthians combined, wouldn't you think we would have at least one example of him addressing crowds of foreigners in tongues speech? For there not to be a single, solitary corroborating example of something Paul said was a regular feature of his spiritual life, is simply too much for me to believe.

someone must be present who can interpret. Only in this way will "anyone in the position of an outsider" (v. 16) understand what you are saying and be built up or edified as a result.

By way of conclusion, let me say this: The preceding argument may yet strike many as odd. After all is said and done, tongues will often continue to appear strange and unappealing to you. That is understandable. But let us never forget what Paul firmly declared at the close of 1 Corinthians 14. No matter how much we may struggle to make sense of this spiritual gift, the apostle is quite clear: "Do not forbid speaking in tongues" (v. 39).

Is the Gift of Tongues a "Sign," and If So, a Sign of What?

Many believe tongues were given to God's people to enable them to evangelize the lost. But there is no evidence that tongues speech in Acts 2 (or elsewhere) served an evangelistic purpose. Nowhere does any biblical author encourage the use of tongues when unbelievers are present in order to win them to saving faith in Christ. In Acts 10, one of only two other instances of tongues speech in Acts, Luke used the related verb form, which is translated "extolling God" (Acts 10:46; see 19:17 where it is said that the Lord Jesus was "extolled"). Also, against the notion that tongues were evangelistic is the fact that when they were spoken at Pentecost, the hearers were left in complete confusion, some openly ridiculing the phenomenon.

When tongues occurred at Pentecost, the people present didn't hear an evangelistic message but doxology or worship. This is consistent with what Paul said in 1 Corinthians 14 where he described tongues as a vertical communication with or to God. As we've already seen, tongues is either prayer to God, praise to God, or a way in which the believer gives thanks to God. In Acts 2 it was only Peter's preaching that brought salvation (see vv. 22–41). Thus, we see that the primary purpose of tongues speech is *address to God* (whether it be in praise or prayer; cf. 1 Cor. 14:2, 14), not to men.

Others insist that tongues was primarily an evangelistic sign-gift for unbelieving Jews or was designed to communicate the gospel to non-Christians. If so, why is it that in two of its three occurrences in Acts, only *believers* were present? Let me ask the same question in slightly different terms. In Acts 10 the only people present when Cornelius and his companions spoke in tongues were the Jewish believers who had accompanied Peter

to Caesarea. There simply was no occasion for tongues to serve an evangelistic purpose given the obvious absence of unbelievers. The same holds true
in Acts 19. The only person explicitly identified as being present when the
disciples of John the Baptist spoke in tongues was the apostle Paul. Even if
there were traveling companions with him, they would have been followers
of Jesus. So again we see that tongues are present but unbelievers are not.
It simply will not hold up to scrutiny to say that tongues are an evangelistic
instrument.

Furthermore, if tongues are always a foreign language designed by God
to be used in sharing the gospel with unbelievers, why did Paul describe his
exercise of this gift in his private devotions when no one else was present
to hear him (see 1 Cor. 14:14–19)? Earlier we looked closely at 1 Corinthians
14:2. This verse carries application for this question as well: If tongues were
designed by God to enable believers to speak to other people in their own language, why would he say in 14:2 that the person who speaks in tongues does
not speak to men but to God? Evangelism is speaking to men. But tongues
speech is speaking to God.

Is Tongues a Sign for Unbelieving Jews?

Virtually every book written against the validity of tongues in today's church
appeals to the idea that the primary (if not sole) purpose of tongues was to
declare God's judgment against Jewish people for having rejected Jesus as the
Messiah. The passage to which they would look for support is 1 Corinthians
14:20–25.[14] There we read,

> Brothers, do not be children in your thinking. Be infants in evil, but in your
> thinking be mature. In the Law it is written, "By people of strange tongues
> and by the lips of foreigners will I speak to this people, and even then they
> will not listen to me, says the Lord." Thus, tongues are a sign not for believ-
> ers but for unbelievers, while prophecy is a sign not for unbelievers but for
> believers. If, therefore, the whole church comes together and all speak in

---

14 For an extensive interaction with and response to the various interpretations of this admittedly difficult
passage, I highly recommend D. A. Carson, *Showing the Spirit: A Theological Exposition of 1 Corinthians 12–14*
(1987; repr., Grand Rapids: Baker, 2019), 140–52.

tongues, and outsiders or unbelievers enter, will they not say that you are out of your minds? But if all prophesy, and an unbeliever or outsider enters, he is convicted by all, he is called to account by all, the secrets of his heart are disclosed, and so, falling on his face, he will worship God and declare that God is really among you.

Paul began by citing a text from the prophecy of Isaiah. In Isaiah 28:11 God declared, "By people of strange tongues and by the lips of foreigners will I speak to this people, and even then they will not listen to me, says the Lord" (1 Cor. 14:21). For us to determine the meaning of this text, we must go back a bit farther in the Old Testament to a warning that God gave to Israel in Deuteronomy 28:49. Deuteronomy 28 is the chapter that lists the many curses or judgments that God will bring against his people Israel if they should fail to "obey the voice" of God and refuse to "do all his commandments and his statutes" (v. 15). If Israel violated the covenant, God would chastise them by sending a foreign enemy speaking a foreign tongue: "The LORD will bring a nation against you from far away, from the end of the earth, swooping down like the eagle, a nation whose language you do not understand" (v. 49). Thus, confusing and confounding speech would serve as a sign of God's judgment against a rebellious people. This is the judgment that Isaiah said had come upon Israel in the eighth century BC when the Assyrians invaded and conquered the Jews (cf. also what happened in the sixth century BC; Jer. 5:15).

Many cessationists argue that God is judging unbelieving Jews in the first century, the sign of which is language they can't understand (i.e., tongues). The purpose of tongues, therefore, is to signify God's judgment against Israel for rejecting the Messiah and thereby to shock them into repentance and faith. Tongues, so goes the argument, is an evangelistic sign gift. Since tongues ceased to function in this capacity when Israel was dispersed in AD 70, the gift was valid only for the first century.

But there are numerous problems with this view. First, we must be alert to the error of reductionism. This is the tendency to take one purpose of a gift, perhaps even the most important and primary purpose of a gift, and *reduce* the gift to *nothing but* that particular purpose. Let's apply that to our text here in 1 Corinthians 14. My point is that even if tongues served as an evangelistic sign gift (a point that I do not believe is true but make for the sake of argument), nowhere does the New Testament restrict or reduce that gift to this one purpose. Simply because tongues is said to function in one capacity does not mean it cannot function in others. To say that my primary task is to preach and teach the Word of God does not mean that is all I do. My responsibility cannot be *reduced* to the ministry of the Word. I also counsel people and lead a large staff and evangelize the lost and undertake numerous other tasks. It's important that we understand spiritual gifts in much the same way. We have already noted that tongues also serve the "common good" of the body of Christ (1 Cor. 12:7) and, when used appropriately, can spiritually edify or build up the person who is speaking or praying (see 1 Cor. 14:4).

Second, if tongues speech were not a spiritual gift for the church at all, why did Paul ever allow it to be exercised and used in the church? If interpreted, tongues speech was entirely permissible. But this seems difficult to explain if its only or primary purpose was to declare judgment against unbelieving Jews.

Third, if uninterpreted tongues were designed to pronounce God's judgment against Jewish people and perhaps stir them to repentance, why would God have made available the accompanying gift of interpretation? Interpretation, it seems, would serve only to undermine this alleged purpose of tongues in declaring judgment against those in the Jewish community who had rejected Jesus as Messiah. The spiritual gift of interpretation makes sense only if tongues speech is profitable and beneficial to Christians in the assembly.

Let's be sure we feel the full weight of this point. Consider again what the cessationist is saying. Unintelligible tongues were given by God to serve as a sign of his judgment against the Jewish people, primarily for the sin of having rejected Jesus as Messiah. But if that is the purpose of tongues, there is no reason why God would also have given the accompanying gift of interpretation. For tongues to achieve their purpose, they must remain uninterpreted and thus confusing. Simply put, this view of the cessationist simply cannot account for why God bestows the gift of interpretation.

Fourth, if God intended tongues speech to serve as a sign for unbelieving Jews, Paul would not have counseled *against* its use when unbelievers are present (1 Cor. 14:23). And yet that is precisely what he did. To speak in uninterpreted tongues when unbelievers are present simply exposes you to the charge of being "out of your minds" (v. 23b). This is why Paul recommended that prophecy, not tongues, be employed when outsiders attend your meetings.

Finally, the contrasts in this context are between believer and non-believer, not Jew and Gentile. Indeed, most commentators concur that the nonbeliever (1 Cor. 14:23–24) is probably a Gentile, not a Jew.

For all these reasons, I conclude that the view that tongues is only (or merely primarily) a sign of judgment on first-century unbelieving Jews is unconvincing. What, then, is the principle that Paul found in Isaiah 28:11 that applied to Corinth and applies to us? It is this: One way in which God brings punishment on people for their unbelief is by speaking to them in an unintelligible language. Speech that cannot be understood is one way that God displays his anger. Incomprehensible language will not guide or instruct or lead to faith and repentance, but only confuse and destroy.

Now, let's apply this to the situation envisioned in first-century Corinth. If outsiders or unbelievers visit your corporate church gathering and you speak in a language they cannot understand, you will simply drive them away. You will be giving a negative "sign" to unbelievers that is entirely wrong, because their hardness of heart has not reached the point where they deserve that severe sign of judgment. So, when you come together (1 Cor. 14:26), if anyone speaks in a tongue, be sure there is an interpretation (v. 27). Otherwise the tongues-speaker should be quiet in the church (v. 28). Prophecy, on the other hand, is a sign of God's presence with believers (v. 22b), and so Paul encouraged its use when unbelievers are present in order that they may see this sign and thereby come to Christian faith (vv. 24–25).

Therefore, in 1 Corinthians 14:20–25 Paul was not talking about the function of the gift of tongues in general, but only about the *negative* result of one particular *abuse* of tongues speech (namely, its use without interpretation in the public assembly). So do not permit uninterpreted tongues speech in church, for in doing so, you run the risk of communicating a negative sign to people that will only drive them away.[15]

The spiritual gift of speaking in tongues has taken something of a beating

---

15 I was greatly helped in my understanding of this text by the comments of Wayne Grudem in his *The Gift of Prophecy in the New Testament and Today*, rev. ed. (Wheaton, IL: Crossway, 2000], 145–54. See also my treatment of this text in *The Language of Heaven: Crucial Questions about Speaking in Tongues* and in *The Beginner's Guide to Spiritual Gifts* (Minneapolis: Bethany House), 167–70.

at the hands of cessationists. But in this chapter we have seen that it is a wonderful gift by which the Spirit enables a Christian to pray, to give thanks, and to worship God in ways that transcend what is possible if we speak only in our native language. I join with the apostle Paul in giving thanks to God for having granted me this marvelous gift.

CHAPTER 13

Does God Want All Christians to Speak in Tongues? And What about the Gift of Interpretation?[1]

Does God intend for every Christian to speak in tongues? This question provokes heated, dogmatic answers, both on the yes and no sides. Most noncharismatic, evangelical believers think it hardly worth the time even to ask the question. For them, the fact that millions of born-again believers do not speak in tongues is experiential confirmation that the answer is decidedly no. How can it be God's "will" that everyone speak in tongues when so many millions of Bible-believing born-again followers of Jesus for the past two thousand years of church history never have? Are they living in disobedience to something God so clearly requires and commands in his Word?

On the other side, most charismatics who answer yes to our question are dumbfounded that anyone would disagree. They believe that Paul's statement in 1 Corinthians 14:5 settles the debate once and for all. There the apostle said, "Now I want you all to speak in tongues." So let's begin there, in 1 Corinthians 14:5, by asking the question this way: Is Paul's expressed "wish" a reflection of his understanding that God's "will" is the same?

---

1 I have addressed this issue in detail in two other publications, on both of which I draw much of what follows. See "Should All Christians Speak in Tongues?" in my book *Tough Topics: Biblical Answers to 25 Challenging Questions* (Wheaton, IL: Crossway, 2013), 276–82; and *The Language of Heaven: Crucial Questions about Speaking in Tongues* (Lake Mary, FL: Charisma House, 2019), 178–87.

No

Those who insist that tongues are not designed by God for all believers appeal to several texts in 1 Corinthians. For example, they direct our attention to 1 Corinthians 7:7 where Paul uses language identical to what is found in 14:5. Paul said this about his own celibacy: "I wish that all were as I myself am. But each has his own gift from God, one of one kind and one of another." Few, if any, would contend that Paul was insisting that all Christians remain single as he was. His "wish," therefore, should not be taken as the expression of an unqualified and universal desire. The same understanding, so they argue, should be applied to Paul's expressed "wish" in 1 Corinthians 14:5 that all Christians speak in tongues.

Yet another argument by those who believe tongues is a gift bestowed on only some Christians is the language Paul employed in 1 Corinthians 12:7–11. There he said that tongues, like the other eight gifts mentioned, are bestowed to individuals as the Holy Spirit wills. If Paul meant that "all" believers were to experience this gift, why did he employ the terminology of "to one is given ... and to another ... to another"? In other words, Paul seems to have suggested that the Spirit sovereignly differentiates among Christians and distributes one or more gifts to this person and yet another, different gift, to this person and yet another gift to that one, and so on.

Those who answer no to our question are insistent that there is no escaping what Paul said in 1 Corinthians 12:28–30. In this text, they believe the apostle clearly argued that all do not speak in tongues any more than all have gifts of healings or all are teachers or apostles. Let's look closely at how Paul framed his question: "Are all apostles? Are all prophets? Are all teachers? Do all work miracles? Do all possess gifts of healing? Do all speak with tongues? Do all interpret? But earnestly desire the higher gifts. And I will show you a still more excellent way" (vv. 29–31).

It's difficult, if not impossible, to escape the conclusion that Paul expected us to respond by saying no. This is reinforced when we take note of how such questions were posed in Greek. But first, consider how we ask questions in English when we already know the answer. English speakers have a way of emphasizing certain words, of elevating our voice, and even utilizing certain facial expressions when we intend for the person listening to know that the answer to our question is decidedly no. For example:

"You're not going to jump off that ledge to your death, are you?"

"Not everyone is a fan of the Dallas Cowboys, are they?"

In each of these cases, we anticipate a negative response: "No."

But in Greek there is a specific grammatical structure designed to elicit a negative response to the question being asked. Such is precisely what Paul employed here in 1 Corinthians 12. The translation provided by the New American Standard Bible makes this slightly more explicit than that of the English Standard Version.

> All are not apostles, are they? All are not prophets, are they? All are not teachers, are they? All are not workers of miracles, are they? All do not have gifts of healings, do they? All do not speak with tongues, do they? All do not interpret, do they?

You can clearly see from the way the questions are phrased that the author wanted you to respond by saying, "No, of course not."

Yes

Many think this passage in 1 Corinthians 12 forever settles the argument. But those who insist on answering yes to our question are quick to remind us that 1 Corinthians 7:7 isn't the only place where Paul used the "I want" or "I wish" terminology. One must also address passages such as these:

> For I do not want you to be unaware, brothers, that our fathers were all under the cloud, and all passed through the sea . . . (1 Cor. 10:1a; actually, a more literal translation would be something along the lines of: "For I do not wish you to be ignorant, brothers . . .")

> But I want you to understand that the head of every man is Christ, the head of a wife is her husband, and the head of Christ is God. (1 Cor. 11:3)

> Now concerning spiritual gifts, brothers, I do not want you to be uninformed. (1 Cor. 12:1)

In each of these three texts, the same Greek verb is used that we find in 1 Corinthians 14:5 ("I want" or "I wish"), and in all of them what the apostle wanted applies equally and universally to every believer. Furthermore, in 1 Corinthians 7 Paul went on to tell us explicitly why his "wish" for universal celibacy could not and should not be fulfilled. It is because "each has his own gift from God" (1 Cor. 7:7b). But in 1 Corinthians 14 no such contextual clues are found that suggest Paul's "wish" or "desire" for all to speak in tongues cannot be fulfilled. Then again, Paul's use of *thelō* in 14:5 may suggest only that this was Paul's *desire*, without telling us whether he (or we) might consider the desire within the realm of possibility. At minimum we may conclude that Paul would be pleased if everyone spoke in tongues. But that doesn't necessarily mean they all should.

Those who believe the answer to our question is yes pose yet another question. "Why," they ask, "would God not want each believer to operate in this particular gift?" In other words, they ask, "Why would God withhold from any of his children a gift that enables them to pray and to praise him so effectively, a gift that also functions to edify them in their faith?" But could not the same question be asked of virtually every other spiritual gift? Why would God not want all of his people to be able to pray for healing with great success, or to teach or to show mercy or to serve or to give generously or to evangelize? In any case, I think we should avoid speculating on what we think God may or may not "want" for all of us unless we have explicit biblical instruction to that effect.

Paul's statement in 1 Corinthians 14:23 also factors into the debate. "If, therefore, the whole church comes together and all speak in tongues, and outsiders or unbelievers enter, will they not say that you are out of your minds?" Paul's question reveals a scenario in the church at Corinth that the apostle found quite problematic. Those who had the gift of tongues were all speaking aloud without the benefit of interpretation. Whether they did this simultaneously or in succession, we don't know. But the problem this posed for unregenerate visitors was obvious. The latter would have no idea of what was being said and would likely conclude that those speaking were mad or deranged or in some sense out of their minds, a scenario hardly conducive to effective evangelism! This most likely accounts for Paul's subsequent demand that only two or three speak in tongues and that there always be an interpretation to follow. But aside from that issue, the argument is that Paul at least envisioned the *hypothetical possibility* that every Christian in Corinth could speak in tongues, even if he advised against it in the corporate meeting of the church. Or could it simply be that he was speaking in deliberately exaggerated language when he said, "all speak in tongues"?

A view that many charismatics are now supporting is that 1 Corinthians 12:7–11 and 12:28–30 refer to the gift of tongues in *public ministry*, that is to say, ministry exercised during the corporate gathering of the entire church, whereas 1 Corinthians 14:5 is describing the gift in *private devotion*. In 12:28 Paul specifically said he was describing what happens "in the church" or "in the assembly" (cf. 1 Cor. 11:18; 14:19, 23, 28, 33, 35). Not everyone is gifted by the Spirit to speak in tongues during the gathered assembly of God's people. But the potential does exist for every believer to pray in tongues in private. These are not two different gifts, however, but two different contexts in which the one gift might be employed. A person who ministers to the entire church in tongues is someone who already uses tongues in his or her prayer life.

Well-known Pentecostal pastor Jack Hayford argues in much the same way, using different terms. He suggests that the *gift* of tongues is (1) limited in distribution (1 Cor. 12:11, 30), and (2) its public exercise is to be closely governed (1 Cor. 14:27–28); while the *grace* of tongues is so broadly available that Paul wished that all enjoyed its blessing (14:5a), which includes (1) distinctive communication with God (14:2); (2) edifying of the believer's private life (14:4); and (3) worship and thanksgiving with beauty and propriety (14:15–17).[2] The difference between these operations of the Holy Spirit is that *not every* Christian has reason to expect he or she will necessarily exercise the public *gift*; while *any* Christian may expect and welcome the private *grace* of spiritual language in his or her personal time of prayer fellowship *with* God (14:2), praiseful worship *before* God (14:15–17), and intercessory prayer *to* God (Rom. 8:26–27).

Paul's point at the end of 1 Corinthians 12 is that not every believer will contribute to the body in precisely the same way. Not everyone will minister a prophetic word, not everyone will teach, and so on. But whether everyone might pray privately in tongues is another matter, not in Paul's purview until chapter 14.

It must be noted, however, that nowhere did Paul or any other New

---

2 Jack Hayford, *The Beauty of Spiritual Language* (Dallas: Word, 1992), 102–6.

Testament author differentiate explicitly between tongues as a "gift" and tongues as a "grace." All "gifts" are expressions of God's "grace" to us through the Holy Spirit. Indeed, as most of my readers are undoubtedly aware, the Greek word for a spiritual "gift" (*charisma*) is clearly related to the Greek word for "grace" (*charis*). All spiritual gifts, and not just tongues, are expressions of divine grace. I must confess a discomfort on my part in establishing a distinction between two expressions of tongues based on a supposed difference in words that nowhere is found in the New Testament.

Those who embrace this view find what they believe is a parallel in Paul's perspective on who may prophesy. "All are not prophets, are they?" (1 Cor. 12:29 NASB). No, of course not. But Paul was quick to say that the potential exists for "all" to prophesy (14:1, 31). Why couldn't the same be true for tongues? Couldn't Paul be saying that whereas all do not speak in tongues as an expression of corporate, public ministry, it is possible that all may speak in tongues as an expression of private praise and prayer? Just as Paul's rhetorical question in 12:29 was not designed to rule out the possibility that all may utter a prophetic word, so also his rhetorical question in 12:30 was not designed to exclude anyone from exercising tongues in their private devotional experience.

One problem with the view that Hayford defends is that when Paul said, "God has appointed *in the church* first apostles, second prophets, third teachers" (emphasis mine), and so on, he wasn't referring to what happened "in the church" gathering or corporate assembly. The phrase, "in the church" means "in the body of Christ" at large (whether that be in Corinth or Thessalonica or Rome or any other place where God's people may be found). However, in several other texts Paul quite clearly had in view the public meeting of God's people (see 1 Cor. 11:18; 14:19, 23, 28, 33, 35). But in the one passage where Paul denied that all have been given the gift of tongues he was referring to "the body of Christ" (12:27), of which we are "individually members." Max Turner also points out,

> The other functions signified in 12:28–30 are surely not restricted to what happens when the Corinthian believers formally assemble. We must assume that prophecy, teaching, healings, miracles, leading and administration, were all both inside and outside the formal "assembly." But all this in turn means that the question of 12:30, "Not all speak in tongues, do

they?" ("No!"), cannot be restricted to mean "Not all have a special gift to speak tongues 'in the assembly,' do they?" It must mean only *some* speak in tongues *at all*, whether privately or in the assembly.[3]

My sense, then, is that Paul was not making a distinction between tongues that are exercised in public and tongues that remain a staple of private devotional prayer. Although there is certainly a variety of "kinds" or "species" of tongues, the difference is not one between private tongues and public tongues.

As you can see, good arguments exist on both sides of the fence when it comes to answering the question of whether God wants all Christians to speak in tongues. I must confess it seems unlikely that God would withhold the gift of tongues from any of his children who passionately and sincerely desire it. My suspicion is that, all things being equal, if you deeply desire this gift, it is probably (but not certainly) because the Holy Spirit has stirred your heart to seek for it. And he has stirred your heart to seek for it because it is his will to bestow it. So, if you long for the gift of tongues, persevere in your prayers. My sense (with no guarantee) is that God will answer you in his time with a satisfying yes.

On the other hand, it is important to remember that as far as we can tell, there is no other spiritual gift that is ever described, defined, or portrayed in the New Testament as one that God bestows, or wants to bestow, on every single Christian. In other words, as I pointed out earlier, few if any would argue that God wants all to have the gift of teaching or the gift of mercy or the gift of leadership, or the gift of evangelism. Why, then, would tongues be unique, the only one among the many *charismata* that God intends for all believers to exercise?

In the final analysis, I'm inclined to conclude that it is not necessarily God's will that all Christians speak in tongues. But I'm open to being persuaded otherwise![4]

---

3 Max Turner, "Early Christian Experience and Theology of 'Tongues': A New Testament Perspective," in *Speaking in Tongues: Multi-Disciplinary Perspectives*, ed. Mark J. Cartledge (Waynesboro, GA: Paternoster, 2006), 27.

4 For those who wish to go deeper, a scholarly and quite helpful discussion of this issue may be found in the *Asian Journal of Pentecostal Studies*. See Max Turner, "Tongues: An Experience for All in the Pauline Churches?" *Asian Journal of Pentecostal Studies* 1.2 (1998): 231–53; Simon K. H. Chan, "A Response to Max Turner," *Asian*

The Interpretation of Tongues

As Paul delineated nine of the gifts of the Spirit in 1 Corinthians 12:8–10, the last on his list was "the interpretation of tongues." Later in that chapter he again referred to interpretation in his denial that any one gift is granted to all Christians (v. 30b). In his instruction on how believers are to arrive at any particular corporate assembly, he said that whereas one may come with a hymn, another with a word of instruction, another with a revelation from God, another with a tongue, one may also come with "an interpretation" (1 Cor. 14:26).

Paul envisioned that in any meeting of God's people "two or at most three" may speak in tongues, "each in turn," which is to say, not simultaneously but one after the other. Once they have concluded, he insisted that "someone interpret" (1 Cor. 14:27b). Although the apostle didn't say so explicitly, it may be that he envisioned only one person to provide the interpretation of all three utterances in tongues. It is entirely possible, on the other hand, that each utterance in tongues will have its own individual interpreter. If no one with the gift of interpretation is present at any particular corporate assembly, no one should speak in tongues.

We have previously taken note of Paul's exhortation to the person who wishes to speak in tongues in public, to the effect that he "should pray that he may interpret" (1 Cor. 14:13). There is no indication in what Paul said that this person had ever interpreted an utterance in tongues before. He or she may have, but it is just as likely that this would be their first experience with this spiritual gift. Paul didn't tell us when the prayer should be uttered, but it seems likely this should occur before the utterance in tongues is given. After all, if there is no interpretation, there should never have been a word in tongues in the first place. It seems only reasonable, then, that the person who is feeling led to speak aloud in tongues should first pray for God to grant him or her the interpretation. If God does not respond to such a prayer by giving the interpretation, the person should then refrain from speaking in tongues altogether.

Journal of Pentecostal Studies 2.2 (1999): 279–81; Robert P. Menzies, "Paul and the Universality of Tongues: A Response to Max Turner," *Asian Journal of Pentecostal Studies* 2.2 (1999): 283–95; and Max Turner, "A Response to the Responses of Menzies and Chan," *Asian Journal of Pentecostal Studies* 2.2 (1999): 297–308.

This procedure appears clear enough, even though not all our questions are given explicit answers by the apostle. But what remains for us to do is to determine, as best we can, precisely how the gift of interpretation functions. What sort of information does it yield? What is the relationship that an interpretation sustains to the utterance in tongues? To those questions we now turn our attention.[5]

What the Gift of Interpretation of Tongues Is Not

We should never confuse the gift of interpretation of tongues with the ability of a person to interpret divine revelation on a broad scale. The person with this gift would not necessarily be extraordinarily capable or skilled in interpreting biblical texts. The science of hermeneutics has principles of interpretation that are easily learned by anyone who has the time and commitment to study them. But educating oneself in the rules that govern how to make sense, for example, of John 3:16, is not what Paul had in mind when he spoke of the gift of interpretation. This gift is the Spirit-empowered ability to interpret what is spoken in *tongues*. There is no indication in Scripture that someone who has this *charisma* would be able to interpret dreams, visions, or other revelatory phenomena.

Although not mentioned in the New Testament, there may well be a spiritual gift of *interpretation*, broadly conceived. I addressed this possibility in chapter 3, where we took up the question of how many spiritual gifts we might reasonably expect God to give. I direct your attention back to that discussion for more on this.

The gift of interpreting tongues must be distinguished from the learned ability to translate a foreign language. I can translate Greek and a good bit of Hebrew and Latin into English, but that is not what Paul had in view. All of us are familiar with scenes at the United Nations or an international political conference where translators are employed to interpret speeches for the representatives of various countries. This is an impressive skill, but it is a natural, learned, human ability. They gained this skill through extensive

---

5   What follows is a revised version of what may be found in my book *The Language of Heaven*. A somewhat abbreviated version is also found in my book *The Beginner's Guide to Spiritual Gifts* (Minneapolis: Bethany House, 2015), 193–98.

education and practice. The gift Paul described, on the other hand, is super-natural, unlearned, and is no less a "manifestation" of the Holy Spirit (1 Cor. 12:7) than the gift of miracles or prophecy.

A somewhat related phenomenon is described in Daniel 5, where a "hand" supernaturally inscribed a message to King Belshazzar, which none of his attendants could interpret. He summoned Daniel who proceeded to interpret the meaning. Whereas the inscription was revelatory, the inter-pretation was not. It was more akin to translation insofar as it was written in Aramaic, a language in which Daniel already had great facility. If the interpretation of tongues was merely the ability to translate a language one previously knew, this would be the only spiritual gift that required no input from or activity of the Holy Spirit.

It would almost appear that Anthony Thiselton's understanding of tongues is a function of his conclusion concerning the nature of interpretation. In an earlier study,[6] and again in his commentary on 1 Corinthians, Thiselton argues that the noun "interpretation" in 1 Corinthians 12:10 and the verb "to interpret" in 14:5 and 13 refer to the ability to put something otherwise unformed and unspoken into articulate speech. He appeals to the use of these terms in both Philo and Josephus, where they denote "the capacity to express in *words* or *articulate speech* wonders which had otherwise left a person speechless, or able to react only emotively with awe or joy."[7] Tongues, says Thiselton, are there-fore utterances that "well up, in experiences of wonder and praise as the Holy Spirit releases inhibitions and censors, in ways which reflect pre-conscious, pre-cognitive yearnings, sighings, or 'building up' which evade cognitive objec-tification and formulation."[8] These inarticulate longings and impulses of praise prompted by the activity of the Spirit (Rom 8:26), are "as yet 'raw' and in need of communicative, intelligible, conscious communication."[9] It is the latter that the gift of interpretation purportedly supplies.

This explanation would seem to entail the conclusion that no one has

6   Anthony Thiselton, "The 'Interpretation' of Tongues: A New Suggestion in the Light of Greek Usage in Philo and Josephus," *JTS* 30 (1979): 15–36.

7   Thiselton, *First Corinthians*, 976.

8   Thiselton, 1108. For this view, see also the work by Gerd Thiessen, *Psychological Aspects of Pauline Theology* (Edinburgh: T&T Clark, 1987), 74–114, 292–341.

9   Thiselton, *First Corinthians*, 1061.

the gift of interpretation alone. Rather, some have tongues while others have *both* tongues *and* interpretation. In other words, claims Thiselton,

> this is why some have the gift of tongues (which liberate and release inner-most sighs to God), and others [in addition to their gift of tongues] have a *further* gift of enabling which allows them to reflect and to put the content of the experience which had generated the inarticulate sign of the Spirit at work into an articulate communicative signal from which all could benefit. Presumably only those who were not content to use tongues only in private were those whom Paul specifically enjoined to pray for this further gift [see 1 Cor. 14:13], or otherwise to remain self-disciplined in public worship.[10]

It may well be that the model of tongues (and the accompanying gift of interpretation) for which Thiselton argues is, to use his own terminology, one of several *species* or *kinds* of tongues (1 Cor. 12:10) envisioned by Paul to be operative in the church. A careful and detailed response to his exegesis is beyond the scope of this book, but at this point I see nothing in his understanding that necessarily precludes the *species* of tongues and interpretation for which I have argued or suggests that tongues was restricted to the apostolic age. In other words, should Thiselton's understanding prove correct, it would have no bearing on the extended question of the perpetuity of either gift.

What the Gift of Interpretation of Tongues Is

So, if the spiritual gift of interpretation of tongues is not the same thing as interpreting Scripture or making sense of dreams, what is it? I would define it as *the Spirit-empowered ability to understand and communicate an otherwise unintelligible public utterance of tongues for the spiritual benefit of the congregation as a whole.* I'm hesitant to use the word *translate* to describe this gift, given the fact that this term may lead people to conclude that there will always be a one-for-one or word-for-word rendering of the tongues utterance into the vernacular of the people. But there is a spectrum from literal translation at one end to broad summation at the other end, whenever the gift of

---

10 Thiselton, 1110.

interpretation is exercised. Interpreting a tongues utterance may take any one of several forms.

For example, someone with this gift *may* provide a literal, word-for-word rendering that corresponds in every conceivable way to the content of the tongue. It would be the same in length and emphasis. If the tongue was delivered in what appear to be five sentences and lasts for forty-five seconds, so, too, would the interpretation.

There may also be a somewhat looser, more fluid rendering that captures the essence of the utterance. Those who engage in the translation of the original text of Scripture into another language, such as English, often refer to this as "dynamic equivalence." The totality of what was spoken in tongues is brought over into the words of the interpreter, but it may not be in a word-for-word form.

At other times something of a commentary is provided in which the interpreter explains (perhaps even exegetes) the tongues utterance. After all, what is said in tongues may be enigmatic or parabolic or symbolic and thus needs an explanation. This is somewhat similar to what happens in an art museum when a scholar or historian "interprets" a painting. He or she may provide comment on the artist's mood and background and even his or her perceived intent in crafting the painting or sculpture.

Then, of course, the interpretation may be closer to what we call a paraphrase of what the tongues utterance means. If I may again appeal to the discipline of Bible translation, I here have in mind what *The Living Bible* provides us as over against the New American Standard translation. The latter is an essentially wooden and quite literal rendering of each word, as much as is possible, while the former is the translator's own effort to bring the original text into the world of the reader in such a way that the latter can make better sense of what the text is saying.

Finally, I suppose someone may interpret an utterance in tongues by giving us a summation of the gist of what was said. No attempt is made to supply a word in the interpretation that corresponds to a precise word in the tongue. Rather, the interpreter takes the utterance in a tongue and reduces it to a much briefer and summarized statement.

There is nothing in what Paul said about the gift of interpretation to preclude the possibility that the Holy Spirit might enable someone to interpret a tongues utterance anywhere along this spectrum. For example, the person with the gift of tongues might speak for five minutes while the interpreter speaks for only three. There is nothing to prevent a single utterance in tongues from being interpreted by two people whose "translations" differ in terms of length and focus. One person might provide a somewhat lengthy, seemingly word-for-word interpretation, while another summarizes its basic content or provides a more practical application of what was spoken in tongues. In any case, the movement is always from the obscurity and unintelligibility of the tongues utterance to clarity and intelligibility of the interpretation, such that everyone in the church can say "Amen" to what was said (1 Cor. 14:16). In this way the entire body is edified.

Think of it this way. If I were to read aloud John 3:16 in the course of a corporate church service and then ask for others to interpret its meaning and apply its truths to our lives, the responses might be noticeably different. One person might lay hold of the word "loved" and unpack the dynamics of God's affection for us that prompted his sending of his Son. Another might choose to talk about the "world" and its need for a savior. One more is led to talk about what it means to "believe" in Jesus or perhaps what John meant by "eternal life." Finally, another chooses to talk about how this verse might be used in sharing the gospel with an unbelieving friend. In each and every case, however, truth is communicated intelligibly based on something in the text of John 3:16. Likewise, when there is an utterance in tongues, differing individuals with the gift of interpretation might conceivably fix their attention on one particular element, word, or phrase, while another is led to make practical application to the lives of those in attendance.

Although Paul did not himself say this in 1 Corinthians, it seems reasonable to think that an interpretation of a tongue should be subject to judgment by the rest of those present in much the same way that a prophetic utterance is to be weighed or evaluated (see 1 Cor. 14:29).

The Content of Interpretation

It would seem reasonable to conclude that the content of the interpretation would depend entirely on the content of the tongues utterance. Therefore, we must ask another question first: *What is said when one speaks in tongues?* Earlier we noted that tongues can be any of the following:

- prayer (1 Cor. 14:2; supplication, petition, intercession, etc.)
- praise (1 Cor. 14:16; cf. Acts 2:11; 10:46)
- thanksgiving (1 Cor. 14:16)

If the interpretation must correspond to the utterance, the former will come forth in the form of prayers, praise, and expressions of gratitude to God. The interpretation will be a *God-ward* utterance, no less than is the tongues utterance on which it is based.

This principle relates directly to the controversial issue of whether there is any such thing as a *message* in tongues, that is, a message directed *horizontally* to people rather than *vertically* to God. The standard view among most charismatic believers is that when an utterance in tongues is interpreted, it becomes the equivalent of prophecy. As such, it is horizontal in its orientation, which is to say, it is directed to other individuals in the church. But if tongues are always prayer, praise, or thanksgiving, would not the interpretation be the same? If a purported interpretation is not heartfelt adoration or some expression of petition or praise, we may justifiably wonder if it is truly from God.

Having said that, I may be mistaken in placing this sort of restriction on the content of tongues speech. Although Paul clearly envisioned it as a form of prayer and as a way in which we both praise God and express our gratitude to him, does this mean that tongues can *never* function in any other way? Must we necessarily limit tongues speech to these three God-ward expressions and rule out any and all *man-ward* utterances? In other words, was Paul, in 1 Corinthians 14, providing us with an *exhaustive* portrayal of what might be communicated when one speaks in tongues? Or might there be other purposes or functions that it serves?[11]

The subject of speaking in tongues and the gift of interpretation will probably remain controversial until Christ returns. The same may also be said about divine healing, to which we now direct our attention.

---

11 This is a question I explore in considerable detail in my book *The Language of Heaven*.

PART 5

FAITH, HEALING, AND MIRACLES

CHAPTER 14

The Spiritual Gift of Faith and Its
Relationship to Healing

The spiritual gift of faith may well be the most enigmatic and misunderstood of all the *charismata*. It is similar to word of wisdom, word of knowledge, and distinguishing between spirits insofar as the only place it is explicitly mentioned is in the list of gifts in 1 Corinthians 12:8–10. There we read that "to another" believer "faith" is given "by the same Spirit" (v. 9). This immediately strikes us as odd given the fact that all Christians have faith, in one form or another. Thus, Paul must be referring to a unique and quite extraordinary manifestation of faith that only some Christians experience.

Given the fact that 1 Corinthians 12:9 is the sole mention of faith as a spiritual gift, we are forced to look elsewhere in the New Testament for possible expressions of it. But first let's remind ourselves of the three kinds of faith a believer might exercise or, better still, the three circumstances in which faith might express itself.

There is, first of all, the faith, belief, or trust that every born-again person exercises when he or she turns to Christ for salvation. Some would call this *converting* faith. This faith is mentioned countless times in the New Testament, such as in Acts 15:9 where Peter declared that God has "cleansed" the hearts of Gentiles in the same way that he did the Jews, "by faith." Or we might refer to it as *saving* or *justifying* faith, given the way Paul said we "have been saved through faith" (Eph. 2:8; see also Rom. 1:16–17; 3:28; 5:1). This is assuredly not what Paul had in mind in 1 Corinthians 12:9. In the latter text, he spoke of a faith that is given "to another" of the many who have come to know Jesus as Savior, but clearly not all.

A second expression of faith in the experience of a Christian is the daily, ongoing, moment-by-moment confidence that we place in Jesus. This is likely what Paul had in mind when he said, "I have been crucified with Christ. It is no longer I who live, but Christ who lives in me. And the life I now live in the flesh I live by faith in the Son of God, who loved me and gave himself for me" (Gal. 2:20). Here the apostle had in view a "faith" that he "now" experienced as he carried out the ministry given to him by God. We might refer to this expression of faith as *constant* or *continuing*, insofar as we trust and believe and rely on Christ throughout the course of each day and in every circumstance. Or perhaps we should call it *sanctifying* faith. This faith is the fruit of the Spirit (Gal. 5:22), the faith that is extolled in Hebrews 11. Although it is found in varying degrees of intensity in each person, no Christian is devoid of it altogether.

My point is that I can have faith, at any time, regarding my status as an adopted child of God (Rom. 8:14–17). I can know and believe, at any time and in all circumstances, that God will never leave me or forsake me (Heb. 13:5). The truth of Romans 8:28, that God is orchestrating all things, even suffering, for my ultimate good and his ultimate glory, is something that warrants my faith throughout the course of my life. But I cannot believe at will, that is to say, at *my* will, that he is going to heal someone for whom I pray. That is a prayer that I can only pray when *God* wills it and enables me to overcome all hesitation and doubt to believe it.

Perhaps we should then call the spiritual gift of faith, *charismatic* faith, insofar as it is said by Paul to be one of the many *charismata* that the Spirit sovereignly bestows on some but not all. Or again, *supernatural* faith may be a more accurate designation. Some may wish to think of it as *spontaneous* faith insofar as it likely happens only on those occasions when the Spirit chooses to bestow it. In other words, the spiritual gift of faith is probably not something a believer experiences on a consistent basis, but is granted on those special occasions when an extraordinary degree of confidence in God's activity is called for.

Jesus may well have had the spiritual gift of faith in mind when he spoke these words to his disciples: "Have faith in God. Truly, I say to you, whoever says to this mountain, 'Be taken up and thrown into the sea, and does not doubt in his heart, but believes that what he says will come to pass, it will be done for him. Therefore I tell you, whatever you ask in prayer, believe that you have received it, and it will be yours" (Mark 11:22–24). Although the "spiritual gift" of faith likely first appeared following Pentecost, what Jesus described here may be analogous to what Paul was talking about in 1 Corinthians 12.

Moving or casting a mountain into the sea was proverbial in those days for the miraculous. After all, why would any Christian want to make a mountain fall into the sea? Our Lord's purpose was to highlight the fact that otherwise humanly impossible things, things that require supernatural and miraculous power, can occur when prayer is filled with faith.

The instantaneous and miraculous destruction of the fig tree (Mark 11:12–14, 20–21) served as an object lesson to the disciples of what can be achieved by faith in God's power. Peter pointed to the tree and said, "Rabbi, look! The fig tree that you cursed has withered" (v. 21). In turn, Jesus said to Peter, "Your comment tells me that you are amazed by the sudden and supernatural withering of the fig tree. But if you have faith in God, all things are possible through prayer."

We should note several things here to help us avoid a misunderstanding of what the spiritual gift of faith is and is not. First, recognize that the "belief" or "faith" that Jesus described is not a case of a Christian forcing himself to believe what he does not really believe. It is not a wrenching of one's brain, a coercing of one's will, a contorting of one's expectations to embrace as real and true something that one's heartfelt conviction says otherwise. Jesus was not telling us that when doubts start to creep in we should put our hands over our ears, close our eyes, and say to those doubts, over and over again, "Lalalalala, I can't hear you. Lalalalala, I can't hear you!" That's not faith. That's "make believe." That's spiritual pretending.

On the other hand, we are responsible to take steps that will facilitate the deepening of faith in our hearts. We can do things, by God's grace, that will expand our confidence in God's goodness and his greatness and help diminish if not drive out our doubts. As I read and study and meditate on the character of God, my confidence in what he can do increases. As I reflect on and ponder the grace and kindness of God, my confidence in his goodness grows and intensifies.

Clearly other factors have to be taken into consideration when we ask God for things in prayer. Faith is not the sole condition for answered prayer.

(1) We have to ask him with the right motives (see James 4:1ff.). (2) We have to be treating our wives with gentleness and kindness and understanding (1 Peter 3:7). (3) We have to clean the slate, so to speak, in our relationships with others. This is the point of Mark 11:25. If you harbor unforgiveness in your heart toward others, it isn't likely that God will answer your prayer, no matter how much alleged faith you think you have (see also Matt. 6:14–15). (4) And we have to ask in accordance with God's will. It doesn't matter if I am somehow able to banish all doubt from my mind and convince myself that I've already received what I asked for, if what I'm asking isn't consistent with the will and character of God, the answer will be no.

It's also important to remember that no amount of faith will force God's hand to do something that is contrary to our welfare. It doesn't matter how persuaded you are or how much faith you have, you simply don't want God to answer every prayer you pray! Look with the benefit of hindsight on some of the things you once believed you needed and were convinced that God would give you. Thank the Lord for saying no to many of these prayers. It would have been devastating if he had said yes. Sometimes God says no to prayers that are offered up in faith because he has something even better in store for us that he plans on giving at a more appropriate time.

My point is simply that it is irresponsible and insensitive to suggest, on the basis of this passage, that if someone doesn't receive from God what they asked for, it is because they are at fault in failing to have enough faith. The absence of faith may well be a factor, but it is not the only factor. There are other things that may more readily account for unanswered prayer.

I am persuaded that the only way anyone can fulfill the condition set forth by Jesus is if God himself chooses to impart to us the faith he requires. Faith, ultimately, is a gift from God. When God wants to bless us with a miraculous answer to our prayer, he will take the initiative to cultivate and build into our hearts the fulfillment of the condition he requires. This may well be precisely what Paul had in view in 1 Corinthians 12.

Another example of "faith" operating in this manner is in 1 Corinthians 13. There Paul insisted on the pervasive presence of love in our relationships with one another in our exercise of all spiritual gifts. He said, "And if I have prophetic powers, and understand all mysteries and all knowledge, and if I have all faith, so as to remove mountains, but have not love, I am nothing" (v. 2). Given the proximity of this passage to chapter 12 of 1 Corinthians, the apostle's reference to the sort of "faith" that can "remove mountains" most likely has in view the spiritual gift of faith.

Note, too, that James's reference to "the prayer of faith" (James 5:15) may also be an allusion to the charismatic gift of faith. Since it is not the case that everyone for whom we pray is healed, notwithstanding the continuing presence of faith in our hearts, James likely was talking about the sort of faith that is spontaneously and sovereignly bestowed by the Spirit when it is God's will to heal the sick. This is not the faith that is easily or regularly experienced by any and all Christians, but the sort that is subject to the timing and purposes of God.

In conclusion, whereas not every member of the body of Christ is granted the "spiritual gift of faith" as a regular, normative reality, any member of the body of Christ is a potential candidate for this particular manifestation of the Spirit. It is a gift, like all others, that we should "earnestly desire" (1 Cor. 14:1) but not one that is in any sense ultimately in our control or up to us to exercise. D. A. Carson differentiates between saving faith and this spontaneous, supernatural faith:

> Saving faith is ultimately grounded in God's gracious and public self-disclosure in Christ Jesus and in the Scriptures; even though the work of the Holy Spirit is required for such faith, faith's object lies in revelatory events and words that are in the public arena. This special faith, however [i.e., the spiritual gift of faith], enables a believer to trust God to bring about certain things for which he or she cannot claim some divine promise recorded in Scripture, or some state of affairs grounded in the very structure of the gospel. One thinks, for instance, of George Muller of Bristol.[1]

Again, says Carson, "[the gift of faith] appears to be the God-given ability, without fakery or platitudinous exhortations to believe what you do not really believe, to trust God for a certain blessing *not* promised in Scripture."[2] Those who testify to having received this gift speak often of a dynamic but ultimately inexplicable surge or eruption of assurance in their hearts that

---

1   D. A. Carson, *Showing the Spirit: A Theological Exposition of 1 Corinthians 12–14* (1987; repr., Grand Rapids: Baker, 2019), 48.
2   Carson, 48n65.

God not only *can* do something powerful in a particular challenging situation but that he *will* do it. Needless to say, there is often a fine line between such extraordinary certainty on the one hand and a presumptuous triumphalism on the other.

Is There Such a Thing as the Spiritual Gift of Healing?

No. There is no such thing as *the* spiritual gift of healing. There never has been and never will be. Obviously, this calls for some explanation. Many Christians, perhaps even most, think of healing in much the same way they do the spiritual gifts of teaching or mercy or evangelism or encouragement. That is to say, they envision a person with the gift of healing as being able to heal all diseases at any time whenever they will. A person with the gift of teaching can teach at the drop of a hat. So, too, with gifts such as mercy and serving, just to mention two. They are gifts that are in our possession and under our control. This is the single most serious mistake when it comes to understanding the spiritual gift of healing.

On numerous occasions I've heard people say, "Well, if the spiritual gift of healing is still valid and operative in our day, we should visit the nearest cancer ward and empty it of its patients." Such thinking betrays a fundamental misconception of how this spiritual gift is described and how it actually functions in the New Testament.

Let's begin with the way Paul referred to this gift in 1 Corinthians 12:9 and again in 12:28 and 12:30. These are the only three places where the gift of healing is mentioned. Note well. I didn't say they are the only three texts where healing is mentioned. Healing is found pervasively in the four gospels and in the book of Acts. But the "gift" or *charisma* of healing is spoken of in only three texts, and in all three instances it is the same terminology: "gifts of healings." Virtually all English translations render this as "gifts of healing" (singular). But Paul quite explicitly employed the plural of both nouns: "gifts [plural] of healings [plural]" (*charismata iamatōn*). This can't be insignificant or merely stylistic. Furthermore, of the nine gifts listed in this paragraph, only healing is mentioned in conjunction with the word "gift(s)." What could this imply?

As I have written elsewhere,[3] evidently Paul did not envision an individ-

---

3   See my book *Practicing the Power: Welcoming the Gifts of the Holy Spirit in Your Life* (Grand Rapids: Zonder-

ual being endowed with one healing gift operative at all times for all diseases. His language suggests either many different gifts or powers of healing, each appropriate to and effective for its related illness, or each occurrence of healing constituting a distinct gift in its own right.

I've had the opportunity on numerous occasions to meet people who have what appears to be a healing anointing for one particular affliction. Some are able to pray more effectively for those with back problems while others see more success when praying for migraine headaches. This may be what Paul had in mind when he spoke of multiple or a plurality of "gifts" of "healings."

As I said above, one of the principal obstacles to a proper understanding of healing is the erroneous assumption that if anyone could *ever* heal, he or she could *always* heal. But in view of the lingering illness of Epaphroditus (Phil. 2:25–30), Timothy (1 Tim. 5:23), Trophimus (2 Tim. 4:20), and perhaps Paul himself (2 Cor. 12:7–10; Gal. 4:13), it is better to view this gift as subject to the will of God, not the will of people. Therefore, a person may be gifted to heal many people but not all. Another may be gifted to heal only one person at one particular time of one particular disease. When asked to pray for the sick, people are often heard to respond, "I can't. I don't have the gift of healing." But if my reading of Paul is correct, there is no such thing as *the* gift of healing, if by that one means the God-given ability to heal everyone of every disease on every occasion. Rather, the Spirit sovereignly distributes a *charisma* of healing for a particular occasion, even though previous prayers for physical restoration under similar circumstances may not have been answered, and even though subsequent prayers for the same affliction may not be answered. In sum, "gifts of healings" are occasional and subject to the sovereign purposes of God.[4]

Few doubt that Paul had a "gift" for healing. But his prayers for Epaphroditus weren't answered, at least not at first (see Phil. 2:25–30). Clearly

---

van, 2017), 73–75; as well as *The Beginner's Guide to Spiritual Gifts* (Minneapolis: Bethany House, 2015), 67–71.

4   D. A. Carson concurs. He refers to "these remarkable plurals [gifts of healings]" as suggesting "that there were *different* gifts of healings: not everyone was getting healed by one person, and perhaps certain persons with *one* of those gifts of healing could by the Lord's grace heal certain diseases or heal a variety of diseases but only at certain times. . . . If a Christian has been granted the *charisma* . . . to heal one particular individual of one particular disease at one time, that Christian should not presume to think that *the* gift of healing has been bestowed on him or her, prompting the founding of a 'healing ministry'" (Carson, *Showing the Spirit*, 49).

Paul could not heal at will. Aside from Jesus, no one else could either! And there is doubt if even Jesus could (read Mark 6:5–6; John 5:19). Some would conclude from Paul's failure to heal his friend that the so-called gift of healing was dying out at this juncture in the life of the church (in spite of the fact that late in his ministry, in Acts 28:9, Paul apparently healed everyone on the island of Malta who came to him). It seems better to conclude that healing, whenever and wherever it occurred, was subject, not to the will of man but to the will of God. No one, not even Paul, could always heal all diseases. If Paul was distressed that Epaphroditus was ill, almost unto death, and that initially his prayers for him were ineffective, I doubt seriously if the apostle would have drawn the same conclusions that modern cessationists do. Paul understood the occasional or circumstantial nature of gifts of healings.

The fact that healing is an expression of divine "mercy" (Phil. 2:27) means that it should never be viewed as a "right" or as something the Christian can claim. There is no place in the life of the believer or the local church for the presumptuous approach to healing that is found in advocates of the health and wealth gospel or in the Word of Faith movement.[5] Healing is not the payment of a debt. God does not *owe* us healing. We don't deserve healing. I believe we should have faith for healing. But there is a vast difference between faith in divine mercy and presumption based on an alleged right. God had "mercy" on Epaphroditus (v. 27), the same word used in the Gospels to describe why Jesus healed people while he was on the earth. God's motive for healing hasn't changed! The primary reason God healed through Jesus prior to Pentecost was because he is a merciful, compassionate God. And the primary reason God continues to heal after Pentecost is because he is a merciful, compassionate God. God is no less merciful, no less compassionate, no less caring when it comes to the physical condition of his people after Pentecost than he was before Pentecost.

There may well be a close connection between gifts of healings and the gift of faith, which immediately precedes it in Paul's list of the *charismata*. As we saw above, the spiritual gift of faith is a unique and extraordinary capacity to believe that God is going to do something quite remarkable for which we don't have an explicit biblical promise.

---

5 For a discussion of whether there is "healing in the atonement," see my book *Tough Topics: Biblical Answers to 25 Challenging Questions* (Wheaton, IL: Crossway, 2013), 295–302.

A personal example will help illustrate what I'm saying. One Sunday a couple came to me before the worship service and asked that the elders of our church anoint their infant son and pray for his healing. After the service we gathered in my office and I anointed him with oil. I don't recall the precise medical name for his condition, but at six months of age he had a serious liver disorder that would require immediate surgery, possibly even a transplant, if something did not change. As we prayed, something very unusual happened. As we laid hands on this young child and prayed, I found myself suddenly filled with an overwhelming and inescapable confidence that he would be healed. It was altogether unexpected. I recall actually trying to doubt, but couldn't. I prayed confidently, filled with a faith unshakable and undeniable. I said to myself, "Lord, you really are going to heal him." Although the family left the room unsure, I was absolutely certain God had healed him. The next morning the doctor agreed. He was totally healed and is a healthy, happy young man in his late twenties today.

Perhaps, then, "the prayer of faith" to which James (5:15) referred is not just any prayer that may be prayed at will, but a uniquely and divinely motivated prayer prompted by the Spirit-wrought conviction that God intends to heal the one for whom prayer is being offered. The faith necessary for healing is itself a gift of God, sovereignly bestowed when he wills. When God chooses to heal, he produces in the hearts of those praying the faith or confidence that such is precisely his intent. The particular kind of faith to which James referred, in response to which God heals, is not the kind that we may exercise at our will. It is the kind of faith that we exercise only when God wills. Thus, there is no reason to think that had I prayed for another afflicted infant boy that day he would necessarily have been healed. The fact that I received a gift for healing on this one occasion is no guarantee that I may pray with equal success on some other occasion.

Many in the church today say they believe that God still heals, but they live as functional deists who rarely if ever actually lay hands on the sick and pray with any degree of expectancy. Jesus laid his hands on the sick (Luke 4:40), as did the early church (Acts 9:17; 28:7–8; cf. Mark 16:18). And so should we.

People often confuse praying expectantly with praying presumptuously. Prayer is presumptuous when the person claims healing without revelatory warrant, or on the unbiblical assumption that God always wills to heal. This then requires them to account for the absence of healing by an appeal either to moral failure or deficiency of faith (usually in the one for whom prayer is offered). People pray expectantly when they humbly petition a merciful God for something they don't deserve but that he delights to give (Luke 11:9–13; cf. Matt. 9:27–31; 20:29–34; Luke 17:13–14). Expectant prayer flows from the recognition that Jesus healed people because he loved them and felt compassion for them (Matt. 14:13–14; 20:34; Mark 1:41–42; Luke 7:11–17), a disposition that nothing in Scripture indicates has changed.

James 5 and Healing

I have three additional comments to make about this passage in James 5. First, James made several key points about the relationship of sickness to sin in verse 15. He wrote, "The prayer offered in faith will restore the one who is sick, and the Lord will raise him up, and *if* he [the sick man] has committed sins, they will be forgiven him" (v. 15 NASB, emphasis added). James was in harmony with Jesus (John 9:1–3) and Paul (2 Cor. 12:1–10) that not all sickness is the direct result of sin. Sometimes it is (1 Cor. 11:27–30; Mark 2:1–12) but not always. The "if" in verse 15 is not designed to suggest that the one who is sick may *never* have sinned. The meaning is that if God should heal him in answer to prayer, this indicates that any sins of the sufferer, which might have been responsible for this particular illness, were forgiven. In other words, if sin were responsible for his sickness, the fact that God healed him physically would be evidence that God had forgiven him spiritually.

Second, the sin James had in mind may have been that of bitterness, resentment, jealousy, anger, or unforgiveness in our relationships with one another, or conceivably any number of sins we may have committed against God. Hence, James advised that we "confess [our] sins to one another" (James 5:16). He probably had in mind either confessing to the person against whom you have sinned or confessing to another believer your more general transgressions, or violations, of biblical laws. What this tells us is that God has chosen to suspend healing mercy on the repentance of his people. When the hurting don't get healed, it may be a result of stubbornness and spiritual insensitivity more than because "God doesn't do that sort of thing anymore."

Finally, we should take careful note of the example of Elijah (see James 5:17–18). As we noted in an earlier chapter, some cessationists believe that biblical miracles were clustered, or concentrated, in only three major periods of history: the days of Moses and Joshua, the time of Elijah and Elisha, and the time of Christ and the apostles. The point of this argument is that Elijah and Elisha, for example, were special, extraordinary, unique individuals who cannot serve as models for us when we pray.

But James said precisely the opposite! The point of verses 17–18 is to counter the argument that Elijah was somehow unique or that because of the period in which he lived he could pray with miraculous success, but we cannot. James wanted readers to know that Elijah was just like you and me. He was a human being with weaknesses, fears, doubts, failures—no less than we. In other words, James said, "Don't let anyone tell you Elijah was in a class by himself. He wasn't. He's just like you. You are just like him. Therefore, pray like he did!"

Don't forget the context: James appealed to the example of Elijah to encourage us when we pray for the sick! The point is that we should pray for miraculous healing with the same faith and expectation with which Elijah prayed for the end of a three-year drought.

If I Have Enough Faith, Will I Always Be Healed?

When it comes to the relationship of our faith to physical healing, Christians will often gravitate to one extreme or the other. Some argue that the sort of faith God honors by granting us healing is altogether devoid of doubt. The believer is called on to drive from his or her conscious thought any possibility that God might not be will to provide healing. One must believe, without hesitation or fear, that God's will is always to heal. Only then will he do so in response to our prayers. Others regard that perspective as bordering on sinful presumption and thus, swinging to the other end of the spectrum, minimize the importance of faith altogether. Faith is largely irrelevant to whether God will heal. He is sovereign and will do what he desires irrespective of our faith or its absence.

The first thing we must consider is the way in which faith is actually described in the New Testament and in the ministry of Jesus. In certain instances healing occurred in the absence of anyone's faith. In John 5:1–9 we read of the man who had been an invalid for thirty-eight years. We see no evidence of faith on his part, either in the will of God relative to his condition or in the ability of Jesus to restore his health. Still, Jesus healed him. It actually comes as something of a surprise that faith is never mentioned anywhere in John's gospel as a prerequisite for healing.

That incident aside, in most cases where Jesus healed, it was in response to someone's faith. Here are a few examples. In the case of a particular paralytic, it was only when Jesus "saw" the "faith" of his friends that he healed the man (Matt. 9:1–8). Jesus restored the sight to two blind men "according to" their "faith" (vv. 28–29). The interesting thing about this incident is that Jesus didn't ask them if they had faith in his will to heal, but only if they believed that he was "able" to heal. When the Canaanite woman called on Jesus to heal her daughter who was severely oppressed by a demon, his response was remarkable: "O woman, great is your faith! Be it done for you as you desire" (Matt. 15:28).

How much faith is required? That may be the wrong question to ask. Perhaps we should focus on the kind or quality of faith, or better still on the object or focus of our confidence. When the father of a young boy asked that Jesus might cast out a demon from his son, our Lord responded by saying, "All things are possible for one who believes" (Mark 9:23). Immediately, "the father of the child cried out and said, 'I believe; help my unbelief!'" (v. 24). Although some measure of faith was present in this man's heart, it was clearly qualified by his own confession of unbelief. Still, Jesus responded by driving out the demon (v. 25).

All doubt about the role of faith should be silenced on reading a text such as this: "He said to her, 'Daughter, your faith has made you well; go in peace, and be healed of your disease'" (Mark 5:34).

When approached by Jairus, whose daughter was near death, Jesus said to him, "Do not fear, only believe" (Mark 5:36). But believe what? That it was the will of Christ to heal her? That Christ possessed the power to heal her? That Jesus would in fact heal her? Jesus said much the same thing to the one leper who returned to give thanks for his healing: "Your faith has made you well" (Luke 17:19). Again, Jesus spoke to blind Bartimaeus and said: "Go your way; your faith has made you well" (Mark 10:52).

It is highly instructive that nowhere in the Gospels or anywhere else in the New Testament are we told to believe that it is always God's will to heal the sick. Jesus never asked that of those whom he healed. He was only concerned that they believed he was able to heal. In light of this, we may identify several expressions of faith, not all of which operate at the same level of confidence. In other words, faith is never monolithic in the Bible, as if every experience of trust in God is the same.

If we should ask why faith appears to play such a crucial role in our response to God, it isn't because God is otherwise lacking and our faith supplies him with the incentive or power to do for us what we ask. Faith is required because faith glorifies God. It redirects our spiritual and emotional energy away from self and to the God who sustains us. Faith is not a force that compels God to act or in any sense "creates our own reality." It is an expression of weakness and utter dependency. The focus of faith is not in our ability to believe but in God's ability to do what otherwise seems impossible. It is not the mere fact of faith, but its focus, that brings results.

We know that faith can have as its focus the reality of God's goodness and his provision for us on a daily basis. We find this expression of faith in the words of the psalmist:

> Behold, the eye of the LORD is on those who fear him,
>> on those who hope in his steadfast love,
> that he may deliver their soul from death
>> and keep them alive in famine.
>
> Our soul waits for the LORD;
>> he is our help and our shield.
> For our heart is glad in him,
>> because we trust in his holy name.
> Let your steadfast love, O LORD, be upon us,
>> even as we hope in you. (Ps. 33:18–22; see also Ps. 147:10–11)

As already noted, Jesus always seems to respond positively to a confession of faith in his ability to heal (see Matt. 9:28–29). We must not overlook what Jesus didn't say in this regard. He did not ask the two blind men, nor anyone else in the course of his ministry, if they believed that it was his will to heal them. He only asked if they believed he was able to do so. The leper in Matthew 8 made no presumption on the will of our Lord, but in faith declared his confidence in his power: "Lord, if you will, you can make me clean" (v. 2). It was the leper's belief that Jesus *could* do it, not necessarily that he *would* do it, that resulted in his healing.

At all times it is essential that we have faith in God's compassion and love for the sick. In other words, our trust is in God's goodness and his commitment to do what is best for his children. "If you then," said Jesus, "who are evil, know how to give good gifts to your children, how much more will the heavenly Father give the Holy Spirit to those who ask him!" (Luke 11:13). This is simply a matter of unwavering confidence in the kindness and mercy of our heavenly Father's heart.

Believing that God actually does heal today is vital. We are nowhere expected to believe that he always will. But if you do not believe that healing is still today a part of God's gracious and merciful provision for his people, it is unlikely (but not impossible) that you will be the recipient of his power in this regard. To cite an obvious example, I don't believe that it is God's design that we discern his will by the casting of lots (see Acts 1:24–26). Therefore, I will not devote my energy in doing so, nor will I have any degree of confidence that, should I choose to cast lots, God will assuredly respond in disclosing his will by such means. Similarly, if you don't believe God still heals, the likelihood is low that you will spend much time in prayer asking him to do so.

But might there be certain occasions when you or I are stirred by the Holy Spirit to believe that it is God's will to heal someone *right now*? Yes. This sort of faith, however, is not the kind that we can crank up at our own initiative or by our own strength. This is likely the kind of faith that Paul had in mind when he spoke of it as a spiritual gift (1 Cor. 12:9) and that James referred to as the "prayer of faith" (James 5:15). This is the sort of faith that we are supernaturally enabled to exercise by God's will, not our own. I can't independently choose to have this sort of faith. I can believe that it is God's will to heal someone at this precise moment only when the Spirit prompts me and empowers me with that degree of unshakable confidence. When God wills to heal, he produces in our hearts the overwhelming and unwavering assurance that such is precisely what is about to occur.

If God Still Heals, Why Doesn't He Always Heal?

God loved the apostle Paul. Yet God sovereignly orchestrated his painful thorn in the flesh and then declined to remove it, notwithstanding Paul's passionate prayer that he be healed. We are not apostles. Yet, as his children, no less so than Paul, God loves us too. We don't know the nature of

Paul's thorn,[6] but each of us has undoubtedly suffered in a similar way, and some considerably worse. We, like Paul, have prayed incessantly to be healed. Or perhaps knowing of a loved one's "thorn," we have prayed for them. And again, like Paul, God declined to remove it. Why?

It's hard to imagine a more difficult, confusing, and controversial topic than why God chooses not to heal in response to the intercessory pleas of his people. I don't profess to have all the answers, but I think I have a few. I'm sure that what follows will provoke many to anger and frustration, while others, I pray, will find a measure of comfort.[7]

In the final analysis, virtually everything about healing remains a mystery. I don't mind saying that I'm weary of those who claim to reduce healing to a formula or a manageable cause-and-effect phenomenon in which we can know with certainty why some are healed and why others are not. I've labored in this chapter to avoid falling into that trap. That said, I would like to suggest that the reason why many are not healed may *possibly* be answered in any one of seven ways.

First, although we must be careful in giving more weight to the role of faith than does the New Testament itself, we also must be willing to acknowledge that occasionally healing does not occur because of the absence of that sort of faith that God delights to honor. This does not mean that every time a person isn't healed it is because of a defective faith, or that if only a more robust and doubt-free faith were in exercise, healing would inevitably follow. But it does mean that faith is very important. How can we conclude otherwise in view of the many texts in which healing is closely linked to someone's faith? I hope you'll take the time to pause and read these passages: Matthew 9:22, 28–29; 15:28; Mark 2:5, 11; 5:34; 9:17–24; 10:52; Luke 17:19; Acts 3:16; 14:8–10; James 5:14–16.

Second, sometimes healing does not occur because of the presence of sin for which there has been no confession or repentance. James 5:15–16 clearly instructs us to confess our sins to one another and pray for one another that we may be healed. Again, please do not conclude from this that each time a person isn't healed it is because he or she has committed some specific sin

---

6 However, I make an effort to identify Paul's "thorn in the flesh" in my book *Tough Topics*, 283–94.

7 What follows is adapted from a chapter in my book *Tough Topics*, titled "Why Doesn't God Always Heal the Sick?" 303–8.

of which they have refused to repent. But in *some* cases (not necessarily all) this is undoubtedly true. We have to reckon with the possibility that lingering bitterness, anger, resentment, envy, or unforgiveness in our hearts and our refusal to confess and repent of such sins is the reason God withholds physical healing from our bodies.

Third, although it sounds odd to many at first hearing, healing may not happen because the sick don't want it to happen. Jesus asked the paralyzed man in John 5:6, "Do you want to be healed?" What on the surface may appear to be a ridiculous question is, on further examination, found to be profoundly insightful.

Some people who suffer from a chronic affliction become accustomed to their illness and to the pattern of life it requires. Their identity is to a large extent wrapped up in their physical disability. I realize that sounds strange to those of us who enjoy robust health. Why would anyone prefer to stay sick? Who wouldn't jump at the opportunity to be healed? But I've actually known a handful of people who in a very real sense enjoy their dependence on others and the special attention it brings them. They are convinced that the only reason people take note of them and show them kindness and compassion is because of their affliction. They fear that if they were healed, they would lose the love on which they've come to depend. Remaining sick is to their way of thinking a small price to pay to retain the kindness and involvement of those who otherwise would ignore them.

Then, of course, in some instances ill people don't want the responsibilities that would come with being healthy. To their way of thinking, it's easier (and perhaps even more profitable) to remain the object of others' beneficence and goodwill than it would be to be healthy and thus expected to get a job and show up from nine to five on a daily basis. This is not a common phenomenon, but it does happen.

Fourth, we must also consider the principle articulated in James 4:2, where we are told, "You do not have, because you do not ask." The simple fact is that some are not healed because they do not pray. Perhaps they pray once or twice and then allow discouragement to paralyze their petitions. Prayer for healing often must be prolonged, sustained, persevering, and combined with fasting.

Fifth, some are not healed because the demonic cause of the affliction has not been addressed. Please do not jump to unwarranted conclusions.

I am not suggesting that all physical disease is demonically induced. Of course, it is interesting, is it not, that in Paul's case God used "a messenger of Satan" to inflict the thorn. There is also the case of the woman in Luke 13 "who had had a disabling spirit [or, a spirit of infirmity] for eighteen years. She was bent over and could not fully straighten herself" (v. 11). According to Jesus, "Satan" had "bound" her (Luke 13:16; see also Acts 10:38). It takes considerable discernment, time, and patience to determine if an illness has a demonic cause, together with even greater commitment to praying for that individual and leading them to address the reasons for their spiritual oppression. When these factors are ignored, healing may not be forthcoming.

Sixth, we must also consider the mystery of divine providence. There are undoubtedly times and seasons in the purposes of God during which his healing power is withdrawn or at least largely diminished. God may have any number of reasons for this to which we are not privy, whether to discipline a wayward and rebellious church or to create a greater desperation for his power or to wean us off excessive dependence on physical comfort and convenience or any number of other possibilities. If this leaves you confused, that's why it's called a mystery!

But what must we say when the problem isn't the absence of faith or the presence of a demon or the refusal to repent or the failure to pray or a lack of desire? How, then, do we account for ongoing physical affliction, as in Paul's case? I strongly urge you to read the next point carefully.

Seventh, often times there are dimensions of spiritual growth and moral development and increase in the knowledge of God in us that God desires *more* than our physical health, experiences that in his wisdom God has determined can be attained *only* by means or in the midst of or in response to less than perfect physical health. In other words, healing the sick is a *good* thing (and we should never cease to pray for it), but often there is a *better* thing that can only be attained by means of physical weakness.

More important to God than our physical health is our spiritual holiness. This isn't to say that the body isn't important. God isn't a gnostic! He values and has redeemed our bodies and now dwells within them as his eternal temple. But while we live in this corrupt and decaying world, inner and spiritual conformity to the image of Christ often comes only at the expense of or at least simultaneous with physical deterioration and suffering (see 2 Cor. 4:16–18).

Let me personalize this principle. If I believe Romans 8:28, that God sovereignly orchestrates all events in my life for my ultimate spiritual good (and preeminently for his ultimate glory), I can only conclude that, all things being equal, if I'm not healed *it is because God values something in me greater than my physical comfort and health* that he, in his infinite wisdom and kindness, knows can only be attained by means of my physical affliction and the lessons of submission, dependency, and trust in God that I learn from it.

In the final analysis, we may never know why a person isn't healed. What, then, ought to be our response? In the first place, don't stop praying! Some people find this difficult to swallow. Many times I've been asked, "Why should Paul bother to pray for release from something that God wills to inflict?" The answer is because *Paul didn't know* what God's will was in this particular case until such time as God chose to make it known. And neither do you or I with regard to any particular illness that we may suffer.

If the Lord had never said in response to Paul's prayer, "No, it isn't my will that you be relieved of this thorn," Paul would have been justified, indeed *required*, to continue to pray for his healing. I once heard my friend Jack Taylor put it this way: "Never cease praying for healing until you are shown otherwise either by divine revelation or death!" If you are able to discern, as did Paul, through some revelatory disclosure or other legitimate biblical means that it is not God's will now or ever to heal you, you may cease asking him to do so. Otherwise, short of death itself, you must persevere in prayer. You never know but that God's ultimate and long-term will for you is complete healing after he has for a season accomplished his short-term sanctifying purpose.

In Paul's case, the only reason he ceased asking for deliverance was because God, in effect, told him to shut up! "No, Paul. I'm not going to heal you. It isn't my will in this instance that you be set free from this affliction. Rather, I have a higher purpose in view: your humility and my Son's glory manifest in the context of your ongoing weakness." Paul, in effect, replied, "Okay, Lord, I'll shut up and submit to your merciful purpose in my life. I know you love me and desire what is ultimately of greatest good for my spiritual growth. Therefore, my prayer now is that you maximize in me the beneficial effects of this pain. Don't let me miss out on any spiritual good that might come my way from this malady. Teach me everything I need to know and sustain me that I might be a platform for the glory of Christ and a source of comfort to other suffering saints."

I'm sure there are other ways to account for why God chooses not to heal, but I trust that these have proven helpful. There is much I do not know about this matter, but of this I'm quite certain: God's grace is sufficient in all circumstances so that we, "for the sake of Christ" (2 Cor. 12:10a), might learn that in our weakness his power is made perfect!

CHAPTER 15

Miracles and the Spiritual Gift of Miracles

As I set before you the spectrum of beliefs about miracles, be aware that each of these views is embraced by professing Christians. I'm not talking about atheists, but about people who claim to know Jesus as Savior and claim to believe the Bible is the Word of God.

First, at one far end of the spectrum are those who argue that miracles no longer occur. They once did, in biblical times, during the Old Testament, during the life and ministry of Jesus, and during the early church as seen in the book of Acts. But God no longer works miracles. Anything that appears to be miraculous can be explained scientifically given enough time and analysis. God always and only operates through normal cause and effect. These people don't deny the reality of the supernatural realm, but they might as well, because anything that anyone might suggest is a miracle often evokes from them condescending scorn. Thus, their response to claims for the miraculous is *cynicism*.

Second, moving a bit farther down the spectrum are those who believe that miracles *might* still occur today, but they are extremely, and I cannot emphasize strongly enough the word *extremely*, rare. Even if miracles might occur today, you should not seek them; you should not pray for them; and your response should be one of heightened *skepticism*. There is a difference between cynicism and skepticism. Cynics are snide and snarky and often treat with scorn anyone who believes in modern-day miracles. Skeptics are simply, well, skeptical. They aren't necessarily mean or nasty, and they don't typically mock those who believe in miracles.

The third perspective is one that affirms that miracles still happen, but when they do happen they occur independently of any human involvement. In other words, God sovereignly works miracles but without the agency of any human being. These are people who believe in miracles but deny that the spiritual gift of working miracles is still operative in our day. There are no miracle workers. These people aren't cynical, nor are they skeptical, but they are *doubtful*. It takes a great deal to convince them that a miracle has occurred. This is the view that I embraced for the first thirty-five years of my life.

The fourth option is the one I embrace today. I believe that miracles still happen. I believe that the spiritual gift of miracles is still operative in the church. I believe that this gift is what I call a circumstantial or occasional gift. That is to say, no Christian can work miracles at will, whenever they please, at any time. Any Christian might be given the power to work a miracle on a particular occasion, dependent on God's sovereign will and his purpose. Miracles are therefore to be prayed for. The spiritual gift of working miracles is one that we should all seek. Whether or not it is given is entirely up to God. And simply because you receive a gift of working a miracle on one occasion does not mean you will always operate or minister at that level of supernatural power. This view is not cynical, not skeptical, or doubtful, but *hopeful* (and prayerful).

The fifth and final option is at the far end of the spectrum from the first view. The first view is that miracles never occur. God never wills to perform supernatural displays of power. This final option argues that God *always* wills to perform miracles in our midst. Not only does God always will to perform them, but he always *will* perform them, and if he doesn't, the fault is always ours. How do these people respond to the claim for the occurrence of a miracle? They are not cynical or skeptical or doubtful or even just hopeful. They are often *gullible*. They tend to be naive and accept without question any and all claims to the miraculous.

John 14:12

Whenever the subject of the miraculous or the spiritual gift of miracles is raised, people immediately turn to the words of Jesus in John 14:12. There he said to his disciples, "Truly, truly, I say to you, whoever believes in me will also do the works that I do; and greater works than these will he do, because I am going to the Father."

Most of the interpretations of John 14:12 are driven by the perceived disparity people feel between what Jesus said would come to pass on the one hand and their own experience on the other. They read this verse and say, "Something's wrong. I don't believe that the followers of Jesus have done the same works Jesus did, far less have they done greater works than he. So how can I navigate around the problem this poses for those of us who believe in the inspiration of the Bible?"

The most popular interpretation in our day is that Jesus's words refer to something other than miraculous deeds and physical healing. The "greater" works Jesus's followers do is a reference to *evangelistic success* in the number of souls saved. After all, whereas Jesus accomplished much in his earthly ministry, the number of people who came to saving faith while in his physical presence was quite small.

Very similar to this is the idea that the works are "greater" because Jesus worked in only one land, whereas his followers work everywhere around the globe. Or perhaps they are "greater" because from this point on they are no longer confined to or flow from only one person. Or again, they are "greater" because Jesus ministered in only a three-year span, whereas his followers are ministering over several centuries. There is a sense in which all those things are true, but do they really account for what he said? I don't think so.

A view I used to embrace is that if the "works" Jesus did, and promised that believers would do, is a reference to miraculous deeds and physical healings, perhaps the complete fulfillment of this word is *yet future*. If what Jesus said was true—and *everything* he said was true—then surely this promise has yet to see its consummate fulfillment. Could it be that it will happen in our generation? This is possible, and I certainly hope it is true. But the answer may lie elsewhere.

A fourth interpretation appeals to Matthew 11:11, where Jesus said that "the one who is least in the kingdom of heaven is greater than he [i.e., greater than John the Baptist]." Why are you and I "greater" than John the Baptist? The answer is that, as great as John was, he never experienced the fullness of the blessings of the kingdom of heaven that came through the death and especially the resurrection of Jesus. John's ministry came too early in redemptive history to permit him to participate in the glory of the new age, which Jesus inaugurated. Thus, the works performed *after* Jesus ascended to the right hand of the Father and sent the Spirit are "greater" because they will occur in a different and more advanced phase of God's plan of salvation, being based on Jesus's finished work of redemption.[1]

In support of this view is the last phrase in John 14:12. There Jesus appears to have attributed the ability of his followers to do "greater" works to the fact that he was "going to the Father." In the context of the Upper Room Discourse (John 13–17), this clearly points us to the gift of the Holy Spirit that was dependent on his ascension to the Father's right hand (see John 14:16, 26; 15:26; 16:7).

I think there is a measure of truth in this. Up until the time that Jesus spoke these words in the upper room, no one had been forgiven of their sins based on the finished work of Jesus on the cross and the empty grave. All salvation up to this point had been in anticipation of what would eventually occur. Salvation was based on faith in the promise of a coming atonement that would forever put away sin. But since Jesus died and arose from the dead and went to his Father and sent the Holy Spirit, salvation is based on faith in the finished historical fact of the atonement for sin.

So what makes the works we do "greater" is that they are done in the aftermath of the final accomplishment of redemption and the outpouring of the Holy Spirit. They are "greater" because they are done in an era or age that doesn't look forward to the payment of a ransom for sin but looks backward at it. The message you preach will be the message not of a promised ransom but a paid ransom, not of a future payment for sin but a finished payment for sin. The works are "greater" because they are performed in the age of fulfillment, the age of the new covenant, an age that transcends anything that has come before in God's redemptive purposes.

Unlike anything that has happened up until now, said Jesus, you will do "works" that point people to a finished work of atonement and an empty grave and a risen and glorified Savior, and you will do it in the fullness of the Spirit's presence and power. On this view, these works are "greater" because of *when* they take place, not because of *what* they are. They occur in the age of the Spirit. They belong to an age of clarity and power with the ascension of Jesus and the descent of the Spirit and the institution of the new covenant.

---

1 This is the view defended by D. A. Carson in two of his commentaries. See D. A. Carson, *The Gospel according to John* (Grand Rapids: Eerdmans, 1991), 495–96; and Carson, *Matthew*, Expositor's Bible Commentary (Grand Rapids: Zondervan, 1984), 263–68.

I think this makes sense, especially when we realize that no one can do "greater" miracles than raising the dead and walking on water and turning a handful of fish and loaves into enough food to feed five thousand. So the word "greater" must be accounted for in terms of a movement from the age of anticipation to the age of fulfillment.

What about the Same, or Equivalent, Works?

But that doesn't solve everything. We still must account for the first half of John 14:12. Let's set aside for a moment the debate over the meaning of "greater" works and address what Jesus meant when he said that we will do the "same" or equivalent works.

Several things must be noted. First, those who perform these works are described as "whoever believes in me." This particular Greek phrase in John's gospel always refers to *all* believers, to *any* person who trusts in Christ, whether apostle or average follower (see John 3:15, 16, 18, 36; 6:35, 40, 47; 7:38; 11:25, 26; 12:44, 46; 14:12). This is crucial for us to grasp. You don't have to be an apostle or a missionary to do the works of Jesus. You don't have to be a pastor or elder or an author. You don't have to be well known or financially successful. It's not one gender to the exclusion of another. You don't have to be a certain age or of a certain ethnicity. You only have to be a believer.

Second, look closely at the immediate context. Jesus said this in John 14:11: "Believe me that I am in the Father and the Father is in me, or else *believe on account of the works* themselves" (emphasis mine). So, the words "believe" and "works" occur together in verse 11 just as they do in verse 12. Jesus's works are designed to help people believe. "Believe on account of the works." In effect, Jesus said, "If my teaching or the message I've proclaimed or how I've interacted with people are leaving doubts in your mind about who I am, look at my works. Look at my deeds. Let the works join with my words and lead you to faith." The "works" that lead to faith, therefore, are something more than "words." They are visible deeds of some sort that have the potential to lead someone to faith in Christ. What might those "works" be? That leads to my third point.

Third, the "works" believers are said to perform may well be *more than* miraculous deeds and physical healings, but they are certainly *not less than* miraculous deeds and healings. I say this because the Greek word translated "work(s)" is used twenty-seven times in the gospel of John. Five of those refer to the work of God the Father in and through Jesus. Some of these refer to the overall purpose of God in Christ, such as bringing salvation to mankind (John 17:4), while others are inclusive of the miracles he performed. Six of the twenty-seven refer to the works or deeds of obedience or disobedience by human beings. The remaining sixteen occurrences all refer to the miracles of Jesus. It might be possible to argue that a few refer to more than miracles, but every one of them certainly does not refer to anything less than miracles. In other words, miracles are always included.

So, if Jesus was referring to average Christians and not just apostles, and if the "works" in view are miracles, what are we to make of this promise? Before I answer that, let me point out one more important fact. Jesus's promise here is not unconditional. Simply because one believes in Jesus does not mean he or she will invariably do the same miraculous deeds that he did. Rather, his point is that the potential for such deeds of supernatural power exists for anyone who is a true believer. But if someone does not believe this text, if someone doubts the reality of the miraculous in our day, if someone denies the ongoing operation of the gifts of the Holy Spirit, if someone lacks any faith or has exceedingly low expectations of what God might do through us today, if someone does not passionately and regularly pray for such works of great power, it is highly unlikely that the works Jesus did will be present in that person's life and ministry.

We must also remember that the apostle Paul plainly taught that the spiritual gift of miracles is not given to every single Christian. "Are all apostles? Are all prophets? Are all teachers? Do all work miracles? Do all possess gifts of healings? Do all speak with tongues? Do all interpret?" (1 Cor. 12:29–30).

The answer Paul was looking for was, no, not all have each of these gifts. Only some do. So anyone who believes in Jesus has the potential to do the works he did, but not every believer will necessarily do miracles. The possibility exists for any who believe in Jesus to do these works, but whether they do is ultimately up to God.

So if Jesus said that those who believe in him will do the same works he did, why hasn't this happened? Listen closely to me: *It has!* Most people argue that Jesus can't mean what he seems to mean because we know it hasn't happened. Believers in Jesus have not, in point of fact, done the same works that he did. I disagree. It *has* happened. And *is* happening.

The Research of Dr. Craig Keener[2]

Dr. Craig Keener, whose PhD is from Duke University, is one of the most highly regarded evangelical New Testament scholars in the world. He is professor of New Testament at Asbury Theological Seminary, and he has written what is widely regarded as the definitive treatment of miracles. It is two volumes, totaling 1,172 pages, and he spends the first 250 pages or so defending the reliability of the miracle accounts in the Bible and then responds at length to the philosophical and theological arguments that some have used to deny the possibility of the miraculous.

Yet by far and away the largest portion of these two volumes is devoted to recording and describing miracles of every sort from all around the world during the present church age, with special attention given to the last approximately 150 years. He cites documented miracles of healing and deliverance in the Philippines, Thailand, Vietnam, Singapore, Malaysia, Myanmar, and Cambodia. Dozens and dozens of documented examples from reliable sources are listed.

He has several hundred examples from churches in India, Sri Lanka, Nepal, Indonesia, South Korea, the Solomon Islands, Samoa, Fiji, Papua New Guinea, New Zealand, and China. The remarkable growth of the church in China is due in large part to the reality of the supernatural as people are confronted with what they simply can't deny: that there is a supernatural God who answers the prayers of his people.

The cases Keener cites involve healings of every imaginable sort: cancerous tumors, congenital blindness, deafness, paralysis, heart disease, kidney disease, tuberculosis, and diabetes, just to mention a few. He even reports several documented cases of people being raised from the dead.

Keener proceeds to devote several chapters and a couple of hundred pages to miracle after miracle after miracle in Africa, throughout Latin America, and in the Caribbean. He focuses specifically on the work of Reinhard Bonnke in Nigeria and Heidi Baker in Mozambique, as well as in the Republic of Congo.

The accounts Keener records from virtually every country in South

---

2   Craig Keener, *Miracles: The Credibility of the New Testament Accounts*, 2 vols. (Grand Rapids: Baker Academic, 2011).

America are stunning, especially in Ecuador and Chile. He also describes dozens of miracles in Cuba.

At this point in the book, he turns his attention to miracles throughout the entire course of Christian history, beginning in the era immediately following the age of the apostles. People who have argued that when the apostles died, miracles ceased, simply have not looked at the evidence. Keener has, and he describes the evidence in great detail. He chronicles miracles throughout the Middle Ages and even into the time of the Reformation. He describes countless miracles in the seventeenth, eighteenth, and nineteenth centuries among a wide variety of Protestant traditions. And his examples are from virtually every Protestant denomination, including Baptist, Presbyterian, Nazarene, Methodist, and Pentecostal, as well as from virtually every theological tradition.

Keener devotes several hundred pages to documenting a wide variety of healing miracles throughout the twentieth and twenty-first centuries. In one ten-page sequence, he documents with great detail no fewer than ninety-five stunning miracles of a wide variety, then brings it to a conclusion by saying, "Such accounts represent only a very small sample of the claims."[3]

Keener then turns his attention to healings of blindness and documents more than 350 instances of healing. He also focuses on a variety of types of paralysis that were healed and several dozen instances of resurrections from the dead. And that's only in volume 1!

Are all the hundreds and hundreds of miraculous claims cited by Keener authentic? Probably not. And he openly concedes that point. But the utmost care was taken in his research, and only the most rigorous standards of medical documentation and eyewitness testimony were utilized. Even if there are many instances that ultimately prove to be false, one simply cannot ignore or deny the thousands of cases Keener cites. And this is only one man's research. I would not be surprised if dozens of volumes of God's miraculous work could be written if there were enough time and people available to record all the miracles. I do not base my interpretation of John 14:12 on Keener's work or that of anyone else. I simply cite Keener's work as evidential confirmation of what I think John 14:12 clearly asserts.

---

3   Keener, 2:505.

What Is a Miracle?

What events in life would qualify as miracles? When you make a trip to an overcrowded mall on Black Friday after Thanksgiving and discover that a space has suddenly opened up for you directly in front of the store where you planned to shop, is *that* a miracle? Should we refer to the majestic and awe-inspiring development of a human being in the womb of her or his mother as a miracle (Ps. 139:13)? Can something that happens with such unbroken *regularity* qualify as a miracle?

Consider this scenario. You suffer a flat tire on your way home from work at midnight on Friday and then discover that you left your cell phone at home. It's more than a little scary being alone and without transportation, when suddenly one of your best friends just happens to drive by and sees you. He tells you that at 11:50 p.m. he had a sudden and irresistible craving for ice cream and rushed out to get some before the grocery store closed at midnight. Is *that* a miracle?

When your close friend is declared cancer-free after a rigorous regimen of radiation and chemotherapy following surgery, at the same time she was the focus of hundreds of fervent prayer requests that she be healed, is that a miracle? If we should conclude that it was God who made effective the radiation and chemo that she received, and that without that medical treatment she would have died, do we call *that* a miracle?

What these examples show us is that the word *miracle* is used somewhat promiscuously and freely to describe everything from the healing of a person blind from birth to a simple answer to prayer, to a providential coincidence when you run into an old friend at the airport whom you haven't seen in twenty years. So what is a good, biblical working definition of a miracle? Max Turner uses the term *miracle* to describe any event that combines the following traits:

> (1) it is an extraordinary or startling observable event, (2) it cannot reasonably be explained in terms of human abilities or other known forces in the world, (3) it is perceived as a direct act of God, and (4) it is usually understood to have symbolic or sign value (e.g., pointing to God as redeemer, judge, and Savior).[4]

---

4   Max Turner, *The Holy Spirit and Spiritual Gifts: Then and Now* (Carlisle: Paternoster, 1996), 272n31.

One factor that has contributed to our confusion about miracles is the unbiblical belief on the part of countless professing Christians that God is largely cut off from the routine affairs of daily life. Although they may not openly assert what we know as *deism*, they live as if God were cut off from the world and rarely engaged with the minutiae of our daily existence. One need only read Psalms 104 and 139 to see how intimately and directly God is involved in everything from the growth of a blade of grass to the development of a fetus in the womb of his or her mother. It is "in" God that "we live and move and have our being" (Acts 17:28). Indeed, "in him all things hold together" (Col. 1:17b). Strictly speaking, then, God does not *intervene* in the affairs of this world. He is actively orchestrating and providentially directing everything that comes to pass (Eph. 1:11; Heb. 1:3). So we must look elsewhere for a proper definition of a miracle.

Perhaps a miracle occurs when God operates directly and apart from any means or instrumentality to accomplish his purposes. On this basis we would point to such events as the resurrection of Jesus from the dead. Yes, the latter was undoubtedly a miracle, but God seems more pleased to make use of means or intermediary causes to produce extraordinary results. He certainly could have produced enough food, *ex nihilo*, to feed the five thousand but preferred instead to make use of the contents of a boy's lunch.

Insofar as God is himself the author of all so-called natural laws, we shouldn't think of miracles as his defiance or superseding of them or his acting in some sense contrary to them. There are no forces in the universe that operate outside of God's providential control and oversight.

Wayne Grudem has proposed a simple but helpful definition that I believe is faithful to the Scriptures: "A miracle," says Grudem, "is a less common kind of God's activity in which he arouses people's awe and wonder and bears witness to himself."[5] No matter how we define a miracle, we must not think that it means a typically absent and uninvolved deity has chosen to intervene or involve himself in otherwise purely human affairs. Rather, as Grudem has suggested, the God who is always omnipresent sovereignly chooses to make his power known in ways that surprise us and alert us to his glory and greatness.

---

5 Wayne Grudem, *Systematic Theology: An Introduction to Biblical Doctrine* (Grand Rapids: Zondervan, 1994), 355. This is a definition that Grudem himself heard from John Frame.

Do "Miracles" Continue but Not the "Gift" of Miracles?

Let's continue our discussion of the spiritual gift of miracles by taking note of Galatians 3:1–5. Here the apostle Paul clearly described both the initial reception of the Spirit at the moment of salvation (v. 2) and the ongoing supply and provision of the Spirit throughout the course of the Christian life (v. 5). The initial gift of the Spirit to the Galatians (and to us as well) is described in verse 2: "Let me ask you only this: Did you receive the Spirit by works of the law or by hearing with faith?" The ongoing and continuous daily supply of the Spirit throughout the course of the Christian life is described in verse 5: "Does he who supplies the Spirit to you and works miracles among you do so by works of the law, or by hearing with faith?" Several important observations are in order.

First, God never gives his Spirit at any time because we have put him in our debt by doing good things. Paul was ruling out any form of legalism or works-based approach to our experience of the Spirit. Twice in this paragraph, first in verse 2 and then again in verse 5, Paul ruled out "works of the law" as the reason why or the instrument through which we experience God's Spirit, whether that be at the point of our conversion or at any time during our Christian lives.

By what means, then, or on what grounds does God give his Spirit to us? That brings me to the second observation. Just as clearly as Paul ruled out works as the reason why we receive God's Spirit, he affirmed that faith is the cause, instrument, as well as the grounds for our experience of the Spirit. Again, in both verse 2 and verse 5, it is "by hearing with faith" that God bestows his Spirit. It is when we believe and trust God and his promises that he is pleased to pour out his Spirit, not only for the purpose of saving us and causing his Spirit to indwell us permanently (v. 2) but also for the purpose of working miracles in our midst.

Third, the faith to which God responds by giving us his Spirit comes by "hearing." Hearing what? Obviously we "hear" the word of God when it is proclaimed or taught or read or communicated and made known in some other fashion. Anytime the truth about God and the gospel of Jesus Christ is heard and believed and trusted and treasured and embraced, God responds by pouring out his Spirit.

Fourth, merely "hearing" isn't enough. We must have "faith" in what we've heard. Simply listening to a sermon or reading the Bible or memorizing Scripture isn't enough. If you don't believe what you've memorized, it serves no good end. God doesn't reward us with the Spirit simply because we're smart or well educated. In both Galatians 3:2 and 3:5 Paul said that our hearing must be the sort that leads to faith. In other words, we have to "believe in" and "trust" and "treasure" in our hearts what God has taught us or said to us in his Word. That's what pleases God. That's what serves as the instrument through which he pours out his Spirit.

Fifth, God is portrayed in verse 5 as "he who supplies the Spirit to you." This is a present tense participle. God is by his very nature (who he is) and also by his choice (what he does) a God who loves to give more of his Spirit to his people when they humble themselves and trust the truth of his Word. This is almost *a badge of identification*. God is saying, "This is who I am. This is what I do. I continually supply the Spirit to my people."

Sixth, we must remember that Paul was writing to Christians. These people in Galatia had already trusted Christ for their salvation. Earlier, in verse 2, Paul referred to the provision of the Spirit that God made to them when they first trusted Jesus for salvation. But now in verse 5 he was saying that God continues to make provision for believing men and women.

I stress this point simply because this is one verse that should forever put to rest the debate about whether God continues after our conversion to supply and provide us with more and more of the Spirit. Paul didn't call this experience in Galatians 3:5 "Spirit baptism" or "Spirit filling." He didn't use the word *anointing*. All that matters is that God is the sort of God whose very nature and purpose are to give more of his Spirit on an ongoing daily basis to his people (see also Phil. 1:19; 1 Thess. 4:8).

Seventh, what specifically is it that God wants us to believe? What is the content or object of our "faith" to which God answers with the extraordinary supply and provision of his Spirit? Paul likely had several things in mind.

Given the larger context and purpose of the letter to the Galatians, he surely had in mind our faith in the finality of Christ's death and resurrection and our confidence in that gracious work of God as the only hope for salvation. Believing that we are justified by faith alone, through grace alone, in Christ alone is central to what we must believe. This is obvious when we read on in Galatians 3:6 where Paul spoke of Abraham "believing" God and being justified as a result.

I also think Paul had in mind our faith and confidence in the character of God. Do you believe God is the sort of God who loves to do wonderful things for his people? Do you believe God is the kind of God who delights to build up and restore and heal? Do you believe that God is of such a character and nature that he has compassion on his people and rejoices to do them good at all times? Believing this about God is crucial to our experience of the supernatural work of the Spirit.

Related to the former point is something we saw in the previous chapter. It concerns our faith that God is *able* to do such things. I would simply remind you that Jesus always responded to that sort of faith with healing and deliverance and blessing (see esp. Matt. 8:2; 9:28–29). The woman with the issue of blood in Mark 5 was healed when she simply touched Jesus's garment. "Your faith has made you well" (v. 34), said Jesus. In other words, "What I enjoy and respond to is your simple confidence and trust in my ability to make a difference in your life."

Simply put, we must labor to believe and trust and bank our souls on the truth of everything God has said in his Word. That is what Paul meant when he spoke of "hearing with faith" here in Galatians 3.

Eighth, God was working miracles among and through these Galatian Christians in the absence of any apostolic influence. As far as we know, there were no apostles present in Galatia when Paul wrote this. Thus, contrary to what most cessationists say, miracles were not exclusively or even primarily the work of apostles but were typically found among ordinary, average Christians like those in first century.

Ninth, notice the close, intertwined connection between believing the Word of God and experiencing the supernatural work of the Spirit. Many today want to create a dividing line between the mind and the ministry of the Spirit. They have bought into a terribly destructive lie that says, "If you want more of the Holy Spirit, put your mind in neutral. Don't clutter up your life with a lot of thinking and theology. Open up yourself to the Spirit by suspending or even suppressing your mental and intellectual activity. Your mind only gets in the way. Thinking does no good."

That is not what Paul said. He said that it is only when we "hear" God's Word and respond in "faith" to what we've heard and learned that God supplies the Spirit to work miracles in our midst. Good theology is the soil in which the supernatural takes root and blossoms in miracles.

The Spiritual Gift of Miracles

The most literal translation of Paul's words in 1 Corinthians 12:10 is "workings of powers" (*energēmata dunameōn*). Although all gifts are "workings" (*energēmata*) or "energizings" by divine power (cf. vv. 6, 11), the word is used here in conjunction with "powers" (*dunamis*) for a particular gift. The word often translated "miracles" in 1 Corinthians 12:10 is actually the Greek word for powers (*dunamis*). Thus, we again have a double plural, "workings of powers," which probably points to a certain variety in these operations.

What are these "workings" or "effectings" or "productions" of "powers"? Whereas all the gifts mentioned in 1 Corinthians 12:8–10 are certainly miraculous, the gift of miracles must primarily encompass other supernatural phenomena as well. Simply put, whereas all healings and prophetic words are displays of power, not all displays of power result in healing or prophetic words. So what kind of displays of supernatural power might Paul have had in mind here?

We should probably include those rare occasions when someone was raised from the dead, as seen, for example, in Acts 9:40 where Peter raised Tabitha from the dead. Paul's prophetic declaration of judgment on Elymas, leaving him temporarily blind (Acts 13:8–11), as well as the instantaneous deaths of Ananias and Sapphira (Acts 5:1–11) may well be included in what the apostle had in mind. Although I've never heard of anyone else turning water into wine or stilling the waves on a raging sea, such power over nature would clearly be instances of miraculous activity. I'm not inclined to include here deliverance from demonic spirits, given the fact that this is a privilege, power, and authority that Jesus appeared to grant to all his followers (Luke 10:17–20). Elijah's fervent prayer "that it might not rain" (James 5:17), together with his subsequent prayer that the rain should resume, would also be a good candidate for the gift of miracles (in spite of the fact that Elijah lived under the old covenant, before the new covenant age in which spiritual gifts were dispersed among God's people).

One often hears the argument that whereas miracles still occur beyond the time of the original apostles, the spiritual gift of miracles has ceased or has been withdrawn by the Spirit from the experience of the church. Is this a valid distinction? On the one hand, I can appreciate the desire of most cessationists to affirm that God is sovereign and can perform miracles according to his will at any time in any age of the church. What I find unacceptable (because it is unbiblical) is the denial that God may still impart the *charisma* of miracles or what Paul referred to, literally, as "workings of powers" (1 Cor. 12:10).

Earlier I described what I believe is the primary reason why most cessationists are reluctant to concede that miraculous gifts of the Spirit are still operative in the church. Simply put, they don't see gifts today that are equivalent in power and effectiveness to those described in the New Testament. On countless occasions I've heard it said, "If the spiritual gift of miracles and the gift of healing (just to mention two of the *charismata*) are designed by God to continue in the life of the church, show me a man or woman who can heal any disease at will; show me a person who operates in the miraculous as Paul or Peter did." In the absence of such New Testament–quality demonstrations of power, the only reasonable conclusion is that God is no longer blessing the church with these gifted individuals. Underlying this conclusion is the notion that if anyone could *ever* heal or perform a miracle, he or she can *always* do so. And since we all acknowledge that the latter does not obtain, such gifts must have ceased early on in the life of the church, most likely soon after the death of the last apostle.

But this argument betrays a fundamental misconception in how spiritual gifts operate. I want to make a case for a distinction in the way we conceive of the many gifts of the Spirit. I freely admit that the terminology I employ in differentiating among the gifts is not found in Scripture. But the nature of these gifts and how they actually functioned in the life of the early church justifies this language. Some gifts are what I call *permanent* or *residential*. They are always present in the person who has received them. They reside with the believer and may be exercised anytime he or she wills to make use of them. Teaching is a perfect example of a permanent or residential gift. I can teach anytime I please. The use of this gift is subject to my will. Other residential gifts include serving, leading, showing mercy, and evangelism, just to mention a few. Those who operate in these giftings will tell you that they can minister to others at all times.

There are, on the other hand, what I refer to as gifts of the Spirit that are *circumstantial* or *occasional*. These gifts are used only when God so wills. They are not at our disposal or subject to our determination. They are empowered by the Spirit in particular circumstances, but not all, on particular occasions of need, but not all. Miracles, healing, faith, and prophecy are examples of circumstantial gifts. The reason why a person may on occasion heal the sick but not always is that whether one is healed is subject to the sovereign will and timing of God. The fact that Paul did not immediately heal Epaphroditus (Phil. 2:25–30), Trophimus (2 Tim. 4:20), Timothy (1 Tim. 5:23), and perhaps himself (2 Cor. 12:1–10), wasn't due to the gift of healing no longer being operative. It simply wasn't God's will at that time for those individuals to be healed of their afflictions.

That prophecy was occasional or circumstantial is seen from the way it is portrayed by Paul in 1 Corinthians 14. There we are told that if someone is to prophesy, they must be the recipient of a revelation from the Spirit, a revelation that in most instances is granted spontaneously (v. 30). No one walks around with revelatory truths or insights in their back pocket, able to speak them at will. This is why the potential exists for anyone to prophesy (see vv. 24, 31). Any believer is potentially the recipient of a revelatory word from God who, in accordance with the guidelines established by Paul, can speak to the edification, encouragement, and consolation of others (v. 3). No one possesses the gift of prophecy as if they can decide when and where and to whom they will prophesy. That is entirely subject to God's will and timing, not ours. He determines when, where, and to whom a revelation will be given. The same would likely apply to the gifts of word of knowledge, word of wisdom, faith, and the discerning of spirits.

If this distinction between gifts that are permanent or residential and those that are occasional or circumstantial is valid, there is no need for the cessationist to affirm that miracles can still occur while denying that the gift of miracles (or healing or prophecy, etc.) has been withdrawn. The latter are not in our authority to be used when we pray or anytime we might will. The infrequent occurrence of the miraculous says nothing about God's design for the cessation of certain gifts. It is the intrinsic nature of the miraculous itself, as subject to God's sovereign will and timing, that accounts for why they either do or do not occur.

Therefore, my reading of the New Testament, as confirmed by experience, indicates that one cannot draw a rigid distinction between a gifted person who ministers in the *charisma* of supernatural power and the alleged isolated occurrence of a miracle produced by a sovereign God. Here is why.

As we just saw, no one in Scripture (aside from Jesus) ministered at will in the miraculous power of the Spirit. In addition, most instances of verifiable miracles in our day come as the result of the prayers of Christian men and women. Healings (such as in James 5) or other miraculous manifestations typically occur through the instrumentality of a believer seeking God and pleading with him in prayer. This by no means denies that God can perform a miracle directly without the use of secondary causes. But when it comes to healing or the exercise of revelatory gifts in particular, it is most often through the impartation *to a particular person* or *persons* of a "gift" for a healing or a word of revelatory insight or some other expression of power.

I rarely hear of a miracle that occurs independently of some Christian man or woman (or a collection of them) praying and pressing into God for a display of his supernatural power. This, I believe, is what Paul had in mind when he spoke of the "gift of miracles" (1 Cor. 12:10). The Holy Spirit, who alone has authority to bestow or withhold all spiritual gifts (v. 11), empowers a person in a particular circumstance to address a unique need in order to accomplish whatever purpose God desires.

A comparison of 1 Corinthians 12:10 with Galatians 3:5 will indicate that both texts have the same phenomenon in view. In the former text, Paul referred to the gift of miracles as "workings of powers" (*energēmata dunameōn*). In the latter passage, God "works miracles" (*energon dunameis*) when his people hear his word and respond in faith. Thus, it is the Spirit who works miracles among us by imparting a *charisma* of power. So when someone asks, "Does God 'work miracles' among us or do gifted men and women 'work miracles' among us?" the answer is indubitably yes!

When we combine this understanding of the nature of the "gift of miracles" with the circumstantial or occasional operation of such miraculous phenomena as bodily healings and revelatory experiences, there is no longer a need to *deny* that such "gifts" continue in the life of the church while *affirming* that miracles still do. Most cessationists don't want to find themselves in the uncomfortable position of doubting, far less denying, that the omnipotent God of the universe *can* do something. They want to be able to justify praying for a miracle when someone is sick without conceding this debate to the continuationists. But this problem disappears when we recognize that God continues to bestow the "gift of miracles" in the same way he did in the early church: rarely, occasionally, and most often (but not always) through a particular Christian person who was seeking God, depending on

God, and interceding for a particular supernatural breakthrough. And thus, this insistence by cessationists that miracles can certainly occur but not through the "gift of miracles," or that healings can occur but not through the "gifts of healings," is a distinction without a difference that serves only to confuse people and muddy the waters in this debate.

PART 6

OTHER GIFTS AND APOSTLESHIP

CHAPTER 16

What about the Spiritual Gifts in Romans 12:6–8 and Ephesians 4:11?

O ur focus in this book has largely been on the gifts listed by Paul in 1 Corinthians 12. But we must not neglect two other lists, one in Romans 12 and the other in Ephesians 4. We begin with Romans 12:3–8.

Spiritual Gifts in Romans 12:3–8

Here is the passage that concerns us.

> For by the grace given to me I say to everyone among you not to think of himself more highly than he ought to think, but to think with sober judgment, each according to the measure of faith that God has assigned. For as in one body we have many members, and the members do not all have the same function, so we, though many, are one body in Christ, and individually members one of another. Having gifts that differ according to the grace given to us, let us use them: if prophecy, in proportion to our faith; if service, in our serving; the one who teaches, in his teaching; the one who exhorts, in his exhortation; the one who contributes, in generosity; the one who leads, with zeal; the one who does acts of mercy, with cheerfulness. (Rom. 12:3–8)

Our primary focus is verses 6–8, but it is always helpful to see a passage in its broader contextual setting.

Before digging into the text, we need to be aware of the viewpoint expressed by Gordon Fee.[1] Fee questions whether the *charismata* in Romans 12:6–8 refer primarily to what we know as "spiritual gifts." He contends that

> it is not at all plain that Paul intended everything that he calls *charismata* in 12:6b–8 to be understood as special gifts *of the Spirit*, at least in the same way that he expressly equates this term with the Spirit's manifestations in 1 Corinthians 12. The list in vv. 6b–8 is so heterogeneous and covers such a broad range of behavior, it seems far more likely that for Paul the emphasis lies on the "grace of God" here being worked out among them in concrete ways, rather than on the empowering of the Spirit for such behavior or on "Spirit gifting" as such. Thus the list includes items such as prophecy, teaching, and exhorting/encouraging, which in 1 Corinthians 12 come under the purview of Spirit *charismata*, as well as various forms of serving others within the believing community (service, contributing to the needs of others, giving aid, and showing mercy), which are never elsewhere in Paul attributed directly to the Spirit as *his* gifts. These latter items move away from the idea of "gifts" per se, at least in terms of Spirit manifestations, to proper ethical behavior, in which the fruit of love finds concrete expression in their midst. That these are indeed the outworking of the Spirit in Pauline theology need not be doubted. What is doubtful is that our translation "gifts *of the Spirit*" is an adequate understanding of Pauline usage. While both enumerations are called *charismata*, only that in 1 Cor. 12:8–10 is tied specifically by Paul himself to the activities of the Spirit in the community.[2]

In other words, according to Fee, "these are concrete expressions of the grace of God at work in the life of individuals for the sake of others; but for him they would not be 'Spiritual gifts,' but *gifts of God* which are *effectively brought into the life of the community by the Spirit*."[3]

As much as I respect Fee, I don't see anything in the text that would lead

---

1 Gordon D. Fee, *God's Empowering Presence: The Holy Spirit in the Letters of Paul* (Peabody, MA: Hendrickson, 1994).

2 Fee, 34–35.

3 Fee, 607.

us to believe that his use of the term *charismata* (Rom. 12:6) is to be taken in a sense different from the way Paul consistently used it in 1 Corinthians 12–14. Unless there is compelling evidence pointing in another direction, we should assume that his use of the term in writing to Rome is the same as his use of it in writing to Corinth. The fact that Paul wrote his epistle to the Romans while in Corinth would only reinforce this point. That Paul referred to expressions of God's "grace" (v. 6) that he did not elsewhere mention in his discussion of spiritual gifts is hardly good grounds for denying that they are genuine *charismata* that are designed to be understood as "manifestations" of the Spirit (v. 7). On Fee's reasoning, we would also be compelled to reject evangelism and pastor-teachers in Ephesians 4 as spiritual gifts insofar as they, like five of the gifts in Romans 12, are not described elsewhere in Paul's letters as "spiritual gifts." Also, given the fact that Paul mentioned here two gifts, prophecy and teaching, that are undeniably listed in 1 Corinthians 12 as "manifestation[s] of the Spirit" (v. 7), the presumptive conclusion is that the other five in Romans 12 are to be understood likewise.

One more observation is in order. We know these gifts are the fruit of God's grace, for Paul declared that they "are according to the grace given to us" (12:6). Thus, as Schreiner correctly notes, "The gifts exercised cannot be attributed to the moral excellence of human beings. They are evidence of the grace of God, who has supplied the church with gifts to strengthen the community."[4] We are now prepared to briefly examine each gift.

Little needs to be said about prophecy, as we examined it at length earlier in the book. One thing, however, should be noted. Prophecy is to be exercised "in proportion to our faith" (Rom. 12:6). Drawing upon Paul's earlier reference to "the measure of faith that God has assigned" (v. 3), Schreiner concludes that Paul is talking about the faith of the prophet. Wayne Grudem agrees with Schreiner and argues that Paul is saying that "some who had the gift of prophecy had a greater measure of faith (that is, a trust or confidence that the Holy Spirit would work or was working in them to bring a revelation which would be the basis of a prophecy)."[5] In other words, there will always be greater and lesser degrees of prophetic ability and consequently greater

---

4   Thomas R. Schreiner, *Romans*, Baker Exegetical Commentary on the New Testament, 2nd ed. (Grand Rapids: Baker Academic, 2018), 637.

5   Wayne Grudem, *The Gift of Prophecy in the New Testament and Today* (Wheaton, IL: Crossway, 2000), 176.

and lesser degrees of prophetic accuracy (which, it seems reasonable to assume, may increase or decrease, depending on the circumstances of that person's life). Thus, prophets are to speak in proportion to the confidence and assurance they have that what they say is truly of God. Prophets are not to speak beyond what God has revealed; they must be careful never to speak on their own authority or from their own resources.[6]

Others, however, have argued that "the faith" (*hē pistis*) refers to those objective truths embodied in the gospel tradition. Thomas Gillespie appeals to three other Pauline texts in which he believes *pistis* with the definite article points to the content of faith (although Rom. 10:8 is questionable). He concludes that "together Galatians 1:23, Romans 10:8, and Philippians 1:27 suggest that when Paul uses *hē pistis* to denote the content of Christian belief, he has in mind the substance and structure of the gospel. This means that in Romans 12:6b prophecy is (1) drawn into the orbit of gospel proclamation, and (2) subjected to the standard provided by the content of this message."[7] However, if this were Paul's meaning, it would be an exceptionally rare usage of *pistis*.

The gift of "service" is the translation of the common term for "ministry" (*diakonia*) that could conceivably be a reference to any or all manner of giving of oneself for the benefit of others. Schreiner thinks it likely has reference to "rendering financial and material assistance."[8] Could Paul here have in mind the office of deacon? Possibly, but whereas *all* deacons serve, there is nothing to suggest that *only* deacons serve. Peter likely had in view this same gift when he spoke of serving "by the strength that God supplies" (1 Peter 4:11).

Those with the gift of serving see a need, a weakness, a person in crisis, or a task that calls for immediate action and instantly feel an impulse from the Spirit to step in and devote their energies to help bring resolution. They typically stay out of the limelight on purpose, preferring to labor anonymously for the sake of those in the body of Christ.

Teaching, as over against prophecy, "depends on an explanation of tradition that is already written, whether that tradition was the Old Testament

6 Adapted from Sam Storms, "A Third Wave View," in *Are Miraculous Gifts for Today? Four Views*, ed. Wayne Grudem (Grand Rapids: Zondervan, 1995), 210.

7 Thomas Gillespie, *The First Theologians: A Study in Early Christian Prophecy* (Grand Rapids: Eerdmans, 1994), 61.

8 Schreiner, *Romans*, 639.

Scriptures, the words and works of Jesus, or catechetical material."[9] It may also include whatever Scripture was already penned and had been recognized as inspired (see 2 Peter 3:15–16). Paul encouraged Timothy to devote himself to other faithful men "who will be able to teach others" (2 Tim. 2:2; cf. 3:10 and Titus 2:1). Teaching appears to be the only spiritual gift required of those who would qualify to serve as elders (1 Tim. 3:2; Titus 1:9). Again, whereas all elders must be able to teach, it is hardly the case that *only* elders teach. A person may have this gift but for whatever reason may not qualify as an elder, or may choose simply not to seek the office. Women also may receive and utilize this gift (Titus 2:3).

Those with this gift are capable of understanding and articulating biblical truth and defending it against the inroads of theological error. Teachers will love to study and are, in most cases, reasonably eloquent, at least to the degree that others can follow their instruction and are persuaded of the truth they communicate.

The gift of "exhortation" is elsewhere linked with teaching (1 Thess. 2:11–13; 1 Tim. 4:13) but here probably emphasizes the application of truths communicated in teaching or the passionate urging and encouraging of people to live out what they know to be true. The word used here may even include the idea of appeal, in which truths that are taught are communicated in such a way that a person is called into action and encouraged to apply biblical doctrine in practical ways.

As for "giving" or "contributing," it is to be done "in [or with] generosity," although the word here can also mean "simplicity." If the latter is in view, Paul would have in mind a person who is careful that their motivation is single and spiritual, altogether for the glory of God and the good of the person(s) to whom their giving is directed, as well as devoid of any desire to gain influence or secure power in the church or put people in their debt (see Matt. 6:2–4). On the other hand, "generosity" is in view when the word is used in 2 Corinthians 8:2 and 9:11, 13.

The one who "leads" likely has in view administrative oversight (see 1 Thess. 5:12; 1 Tim. 3:4–5, 12; 5:17). It should be carried out with diligence, not laziness. Since Paul did not specify over whom or what one would lead,

---

9 Schreiner, 640. For an excellent discussion highlighting the differences between teaching and prophecy, see Grudem, *The Gift of Prophecy in the New Testament and Today*, 113–24.

we should not restrict this gift to those who are elders or pastors. Although elders in the local church assuredly lead (see 1 Thess. 5:12; 1 Tim. 5:17), one need not be an elder to possess and faithfully and fruitfully exercise this gift.[10]

The gift of mercy finds expression in any number of contexts, but probably has in view ministry to the sick or those who are discouraged and depressed, perhaps even suffering economic hardship. Those with this gift typically are deeply compassionate and empathize with those who are suffering. Paul encouraged them to fulfill this ministry "with cheerfulness," a word that he also employed in 2 Corinthians 9:7 to emphasize the proper attitude in our financial stewardship. One must display mercy joyfully, not begrudgingly or reluctantly, as if one were discharging a debt or acting solely from a sense of moral duty.

Ephesians 4:11–16

And he gave the apostles, the prophets, the evangelists, the shepherds and teachers, to equip the saints for the work of ministry, for building up the body of Christ, until we all attain to the unity of the faith and of the knowledge of the Son of God, to mature manhood, to the measure of the stature of the fullness of Christ, so that we may no longer be children, tossed to and fro by the waves and carried about by every wind of doctrine, by human cunning, by craftiness in deceitful schemes. Rather, speaking the truth in love, we are to grow up in every way into him who is the head, into Christ, from whom the whole body, joined and held together by every joint with which it is equipped, when each part is working properly, makes the body grow so that it builds itself up in love. (Eph. 4:11–16)

Here we see that God not only gives "grace" (Eph. 4:7) to people, but he also gives people to people who are "graced" with the ability to edify and strengthen one another. Nothing needs to be said here about apostles and prophets, as we've examined these gifts in detail elsewhere in this book.

---

10 Fee suggests that this word, translated "leads," refers more to caring for others than to authoritative government or oversight. Situated as it is between giving and showing mercy, he believes the emphasis is on the pastoral dimension that those in leadership demonstrate (Fee, *God's Empowering Presence*, 604n395).

The only two other occurrences of the noun translated "evangelists" (plural of *euangelistēs*) are found in Acts 21:8 (Philip is called "the evangelist") and 2 Timothy 4:5 (where Paul exhorted his spiritual son to do the work of an "evangelist"). Were these individuals itinerant ministers engaged in church planting, or were they gifted individuals who resided permanently in their own local assembly? There seems to be no reason to choose one or the other. In any case, they were empowered by the Spirit to labor in gospel proclamation and were likely those who, on average, saw more genuine conversions than other Christians who shared their faith.

It should be noted that the definite article ("the") appears before each of the first three: apostles, prophets, and evangelists, whereas "shepherds" (ESV; or pastors) and "teachers" are linked by a single article. Some grammarians contend this means they constitute one gift, not two, hence: *pastor-teachers*.[11] At minimum, we should recognize some sort of overlap between the two. It does raise the question of whether someone can be a "pastor" without also being a "teacher" (an unlikely scenario; it is difficult to see how a person who can't teach could pastor or shepherd the people of God). Certainly someone might have the gift of teaching (as we saw in Rom. 12:7 where it stands alone) without serving as a pastor.

This is the only place in the New Testament where the noun *poimēn*, "shepherd" or "pastor" is used. However, the cognate verb form is used in Acts 20:28 and 1 Peter 5:1–4 (see also John 21:16) where elders are commanded to "pastor" or to "shepherd" God's people. If Paul intended us to understand "pastoring" more as a spiritual gift and less as an office in the church, we might be justified in drawing these conclusions:

- All pastors are teachers,
- but not all teachers are pastors.
- All elders are pastors,
- but not all pastors are elders.
- All elders are teachers,
- but not all teachers are elders.

---

11 See the discussion in Daniel B. Wallace, *Greek Grammar beyond the Basics: An Exegetical Syntax of the New Testament* (Grand Rapids: Zondervan, 1996), 284.

Two related questions need to be answered. First, "Do these persons receive the name they have been given simply because they perform certain functions from time to time or also because they occupy some clearly defined position within their communities?"[12] Second, if the latter is the case, are these four or five "official giftings" to be viewed as comprising some sort of unique church authority, apart from which the local church cannot fully function, or are they listed here simply as random representatives of the many and various spiritual gifts bestowed by the Spirit?

I'm inclined to embrace the second option. Contrary to the opinion of many, especially in the Pentecostal and charismatic branch of the evangelical family, I see nothing here that would indicate Paul is providing us with a blueprint for local church government, as if to say that for a church to be properly aligned and functioning at a high level of effectiveness, there must always be at least one of these four or five individuals present and ministering in every local church. Thus, I see no reason why we should not view this list in precisely the same way we read the lists in 1 Corinthians 12:8–10, 28–30 and in Romans 12:6–8, namely, as representative. In other words, Paul could as easily have included in Ephesians 4:11 such gifts as exhortation, leading, giving, or speaking in tongues, and in doing so secure the same result.

A brief word is in order concerning the function or purpose of these gifts. Ephesians 4:12 consists of three prepositional phrases: (1) "to equip the saints," (2) "for the work of ministry," and (3) "for building up the body of Christ." There are two ways to interpret these phrases and thus the purpose of the gifts in verse 11. Grammatically speaking, either one is possible.

The most popular view is that the first and second phrases are to be taken together, as expressing one idea. Thus, the gifted people of verse 11 have been given to equip the saints for the work of ministry. That is to say, all believers are the ones who do the work of ministry, having been equipped to do so by the gifted people of verse 11. This will then contribute to the building up of the body of Christ. On this view, verse 12 is declaring that all believers, and not just a select few with special gifts, have received grace for ministry.

Another interpretation is that all three prepositional phrases describe what the gifted people of verse 11 do in the church. Apostles, prophets, evangelists, pastors, and teachers (or pastor-teachers) have been given to the

12 Andrew T. Lincoln, *Ephesians*, Word Biblical Commentary (Dallas: Word, 1990), 252.

church so that they (the gifted people of v. 11) might equip the saints, so that they (the gifted people of v. 11) might do the work of ministry, so that they (the gifted people of v. 11) might build up the body of Christ. Andrew Lincoln advocates this view and says, "All believers are to be brought to a state of completion, and it is the ministers Christ has given who are the means to this end as they exercise their ministries of proclamation, teaching, and leadership."[13]

If this second view is correct, one need not fear that all other believers are relegated to so-called lay status in the church. Again, verses 7 and 16 both explicitly assert that all Christians have been gifted in order that they might serve and minister and contribute to the growth and well-being of the body of Christ.

What needs to be noted is that the proper use of spiritual gifts can greatly reduce spiritual immaturity in the body, portrayed here by the word translated "children" (v. 14a), a term set in contrast to the "mature man" of verse 13. We are to imitate children in their humility and innocence but not in their ignorance and instability. For Paul "immaturity is evidenced in insta-bility, rootlessness, lack of direction, doctrinal vacillation, and susceptibility to manipulation and error."[14] Immaturity is especially evident when believers are easily duped by false teaching and always seem to embrace whatever new theological fad is being promoted. "Every wind of doctrine" in verse 14 is in obvious contrast with the "unity of the faith" in verse 13. In other words, *at the heart of childish immaturity is the lack of theological discernment.* And it is the proper exercise of spiritual gifts in the local church that provides a remedy to this affliction from which so many Christians suffer.

---

13 Lincoln, *Ephesians*, 254.
14 Lincoln, *Ephesians*, 257.

CHAPTER 17

Is Apostleship a Spiritual Gift, an Office, or Both?

Most people simply assume that apostleship is a spiritual gift in much the same way as is prophecy or teaching or mercy. And yet nowhere in the New Testament is the term *charisma* ever applied to the word *apostle*. An equal number of people, perhaps more, insist that of all the spiritual gifts mentioned in the New Testament, apostleship is assuredly at least one that has been withdrawn from the life of the local church. Cessationists believe that this may well open the door to acknowledging that other spiritual gifts were likewise temporary.

But is apostleship a spiritual gift?[1] Although not a strict cessationist, Robert Saucy points out that apostles "are listed along with prophets and teachers whom all agree were individuals who regularly exercised the corresponding gifts of prophecy and teaching (cf. 1 Cor. 12:28–29; Eph. 4:11). Even as prophets and teachers were such by corresponding spiritual gifts which they expressed, so were apostles."[2]

It is easy to understand this with regard to prophets and teachers and other similar gifts. Exhorters are those who exhort, teachers teach, healers heal, those who have the gift of faith exercise extraordinary faith, and so on. But how does an "apostle" (noun) "apostle" (verb)? Whereas Saucy insists that apostleship is a spiritual gift, he never defines it. The closest he comes

---

1 Some of this chapter is adapted from "A Third Wave View," my contribution to the book *Are Miraculous Gifts for Today? Four Views*, ed. Wayne Grudem (Grand Rapids: Zondervan, 1995), 156–59, and is used here with permission.

2 Robert Saucy, "An Open but Cautious View," in *Are Miraculous Gifts for Today? Four Views*, ed. Wayne Grudem (Grand Rapids: Zondervan, 1995), 101.

to providing a definition is when he says that "while the apostles exercised various gifts common to others (such as prophecy and teaching), they were also endowed with a unique spiritual gift that enabled them to minister as apostles."[3]

But what does it mean to minister as an apostle? One ministers as a discerner of spirits by discerning spirits. One ministers as a giver by giving. However, to say that one is enabled to minister as an apostle does not tell me what the gift of *apostle-ing* (to coin a term) is. As Jack Deere explains,

> It is virtually impossible to define the "gift" of apostleship in the same way that the other gifts can be defined. We can easily conceive of someone exercising the gift of prophecy without being a prophet. The same is true for all the other gifts. But how could someone come to a meeting of a local assembly and exercise the gift of apostleship in that meeting without actually being an apostle? An apostle in an assembly might teach, or prophesy, or heal, or lead, or administrate. But what would it mean to exercise the gift of apostleship? We simply cannot think of apostleship apart from the historical apostles. In the New Testament an apostle is not a spiritual gift but a person who had a divinely given commission and ministry.[4]

As we saw in an earlier chapter, spiritual gifts, as described in 1 Corinthians 12:7–10, are divinely energized deeds that are performed. But how does one do *apostle-ing*? I have no problem with how one might speak prophetically or display mercy or provide encouragement to another believer. But apostleship, it would seem, is not an inner working of the Holy Spirit through a human vessel, but an office or position of authority to which one is called by Christ Jesus himself.

This raises the question of the criteria for apostleship, which inescapably sets it apart from all spiritual gifts. We will take up that issue in the following chapter. But if apostleship were a *charisma*, it would be the only one for which a person must meet certain qualifying standards. Paul described the *charismata* as if the potential always exists for any person to be the recipient of any gift, depending on the sovereign will of the Spirit (1 Cor. 12:11). Not

---

3 Saucy, 102.
4 Jack Deere, *Surprised by the Power of the Spirit* (Grand Rapids: Zondervan, 1993), 242.

so with apostleship. Although it is increasingly coming under close scrutiny (see the next chapter), many continue to believe that to qualify as an apostle one must be both "an eye and earwitness to the resurrection of Christ" and receive a personal commission from Jesus himself (Acts 1:22–26; 1 Cor. 9:1–2; 15:7–9; cf. also Rom. 1:1, 5; 1 Cor. 1:1; 2 Cor. 1:1; Gal. 1:1). Thus, if these are absolute requirements (which I have come to increasingly doubt), unlike the other *charismata*, only a select few who met specific conditions could even be considered as possible apostles.

There is yet another, related, reason why it is unlikely that Paul thought of apostleship as a spiritual gift. I have in mind his repeated exhortation to "earnestly desire the higher gifts" (1 Cor. 12:31; cf. 14:1, 12). The *charismata* are to be desired and prayed for (1 Cor. 14:13). In fact, we are especially to desire those gifts that are most effective in edifying the church (in this regard, see 1 Cor. 14:12). Most scholars believe the list in 1 Corinthians 12:28–29, at the top of which is apostleship, is prioritized according to this principle. But if apostleship is a gift, like prophecy or teaching, Paul would be in the awkward position of encouraging all Christians to desire, above all else, that they might be apostles! Yet, as noted above, if the traditional view of the requirements for apostleship is maintained, this is not something that could be prayed for or desired or in any sense sought after. Either you are an eye and earwitness of Christ's resurrection or you are not. Either you have received a personal commission from Jesus or you have not. Of course, if we were to discover that these were requirements only for the original Twelve (plus Paul and perhaps Barnabas, Silas, and James), the problem would not be so acute.

In a word, whereas apostles themselves certainly received *charismata* such as the ability to prophesy, to heal, to show mercy, and so on, apostleship per se is not a *charisma*. Apostleship is not an enabling power; it is an ecclesiastical position.

The reason why many wish to classify apostleship as a spiritual gift is not hard to see. Robert Saucy writes, "If the *charisma* of being an apostle did not continue in the church, then we must acknowledge that not all of the spiritual gifts operative in the New Testament church have continued throughout history. Furthermore, this fact creates the possibility that other *charismata* have also ceased or changed."[5] I am happy to concede the possibility that all

---

5   Saucy, "An Open but Cautious View," 102.

of the *charismata* have ceased. But it is a possibility I will entertain only if something in Scripture explicitly asserts them to be temporary or defines these gifts in such a way that necessarily excludes them from subsequent church life. There is, however, nothing inherent in any of the gifts that either suggests or implies that they were temporary. I should also point out that this logic cuts both ways. If the cessationist wants to argue that the cessation of apostleship opens the door for other gifts to have been temporary, the continuationist can argue that the continuation of teaching or mercy or evangelism opens the door for other gifts to have been permanent. It's a weak argument either way.

Furthermore, this sort of argument is like saying the potential exists for *no* practice of the early church to be valid today simply because we acknowledge that *some* are not. But we all admit that such a hypothetical scenario has no ultimate theological or practical bearing on the continuing validity of any particular activity. Each practice must be evaluated for what it is and why God ordained it. Therefore, if the New Testament explicitly defines a spiritual gift as exclusively tied to the first century and consequently invalid for any Christian in any subsequent period of church history, I will be the first to declare myself a cessationist (insofar as that *one* gift is concerned). However, nothing that any cessationist has written leads me to believe that any of the *charismata* fall into that category.

I trust that greater clarity will be ours once we determine the necessary qualifications for being an apostle. This will shed considerable light on whether we conclude that apostleship is a spiritual gift or an office or in some sense both. At this stage, I'm inclined to view the apostolate as something of an *office*, in spite of the fact that no such terminology is ever applied to it in the New Testament. Still, though, apostles are people who were appointed to their position (Mark 3:13, 16). In these verses Jesus uses the verb *poieō*, which can mean anything from "make" to "perform" to "appoint" (see also Heb. 3:2, where *poieō* is used to describe Jesus as being "appointed" to his task by the Father). There is nothing technical about the term, and we should be reluctant to invest too much ecclesiastical significance in it. There are, of course, numerous places where apostles are described as being "called" and "sent" (Rom. 1:1; see 1 Cor. 1:1 where Paul described himself as "called by the will of God to be an apostle"). In 1 Timothy 1:1 Paul used the word "command" or "injunction" (*epitagē*) to undergird the basis of his apostleship.

The English Standard Version rendering of 1 Timothy 3:1 is somewhat misleading. There we read that "If anyone aspires to the office of overseer, he desires a noble task." The word "office" here is not represented by any word in the Greek text. The translators obviously understand the position of bishop or overseer or elder as one that entails some measure of authority; hence, their insertion of the word "office" into the text. It's not unreasonable to think that the New Testament authors viewed the apostolate in much the same way. It is a "work" or an "assignment" or a "position of authority" to which a person may be called by God.

Whereas it is certainly the case that God has graciously given apostles to the church for its guidance and edification (Eph. 4:11), apostleship itself does not appear to qualify as a *charisma* in the same way that other manifestations of the Spirit do. Rather, much in the same way as we regard elders and deacons, apostles are those who have been called, commissioned, and appointed to a position ("office"?) of authority for the building up of the body of Christ.

A Definition

So how might we define an apostle? Is there a uniform definition that would apply to all in the New Testament (and perhaps in our day) who have been called or appointed to this office? J. B. Lightfoot, in his widely regarded essay on the apostolate, contended that an apostle was "not only the messenger, but the delegate of the person who sends him. He is entrusted with a mission, [and] has powers conferred upon him."[6]

Some craft their definition based on the lexical meaning of the Greek verb *apostellō* and thus take *apostolos* to mean "one who is sent." Others, however, have come to recognize that any definition must include the notion of being commissioned as an authorized representative or delegate of the one who sent him.[7] Thus, an apostle is one who has, in a manner of speaking, been

---

6   J. B. Lightfoot, "The Name and Office of an Apostle," in Lightfoot, *The Epistle of St. Paul to the Galatians* (Grand Rapids: Zondervan, 1975), 92.

7   Frank Chan points out that some, such as Lightfoot, contend that the Christian *apostolos* "functioned in a manner parallel to the Jewish *shaliach* ('agent')—in Jewish society the legally commissioned representative who acted in the stead of his client (m. Ber. 5:5). Although some scholars have rejected Lightfoot's *apostolos-shaliach* connection as anachronistic, the analogy nevertheless serves well in conveying 'divinely delegated authority' as the central feature of apostleship, as it has always been understood (including by cessationists)"

granted the power of attorney. What he says and does is discharged on behalf of the one who sent or commissioned him. In this way, says Frank Chan,

> any actions he performs on behalf of his client are as if performed by the client himself, i.e., they are authoritative and binding. Apostles of Jesus Christ, in an analogous way, perform their assigned ministries as representatives of Jesus Christ. In matters of the Spirit, they possess Christ's authority to the degree that they are faithful to the commission they've been given.[8]

Chan proceeds to define apostles as

> remarkable leaders sent by God to establish new spheres of ministry by setting up the key governmental structures necessary for those ministries.... The "sending" idea, along with "governmental structures" idea, emphasizes the way apostles are ground-breakers and pioneers, visionary and entrepreneurial. By "spheres of ministry" we acknowledge, as did Paul (2 Cor 10:13), that the spiritual gift of apostleship is not limitless divine authority, but divine authority within an assigned boundary.[9]

The Qualifications or Requirements for Being an Apostle

I question whether there would be much of a controversy over the subject of apostleship were it not for the emergence of what is called the New Apostolic Reformation.[10] Without going into detail regarding this movement, it has

---

("The Apostleship of Jesus as the Basis for Redefining Apostleship along Non-Cessationist Lines," a paper for the 58th annual meeting of the Evangelical Theological Society, November 17, 2006).

8   Frank Chan, from an unpublished paper, "The Office of Apostle," August 2001, used here with permission.

9   Frank Chan, unpublished paper, "Apostles and Prophets as the Foundation of the Church: Rethinking a Popular Cessationist Argument from Ephesians 2:20," used here with permission.

10   For more information on the so-called NAR, see two books by C. Peter Wagner: *Churchquake! How the New Apostolic Reformation Is Shaking Up the Church as We Know It* (Ventura, CA: Regal, 1996); and *Apostles and Prophets: The Foundation of the Church* (Ventura, CA: Regal, 2000). In addition, one should consult David Cartledge, *The Apostolic Revolution: The Restoration of Apostles and Prophets in the Assemblies of God in Australia* (Chester Hill, NSW, Australia: Paraclete Institute, 2000); Donald E. Miller, *Reinventing American Protestantism: Christianity in the New Millennium* (Berkeley: University of California Press, 1996). For a rigorous critique of the movement, see the books by R. Douglas Geivett and Holly Pivec, *A New Apostolic Reformation? A Biblical Response to a Worldwide Movement* (Wooster, OH: Weaver, 2014), and *God's Super-Apostles: Encountering the*

provoked heated dialogue about whether apostles are still active in the church today and, if so, what might be the nature and extent of their authority.

The New Testament is clear regarding the original group of twelve apostles, chosen by Jesus (Mark 3:13–19) to "be with him" (v. 14). Luke recorded that Jesus "called his disciples and chose from them twelve, whom he named apostles" (Luke 6:13). After the death of Judas Iscariot, Matthias was selected to replace him through the casting of lots (Acts 1:21–26). These men are likely the ones whose names are inscribed on the twelve foundations of the wall of the new Jerusalem (Rev. 21:14). Although the original Twelve comprise a unique and unchanging group, others are undeniably identified as apostles. Among these we would include Paul, whose calling into the apostolate is clearly described in the New Testament (see Rom. 1:1; Col. 1:1). Paul described himself as "an apostle—not from men nor through man, but through Jesus Christ and God the Father" (Gal. 1:1).

But as we move beyond Paul, we encounter considerable controversy. The questions that must be answered are: Who else in the New Testament is identified as an apostle, what does this tell us about the qualifications or criteria for being an apostle, and is it possible that God still intends for apostles to be active in the church today?

It seems evident from Ephesians 2:19–20 that some apostles served in a foundational role. As Paul explained, "the household of God" or the church is "built on the foundation of the apostles and prophets, Christ Jesus himself being the cornerstone." These apostles spoke and wrote the theological and ethical truths that are morally binding on the beliefs and behavior of all Christians in every age. But there would appear to be others who are legitimately called "apostles" who did not function in this capacity.

Barnabas was most likely an apostle, as seems clear from the way he is described in Acts 11:22ff.; 13:1–3; 1 Corinthians 9:1–6; and Galatians 2:1. In fact, Barnabas is explicitly called an apostle in Acts 14:14. Numerous texts suggest that Silas (also known as Silvanus) was an apostle (see Acts 15:22ff.; 16:19ff.; 1 Thess. 1:1). In 1 Thessalonians 2:4–7 Paul appeared to include both Silas and Timothy among those he described as apostles. The primary reason for excluding Timothy was the belief that to be an apostle one had to have been an eyewitness to the risen Christ. But if the latter qualification only

---

Worldwide Prophets and Apostles Movement (Wooster, OH: Weaver, 2014).

applied to the original Twelve and Paul (more on this later), it would have no bearing on Timothy's call to the apostolate. Paul explicitly called James, the brother of Jesus, an apostle in Galatians 1:19.

Titus is also often mentioned as a possible apostle, given his prominent role alongside Paul. Although not explicitly called an apostle, his authority as one who labored with Paul suggests that he, too, was regarded as one (see esp. 2 Cor. 2:12–13; 7:6, 13, 14; 8:6, 16; Gal. 2:1ff.; 2 Tim. 4:10; Titus 1:5). Paul also spoke of "our brothers" who were "messengers [lit., apostles] of the churches" (2 Cor. 8:23). Many insist that here the word "apostle" is used in a nontechnical sense of someone who served as an ambassador of a particular local church. Again, though, this appears to be the result of a prior belief that an apostle must have been an eye and earwitness of the risen Christ. The same argument is used to exclude Epaphroditus as an apostle, even though the term is specifically applied to him (Phil. 2:25).

A fascinating and instructive reference is found in 2 Corinthians 11:13, where Paul warned the church about "false apostles" who disguise themselves "as apostles of Christ." If seeing the risen Christ was a qualification for anyone who claimed to be an apostle, we would have expected Paul to exclude them on that basis. But he instead pointed to their "deceitful" ways (v. 13) and their "deeds" that warrant judgment (v. 15).

In Paul's greetings to the saints in Rome, he included the following: "Greet Andronicus and Junia [or Junias], my kinsmen and my fellow prisoners. They are well known to the apostles, and they were in Christ before me" (Rom. 16:7). Some translations render this "well known *among* the apostles," thus implying that both Andronicus and Junia(s) were themselves apostles. Several questions must be addressed.

First, is Junia(s) masculine or feminine? If feminine, then they are most likely husband and wife. Recent examination of extensive Greek literature outside the Bible gives little help. The word *Junias* turned up only twice as a woman's name and only once as a man's name. If Junia(s) was a woman, do we have reference here to a female apostle? If so, it would be difficult to restrict women from holding senior governmental authority in the local church insofar as the office of apostle in the New Testament was the pinnacle of spiritual authority.

Second, how should we translate the passage: "well known *to* the apostles" or "well known *among* the apostles"? The latter would suggest that Andronicus and Junia(s) were themselves apostles, well known in that unique circle of believers. The former would suggest that the apostles, such as Paul, knew these two people quite well. The point has been made that "since Andronicus and Junia(s) were Christians before Paul was, it may be that their longstanding ministry (reaching back before Paul's) is precisely what Paul might have in mind when he says 'of note among the apostles.' They may well have been known among the apostles before Paul was even converted."[11] However, recent analysis of the grammar of this text has suggested that this particular construction should be rendered "well known *to* the apostles."[12] There is, therefore, questionable support for the idea that Junia(s), whether male or female, was an apostle.[13]

An especially instructive passage is found in 1 Corinthians 4:9 where Paul said that "God has exhibited us apostles as last of all," a reference that most likely would include Apollos (see also 1 Cor. 1:12; 3:4ff.; 16:12). Opposition to this conclusion is the almost inescapable evidence that Apollos had not seen the risen Christ. He is described in Acts 18:24 as being "a native of Alexandria." Most also contend that his late conversion precluded the possibility that he had seen the risen Lord. Some would insist that if Paul did regard him as an apostle, it could only be because he believed Apollos had actually seen the risen Christ. But this seems highly unlikely.

The most prudent way forward for us would be to pause our investigation of who was or was not an apostle and turn to the question of the supposed qualifications for the office. If having been an eye and earwitness to the risen Christ was a *sine qua non* of apostolic calling, we would have to exclude both Apollos and Timothy from that group. But the evidence for this view may be less persuasive than previously thought. So, to that we now turn our attention.

---

11 John Piper and Wayne Grudem, "An Overview of Central Concerns: Questions and Answers," *Recovering Biblical Manhood and Womanhood: A Response to Evangelical Feminism*, ed. John Piper and Wayne Grudem (Wheaton, IL: Crossway, 1991), 80.

12 See M. H. Burer and D. B. Wallace, "Was Junias Really an Apostle? A Reexamination of Romans 16:7," *New Testament Studies* 47 (2001): 76–91. This article was followed by another, authored by Burer: "'episēmoi en tois apostolois' in Rom 16:7 as 'well known to the apostles'; further defense and new evidence," *JETS* 58.4 (2015): 731–55.

13 Those who are inclined to identify Junia(s) as an apostle also suggest that she or he would have been so designated much in the way the ambassadors or representatives in 2 Corinthians 8:23 and Epaphroditus in Philippians 2:25 were "apostles."

CHAPTER 18

The Qualifications for Apostleship, or Are There Apostles in the Church Today?

The most popular view among evangelicals is that to qualify as an apostle, two specific criteria must be met. First, the individual must have been an eye and earwitness of the risen Christ.[1] This is based on three texts. The first is Acts 1:21–22: "So one of the men who have accompanied us during all the time that the Lord Jesus went in and out among us, beginning from the baptism of John until the day when he was taken up from us—one of these men must become with us a witness to his resurrection." Of the two men who met these criteria, Matthias and Barsabbas, the former was selected by lot.

In the second text, Paul spoke of his apostleship in this manner: "Am I not free? Am I not an apostle? Have I not seen Jesus our Lord? Are not you my workmanship in the Lord? If to others I am not an apostle, at least I am to you, for you are the seal of my apostleship in the Lord" (1 Cor. 9:1–2). Finally, Paul pointed to the fact that the risen Christ "appeared also to me" (15:8).

A second purported qualification is having been personally called and commissioned by Christ to this office. This is not as clear as the former criterion but seems to be implied by such texts as Mark 3:14 and 16 where Jesus is said to have "appointed" the Twelve as apostles. Paul described himself as having been "called to be an apostle, set apart for the gospel of God" (Rom. 1:1; see also 1 Cor. 1:1; Gal. 1:1, 11–12, 15–17).

---

1 Appeal is most often made to the classic essay by J. B. Lightfoot, "The Name and Office of an Apostle," in *The Epistle of St. Paul to the Galatians* (Grand Rapids: Zondervan, 1975), 92–101.

If these two qualifications (especially the first) are essential for the apostolate, then neither Apollos nor Timothy can be included in that group. Or if they are included, they would be apostles of a different and somewhat lower order of importance and authority. But are these texts cited above decisive?

Some also insist that an essential part of apostleship is the authority to write inspired Scripture. There are three problems with this view. First, Scripture nowhere asserts that all apostles could write Scripture simply because they were apostles. Second, several of the apostles did not, in fact, write Scripture. Does this disqualify them from holding this position? Third, people other than apostles did, in fact, write Scripture: Mark, Luke, the author of Hebrews, and most likely Jude.[2] There is no explicit or conclusive evidence that apostleship per se entailed the authority to write Scripture or required that one do so. Therefore, it is conceivable that God could raise up apostles subsequent to the closing of the biblical canon without threatening the latter's finality and sufficiency. The canon is closed, not because God has stopped speaking, nor because there are no more apostles, but because God sovereignly closed it. God simply ceased inspiring and preserving canonical revelation. Basing the finality of the canon on the cessation of apostleship is disastrous. How can the absence of apostles guarantee the closing of the canon when nonapostles wrote Scripture? Such a view would require us to assert, absurdly, that as long as there are nonapostolic Christians, the canon is open!

1 Corinthians 9:1–6

We begin our evaluation of the traditional view with 1 Corinthians 9. There we read the following:

> Am I not free? Am I not an apostle? Have I not seen Jesus our Lord? Are not you my workmanship in the Lord? If to others I am not an apostle, at least I am to you, for you are the seal of my apostleship in the Lord.
> This is my defense to those who would examine me. Do we not have

---

2 Some would reject Jude as an apostle in light of his comment in Jude 17–18: "But you must remember, beloved, the predictions of the apostles of our Lord Jesus Christ. They said to you, 'In the last time there will be scoffers, following their own ungodly passions.'"

the right to eat and drink? Do we not have the right to take along a believing wife, as do the other apostles and the brothers of the Lord and Cephas? Or is it only Barnabas and I who have no right to refrain from working for a living? (vv. 1–6)

What are we to make of this? I can do no better than cite Andrew Wilson and his response to the argument that Paul was setting forth a necessary condition for anyone who claimed to be an apostle.[3] He writes,

The point at issue in 9:1–2 is not "what qualifies anyone to be an apostle," but "what guarantees that Paul is an apostle," and as such has more to do with *sufficient* conditions for apostleship than *necessary* ones.[4] In 9:1, for example, Paul asserts his freedom (1a) on the basis of his apostleship (1b); his apostleship is a sufficient condition for his Christian freedom, but it is not a necessary one, for (to Paul) all Christians are free, whether they are apostles or not. Similarly, Paul's apostleship (1b) is grounded both in his commission from the risen Jesus (1c), and in the Corinthians themselves (1d), who by their very existence as believers authenticate Paul's apostolic ministry (2). In context, Paul is not saying that either of these things are *necessary* conditions for *all* apostleship; he may or may not believe that, but it is not what he is saying here. Rather, he is saying that between them, they constitute *sufficient* conditions for *his* apostleship. In fact, in modern scholarship, it is generally agreed that Paul's point here has to do with establishing his freedom, not with providing qualifications for all apostles in all places at all times.[5]

We must not overlook the fact that Paul didn't simply appeal to his having seen Jesus after his resurrection. He also said, "Am I not free?" (v. 1a), by which he meant financially independent. "Yet no one infers from this that monetary self-sufficiency is a requirement for apostleship! It would seem

---

3   See Andrew Wilson, "Apostle Apollos?" in *JETS* 56.2 (2013): 325–35.

4   Here Wilson points to 2 Corinthians 11:7–13, "where he indicates that [Paul's] refusal to accept money from the Corinthians, in contrast to the super-apostles who take it happily, undermines their claim to apostleship and reinforces his. He does not, however, regard this as a necessary condition for genuine apostleship (1 Cor. 9:3–14)" (Wilson, 332n24).

5   Wilson, 332–33.

that Paul is listing items that are relevant to apostleship in his time and circumstance, not items that are definitional to it."[6]

We should also take into consideration verses 3–6, which suggest that Paul was just as concerned with asserting the apostolic rights of Barnabas, yet nothing is said about the latter having seen the risen Jesus. Some will respond by suggesting that Barnabas was among the "more than five hundred brothers" to whom Jesus appeared or perhaps is included among "all the apostles" who likewise saw Jesus following his resurrection (see 1 Cor. 15:6–7). But there is no way to prove this is the case unless one reads all these texts through the lens of a prior assumption that seeing the risen Christ was essential to the apostolic office.

There is also the possibility that Paul's point in 1 Corinthians 9 is simply to establish the fact that he was not in any way less an apostle than those who *had* seen the risen Christ, specifically the Twelve. His point would be that he had the same rights and authority as Peter and James and John. Perhaps someone in Corinth was bringing Paul's claim to apostolicity into question on the basis of his being a secondary, less authoritative apostle than those who walked and ministered with Jesus for three years. If so, Paul's comments here in 1 Corinthians 9 would be less a statement about the qualifications for all apostles and more an assertion of his own rights as equal to those of Peter and the other eleven.

Or to put it in other words, Paul's apostolic ministry should not be questioned, for he had been commissioned by Jesus and had a consistent and fruitful track record in having established the Corinthian church and in being largely responsible for the conversion of its members. These two factors are sufficient to justify *his* apostolic authority but are not designed to set forth absolutely necessary conditions for any other who may claim to be an apostle.

Frank Chan has suggested that Paul's language here may possibly reflect the perspective of the apostolic office as it existed in Jerusalem, but not necessarily in other geographic regions at a later time in the development of the early church. Paul, then, may well have been giving "lip service" to this

---

6 Frank Chan, "The Apostleship of Jesus as the Basis for Redefining Apostleship along Non-Cessationist Lines," unpublished paper delivered at the 58th annual meeting of the Evangelical Theological Society, November 17, 2006, 6n25.

concept of apostleship in 1 Corinthians 9:1 "in part because his opponents at Corinth, who had ties to Jerusalem and who were probably eyewitnesses of the resurrection themselves (cf. 2 Cor. 5:16), held this view."[7] Thus, it may be that by the time Paul referred to Andronicus and Junia(s) as apostles in Romans 16:7 (on the dubious assumption that he actually did), "he had abandoned this early 'ruling apostle' concept and embraced an Antioch-based 'missionary apostle' concept, one that did *not* require apostles to be eyewitnesses of the resurrection, but did require apostles to be willing to sacrifice and suffer for their calling."[8] In fact, it is on this basis that we may be justified in actually viewing Timothy as an apostle.

Acts 1:21–26

But what might be said regarding Acts 1 and the choice of Matthias to replace Judas?

> "So one of the men who have accompanied us during all the time that the Lord Jesus went in and out among us, beginning from the baptism of John until the day when he was taken up from us—one of these men must become with us a witness to his resurrection." And they put forward two, Joseph called Barsabbas, who was also called Justus, and Matthias. And they prayed and said, "You, Lord, who know the hearts of all, show which one of these two you have chosen to take the place in this ministry and apostleship from which Judas turned aside to go to his own place." And they cast lots for them, and the lot fell on Matthias, and he was numbered with the eleven apostles. (Acts 1:21–26)

Once again, Wilson speaks decisively to the point:

> The stipulations for apostolic ministry given in Acts 1:22–23 applied to the final member of the twelve, not to others such as Paul—and they would of

---

7 Frank Chan, "'Apostles' in 1 Cor 12:28–29 and 1 Cor 4:9: Founding Fathers of the Universal Church or Foundation-Building Leaders at Corinth?" unpublished paper delivered at the 61st Annual Meeting of the Evangelical Theological Society, November 19, 2009, 3n8.

8 Chan, 3n8.

course have excluded Paul himself, had they been applied . . . [for] the last member of the twelve had to have been with the disciples "during all the time that the Lord Jesus went in and out among us, beginning from the baptism of John," a requirement that, quite obviously, Paul did not satisfy. So to read 1 Cor 9:1 through the lenses of Acts 1:21–22, as if they are both saying more or less the same thing, is to ignore a difference between them so large that it would have excluded the author of 1 Corinthians himself. It does not, therefore, seem that the Lukan material gives us a good reason to deny that Paul regarded Apollos as an apostle, for the context of Acts 1:21–22 is substantially different to that of 1 Cor 9:1.[9]

Frank Chan agrees: "It is entirely conceivable that Luke could have regarded the eyewitness stipulation to be a fitting requirement for the apostolic ministry at the *outset* of the Christian mission (a *description*), but *not* necessarily a fitting requirement for *all* times (a *prescription*), especially in light of the changing circumstances faced by the Christian mission as it expanded."[10] Chan's point is that in the early days of the church's existence in and around Jerusalem, the authenticity of the witness borne by the apostles was quite important. But, says Chan, "as the church moved further and further from Jerusalem geographically and from the resurrection chronologically, is it not understandable that the spiritual authority to preach the gospel, heal the sick, establish churches (what apostles do) did not require a firsthand knowledge of an event in 30 AD, but a firsthand knowledge of the risen Christ himself as manifested in the power of the Holy Spirit?"[11]

Thus, it seems quite likely to me that the criteria set forth here in Acts 1 were designed for a special category of apostle, namely, the Twelve whose names are to appear on the foundations of the wall of the new Jerusalem (Rev. 21:14). The evidence we have examined in the previous chapter and now in this one indicates that whereas the Twelve *perhaps* had to have seen the risen Christ, there is little reason to think that this qualification would have extended to all other apostles.

---

9 Wilson, "Apostle Apollos?" 333.
10 Frank Chan, "Flaws in J. B. Lightfoot's Cessationist Concept of Apostleship: A Critique of the So-Called 'Eyewitness of the Resurrection' Requirement," unpublished paper delivered at the 60th Annual Meeting of the Evangelical Theological Society, November 18, 2008, 6 (emphases original).
11 Chan, n. 23.

The reason for concluding that any potential candidate to replace Judas Iscariot among the Twelve had to have been an eyewitness of the risen Christ is implicit in something we read in Acts 1:21–22. According to Peter, whomever the Lord might select for this position had to "have accompanied us during all the time that the Lord Jesus went in and out among us, beginning from the baptism of John until the day when he was taken up from us" (which, as earlier noted, would have ruled out Paul). If it were required that this individual be present with the apostles until the ascension of Jesus, he obviously would have, at some point, seen the risen Christ himself. He would thus have joined the Eleven in bearing witness to "his resurrection" (Acts 1:22b). The latter, of course, is a reference to what the apostles would do in their subsequent ministry. Being a "witness to his resurrection" means that he bears witness to or makes known to others that Jesus is in fact alive from the dead. All of us even today are called to be a "witness to his resurrection." You can't "become" a witness to something that has already occurred. You can only bear witness to it, which is to say, preach it and make it known to others, and anyone can do this who knows Christ as Lord and Savior. To be clear, the text doesn't explicitly say that this person was an eyewitness to the resurrection in the sense that he saw the risen Christ. Although certainly implied, the point is that this person must become a witness to or on behalf of or concerning the truth of the resurrection of Jesus. Thus, what we have here is a declaration of what *would* transpire in the *future*. In any case, as previously argued, whereas the requirement of having seen the risen Christ was essential for becoming one of the Twelve, it goes beyond what is stated in Acts to insist that this was also a requirement for all subsequent apostles.

1 Corinthians 15:7–9

We are left, finally, with 1 Corinthians 15:7–9. There we read,

> Then he appeared to James, then to all the apostles. Last of all, as to one untimely born, he appeared also to me. For I am the least of the apostles, unworthy to be called an apostle, because I persecuted the church of God.

The most common understanding is that the word translated "last of all" means that once Jesus, after his resurrection, appeared to Paul, he thereafter appeared to no one else.[12] And since seeing the risen Christ is supposedly a necessary condition for being an apostle, Paul was effectively closing down the apostolate to any and all subsequent claims to the office. Likewise, Paul Barnett argues from this that "Paul himself sought to establish the limited extent of the numbers of apostles. His careful words that Christ 'appeared to me last of all' . . . serve to show that while there were apostles before him, there were no apostles after him. According to Paul he is both 'the least' and 'the last' of the apostles."[13]

Let us assume, for the sake of argument, that Paul was claiming to be the last to have experienced a postresurrection appearance of Jesus. Even then, "it is by no means clear that he believed he was therefore the last ever *apostolos*."[14] The latter point can only be asserted if, contrary to what we have seen, being an eye and earwitness to the risen Christ was a necessary condition for *anyone* being an apostle.

But this verse may be understood differently. As noted, Paul was listing those to whom Jesus appeared in order to prove his bodily resurrection. One reason we know that Christ was raised physically from the dead is because there were hundreds of eyewitnesses who would testify to that fact. Paul was one of them. *He mentioned himself among these who had seen Christ alive not to prove that he was an apostle but to demonstrate that Christ was truly raised.* Jesus appeared to Peter, then the Twelve, after that to more than five hundred brethren, then to James, then to other apostles, and last of all, that is, last among all those mentioned here to whom he appeared following his resurrection, to Paul. Paul was the last to whom Jesus had appeared to that point in time, but nothing in the text suggests that Jesus could not or would not appear to someone subsequent to Paul. In other words, Paul was not describing Jesus's postresurrection appearances in order to prove his or anyone else's apostleship, but to prove that Jesus did in fact rise from the dead. After all, he mentioned his appearing to more than five hundred people, none of whom were apostles. Let it be said, however, that even if this interpretation of "last of all" is incorrect, nothing in what Paul said rules out the possibility of apostles subsequent to him in church history.

---

12 This is the conclusion reached by Peter Jones, "1 Corinthians 15:8: Paul the Last Apostle," *TynBul* 36 (1985): 3–34.

13 "Apostle," in *Dictionary of Paul and His Letters* (Downers Grove, IL: IVP, 1993), 50.

14 Wilson, "Apostle Apollos?" 334.

The Personal Call and Commission of Christ

As for the purported "personal call" from Christ or "commissioning" by him as a necessary qualification for being an apostle, there is no doubt that Paul based his apostleship at least in part on his having received one. We need not rehearse the many texts where this is either asserted or implied (see Acts 9:15; 26:12–18; Rom. 1:1; 1 Cor. 1:1; Gal. 1:1; 1 Tim. 1:1).

But by what means would the personal "call" or "commission" to the office of apostle have come to others? I see no reason why we should restrict this to a personal visitation from Christ (such as that experienced by Paul on the Damascus Road) or by means of a "voice" from heaven. After all, it appears that Matthias was appointed to the office without either of these, being set apart solely by the casting of lots (Acts 1:21–26). The latter, of course, would have clearly constituted a decisive and unmistakable call to the office. In any case, there would surely have been some sense in one's heart that Christ was commissioning a person to this task, however subjective that may feel. In other words, the calling by Christ might perhaps be discerned through what is known as the *internal testimony of the Spirit*. This would hardly stand alone as investing a person with apostolic authority. There would need to be confirmation or some form of validation by the church, especially the elders, as they acknowledged the gifts and character of the individual and placed their blessing on him. Beyond that we can only speculate.

Thus far we have examined the nature of the apostolic office, and particularly the qualifications laid out in the New Testament for an apostle. I brought into serious question the traditional evangelical view that to be an apostle one must have seen the risen Christ, although it is certainly the case that one must have been the recipient, by some means, of a personal call or commission from Christ himself. We now turn our attention to the twofold question of whether men such as Apollos, Timothy, and Titus might have qualified as apostles, and whether such apostles still exist in the church today.

The Case for Apollos (as well as for Timothy and Titus)

Do Paul's comments in 1 Corinthians 4:6–9 suggest that he regarded Apollos as an apostle? I believe the answer is yes. Here is what Paul wrote:

> I have applied all these things to myself and Apollos for your benefit, brothers, that you may learn by us not to go beyond what is written, that none of you may be puffed up in favor of one against another. For who sees anything different in you? What do you have that you did not receive? If then you received it, why do you boast as if you did not receive it?
>
> Already you have all you want! Already you have become rich! Without us you have become kings! And would that you did reign, so that we might share the rule with you! For I think that God has exhibited us apostles as last of all, like men sentenced to death, because we have become a spectacle to the world, to angels, and to men.

First, when Paul spoke of God having exhibited "us apostles" last of all (v. 9), "the wider context of 3:5–4:21 indicates that the subjects" of "us" are Paul and Apollos and possibly also Cephas (Peter).[15] The "we" in 1 Corinthians 3:9 and the "us" in 4:1 certainly include Paul and Apollos, and there is no indication that this has changed when we arrive at 4:9.

Second, in verse 6 Paul was clearly including Apollos in the "us" by whom the Corinthians had learned "not to go beyond what is written." Why would we not conclude, then, that the "us" in verse 8a and the "we" in verse 8b include Apollos? And if they do, and only special pleading would suggest otherwise, it seems reasonable that Paul had Apollos in mind in verse 9 when he spoke explicitly about "us apostles."

Third, since the Corinthians had divided into factions, aligning themselves with either Paul, Cephas (Peter), or Apollos (1 Cor. 3:4–9), it seems reasonable to conclude that they regarded the latter, no less than the former two, as an apostle. If Paul believed the Corinthians were wrong in drawing this conclusion,

> if, in his view, Apollos was not an apostle because he had not seen the risen Jesus—then Paul would probably not have reasoned the way he did, affirming the similarities between himself and Apollos throughout 1:10–4:21, and seamlessly moving from talking about the two of them to talking about "us apostles." It therefore seems probable (a) that the Corinthians believed that

---

15 Wilson, 329.

Apollos was an *apostolos* ... and (b) that Paul did not attempt to correct their view. The only obvious explanation for this is that he shared it.[16]

What, then, are the possible conclusions we might derive from this passage? I think Andrew Wilson has identified them. "Either (1) Paul did not regard Apollos as an apostle; (2) Paul believed Apollos had witnessed the resurrected Jesus; or (3) for Paul, witnessing the risen Christ was not a necessary condition for all apostleship."[17] When we view 1 Corinthians 4 in the light of all the other evidence we've examined, I'm inclined to believe that the third of these options is most likely.

A similar case can be made for Timothy and Titus as apostles, even though neither of them witnessed the risen Christ or received a personal commission from him. And like Apollos, neither of them wrote Scripture.

As for Timothy, there is a dispute among scholars as to whether the first-person plural "we ... as apostles of Christ" in 1 Thessalonians 2:6–7 includes, in addition to Paul, both Silvanus (Silas) and Timothy, or only Silas. In 1 Thessalonians 3:2 Paul said that "we" sent "Timothy, our brother and God's coworker in the gospel of Christ." Clearly the "we" in this text, as well as in 3:6, does not include Timothy. Likewise, in 2:2 Paul said, "We had already suffered ... in Philippi," a statement that would have included Silas but not Timothy (see Acts 16:19). However, there is no explicit contextual clue in 2:6–7 that Paul was referring only to himself, or to himself and Silas to the exclusion of Timothy. Given the fact that the epistle is from "Paul, Silvanus, and Timothy" (1:1), the most natural assumption is that all three are in view in the "we ... as apostles of Christ" in 2:6b. But it would be unwise to be dogmatic on this point.[18]

In an unpublished paper made available to me by the author, Frank Chan points out that Timothy

has clearly played a foundation-laying role at the church at Corinth (2 Cor 2:19). Though there is no evidence of a direct commission from God or

---

16 Wilson, 331.

17 Wilson, 325.

18 Wayne Grudem has argued at length that Timothy was not an apostle. See his evidence in *Systematic Theology: An Introduction to Biblical Doctrine* (Grand Rapids: Zondervan, 1994), 905–12.

Christ, there was one occasion during which Paul and other elders laid hands upon Timothy, imparting some spiritual gift to him (2 Tim 1:6; cf. 1 Tim 4:14). At Ephesus, Timothy is serving in authority *over elders*, apparently functioning in Paul's stead with Paul's authority, ensuring that the teaching elders are paid (1 Tim 5:17), evaluating accusations against elders (1 Tim 5:18), laying hands on new elders (1 Tim 5:22) and commanding certain men (probably elders) to stop their false teaching (1 Tim 1:3). To maintain the non-apostolic status of Timothy because he is a *second-generation* early church leader seems arbitrary.[19]

Still, though, a possible indication that Timothy was not an apostle is the way Paul regularly excluded him from the title in the opening greetings of his epistles. In several of these, Paul identified himself as an "apostle" but referred to Timothy only as "our brother" (see 2 Cor. 1:1; Col. 1:1; Philem. 1). In Philippians 1:1 he opened with the words, "Paul and Timothy, servants of Jesus Christ." In any case, if Timothy was not an apostle, it would not have been due to his not having seen the risen Christ but to the fact that Christ had simply not called him to that office.[20]

As noted earlier, Paul also spoke of other men who were "messengers of the churches" (2 Cor. 8:23). The English Standard Version translates *apostoloi* as "messengers" on the assumption that such men would not have met the required conditions for being an apostle. Once again, we see how this prior assumption regarding the qualifications for being an apostle exerted a controlling influence not only over interpretation of the text but also its translation. The fact is that of the eighty instances in which the word *apostle* is used in the New Testament, only four could possibly refer to nonapostolic "messengers" (see John 13:16; Phil. 2:25; 2 Cor. 8:23; and possibly Rom. 16:7). And of these four, only the text in John 13:16 most assuredly does.

We must also reckon with what Paul said in 1 Corinthians 12:28. Those who argue that there were few apostles in the early church, perhaps no more

---

19 Chan explores this perspective on Timothy in greater detail in his unpublished paper, "Flaws in J. B. Lightfoot's Cessationist Concept of Apostleship," 13–15.

20 On the other hand, it is entirely possible that Paul mentioned himself and Timothy in this manner to draw attention to the difference between the primary author of the letter (Paul) and a secondary contributor (Timothy).

than fifteen (the Twelve, plus Paul, Barnabas, and James) cannot explain Paul's reference to apostles as given to local churches for their edification. Even if the number of apostles is expanded to twenty or more, Paul appears to have envisioned each local church profiting spiritually from the ministry and leadership of at least one apostle. In other words, if apostles are among the many gifts (or offices) God has granted to all of his churches, there would necessarily be a multitude of them, perhaps numbering in the hundreds. Frank Chan then poses this question:

> Why would Paul list "apostles" in 1 Cor 12:28 as one of the spiritual gifts that edify the body, if he did not conceive of the gift operating and having some effect "for the common good" at the level of the *local* congregation? Could it be that Paul assumed apostles normally were known by and intimately connected to local churches—a difficult idea to grasp if there were only fifteen in the entire known Christian world?[21]

And we mustn't forget that the original band of apostles ministered some thirty years in Judea, prior to the time that Paul wrote to the Corinthians. Is it feasible that it is only these few apostles that Paul had in mind when he encouraged the Corinthian believers to embrace "apostles" as one of the primary blessings and sources of encouragement and edification given by God to the church?

In a related vein, the same question can be asked of Paul's words in Ephesians 4:11. Did Paul here refer only to a mere fifteen to twenty individuals? His point in this passage is to list five (or perhaps only four, if pastor and teacher are one gift) ministries on which individual Christians in all local churches may depend for the sort of equipping and encouragement that will enable them to grow up into Christlike maturity. And if one responds by saying that *apostolos* in Ephesians 4:11 has in view only messengers, missionaries, or ambassadors, why would Paul list apostles both here and in 1 Corinthians 12:28 as first or "highest" among the many ministries of the church? Then there is also Paul's reference in 1 Corinthians 15:5, 7 to "all the apostles," who were in all likelihood separate from the Twelve, James, and himself. Who might they be? This text, together with

---

21 Chan, "The Apostleship of Jesus as the Basis for Redefining Apostleship along Non-Cessationist Lines."

Paul's reference to "the other apostles" in 1 Corinthians 9:5, strongly suggests that there were considerably more apostles in the early church than a mere fifteen or twenty.

What might we conclude, then, regarding the tendency within conservative evangelicalism to divide the apostolic office into two types? In an article I wrote many years ago, I defended the notion that there were so-called capital *A* apostles who were required to have been eye and earwitnesses of the risen Christ. These would include the Eleven, plus Matthias, James, Barnabas, possibly Silas, and definitely Paul. I also argued that there were so-called lowercase *a* apostles who functioned in a significantly less authoritative role as emissaries, ambassadors, or messengers on behalf of local churches. The only individuals who might be included under this second category are Epaphroditus, the individuals mentioned in 2 Corinthians 8:23, and possibly Andronicus and Junia(s) (although, as noted earlier, the latter two were likely not designated as "apostles" in Romans 16:7). These lowercase *a* apostles were not required to have seen the risen Christ or to have been personally commissioned by him. It was enough that a local church appointed them to their particular ministries.

But, as Wilson has so persuasively argued,

> Apollos makes this very neat approach somewhat less straightforward. Here we appear to have a man who did not witness the resurrection or receive a personal commission from Jesus, and who never wrote Scripture . . . yet nonetheless had a substantial role in the establishment of the Corinthian church, and was placed in the same foolish, cruciform, scum-of-the-earth group of apostles as Paul himself. He clearly did not have the same experience or commission as Paul or the twelve, yet he does not seem to be a mere "messenger of the churches" either.[22]

The designation of Apollos as an apostle in this way not only points to the diversity of ways in which the word is used in the New Testament but also reinforces the distinct possibility (probability?) that whereas appearances of the risen Christ may have ended with Paul's experience on the Damascus Road, apostleship did not.

---

22 Wilson, "Apostle Apollos?" 335.

Apostles in the Church Today?

If being an eyewitness to the risen Christ is not a requirement for the office of apostle, except for those who comprised the original Twelve, what then are the qualifications that one must meet, or perhaps the characteristics in life and ministry that one must display? Whereas the presence of these features noted below do not make one an apostle, their absence may well call into question the authenticity of one's claim to that office. One would be hard-pressed to find an apostle in the New Testament whose life was not characterized by these features.

1. Success in ministry (1 Cor. 9:2; cf. 2 Cor. 3:1–3; but nonapostles also have great evangelistic success; see Philip in Acts 8).
2. Having received a personal call from Christ or commission to the office (be it face-to-face, as with the original Twelve, or by revelation, or by some other subjective means; although the appointment of Matthias to the office is described without any reference to this personal call; we can only assume that it had happened in some manner prior to the events of Acts 1).
3. Signs and wonders (Acts 5:12; Rom. 15:19; 2 Cor. 12:12; but nonapostles also performed signs and wonders; see Stephen in Acts 6 and Philip in Acts 8).
4. Extreme suffering (2 Cor. 4:7–15; 11:23–33; Col. 1:24; then again, countless others also suffer).
5. Christlike life and humility (2 Cor. 1:12; 2:17; 3:4–6; 4:2; 5:11; 6:3–13; 7:2; 10:13–18; 11:6, 23–28).
6. Related to the previous point is the issue of moral and spiritual character that appears to be critical in ascertaining who has or has not been appointed to the office of apostle. In the New Testament those called as apostles are consistently praised for being good men, full of the Spirit and full of faith (as with Barnabas; see Acts 11:24). Apostles must have a servant's heart (1 Cor. 3:5; 2 Cor. 12:15), always ready to lay down their lives for the sake of the sheep.
7. Although no specific spiritual gift is ever said to be essential to apostolic ministry, one can only assume that an apostle would have been able to teach. Apollos is portrayed as "an eloquent man, competent

in the Scriptures" who "spoke and taught accurately the things concerning Jesus" (Acts 18:24–25). Paul, and perhaps also inclusive of Silas and Timothy, "exhorted" and "encouraged" the believers in Thessalonica on how "to walk in a manner worthy of God" (1 Thess. 2:12; see also Acts 11:23, 26). And it's hard to imagine discharging successful apostolic ministry without the spiritual gift of leadership (Rom. 12:8) and perhaps also administration (1 Cor. 12:28).

8. God-orchestrated stigma (1 Cor. 4:9–13; 2 Cor. 6:3–10; 12:1–10).

If we were to conclude that apostleship is in some sense a spiritual gift (although I continue to have my doubts), we should probably define it as the empowering presence of the Spirit that enables a person to do the kind of work or discharge the kind of ministry that we see in Paul, Barnabas, Silas, and perhaps also Timothy and Titus. This would include bringing wisdom to bear in a local church on whatever issue or crisis it may face. Apostles evangelize where the gospel has not yet extended (Acts 16:11ff.). They plant churches. They exhort, instruct, and admonish believers in the local church (20:31). They provide spiritual wisdom and guidance for decision-making and the adjudication of church discipline. They hold elders and the people in local churches accountable to the doctrinal standards that have been set forth in Scripture. This does not mean that an apostle could overrule the duly appointed authority of the elders. It does mean that if the elders of a local congregation recognize an apostolic calling of God on a person, they are free to seek his input, guidance, and instruction. An apostle would then be active in helping bring clarity to biblical doctrine and its proper application.

Finally, what might we conclude about the *duration* of the apostolic office? Nothing in the qualifications for being an apostle require that we limit its validity to the first century. Nowhere else in the New Testament is the apostolate said to be restricted to the early church. It is, of course, undeniably the case that certain expressions of apostolic ministry, such as the authority granted to some to lay the theological and ethical foundations for the church universal, were necessarily time bound. But once the apostles ceased to function in this capacity does not mean they ceased to function in a variety of others.

Ephesians 4:11–13 is quite explicit that the risen Christ has blessed his people not only with prophets, evangelists, pastors, and teachers, but also with apostles "to equip the saints for the work of ministry, for building up the body of Christ, *until* we all attain to the unity of the faith and of the knowledge of the Son of God, to mature manhood, to the measure of the stature of the fullness of Christ" (emphasis mine). As long as immaturity remains, so do the gifts and/or ministerial offices God gave us to overcome it. Until such time as we reach "the stature of the fullness of Christ," and I daresay that won't be until Christ himself appears to consummate our salvation, the five gifts of Ephesians 4:11 (and by extended implication, all the other gifts as well), will be present and operational in the lives of God's people.

Some would argue against this by contending that the ministry or influence of the original apostles continues in the life of the church in subsequent centuries by means of their writings. The *inspired documents* of the apostolate are the way in which their ministry is perpetuated. Of course, there is a sense in which that is true. But as cogent as this may initially sound, the fact is that Paul did not speak in this passage of documents or epistles but of actual men who were appointed or gifted to function in their capacity as apostles, much in the same way as he envisioned *people* who were prophets, evangelists, pastors, and teachers being actively present in the church until such time as the church attains its full maturity.

The precise role and the extent of apostolic authority that such people would express in the modern church is something that goes beyond the limits of what I can address in this book. But we should remember that not even the New Testament apostles possessed universal authority. In fact, Paul said to the Corinthians, "If to others I am not an apostle, at least I am to you, for you are the seal of my apostleship in the Lord" (1 Cor. 9:2). Similarly, in 2 Corinthians 10:13–18, Paul refused to "boast beyond limits, but [would] boast only with regard to the area of influence God assigned" to him (v. 13). Insofar as Paul was an inspired author of Scripture, his influence is comprehensive, but in terms of personal oversight of particular local churches, his authority was limited.

And I see no reason why we should live in fear of apostolic authority any more than we do of the authority that God has invested in those who serve as pastors and elders in the local church (see Acts 20:28; 1 Thess. 5:12–13; Heb. 13:17; 1 Peter 5:1–5). The fact that someone might overextend their authority and abuse it to the detriment of the people of God is, in itself, hardly a reason to reject altogether the reality and need for properly recognized spiritual authority in the life of the local church.

Conclusion

The variety of theological issues over which Christians have divided, often with less than charity and patience, is quite staggering. One can readily point to complementarians and their disagreement with egalitarians, or those who embrace a pretribulation rapture and their argument with those who affirm a posttribulation return of Christ. Young-earth creationists dispute the conclusions of those who believe in an old earth, and paedobaptists and credo-baptists regularly find new ways of refuting the other's perspective. Calvinists and Arminians, premillennialists and amillennialists continue to crank out books at an alarming rate, claiming to have demonstrated beyond question the errors of the opposing side.

And then there is the debate that undergirds so much of what I've written in this book. Are tongues for today? Does God still bestow gifts of healing? Is the gift of miracles one that God continues to distribute to his people? Is the Bible sufficient, and if so, how might one defend the contemporary validity of revelatory gifts of the Spirit? My aim in this book was certainly not to pour more fuel on the already raging fire of disagreement on this subject (although some will conclude that such is precisely what I've done!). I'm neither naive nor optimistic enough to think that what I've written will resolve the issue for everyone. But I do hope that it will contribute in some small measure to easing the tension over spiritual gifts that so often tends to put continuationists and cessationists at each other's throats.

My strong belief in the continuation of all spiritual gifts into the present day has only intensified with the research and reflection that went into what you've just read. That doesn't mean that my cessationist friends don't have good arguments. They do. It's just that I don't find them persuasive. But, at the end of the day, whatever disagreements remain, and I'm quite sure they will, I pray they would not become the cause of acrimony or harsh criticism or, God forbid, the sort of bitter schism that serves only to bring reproach on the name of our Lord Jesus Christ.

As much as I value all the spiritual gifts and pray for their biblically based, Christ-exalting use in the body of Christ, I want to remind us all of something that my friend Craig Keener, a passionate and articulate advocate of the view that I have unpacked in this book, wrote in an article that appeared on his website on April 29, 2019 (www.craigkeener.com). His sober words are a reminder that spiritual gifts are not the most important or longlasting thing in the world, but neither are they to be treated with indifference or scorn. "The gifts pass away at Jesus's return ([1 Cor.] 13:8, 10, 12)," he wisely notes, but "not because they are bad or in the present unnecessary. They pass away because they are surpassed by something infinitely more wonderful."[1] So, as we together await with eager anticipation the arrival of "the perfect," may we love, encourage, instruct, and pray for one another to the glory of God the Father, in the name of our Lord Jesus Christ, through the power of his Holy Spirit.

---

1 Craig Keener, "Spiritual Gifts in 1 Cor 12–14 (part 2)," April 2019, www.craigkeener.com/spiritual-gifts-in-1-cor-12-14-part-2/.

Does God Give Spiritual Gifts to Non-Christians?

Your immediate response to this question may well be, "Of course not! Are you kidding?" It seems patently obvious that spiritual gifts are intended only for Christians. After all, as we've already seen, they are expressions of God's grace, they are manifestations of the Holy Spirit, and their purpose is primarily to encourage and edify other believers in the body of Christ. So how can anyone even suggest that God might grant a spiritual gift to someone who remains in unbelief and rebellion against the gospel?

That's a fair question. But there is more to this than most people are aware. For example, what are we to make of Jesus's comments at the close of the Sermon on the Mount? He said this of nonbelievers:

> "Not everyone who says to me, 'Lord, Lord,' will enter the kingdom of heaven, but the one who does the will of my Father who is in heaven. On that day many will say to me, 'Lord, Lord, did we not prophesy in your name, and cast out demons in your name, and do many mighty works in your name?' And then will I declare to them, 'I never knew you; depart from me, you workers of lawlessness.'" (Matt. 7:21–23)[1]

---

1   I should also mention in passing the case of the woman Jezebel in Revelation 2:20–23. Here we read that she "calls herself a prophetess" (v. 20). I can't imagine Jesus using this language if her prophetic gift was of the Holy Spirit. Some contend she was a born-again believer who had simply gone astray, but I suggest that her behavior and beliefs are an indication that whatever claims she made to being saved and prophetically gifted were spurious. This isn't to say she didn't have a supernatural power, but as this chapter indicates, the latter need not always be from God.

Then we have Jesus's words in the Olivet Discourse. There he issued this warning concerning the emergence of false prophets: "For false christs and false prophets will arise and perform great signs and wonders, so as to lead astray, if possible, even the elect" (Matt. 24:24; cf. Mark 13:22).

Paul referred to the "coming of the lawless one," evidently a reference to the Antichrist, and said that his appearance would be "by the activity of Satan with all power and false signs and wonders" (2 Thess. 2:9). Are these "signs and wonders" called "false" because they are not, in point of fact, actual supernatural signs and wonders? In other words, are they sleight of hand, magical tricks that are designed to look like the real deal but in fact are easily explained by appeal to the laws of physics? It is interesting that immediately following this description of the "lawless" one's activity, Paul brought up the "wicked deception" (v. 10) perpetrated by Satan. Or are these signs and wonders false in the sense that they mislead and promote heretical doctrines? The message they promote may be what is "false," and not necessarily the reality of their supernatural origin.

This discussion raises several additional questions, such as, can Satan perform genuine supernatural deeds? Some deny that he can, for they fear this would compromise the capacity of Christ's signs and wonders to bear witness to his identity. There seems to be no argument that angels, as well as demons, can do supernatural things when empowered and commissioned by God to do so. Satan exerted control over the forces of nature when he launched his attack against Job, but only then with God's permission. I don't want to digress into a discussion of Satan's power or that of other demonic beings, but it seems likely that they do have the power to produce effects that cannot be accounted for by appeal to any physical cause.[2]

In Jesus's statement in the Olivet Discourse, he didn't refer to these signs and wonders as "false" but only described them as "great." He did, however, warn us that the aim of such "miraculous" deeds is to "lead astray" or deceive the elect, were that possible.

Let's return for a moment to Jesus's words in Matthew 7. Clearly he was talking about unbelievers, people whom Jesus "never knew." So what did Jesus mean when he quoted their claim that they prophesied and performed

2   See my discussion of the power and activity of Satan and demons in my book *Tough Topics: Biblical Answers to 25 Challenging Questions* (Wheaton, IL: Crossway, 2013), 137–65.

mighty works in his name? Neither Jesus nor Matthew provided us with an answer, but it may be that these people did so with God's permission, as was the case with Judas Iscariot in the New Testament. Nowhere in the four gospels are we told that only the other eleven apostles operated in signs and wonders. The assumption is that Judas Iscariot would have prophesied, healed the sick, and cast out demons along with the others.

On the other hand, Jesus may not have been endorsing the truth of their claim, but merely citing it to highlight how grievous their unbelief really was. In other words, they were lying about operating in miraculous gifts and supernatural power. For Jesus to have inserted, as it were, a parenthetical rebuttal, declaring, "Oh, but of course, their so-called prophetic words and mighty works never really happened at all," would have distracted his audience from the main point he wanted to communicate.

Let's note also a handful of texts where it appears that certain unbelieving individuals were successful in deliverance ministry. Jesus was accused by the religious leaders of casting out demons by "the prince of demons" (Matt. 12:24), to which he responded, "And if I cast out demons by Beelzebul, by whom do your sons cast them out?" (v. 27). Again, in Mark 9:38 the disciples reported to Jesus that they "saw someone casting out demons in your name." Our Lord's response in verses 39–41 seems to acknowledge that this was a legitimate exorcism. On the other hand, the seven sons of a Jewish high priest named Sceva likewise "undertook to invoke the name of the Lord Jesus over those who had evil spirits" (Acts 19:13). But the demon scoffed at their attempt to cast him (it?) out and "overpowered them, so that they fled out of the house naked and wounded" (v. 16). This latter case clearly indicates that not all efforts to cast out demons in the name of Jesus were successful!

And what shall we say about the terms used in Hebrews 6:4–5, where people are described as having "once been enlightened" and "have tasted the heavenly gift, and have shared in the Holy Spirit" and "have tasted the goodness of the word of God and the powers of the age to come"? Is it possible for these experiences to be true of people who have been repeatedly exposed to the gospel and to the benefits it brings, yet without personally embracing the person of Christ as Lord and Savior (think Judas Iscariot)? As we seek to answer this question, we need to keep in mind the extent to which the Holy Spirit can minister to, exert his influence upon, and richly bless people with extraordinary experiences and opportunities without actually causing them to be born again and without imparting to them the gift of saving faith in Jesus Christ.

They have "once been enlightened" (Heb. 6:4). Have true Christians been "enlightened"? Yes. But this term need mean no more than to hear the gospel, to learn, or to understand. Countless non-Christians who grew up in church, perhaps attended a Christian college or seminary, understand a great deal about the Christian faith. The Holy Spirit can actually enlighten them and give them insight, which they in turn ultimately reject. Merely understanding Christian doctrines does not prove one is saved!

All of us know people, perhaps family members, who have been repeatedly exposed to the truth of the gospel, understand what it means, can articulate the claims of Christ with remarkable precision, yet refuse to put their trust in him as Lord and Savior. Thus, whereas all true Christians have been enlightened, not all those who are enlightened are true Christians.

I should also point out that in the years immediately following the death of the apostles, the term *enlightened* was frequently used to describe Christian baptism. It isn't used that way in Scripture, but it is often found in the early church fathers in reference to what one experiences in the waters of baptism. Some have argued as well that the phrase "tasted the heavenly gift" is a reference to eating and drinking the bread and wine of the Lord's Supper. If so, our author would be saying that these people have been baptized and have regularly participated in the Lord's Supper, but never came fully and finally to saving faith in Christ. This interpretation is doubtful, but it is worth noting.

Here we will combine three of these phrases: they have "tasted the heavenly gift" and "the goodness of the word of God" and "the powers of the age to come" (Heb. 6:4–5). This certainly points to a genuine spiritual experience. But must we conclude that it was a genuine *saving* or *redemptive* spiritual experience? These are not strangers to the gospel or to the church. These are people who have come under conviction of the Holy Spirit, who have experienced some degree of blessing both through common grace and through their close, intimate contact with genuine believers.

Perhaps they have been healed (remember, the vast majority whom Jesus healed were not saved). Perhaps a demon has been cast out. They have heard the Word of God and have come to taste and feel and enjoy something of its power and beauty and truth. They have felt the wooing of the Spirit and have seen great and wonderful things in the body of Christ. These, then, "have tasted" the power and blessings of the new covenant, but they have not personally prized, cherished, embraced, loved, trusted, treasured, or savored the atoning death of Jesus as their only hope for eternal life.

They have also "shared in the Holy Spirit." Whereas the word translated "shared" or "partaken" can certainly refer to a saving participation in Christ (cf. Heb. 3:14), it can also refer to a looser association or participation (see Luke 5:7; Heb. 1:9, translated "comrades" or "companions"). These people had in some way come to share in some aspect of the Holy Spirit and his ministry. But in what way? Must we conclude that it was a "saving" way?

I believe that the people described in Hebrews 6:4–5 who, according to verse 6, "have fallen away" are not now and never were born-again believers. They are not Christians who have "lost" their salvation. They are non-Christians who perhaps made a profession of faith in Jesus, perhaps became members of a church, perhaps even participated in leadership, were probably baptized and came often to the Lord's Table, and then willfully and with a hard heart turned away and rejected everything they had come to know.

The spiritual state and experience of those described in Hebrews 6:4–6 is virtually identical to that of the first three of four soils in the parable of the sower (see Matt. 13:3–23; Mark 4:1–9; Luke 8:4–15). In that parable, only the fourth soil is called "good" and subsequently bears fruit. The other three represent those who hear the gospel and respond with varying degrees of understanding, interest, and joy, none of which, however, bear fruit that would testify of genuine spiritual life. That is to say, they experienced "enlightenment" and "tasted" the goodness and power of the ministry of the Spirit and the blessings of the kingdom yet turned their backs on the truth when trials, troubles, or temptations came their way. Their apostasy was proof of the falsity of their initial "faith" (see esp. John 8:31; Heb. 3:6,14; 1 John 2:19).

The point of citing Hebrews 6 is simply to suggest that the sharing in the Holy Spirit and the tasting of the powers of the age to come that these people experienced, may (I repeat, *may*) suggest that they also operated to some degree in what may be called gifts of the Holy Spirit.

Perhaps the best case for demonstrating that non-Christians might be recipients of a spiritual gift is found in the events of Pentecost as described in Acts 2:5–13. On that day, the disciples of Jesus were filled with the Spirit, spoke in tongues, and prophesied. The unbelieving multitude was bewildered, "because each one was hearing them speak in his own language" (Acts 2:6).

Some insist that the tongues in Acts 2 were not human languages.[3] They contend that Luke was describing not the hearing *of* one's own language but the hearing *in* one's own language. In other words, what occurred at Pentecost wasn't so much a miracle of speaking but a miracle of hearing. At the same moment that "other tongues" were spoken through the Holy Spirit, they were immediately translated by the same Holy Spirit into the many languages of the multitude.[4] Thus, there was no identifiable linguistic content or structure to what the disciples said. What made their speech intelligible wasn't the fact they were speaking in the actual languages of the people present at Pentecost, but rather the work of the Spirit in the minds of the latter by which they were enabled to "hear" these utterances in their native tongues. Three times in Acts 2 Luke said that those present were "hearing" (v. 6) them speak in their own language. Again, they asked, "And how is it that we hear, each of us in his own native language?" (v. 8). Finally, they said, "We hear them telling in our own tongues the mighty works of God" (v. 11). Thus, J. Rodman Williams argues that there is *both* a miracle of "speech"—other, different, spiritual tongues—*and* a miracle of "understanding," each facilitated by the Holy Spirit.

If this view is correct, a miraculous *charisma* of the Holy Spirit (namely, the gift of interpretation) was given to every *unbeliever* present on the day of Pentecost. But as D. A. Carson has noted, it is Luke's purpose "to associate the descent of the Spirit with the Spirit's activity *among the believers*, not to postulate a miracle of the Spirit *among those who were still unbelievers*."[5] Nothing in the text explicitly speaks of the Holy Spirit descending on the crowd, but rather on the disciples. Or, as Max Turner puts it, surely Luke "would not wish to suggest that the apostolic band merely prattled incomprehensibly, while God

3   The following discussion of Acts 2 is adapted from my book *The Language of Heaven: Crucial Questions about Speaking in Tongues* (Lake Mary, FL: Charisma House, 2019), and is used here with permission.

4   See J. Rodman Williams, *Renewal Theology: Salvation, the Holy Spirit, and Christian Living* (Grand Rapids: Zondervan, 1990), 2:215. Others who find in Acts 2 a miracle of "hearing" include Luke T. Johnson, "Tongues, Gift of," in *The Anchor Bible Dictionary* (New York: Doubleday, 1992), 6:597, and more recently Anthony Thiselton, *The First Epistle to the Corinthians* (Grand Rapids: Eerdmans, 2000), 977.

5   D. A. Carson, *Showing the Spirit: A Theological Exposition of 1 Corinthians 12–14* (1987; repr., Grand Rapids: Baker, 2019), 181, emphasis his.

worked the yet greater miracle of interpretation of tongues in the *un*believers."[6]
One should also note that "Luke reports their speaking 'other languages' before
mentioning that anyone hears them (2:4)."[7]

I'm led to conclude, then, that the incident on the day of Pentecost is not
an example of nonbelievers being granted a spiritual gift.

But we must reckon with our Lord's words in Matthew 7 and again in
Matthew 24. Might one explanation be that these were genuine works of
supernatural power that we should attribute to what theologians refer to as
common grace? This is the gracious and enabling power of the Holy Spirit
at work in unbelievers, empowering them to do countless things that are
beneficial and good and helpful, even though they remain unregenerate and
lost in sin. People often lose sight of how much the Holy Spirit accomplishes
for and through non-Christians, short of salvation itself. This is worthy of
deeper exploration.

Common Grace and Spiritual Gifts[8]

If the unregenerate man or woman is spiritually blind and hostile to the
gospel, unable in their own strength to "understand" the things of God or to
"seek" for him, and cannot do anything "good" (Rom. 3:11–12), how is it that
they nonetheless perform great deeds of civil morality and produce great
works of art, music, and governmental policy? The explanation provided by
Scripture is that, in spite of their *total depravity*, God not only restrains the
full manifestation of the evil tendencies of the human heart but also, on
a more positive note, enables non-Christians to perform deeds of relative
"good."

The verdict of the apostle Paul on the universal condition of humanity
is, to say the least, a bleak one (see Rom. 3:10b–18). But, as John Murray has
observed, this apostolic assessment of human nature forces us to deal with
a series of insistent questions:

---

6   Max Turner, *The Holy Spirit and Spiritual Gifts* (Peabody, MA: Hendrickson, 1998), 223.

7   Craig S. Keener, *Acts: An Exegetical Commentary, Volume 1* (Grand Rapids: Baker Academic, 2012), 823.

8   The following discussion is adapted from my book *Chosen for Life: The Case for Divine Election* (Wheaton,
IL: Crossway, 2007), 54–59, and is used here with permission.

> How is it that men who still lie under the wrath and curse of God and are heirs of hell enjoy so many good gifts at the hand of God? How is it that men who are not savingly renewed by the Spirit of God nevertheless exhibit so many qualities, gifts and accomplishments that promote the preservation, temporal happiness, cultural progress, social and economic improvement of themselves and of others? How is it that races and peoples that have been apparently untouched by the redemptive and regenerative influences of the gospel contribute so much to what we call human civilization? To put the question most comprehensively: how is it that this sin-cursed world enjoys so much favour and kindness at the hand of its holy and ever-blessed Creator?[9]

The answer given by those in the Reformed tradition is an appeal to what theologians call God's "common grace." It is *common* in the sense that it is universally present among mankind, in varying degrees, of course. Common grace must therefore be distinguished from God's special, saving, or redemptive grace, the grace by which he draws the elect to faith in Christ and preserves them in their status as adopted spiritual sons and daughters. Common grace has been defined in various ways. According to Charles Hodge, the Bible teaches that

> the Holy Spirit as the Spirit of truth, of holiness, and of life in all its forms, is present with every human mind, enforcing truth, restraining from evil, exciting to good, and imparting wisdom or strength, when, where, and in what measure seemeth to Him good. . . . This is what in theology is called common grace.[10]

Abraham Kuyper defines common grace as

> that act of God by which negatively He curbs the operations of Satan, death, and sin, and by which positively He creates an intermediate state

---

9   John Murray, "Common Grace," in *Collected Writings of John Murray*, 4 vols. (Edinburgh: Banner of Truth, 1977), 2:93.

10   Charles Hodge, *Systematic Theology*, 3 vols. (Grand Rapids: Eerdmans, 1970), 2:667.

for this cosmos, as well as for our human race, which is and continues to be deeply and radically sinful, but in which sin cannot work out its end.[11]

A simpler and more direct definition of common grace is given by John Murray. Common grace, he writes,

is every favour of whatever kind or degree, falling short of salvation, which this undeserving and sin-cursed world enjoys at the hand of God.[12]

I'll make use of Murray's definition as we seek to identify the variety of ways in which common grace operates.

The first aspect of common grace is what we might call negative or preventative. Its essential characteristic is that of *restraint*. Although the restraint that God places on sin and its effects is neither complete (else no sin would exist at all) nor uniform (else all men would be equally evil or good), it is of such a nature that the expression and effects of human depravity are not permitted to reach the maximum height of which they are capable. The notion of common grace as restraint is operative in several areas. As already noted, God exercises restraint on *the sin of man*. Murray explains, "God places restraint upon the workings of human depravity and thus prevents the unholy affections and principles of men from manifesting all the potentialities inherent in them. He prevents depravity from bursting forth in all its vehemence and violence."[13]

The "mark" that God placed on Cain, "lest any who found him should attack him" (Gen. 4:15), is one example. God told Abimelech, king of Gerar, that "it was I who kept you from sinning" when the king considered having sexual relations with Sarah, Abraham's wife (Gen. 20:6; see also 2 Kings 19:27–28). The apostle Paul referred to the one "who now restrains" the revelation of the lawless one (2 Thess. 2:7). In each of these cases, God (most likely the Holy Spirit) exerts a preventative influence on what would otherwise be acts of evil.

---

11 Abraham Kuyper, *Principles of Sacred Theology*, trans. J. Hendrik De Vries (Grand Rapids: Eerdmans, 1969), 279.

12 Murray, "Common Grace," 2:96.

13 Murray, 2:98.

Another expression of common grace is God's merciful determination to suspend the immediate manifestation of his wrath and judgment warranted by human sin. We see this in texts such as Genesis 6:3; Acts 17:30; Romans 2:4; 1 Peter 3:20; and 2 Peter 3:9. In similar fashion, God exerts a restraining influence on the destructive tendencies in the natural creation.

Our primary concern, however, is with the more positive and constructive effects of common grace. It is in this regard that we ask whether God might bestow certain spiritual gifts on the unregenerate. There are numerous biblical texts where God is portrayed as pouring out both physical and spiritual blessings on the nonelect, as well as texts that suggest he endows them with remarkable capacities and talents (see Pss. 65:9–13; 104:10–30; 145:1–16). It's important to remember, however, that these blessings, whatever their nature, do not entail or guarantee the salvation of the recipient. Furthermore, as Murray perceptibly notes, God not only restrains evil in unregenerate souls but also endows them with

> gifts, talents, and aptitudes; he stimulates them with interest and purpose to the practice of virtues, the pursuance of worthy tasks, and the cultivation of arts and sciences that occupy the time, activity and energy of men and that make for the benefit and civilization of the human race. He ordains institutions for the protection and promotion of right, the preservation of liberty, the advance of knowledge and the improvement of physical and moral conditions. We may regard these interests, pursuits and institutions as exercising both an expulsive and impulsive influence. Occupying the energy, activity and time of men they prevent the indulgence of less noble and ignoble pursuits and they exercise an ameliorating, moralizing, stabilizing and civilizing influence upon the social organism.[14]

We read about this manifestation of common grace in Genesis 39:5 where God is said to have "blessed the Egyptian's house for Joseph's sake." At Lystra, Paul declared that God "did good by giving you rains from heaven and fruitful seasons, satisfying your hearts with food and gladness" (Acts 14:17). Jesus himself said that God "makes his sun rise on the evil and on the good, and sends rain on the just and on the unjust" (Matt. 5:45). The Father

---

14 Murray, 2:102–3.

is described as being "kind to the ungrateful and the evil" (Luke 6:35; see Luke 16:25). It is only because of such operations of common grace that the non-Christian may be said to perform "good" (cf. 2 Kings 10:30; 12:2; Matt. 5:46; Luke 6:33; Rom. 2:14–15). However, Murray reminds us that "the good attributed to unregenerate men is after all only relative good. It is not good in the sense of meeting in motivation, principle and aim the requirements of God's law and the demands of his holiness,"[15] and thus can in no way commend them to the righteousness of the Father. We must never lose sight of the fact that all such operations of "grace" (so-called because undeserved) are nonsaving, being neither in design nor effect such as would produce new life in Christ.

Conclusion

Could it be, then, that by means of his bountiful display of common grace toward an unbelieving world, the Spirit at times mercifully bestows on the non-Christian at least some capacity to operate in supernatural power that may bear some degree of resemblance to the *charismata* that are given to those who are born-again? If true, this would certainly account for what we see in the life of Judas as well as in the experience of those we read about in Matthew 7:21–23. But the *charismata* themselves are reserved for God's children, those who have also been made the merciful recipients of God's saving, special grace.

---

15 Murray, 2:107.

What Is the Future of Charismatic Renewal?

ASSESSING ITS STRENGTHS AND WEAKNESSES

A s we bring our discussion of spiritual gifts to a conclusion, it would be helpful to examine the emergence of what is known as charismatic renewal and to highlight both its strengths and weaknesses, as well as its future prospects.

What Is Charismatic Spirituality?

In his book *Encountering the Spirit: The Charismatic Tradition*, Mark Cartledge contends that "the central motif of the charismatic tradition is the 'encounter with the Spirit' both corporately within the worshipping life of the Church and individually through personal devotion and ongoing work and witness in the world."[1] Thus, the charismatic tradition anticipates continual encounters with the Spirit as part of the ongoing life of the believer. Charismatics "expect God to reveal his glory in worship, to answer prayer, to perform miracles, to speak directly by means of dreams and visions and prophecy."[2] Cartledge sums it up best in saying that at the core of charismatic spirituality is the

---

1 Mark Cartledge, *Encountering the Spirit* (London: Darton, Longman and Todd, 2006), 16.
2 Cartledge, 28–29.

conviction that "God is not absent but deeply present. . . . God loves to give himself to his people!"[3]

Cartledge identifies four themes that constitute the heart of charismatic spirituality. The first is worship, which is most often characterized by informality, contemporary music, freedom, full participation (rather than the performance orientation of more liturgical traditions), "an energetic engagement with praise,"[4] prayer ministry, and spontaneity that allows for contributions from the congregation that may include "the use of spiritual gifts such as prophecy or speaking in tongues, or . . . the opportunity to give a testimony for the encouragement of those present."[5]

A second consistent theme is what Cartledge calls inspired speech, such as "reception of revelation through 'words,' pictures, visions and dreams; the relay of that revelation through prophetic messages, words of wisdom and words of knowledge; as well as the inspiration in prayer, testimony and preaching."[6] He is quick to point out, however, "that most Pentecostal and Charismatic leaders, following the injunctions of Paul, take seriously the need to discern the nature of inspired speech."[7] All inspired speech, therefore, is "relativised" and does not "give a platform for claims to new revelation."[8]

The third dimension of charismatic spirituality noted by Cartledge is what he calls the sanctified life. It is certainly the case that modern Pentecostalism can trace its theological roots, at least in part, to John Wesley and the National Holiness movement, but I struggle to see this feature as being essential to the contemporary charismatic movement. Whereas charismatic believers are assuredly committed to the principles and practice of holiness and pursuit of a life consecrated to God, there is nothing especially unique in their approach that would set them apart from the mainstream of evangelical Protestantism.

Fourth, "charismatic spirituality has often been associated with forms of apocalypticism: end-time expectations about the consummation of the kingdom of God. To some extent this is still prevalent but cannot be said

---

3   Cartledge, 29.
4   Cartledge, 58.
5   Cartledge, 58.
6   Cartledge, 69.
7   Cartledge, 84.
8   Cartledge, 85.

to permeate every expression of the tradition."[9] What is pervasive among charismatics is the recognition of the "already / not yet" dimension of the kingdom's presence, due to the influence of George Ladd and the way his perspective was embraced and articulated by the late John Wimber.

My primary criticism is that I'm not convinced that the four themes cited by Cartledge as indicative of charismatic spirituality are the most accurate way of portraying this tradition. I agree that worship and inspired speech are essential distinctives, but the notions of holiness of life and "apocalypticism" are less evident. Even when they are present among charismatics, they are no more prominent than one would find in many Baptist denominations or even among the Nazarenes. I think it would be more accurate to emphasize the concept of *power* in Christian experience and ministry as a distinctive feature of the charismatic tradition (whether in signs and wonders, healing, or the more routine exercise of the *charismata* in corporate church life). In addition, the concept of divine *immanence* and the relational intimacy that it produces is far more a factor in the typical charismatic church than either of the other two emphases noted by Cartledge.

Assessing Both the Strengths and Weaknesses in Charismatic Renewal

What might we identify as some of the strengths and weaknesses that charismatic renewal has brought to the evangelical church? Although by no means exhaustive, I would suggest the following ten things.

1. The charismatic tradition has done well in emphasizing the role of authentic *experience* in Christian living. Charismatics are to be applauded for bringing a more *holistic* approach to our relationship with God. In doing so, the dualism between body and spirit, as well as between the affective and cognitive dimensions, has been overcome. On the other hand, this has led at times to a de-emphasis on the mind (even a "demonizing" of it) and a failure to appreciate the necessity of a rigorous intellectual engagement with the faith.

2. The charismatic renewal has also contributed greatly to a biblical

---

9   Cartledge, 101.

egalitarianism in terms of the distribution of spiritual gifts and the breaking down of socioeconomic and educational barriers that tended to reinforce the older distinctions between clergy and laity. On the other hand, one can also see the emergence of an unbiblical egalitarianism that fails to acknowledge the complementary but differing roles and levels of authority that God has ordained for men and women.

3. Whereas much of mainstream evangelicalism can become mired in an *underrealized eschatology* that breeds defeatism, passive acquiescence to the status quo, and a loss of the joy that comes with experiencing the power and privilege of what we *already* have in Christ, the charismatic tradition can be guilty of an *overrealized eschatology* that breeds naive triumphalism, presumptuous prayer, and an unrealistic expectation of spiritual and physical blessings that are *not yet* God's purpose to bestow. Thus, whereas evangelical cessationists often fail to recognize and act upon the authority that is already ours in Christ, evangelical continuationists just as frequently fall short in acknowledging how a theology of weakness can serve the greater glory of God.

4. Charismatics are to be applauded for their focus on the *Old Testament* and its *narrative* portrayal of the immediacy of God in the lives of his people, primarily as expressed in signs, wonders, and prophetic revelation. But they often fall into the trap of applying old covenant models for ministry and leadership to people living under the new covenant. Even more egregious is the tendency to elevate old covenant types and shadows while failing to recognize their antitypical fulfillment in Jesus in the new covenant.

5. The charismatic tradition has awakened the evangelical world to the reality of spiritual warfare and to the authority of the believer over all the power of the enemy (Luke 10:1–20). They, far more than most, have come to grips, both in terms of theological belief and actual practical strategy, with Paul's warning about where our real enemies are to be found ("We do not wrestle against flesh and blood, but against the rulers, against the authorities, against the cosmic powers over this present darkness, against the spiritual forces of evil in the heavenly places," Eph. 6:12). However, in their zeal to do justice to the presence

and activity of the demonic, they have tended to demonize the flesh. That is to say, if secular scientists are guilty of looking for a genetic or biochemical cause for all human misbehavior, some forms of charismatic hyperspirituality look for a demonic explanation. The result is that sins of the flesh are reduced to "spirits" of lust, nicotine, envy, homosexuality, alcoholism, and so on. Similarly, among charismatics "the category of creation or nature can be lost in a worldview that sees reality in the dichotomous terms of light and darkness, or the spiritual kingdom of God versus the spiritual kingdom of Satan. This cosmological dualism can fuel spiritual warfare, but it also misses the important category of creation as good but fallen."[10]

6. Although the charismatic renewal is responsible to some degree for bringing to light the reality of the spiritual realm in a world dominated by scientific naturalism, it is also at times guilty of a modern form of gnosticism. This hyperspirituality has led to a neglect of the routine disciplines of Christian living and the ordinary means of grace, a failure to appreciate the presence of God in natural processes, and a loss of appreciation for the beauty and value of the material creation.

7. Charismatics are to be applauded for their emphasis on spiritual gifts, especially that of prophecy and the reality that God still speaks. Sadly, though, this gift has often been turned into a crystal ball for routine daily decision-making. And notwithstanding their protests to the contrary, a minority among charismatics are somewhat inclined to elevate the spoken word of God over the written word of canonical Scripture.

8. The charismatic renewal has rightly brought to our attention the reality and importance of multiple postconversion encounters with the Holy Spirit. These experiences can serve to impart spiritual gifts, empower believers for ministry and witness, and enhance and deepen our intimacy with the Father. But they can also be distorted by becoming badges of spiritual superiority. The desire (which can all too often degenerate into an unhealthy craving) for fresh encounters with the Spirit can easily be used as an excuse for the neglect of healthy involvement in a local church, while the believer moves from

---

10 Cartledge, 135.

conference to conference, revival to revival, ostensibly in search of the next "great move of God."

9. Whereas the charismatic tradition is correct in insisting that the apostolic office is in some way still valid for the church today, it has given unhealthy credence to an effort by some to restructure local church leadership on a foundation other than that of the elder/deacon pattern so clearly endorsed in the New Testament epistles.

10. Whereas charismatics have rightly turned our attention to the importance of revival and power encounters with the Spirit that often lead to deliverance, healing, and renewed fellowship with God, they have also drawn unbiblical connections between physical manifestations and spiritual maturity, as if the presence of the former is a clear sign of the latter.[11]

Prospects for the Future

If the charismatic renewal is not only to thrive in the days ahead but also expand its influence in the broader evangelical world, several things must occur. Included among these, in no particular order, are the following.

1. Charismatics must return to a robust view of the gospel and how it functions to shape all of life and belief. Although there are notable and laudatory exceptions to this, many Pentecostal and charismatic churches fall short in their understanding and proclamation of the gospel. They likewise fail to articulate the many ways in which the gospel serves not merely as a doorway into the kingdom of God but as the governing principle for everyday ethical responsibilities, from how one relates to his or her spouse, to the use of one's finances, and to the importance of forgiving one another in the body of Christ.

2. There is a great need in charismatic circles for a more explicitly christological center to theology and ministry. In other words, without diminishing their emphasis on the Holy Spirit, charismatics must elevate their focus on Jesus Christ: his life, death, resurrection,

---

11 In this regard, I highly recommend the insightful and profoundly practical book by Andrew K. Gabriel, *Simply Spirit-Filled: Experiencing God in the Presence and Power of the Holy Spirit* (Nashville: Emanate, 2019).

and exaltation. In a sense, pneumatology must be subservient to Christology.

3. Charismatics are notoriously weak when it comes to ecclesiology. This is seen in: (a) the tendency to embrace structures of local church leadership that are alien to the New Testament pattern; (b) a flippant and casual approach to both church membership and discipline; (c) a low view of the nature and priority of the sacraments; and (d) an overall failure to recognize the centrality of the local church as God's primary means for expanding the kingdom and exalting his Son (see Eph. 3:10).

4. Charismatics must turn from a man-centered (anthropocentric) orientation to a more biblically robust God-centered or theocentric perspective on the faith. This should express itself in at least three ways: (a) a thorough refutation of open theism, which, sadly, has infected much of the charismatic world; (b) a comparatively more reformed understanding of soteriology (although this need not entail full-blown five-point Calvinism); and (c) a recognition of the centrality of God's glory as the ultimate purpose for both creation and redemption.

5. There is a great need in the charismatic world for a scripturally shaped and pastorally sensitive theology of suffering, one that does not undermine or compromise its equally important belief in the reality of divine healing. Mark Cartledge puts it this way: "With the emphasis on power and the immediacy of the transcendent within the immanent, the charismatic tradition can err on the side of expecting too much now."[12] Thus, often the result is that "the power of the resurrection can eclipse the weakness of the cross . . . [and] success and celebrity status can be sought as signs of power and blessing rather than a commitment to suffering and weakness in the ordinary of everyday life."[13]

The essence of *charismatic triumphalism* is the belief that the overt and consummate victories that we will experience only in the age to come are available to us now. We are encouraged to rejoice

---

12 Cartledge, *Encountering the Spirit*, 135.
13 Cartledge, 135.

that we have authority over demonic spirits (cf. Luke 10:17–20), that we have been blessed "with every spiritual blessing in the heavenly places" (Eph. 1:3) and have been "raised" up with Christ and are "seated" together "with him" (Eph. 2:6). We who believe "that Jesus is the Son of God" have "overcome" the world (1 John 5:5). And Jesus himself promises great and glorious rewards "to the one who conquers" now (Rev. 2:7, 11, et al.).

Where many often go astray is in their claim that such truths necessarily entail visible and irreversible victories in the present that result in a life free from persecution, suffering, or demonic assault. It's the notion that since I'm a "child of the King" I have a *right* to live in financial prosperity and complete physical health, free from that "groaning" under the lingering curse of the fall which Paul appears to indicate will continue until the return of Christ (cf. Rom. 8:18–25).

The nature of this *toxic triumphalism* is nowhere better seen than in 2 Corinthians 13:1–4. There Paul wrote,

> This is the third time I am coming to you. Every charge must be established by the evidence of two or three witnesses. I warned those who sinned before and all the others, and I warn them now while absent, as I did when present on my second visit, that if I come again I will not spare them—since you seek proof that Christ is speaking in me. He is not weak in dealing with you, but is powerful among you. For he was crucified in weakness, but lives by the power of God. For we also are weak in him, but in dealing with you we will live with him by the power of God.

D. A. Carson explains, "They were so sub-Christian in their thinking that Christlike gentleness and meekness meant little to them. They preferred manifestations of power, however exploitative and arbitrary they might be ([2 Cor.] 11:20). Paul's gentleness they therefore misjudged as weakness, preferring the triumphalistic pushiness of the false apostles. Paul responds by saying that if it is power they want to see as the absolute criterion of genuine apostolicity, they may get more than they bargained for: he may be forced to display the power of the resurrected Christ, speaking through him in the thunderous tones of punishment, another version perhaps of the judgment meted out to Ananias and Sapphira."[14]

Paul's point is that his life and especially his relationship to the Corinthians mirror that of Christ. Jesus, said Paul, was the supreme embodiment and example of both weakness (in his crucifixion) and strength (in his resurrection and exaltation). Jesus was "obedient to the point of death" (Phil. 2:8b) and refused to retaliate or react against his accusers (Matt. 26:52, 67–68; 27:11–14, 27–31; 1 Peter 2:23). Herein was his "weakness" as well as the public demonstration of his essential mortality. But unlike us, he did not remain in weakness but came to life again through the resurrection "power of God" (2 Cor. 13:4a).

Yes, said Paul, I am weak, as Jesus was, a weakness you've despised and used to undermine my credibility. But "in dealing with you we will live with him by the power of God" (2 Cor. 13:4b). The phrase "we will live with him" is not, as most triumphalists would prefer, a reference to the final resurrection and our hope of living in Christ's presence in the age to come. Rather, "Paul is speaking of his imminent visit to Corinth when, in unison with Christ and with God's power, he would act decisively and vigorously against unrepentant evildoers within the congregation."[15]

6. Charismatics cannot afford to be identified with the more extreme forms of eschatological Zionism. The most effective antidote to this widespread error is a recognition of the way in which Jesus became the antitypical fulfillment of the many shadows, symbols, and typological adumbrations of the Old Testament. If charismatics do not come to understand how the New Testament interprets and fulfills the Old Testament prophetic word, it will remain hopelessly mired in the darkness of dispensationalism and the many errors it spawns.

7. Charismatics must cease paying mere lip service to the convergence of Word and Spirit. There has been in many charismatic circles a loss of the functional authority of Scripture. The simple but sad fact is that

---

14 D. A. Carson, *From Triumphalism to Maturity: An Exposition of 2 Corinthians 10–13* (Grand Rapids: Baker, 1984), 174.

15 Murray J. Harris, *The Second Epistle to the Corinthians: A Commentary on the Greek Text* (Grand Rapids: Eerdmans, 2005), 916.

cessationists are right: charismatics, in general, have often failed to subject all claims of prophetic revelation or spiritual power encounters to the final standard of biblical authority.[16]

8. A repudiation of all expressions of *manipulative and hyperspiritual sensationalism* is essential.[17] Hankering after the spectacular and spellbinding display of what pretends to be supernatural power is anathema to the teaching of God's Word. Worse still are the deceitful tactics utilized by some celebrities in the charismatic subculture (I hardly need to name names). They are undoubtedly in the minority, but their high profile and outlandish claims often lead many to think that this is standard practice among those who believe in the contemporary validity of spiritual gifts.

9. The charismatic movement must vocally distance itself from the so-called health and wealth gospel, as well as from the extremes of the Word of Faith movement. Contrary to what many have concluded, these are not mainstream charismatic convictions. They are serious aberrations from the teaching of Scripture, and their deviant doctrines (often promulgated largely for monetary gain) must be exposed and repudiated.[18]

10. Finally, there is in the charismatic world an unhealthy hankering for whatever is new and bizarre, often without regard for the history of

---

16 See my article "When Word Meets Spirit," in *Charisma* 44.3 (October 2018): 34–38.

17 I devoted an entire chapter to this problem in my book *Practicing the Power* (Grand Rapids: Zondervan, 2017), 192–212.

18 There are several well-written refutations of these aberrations from charismatic belief and practice, among which are Bruce Barron, *The Health and Wealth Gospel* (Downers Grove, IL: InterVarsity, 1987); Michael L. Brown, *Whatever Happened to the Power of God?* (Shippensburg, PA: Destiny Image, 1991), and *Playing with Holy Fire: A Wake-Up Call to the Pentecostal-Charismatic Church* (Lake Mary, FL: Charisma House, 2018); Charles Farah, *From the Pinnacle of the Temple* (Plainfield, NJ: Logos International, n.d.); David W. Jones and Russell S. Woodbridge, *Health, Wealth & Happiness: Has the Prosperity Gospel Overshadowed the Gospel of Christ?* (Grand Rapids: Kregel, 2011); D. R. McConnell, *A Different Gospel: A Historical and Biblical Analysis of the Modern Faith Movement* (Peabody, MA: Hendrickson, 1988); and Andrew Perriman, ed., *Faith, Health and Prosperity: A Report on "Word of Faith" and "Positive Confession" Theologies by ACUTE (the Evangelical Alliance Commission on Unity and Truth among Evangelicals* (Carlisle: Paternoster, 2003). Although I have several substantive disagreements with his books, one should also consult Costi W. Hinn (with Anthony G. Wood), *Defining Deception: Freeing the Church from the Mystical-Miracle Movement* (El Cajon, CA: Southern California Seminary Press, 2018); and Costi W. Hinn, *God, Greed, and the (Prosperity) Gospel: How Truth Overwhelms a Life Built on Lies* (Grand Rapids: Zondervan, 2019).

the Christian church and the consensus that has developed around the "Great Tradition" and the ecumenical creeds of the past. In a word, charismatics tend to fall prey to what C. S. Lewis referred to as chronological snobbery. In the days ahead, charismatics must be willing to look backward as readily and eagerly as they look forward, and to learn from our forefathers in the faith.

Subject Index

administration, gift of, 37, 43, 135

Agabus, 163, 177, 182, 182n. 12, 183, 185

Aidan, 143

Ambrose, 139

Andronicus, 297, 303, 312

Ansgar, 143

Anthony of Padua, 143

apocalypticism, 331–32

Apollinarius, 133

Apollos, 298, 300, 304, 307–9, 312, 313

apostles, the

    authority of to write inspired
      Scripture, 300

    as called by God, 293–94, 294n. 7,
      296, 297, 299, 307, 313

    in the church today, 313–15

    distinguishing marks of, 80–81

    as eyewitness to Jesus, 292, 296,
      297, 298, 299, 302, 304, 305, 306,
      307, 312

    false, 78, 81, 297

    as foundation of the church,
      170–71, 296

    and God's power, 8

    Holy Spirit working through, 7

    and leadership, 314

    as messengers, 297, 310, 311, 312

    signs and wonders as authentica-
      tion of, 72, 77–79, 80, 81, 84, 98,
      99, 313

    and spiritual gifts, 27, 44–45,
      77–79, 292, 313–14

    and teaching, 313

apostleship

    cessationist view of, 290, 293,
      294n. 7

    criteria for, 291–92, 293, 294n. 7,
      295–98, 299–315

    defining, 290–91, 294–95

    gift of, 35, 36, 37, 43, 70, 137,
      290–91, 290–98, 311, 314

    as office, 291, 292, 293, 294, 314

    Paul and, 35, 36, 80–81, 292, 296,
      299, 301–2, 301n. 4, 302, 305–6,
      311, 315

Aquinas, Thomas, 143

Ash, James, 124, 125

Athanasius, 136

Athenagoras, 133

Augustine, 127, 139–40, 141

Baker, Heidi, 266

doubt and, 261

evangelistic purpose of, 99–100

gift of, 35, 37, 40, 43, 261, 265,
   273–77

and God's glory, 99, 269

Holy Spirit enablement of, 19

of Jesus, 10, 11, 99, 100, 265

John 14:12 and, 261–64

in the Middle Ages, 143, 267

not exclusive to apostles, 44, 45,
   80, 81, 82, 105, 264, 272

as occasional gift, 261, 276

Paul and, 11, 35, 46, 78, 79, 80, 82,
   99, 117, 200, 265, 272, 276

as power, 10, 11

purpose of, 27, 264, 269

in the Reformation, 267

as serving gift, 43

skepticism and, 260

spectrum of beliefs about, 260–61

what is, 268–69

Montague, George T., 128, 134

Montanist controversy, the, 131–34, 136

Montanus, 132, 133, 168

Murray, John, 325–26, 327, 328, 329

New Apostolic Reformation, the,
   295–96

Novatian, 135

offices, 45

Oliver, Jeff, 128, 140

Origen, 134, 135

Pachomius, 136

pastoring, gift of, 36, 37, 100, 287

pastoring-teaching, gift of, 36, 37,
   283, 287, 288

Paul

and apostleship, 35, 36, 80–81,
   296, 292, 299, 301–2, 301n. 4,
   302, 305–6, 311, 315

calling of as apostle, 78. 79, 296,
   299, 302, 307

and celibacy, 226, 228

and the *charismata*, 21, 24, 291

and discernment of spirits,
   198–201

and evangelism, gift of, 100, 287

and faith, gift of, 35, 36, 40,
   241–42, 244–45, 254

and giving, gift of, 34, 36, 281, 285

and God's power, 5, 7, 9, 10–11, 21,
   22, 25

and grace, 25

and healing, gift of, 35, 40, 46, 136,
   246–48, 254

Holy spirit working through, 7, 9

and immaturity, 289

and impartation of spiritual gifts,
   48, 56, 60

and interpretation of tongues, gift
   of, 27, 35, 41

and love, 16, 48, 52, 71, 117, 186,
   195, 210, 242, 244

and miracles, 11, 35, 46, 78, 79, 80,
   82, 99, 117, 200, 265, 272, 276

and number of spiritual gifts
   given to people, 46–47

and pastoring, gift of, 100, 287

pride of, 53

and prophecy, gift of, 27, 34–36,

Scripture Index